Logic: A Philosophical Introduction

JACK KAMINSKY
State Universtity of New York
at Binghamton

Logic: A Philosophical Introduction

ALICE KAMINSKY
State University of New York,
College at Cortland

ADDISON-WESLEY
PUBLISHING COMPANY
Reading, Massachusetts · Menlo Park, California
London · Amsterdam · Don Mills, Ontario · Sydney

ISBN 0-201-03576-6
BCDEFGHIJ-MA-798765

Preface

Many books now deal with contemporary logic. But since contemporary logic is primarily symbolic and mathematical, most texts are written for the mathematics student or at least for the student who is fascinated by mathematical manipulations. However, logic is not merely the concern of mathematicians. Everyone uses logic to some degree, both in his professional life as well as in his day-to-day living. The student of literature, of biology, of psychology, or of just ordinary "human nature," must eventually ask himself or others whether what he believes is logical or illogical, correctly or incorrectly reasoned. Thus, just as everyone ought to have at least some information about what is happening in the sciences or in medicine in order to be better able to deal with any illnesses that might affect him, so also should he know what is happening in logic in order to be better able to deal with the countless number of arguments constantly offered by newspapers, books, journals, politicians, teachers, and others. In this book we are concerned with giving the average reader, one who is not mathematically inclined, some insight into what is occurring in contemporary logic. Although some reliance on symbolic techniques occurs, and one or two sections of the book do employ a fairly substantial amount of symbolism, for the most part there is an explicit attempt to verbalize as much of contemporary logic as possible and to indicate, in what we hope is very ordinary language, how contemporary logic operates. For this reason we try to take a leisurely pace. We try to stop whenever possible to discuss what we are doing and why it is important.

A leisurely pace, however, does not mean a lackadaisical approach. Much of what would be found in other introductory logic texts is here as well. But what we have tried to do is to approach logic in terms of its relevance, not simply in relation to mathematics, but in relation to important problems in language, philosophy, literature, and just plain common sense. Thus this book does not avoid, as do most of the logic books, the controversial philosophical, linguistic, and other speculative issues which arise in the study of logic. This does not mean that we offer any definitive analyses of these issues. But we try to give enough insight to interest the reader and make him want to go on to study the great philosophical problems of Western civilization.

The chapters are so arranged that they lead gradually into a study of the techniques of contemporary symbolic logic. The most difficult chapter is probably Chapter 13, which attempts to apply a modified form of W. V. Quine's canonical and main methods to various complicated arguments. Other techniques are used besides those worked out by Quine, and undoubtedly there are those who prefer to use a system of natural deduction. But we have chosen Quine's method because it is less complicated—especially in the light of changes he has made in the third edition of his *Methods of Logic*—than the natural deduction techniques. Those who have used logic texts which employ natural deduction know that the various modifications and conditions required prior to application are constant sources of confusion to the introductory student.

The canonical, or *C* method as we call it here, is also fairly complex but we think it is easier than other techniques. A second reason for selecting Quine's method is that we do believe it will eventually supersede most other techniques. The full development of the canonical method leads to what Quine calls the main method which, as he indicates, is a decisive procedure for testing the validity of the most complicated kinds of arguments. Our book gives the student an introduction to this procedure.

We are indebted to various readers whose detailed criticisms helped us immensely. We are also indebted to such major logicians as I. Copi and especially W. V. Quine, whose work has been of inestimable value to us.

Cortland, New York   J. K

March 1974   A. R. K.

Contents

1

Introduction

Sociologists and anthropologists frequently make the point that one major characteristic distinguishes men from animals: men have a far greater capacity to make tools. Most animals can remold their environments in some way to survive the hardships of weather and food shortages. For example, birds build nests that will withstand ferocious storms, and they do this before such storms actually occur. But this ability to make tools for survival is most advanced in human beings, who produce such remarkable instruments that living can involve pleasurable and aesthetic, as well as survival activities. Art, literature, and all the other humanistic fields appear in profusion only when human survival is made relatively secure. If we mean by a tool anything created by man to help him control a frequently hostile environment, then language is probably the most crucial of all human tools. People using a language can work together and thus create what any one man could not normally accomplish. By means of words, men seem to bring possible futures into the present and examine them prior to their actual occurrence. In this sense language serves us as the crystal ball serves the fortune teller, since it is the major instrument through which we may create in imagination what might possibly occur later. We were able to talk and write about landing on the moon long before we actually accomplished it.

Oddly enough, even though language is such an important part of our lives, its origin remains a mystery. Why did the sounds made by the human throat become the source for the construction of a language? Why didn't hand motions or facial expressions serve as the original basis for communication? Some have maintained that language is instinctive and that therefore we begin to speak in the same way we gradually begin to walk. We are born with vocal cords and other biological equipment which under the proper stimuli lead to the production of certain kinds of sounds that become parts of linguistic expression.

This is a very questionable theory. First of all, it is highly dubious whether the vocal cords or any other parts of the human body function primarily to produce linguistic sounds. As R. M. S. Heffner has indicated, all the biological parts which are utilized for speech making have other more crucial functions. Thus, he notes, the mechanism of the larynx and the so-called vocal cords is necessary for the process of normal elimination from the alimentary canal; it also has an important function in normal childbirth. Furthermore, without this mechanism our arm movements would be severely limited.

A great many of the muscular actions of our arms depend upon the creation of a partial vacuum beneath the vocal bands. Without these two valvular controls of the opening of the larynx [vocal cords] the human animal would have very little power above the hips. He could not lift himself, or any object of size, with his arms.[1]

In other words, those biological organs which seem to be primarily designed for speech turn out to have other more basic functions.

Second, while a child will learn to walk without help, he cannot learn a language without help. We begin to speak not instinctively but by imitating the sounds made by our parents, relatives, and society in general. Thus many linguists now regard the creation of a language as a conventional habit picked up by imitation. But exactly how did this conventional habit take hold? Did men who were originally without language suddenly begin to employ sounds as signs of things and occurrences? Were human beings ever able to function without any linguistic resources? Some linguists believe that even the most primitive men had some rudimentary means of linguistic communication. We do not know whether men actually lived together at one time without using a language any more than we know why a language which utilizes the vocal cords should have arisen at all. A language could consist of hand motions, or eye motions, or whistling. It is not difficult to imagine a kind of communication which utilizes the various movements of fingers; the deaf do have such a language.

Several theories have been offered to explain why sounds from the vocal cords became the primary means of forming a language. The explanation that would be most palatable to the religious world would be the view that God created language as well as man during those early six days of creation, and that He recognized that vocal sounds would be most beneficial. (It would, of course, be rather difficult to determine whether these early humans spoke Hebrew, Greek, Arabic, Zulu, or Sanskrit.) However, most linguists prefer a natural rather than a supernatural explanation. They use the following, rather colorful, terms to describe frequently overlapping theories about the origin of speech.

The *bow-wow* theory claims that speech arose from man's conscious imitation of the sounds of nature as a way of signaling to others the presence of certain animals or other potential dangers. This onomatopoeic process is still evident today when a child calls a dog a "bow-wow," or a train a "choo-choo." The *pooh-pooh* theory is the nickname for the view that language results from instinctive vocal ejaculations, such as "pooh," "oh," "ah," etc., caused by

---

1. R.M.S. Heffner, *General Phonetics*. Madison: University of Wisconsin Press, 1964, p. 23.

feelings of pain, pleasure, surprise, contempt, and so on. In this way sounds became associated with happy or unhappy events and were gradually utilized to signify a particular object or occurrence. According to the *sing-song* hypothesis, men at an early stage adopted mechanical chanting in order to show respect to the gods (although it is not clear why chanting, rather than something else, should be chosen to honor the gods). This chanting was gradually modified and words were formed. The *yo-he-ho* and the *ta-ta* theories both explain the origin of speech in terms of kinesthetic activity. The yo-he-ho-ists believe that primitive physical exertions were accompanied by instinctive sounds, perhaps grunts, which gradually became words. The ta-ta school maintains that the vocal cords are biologically connected to the body, and sounds automatically arise when the body moves. Out of these sounds arose language.

These are all interesting conjectures, and perhaps one or more of them is correct. But scientific linguistics obviously still awaits the kind of evidence which will enable it to give a warranted account of the genesis of language.

We marvel at the communication systems of bees and dolphins, but of course their systems are not comparable to ours. We are able to use language not only to satisfy the practical needs of everyday living, but also to create the works of art, science, and philosophy that serve to enrich human existence. It is not known whether animals and insects, such as the dolphin and the bee, would become extinct if they lost the power of communication. But our reliance on language is so extensive that some linguists have claimed that man would die out if he were unable to speak or write.

On the other hand, language has been blamed for many of the evils in this world: misunderstandings, quarrels, wars. Many have been disheartened by the ambiguities and obscurities inherent in our system of communication. In this connection we are reminded of the Professors of Language in *Gulliver's Travels*, who are so distrustful of the words they use that they carry with them the objects which the words are meant to designate. This distrust of language has been shared by such philosophers as Locke, Berkeley, Santayana, Whitehead, and Wittgenstein. Brigham Young offers us an extreme example of logophobia when he states: "I long for the time that a point of the finger, or motion of the hand, will express every idea without utterance."[2] It might be noted that mutes have this ability to "express every idea without utterance," but they would hardly describe their means of communication as ideal.

---

2. Max Black, *The Labyrinth of Language*. New York: Frederick A. Praeger, 1968, p. 116; quoted from Brigham Young's *Journal of Discourses*.

Even though the objections to language do have some validity, they are insignificant in view of the many benefits language has bestowed upon men. Try to imagine a world inhabited by Gulliver's linguists as they scurry about to express their view of an atom by carrying an atom; or try to imagine the kind of objects they would require in order to formulate Einstein's theory of relativity or the mathematical notion of an irrational number. Apparently nothing can serve as an adequate substitute for that versatile phenomenon, language.

The functions of language are many and diverse. It enables us to communicate to others our experiences and desires; it enables us to release emotional tensions; in the hands of great writers like Shakespeare, Milton, and Proust, it is the means for achieving unique and sublime aesthetic effects. Wittgenstein has classified the functions of language in the following way:

giving orders and obeying them

describing the appearance of an object or giving its measurements

constructing an object from a description (a drawing)

reporting an event

speculating about an event

forming and testing an hypothesis

presenting the results of an experiment in tables and diagrams

making up a story and reading it

play acting

singing catches

guessing riddles

making a joke; telling it

solving a problem in practical arithmethic

translating from one language into another

asking, thanking, cursing, greeting, praying[3]

Undoubtedly there are other functions that can be added to this list, for example, persuading and frightening. Language is often employed to persuade someone to do something or to frighten him. But perhaps the most important function—one that makes possible not only much of scientific theory, but

---

3. Ludwig Wittgenstein, *Philosophical Investigations*, Third Edition. New York: MacMillan, 1969, pp. 11–12.

also much of our everyday planning—is the use of language to draw inferences and to test beliefs. Only as our thoughts and speculations are formed into words and then into sentences can we begin to ask what is true and what is false, and whether new or additional information can be drawn from the data already in our possession. In terms of everyday living this fact is clearly exhibited. The acts of observing phenomena of the most intricate sort and of conducting laboratory tests become most meaningful when these phenomena and experimental data are described by words and thereby exposed to the tests of scientific rejection or acceptance. Only when a theory or hypothesis has been verbalized can we begin to ask whether the evidence involved does really substantiate the conclusion, or whether further information can be inferred from the theory or hypothesis, or whether an implicit contradiction is present. This inferential characteristic of language, which enables us to sift through information and to determine what is most reliable, makes language essential as an instrument for human survival.

There are those, of course, who believe in other ways of drawing inferences and ascertaining truth, such as through the processes of intuition, revelation, clairvoyance, and other mystical or supernatural approaches. The Zen Buddhists are supposed to be wise men who obtain knowledge through silence, meditation, and intuition. But if the Eastern wise man remains mute, how are we to judge whether he really is wise? The most profound theory must eventually be articulated, for otherwise how are we to judge whether it is profound? Even the hairiest and most solemn-looking mystic has to say something if he wants to convey his wisdom to more than the silent circle with whom he communes. And when he uses words, he is as responsible as the ordinary man for making sense. An essential aspect of making sense is communicating logically; that is, abiding by the rules for drawing inferences and distinguishing truth from falsity. A Timothy Leary can tell us that LSD is man's pathway to God, but the moment that he moves from feeling to talking, the moment that he advises others to believe something because of certain reasons, then he, like any other fallible mortal, becomes subject to the same implicit rules of logical inference which all men are obligated to utilize when they use a language system. He has to demonstrate that his evidence is legitimate, his conclusions are correct. In other words, he has to convince us that what he affirms is neither linguistically obscure nor logically untenable.

Through the ages man has relied upon various means for validating his beliefs. Besides using words and phrases as magic formulas he has prostrated himself before the stars, the moon, the sun, pieces of wood designed in the form of deities, statues, beads, rabbits' feet, old coins, old clothes, cows, snakes, mirrors, toads, salt, shawls, water, phallic symbols, and an indefinite number of other interesting phenomena. But such reliance on the magical properties of things, whether they be words or objects, has not proved very satisfactory. In the last resort, beliefs are best validated by an inspection of the verbally stated or written reasons that permit evidence to be questioned and inference to be checked. It might be argued that as an instrument of inference, language is quite fallible and the rules that express the relation of evidence to conclusion are often vaguely stated, if they are stated at all. In fact, in all languages except special ones formulated by logicians and mathematicians, the rules governing inference are implicit and only careful analysis can bring to light whether a given argument is or is not legitimate. Of course, an ideal system of communication could be formed if an omnipotent God were to inform us once and for all of the rules of inference a language ought to have. But unfortunately there has been some difficulty through the years in obtaining this information; thus we are constantly employing an imperfect instrument. But this is not sufficient cause for despair. After all, no tool is perfect, and it is better to use an imperfect one and attempt to improve it rather than to reject it. For better or worse, we argue, discuss, analyze, and inform by means of words, and thus our only hope is to clarify our understanding of what a language is, how it can be improved, and what the rules are that govern the giving of reasons and the justification for beliefs.

It is important to recognize at the outset that what we call logical inference is not to be confused with the psychological activity known as *thinking*. Much confusion exists concerning the puzzling question of what occurs in the mind when thinking is in process. Elaborate theories expounded by philosophers and psychologists have attempted to describe what the mind is and what its contents are. Some contend that both physical and mental things reside in the head, while others claim that mental entities do not exist. But we are not concerned with this question. When we ask whether something logically follows from something else, we are not concerned with what is going on in anyone's head. What is actually in the mind of a political orator may never be known (perhaps this is fortunate), but when he speaks or writes, what he states can be known and can be judged in terms of whether a given sentence does or does not follow from some other sentence. We may never be able to look into a man's mind, and therefore we may never be sure that we know exactly what he might mean, but we can look at and ask questions about the words and sentences he uses.

What we intend to do in this book, then, is to deal with those features of a language that determine its inferential, that is, its logical structure. More specifically, we shall be concerned with examining many of those linguistic expressions that seem to offer a clue that inference is occurring. Thus, for example, words like *therefore, then, if, hence* (as well as their counterparts in foreign languages) would seem to play some special role when we want to state that something logically follows from something else. In the statement "If what you say is true, then John Doe is guilty," the words *if* and *then* are ways of indicating that the statement "John Doe is guilty" is to be inferred from "what you say is true." In fact, *if* and *then* would seem to be governed by certain implicit rules, for in the majority of cases it would be wrong to interchange the words following *if* with the words following *then*. To say "If I walk in the rain, then I catch a cold" obviously is not the same as saying "If I catch a cold, then I walk in the rain." Another rule allows us to eliminate the *if-then* grammatical construction entirely and equate "If I walk in the rain, then I catch a cold" with "Either I do not walk in the rain, or I catch a cold." We shall attempt to examine the rules that govern the use of such terms as *if* and *then*.

Along the way we shall also attempt to deal with what logic books usually ignore—namely, the philosophical and linguistic problems that arise out of a concern with logic. In recent times a major focus of interest has been the relation of logic to mathematics. Since the advent of Russell's and Whitehead's monumental work, *Principia Mathematica*,[4] which seeks to show how mathematics can be derived from purely logical foundations, logicians have tended to overemphasize the relation of logic to mathematics and to underemphasize the philosophical and linguistic problems engendered by an examination of logic. It may be very important to show that all mathematical truths are really reducible to truths of logic. But it would seem just as important to ask what it is that logical truths themselves are. There is a tendency to think that if a statement is logically true, then it is necessarily true, that is, it is incapable of ever being falsified. But how is this to be squared with the views of natural and social scientists who maintain that the only assertions which are scientifically acceptable are those that are capable of being falsified? Absolute truths are no longer to be tolerated in scientific inquiry. But would this mean that logic is not to be utilized in scientific inquiry? This would surely be absurd. What, then, is the answer?

Logic, it is said, is supposed to deal with meaningful sentences. We usually assume we know what sentences and meanings are, but when we attempt to explain what they really are, we are forced to deal with some of the most

---

4. Bertrand Russell and Alfred North Whitehead, *Principia Mathematica*, Second Edition. Cambridge University Press, 1925–27, 3 vols.

profound philosophical problems. Sentences are very difficult to define, and meanings turn out to be ephemeral entities that constantly elude clarification. Our treatment will concern itself with these very issues which have been ignored by those who emphasize the mathematical aspects of logical inquiry.

Exercises

1. What are the most important functions of a language?

2. According to a report in the *New York Times* (October 24, 1970, p. 33), some young people gathered together in a dark, incense-filled room in Wilton, Connecticut, on October 23, 1970. With their eyes closed and their palms pressed together, they prayed silently Then from the back of the room there was a sound, "... at first low, then rising in volume until it resounded from the beamed ceiling like a foghorn 'oooOOOMMMMMMM!' The sound, from the Sanskrit word 'Aum,' is said to be the divine syllable that accompanied the creation of the universe. It is intoned every Monday night here during meditations held by an Indian guru named Sri Chinmoy Kumar Ghose."

    Discuss how in the above example, language is used to (1) release tensions and (2) control the beliefs and actions of people. Can you give any other examples of how language is used to release tensions and control people?

3. Can a civilization rely on something else besides speech or writing to communicate?

4. Do you think that the present civilization on earth would survive if we suddenly lost the power to speak or write?

5. Describe the various theories which attempt to account for the genesis of language. Which seem to you to be the most naive and which seem to have some relevance?

6. Certain languages such as Esperanto, Interlingua Ido, and Basic English have been formulated to serve as a universal or auxiliary language to facilitate communication between peoples of the world. Do you believe that the adoption of a universal language might help to minimize the misunderstandings that cause wars and conflict among nations?

7. What is *thinking*? Think hard about something. If someone asks you what you are thinking about, you answer by using words and sentences. Then is thinking equivalent to words and sentences?

8. Can one think without language?

9. The language employed by Gulliver's linguists is a clumsy device, but would it not have the advantage of being very precise since whatever is being described must be present? Discuss.

10. Discuss what you mean when you say that someone is "illogical."

SUPPLEMENTARY READINGS

Butler, Samuel, "Thought and Language," in Max Black (ed.), *The Importance of Language*. Englewood Cliffs, N.J.: Prentice-Hall, 1962.

Russell, Bertrand, "Language," in E. Nagel and R. B. Brandt, (eds.), *Meaning and Knowledge*. New York: Harcourt, Brace, and World, 1965.

Schlauch, Margaret, *The Gift of Tongues*. New York: Viking Press, 1945. Chapter 1, "Language as Communication."

Wenner, Adrian M., "Sound Communication in Honeybees," *Scientific American*, CCX (1964), 116–22.

2

Types
of
Discourse

INFERENTIAL DISCOURSE

To discuss inferential discourse, we must first establish what it is and how it is to be distinguished from other kinds of discourse. Perhaps the best way to begin the explanation of inference is to observe some examples in which inference is taking place and compare them with others in which inference is either nonexistent or subservient to some other linguistic function.

Consider the following:

> The new obscenity law permits publication of works formerly condemned as pornographic. Sexual permissiveness is no longer condemned, and in some cases immorality is condoned. The new obscenity law is certainly fostering moral corruption.

Here the writer is presenting us with an *argument*; that is, he is telling us that on the basis of certain *reasons*, or *evidence*, or *premises* (we shall use *reason, evidence,* as well as *premise* interchangeably) a given *conclusion* correctly follows. Specifically, the conclusion is: "The new obscenity law is certainly fostering moral corruption." The reasons, according to the writer, are: "The new obscenity law permits publication of works formerly condemned as pornographic. Sexual permissiveness is no longer condemned, and in some cases immorality is condoned." Whenever one is concerned primarily with giving reasons or evidence for some particular belief, he becomes involved in an inference-producing discourse. Discourses of this kind, arguments as we have called them, will be our main concern in this book.

In many of the arguments that are encountered, the word *therefore* is used, either implicitly—as in the example above—or explicitly, and this gives us an immediate clue as to what part of the argument is evidence and what part is conclusion. In the statement "He felt dizzy and he fainted; therefore he is sick," the word *therefore* is an immediate sign to anyone who understands English that evidence is being given and a conclusion is being drawn. The evidence may not be adequate or believable, and the conclusion may not be warranted. History abounds with examples of people who accepted certain beliefs using very flimsy evidence and lacking knowledge of logic. But the word *therefore*, or one of the following substitutes for it, is indication that argumentative discourse is being offered.

so	*thus*
hence	*it follows that*
consequently	*as a result*

accordingly	*then* (when it does not refer to time)

Sometimes arguments are recognized not by an implicit or explicit use of *therefore*, which usually indicates that the conclusion follows directly after the word, but by the use of other words that indicate evidence or reasons are being given. Thus in "He will win since he is strong" the word *since* indicates that what follows it, in this case "he is strong," is to be regarded as evidence, or as a reason. And since only "he will win" is left, then this must be the conclusion for which "he is strong" is evidence. Some other words that play a role similar to *since* are:

for	*as*
if	*considering that*
taking into account that	*on the basis of*
due to the fact that	*because*

Discourse—especially argumentative discourse—might be much clearer and more easily evaluated for its logical rigor if we either (1) constantly included the words that signified what was to be taken as evidence and what as conclusion or (2) had some rule that specified the order of evidence and conclusion; a rule, for example, that told us that evidence must come first in a sentence and conclusion last. But consider the following four examples:

1. We should keep him out of government; he is an atheist and a homosexual.

2. He is an atheist and a homosexual; we should keep him out of government.

3. He is an atheist. Therefore we should keep him out of government. He is also a homosexual.

4. He is an atheist and a homosexual. We keep anyone out of government who is an atheist and a homosexual.

In example 1, there are no words which indicate the sentence which is evidence and the sentence which is a conclusion. Only one who was aware that atheists and homosexuals are frequently disqualified from government service would be immediately ready to take "he is an atheist and a homosexual" as evidence or reasons for "we ought to keep him out of government." Note also that here the reasons occur *after* the conclusion has been given.

In example 2, again there are no words which signal what is the evidence and what is the conclusion. Here also only prior information permits us to assume what is the evidence and what is the conclusion. The reasons in this example occur *before* the conclusion. In example 3, the use of *therefore* does tell us what the conclusion is. But the reasons appear both *before* and *after* the conclusion. Finally, in 4, no words are given by which to distinguish evidence from conclusion; in fact the conclusion itself is omitted! Both statements in example 4 are reasons, and the omitted conclusion ("we ought to keep him out of government") is presumed to be obvious. But it is obvious only because we have prior knowledge about atheists, homosexuals, and governments.

Thus we are not too scrupulous about where we place reasons and conclusions. In our writing and conversation it is often quite difficult not only to distinguish the reasons from the conclusions, but also to decide whether the discourse is an argument.

Examples 1, 2, and 4 above are regarded as arguments only because we are familiar with certain social and governmental facts. But is the following example an argument or merely a series of sentences?

5. He sleeps very little. He does not eat much. He does not feel very well.

If these statements offer reasons for a conclusion, then which sentence is the conclusion and which ones are the reasons? Example 5 could mean:

6. He sleeps very little and does not eat much. Therefore he does not feel well.

7. He sleeps very little and does not feel very well. Therefore he does not eat much.

8. He does not eat much and he does not feel very well. Therefore he sleeps very little.

Unless the word *therefore* is specifically given, or unless some broader context clarifies the meaning, there is no way of knowing how example 5 is to be understood. We frequently employ language in this ambiguous way, and if we wish to communicate effectively, we are then obligated to make explicit the precise meanings intended.

Let us examine the first paragraph of Book I of Aristotle's *Politics*.

Every state is a community of some kind, and every community is established with a view to some good; for mankind always act in order to obtain that which they think good. But, if all communities aim at some good, the state or political community, which is the highest of all, and which embraces all the rest, aims at good in a greater degree than any other, and at the highest good.

What is the conclusion of this passage? A careful reading would reveal that it really contains *two* conclusions. The use of *for* in the first sentence reveals to us that "mankind always act in order to obtain that which they think good" is the evidence and therefore the rest of the sentence, "every state is a community of some kind, and every community is established with a view to some good," is the conclusion. But the second sentence also contains a conclusion. By noticing where *if* is located, and by making explicit the word *therefore* which is meant to appear directly before *the state*, we can then identify the conclusion. Once the reasons and the conclusions of a given argument have been identified, then it is possible to ask whether the reasons given are any good; that is, whether they are true or false, whether the conclusion does indeed follow from them. And until this kind of identification is made there is no way of judging whether or not we ought to believe what Aristotle (or anyone else, for that matter) wants us to believe.

The Aristotle passage, by its use of the key terms *for* and *if*, has at least the virtue of containing identifiable conclusions. But very often a writer does not give the conclusion explicitly, either because he feels the tone and context of the writing make the conclusion obvious or because an explicit expression of the conclusion might be too controversial. Thus some conservative writer in a magazine might state: "John Jones, who was a strong opponent of the Vietnam War, has been shown to be a card-carrying Communist." By relating Jones's view of the war to the fact that he is a Communist, the magazine serves to foster the prejudicial belief a reader might have that all those who opposed the Vietnam War are Communists. But as long as the belief is left implicit, it does not have to be defended in the way an explicit belief would be. If the writer had said, "John Jones, who was a strong opponent of the Vietnam War, has finally been shown to be a card-carrying Communist, and this proves that all those who opposed the Vietnam War are Communists," the statement would be quickly rejected by all thinking persons. It is safer, although not necessarily more honest, to keep conclusions implicit.

Not only do we have to deal with implicit conclusions, but we also encounter discourses which at first glance do not seem to contain any arguments. In such instances the context as a whole must be examined to determine whether or not an argument is implicit in the discourse. The following comment on Henry James was written by Ford Maddox Ford.

He saw the "common people" lying like a dark sea round the raft of the privileged. They excited his piqued wonder, his ardent curiosity, he built the most elaborate theories all over and round them, he observed enough of them to be able to give characteristics, phrases, and turns of mind to the retainers of the Privileged, but he never could be brought to think that he knew enough about them to let him project their lives onto paper. He noted admirably the very phraseology of Mrs. Wicks, the faithful attendant of Maisie who lived forever in fear of being "spoken to," and with equal admirableness the point of view of poor Brooksmith, the gentleman's valet who "never *had* got his spirits up" after the loss of his one wonderful master. But if, as happens to us today, he had been confronted by a Radical Left clamouring that he must write about the proletariat or be lost, he would just for ever have dismissed his faithful amanuensis and relapsed into mournful silence.[1]

No one sentence in this passage can be identified as the conclusion. Even indicator terms such as *since*, *if*, and *therefore* are missing. Ford might be taken to be merely reporting the fact that James does not write about the common people. But not everything Ford has written here is factual. In the last sentence he states what he *believes* James might have done had he been alive today. Furthermore, even in reporting James's aversion to writing about ordinary people, Ford goes on to stress this fact and to exaggerate it to the point of claiming that James would not have written anything at all had he been required to write about common people. James saw them "like a dark sea around the raft of the privileged"; they were the "proletariat" about whom the "radical left" were "clamouring" that we must write. The use of such picturesque and emotional language should immediately make us suspect that Ford is doing more than merely giving us factual information about James. Ford wants us to take a certain view towards James, to draw some conclusion concerning James's ability as a writer. But what this conclusion is can only be conjectured from the above selection. The following arguments are all possible:

1. Since James does not write about the common people, he is a poor writer.

2. Since James does not write about the common people, he is a limited writer.

3. James does not write about common people, but he still has significant literary virtues. Therefore he is a great writer.

4. Henry James is a great writer because he does not write about common people.

---

1. Ford Maddox Ford, *Portraits from Life*, "Henry James, The Master." Chicago: Henry Regnery Company, 1937, pp. 9–10.

5. Henry James is to be condemned as a human being because he does not concern himself with common people; he is a snob.

To discover which conclusion Ford had in mind, the reader would have to read the entire context in which it appears. He would then realize that it contains a somewhat malicious portrait of James and that most likely Ford intended to defend either arguments 2, or 5. But Ford himself never gives us an explicit statement of his argument and the reason for this is quite clear. When made explicit the arguments might easily be refuted and dismissed. But by leaving the argument unsaid, Ford gives the reader a vague feeling that something is seriously wrong with James and his art, a feeling which Ford wishes to instill without having to argue seriously about whether he is right or wrong.

Since any kind of discourse can have some implicit conclusion, one should always ask:

What is the point that is being made?

What is the speaker (or writer) trying to prove?

Is there something the speaker wants us to believe even though he does not explicitly tell us what it is?

If he does not want to make it explicit, then why is he concealing it?

Once we have distinguished the reasons and the conclusions in a given argument we are on our way to determining whether the argument is satisfactory, for, as we shall see, there are specific means by which we can tell whether or not a given conclusion does follow logically from a given set of premises. But an argument is not to be labeled satisfactory simply because its conclusion and its premises are formed in accordance with the rules of logic.

A *valid* argument should be distinguished from a *sound* one. An argument is valid when the premises and conclusion are so organized that the conclusion follows necessarily from the premises. More specifically, when we are concerned with validity we are not concerned with whether the argument is a good one or not, but simply with its organization. An example will make this point clear. The following argument (A) is valid.

All men are idiots.

No idiots are politicians.   (A)

Therefore no men are politicians.

This argument is valid not because its premises are true (we suspect they are both false) but because the premises and the conclusion are all embedded in a certain *form*. But what is this so-called form?

In later chapters we shall have more to say about the form or framework contained in every argument. But here we can at least make some general observations. In the above argument concerning idiots and politicians there are two interesting features. First, some of the words are *descriptive* in the sense that they refer to or describe something. Thus *men*, *idiots*, and *politicians* are descriptive words. They refer to men, idiots, and politicians. On the other hand, some of the words are not descriptive at all; they are what we shall later call *syntactical* or *connector* words that form a framework in which descriptive words are embedded. Thus *all*, *are*, *no*, and *therefore* do not describe anything. No one has ever seen an all, or an are, or a no, or a therefore. Now if we extract each descriptive word and replace it by a specific letter, the above argument will look like this:

All *X* are *Y*.

No *Y* are *Z*.

Therefore no *X* are *Z*.

Here the *X*, *Y*, and *Z* stand for the particular descriptive words of the argument, and once we make this replacement of letters for words the form of the argument is now quite clearly given. It is the particular arrangement of descriptive words in relation to connector words. Thus note the following characteristics of this form: (1) The two premises start with *all* and *no* respectively. (2) The conclusion, if we ignore the word *therefore*, starts with *no*. (3) *X* is a subject in the first premise and a subject in the conclusion; *Y* is a predicate in the first premise and a subject in the second premise; *Z* is a predicate in the second premise and a predicate in the conclusion.

This particular kind of arrangement of the descriptive words and the connector words shows the form of the argument and ought to be distinguished from the form of other arguments such as (B):

All idiots are men.

No idiots are politicians.   (B)

Therefore no men are politicians.

In this case the form is exhibited as:

All *Y* is *X*.

No *Y* is *Z*.

Therefore no *X* is *Z*.

Here the arrangement is such that the two premises begin with *all* and *no* and the conclusion with *no*, just as in the first form, but the arrangements of the *X*, *Y*, and *Z* are different. In this form, *X* is a predicate in the first premise even though it is still a subject in the conclusion; *Y* is a subject in both premises, while *Z* remains a predicate in both the second premise and the conclusion.

The following argument (C) presents still another form that is distinct from the ones we have just examined:

Some men are idiots.

Politicians are idiots.   (C)

Therefore all men are politicians.

And the form is:

Some *X* is *Y*.

No *Z* is *Y*.

Therefore all *X* is *Z*.

Here, of course, the contrast of forms is quite evident. First, the premises start with *some* and *no* and the conclusion with *all*; *X* is a subject in the first premise and a subject in the conclusion; *Y* is a predicate in both premises; finally, *Z* is a subject in the second premise and a predicate in the conclusion. Thus the form of an argument is dependent upon the specific arrangement of the connector and descriptive terms.

The ability to determine the form of an argument is important, for the form shows us whether or not an argument is valid. Thus (A) above is valid while (B) and (C) are invalid, not because we are dealing with men, idiots, and politicians but because (A) has a certain form that always permits it to be called valid while (B) and (C) have forms which, regardless of what descriptive terms they may contain, will always be invalid. What the rules are that make one form valid (that is, logically correct) and another form invalid (that is, logically incorrect) is, of course, what we shall be discovering when we examine the rules of logical inference. But here it can be indicated that if a conclusion correctly follows from certain premises, if the argument is valid, it is not due to the truth or falsity of the premises, but simply because the premises and the conclusion are formed and arranged in a certain way.

Obviously the best argument is not only logically correct, but also uses true premises. In the final analysis we want our arguments to tell us what is true. Thus the best argument is *sound*; that is, the argument is valid and the premises are true. For if the premises are true and the logic is correct, then the conclusion must be true. This is the only connection between logical form and truth. If an argument is valid and if its premises are true, then the conclusion will also be true.

For this reason there are always two questions that must be asked of any argument: (1) Does the conclusion follow logically from the premises? (2) Are the premises true? On this analysis Aristotle's logic may be impeccable, but we would still be required to ask whether the premises of his argument are to be taken as true. *Do* all communities aim at some good, and is it true that men always act in order to obtain that which they think good? (Would you accept these premises as true?)

OTHER KINDS OF DISCOURSE

We have been discussing argumentative discourse, but there are other kinds of discourse. Language is used for different purposes. Sometimes we tell stories, real or imaginary, with the objective of relating what happens rather than proving some point. This is called *narrative* discourse. Examples of this type may range from the simple forms found in fairy tales, fables, anecdotes, and sketches to the more complex types such as autobiography, biography, short stories, plays, novels, poetry, and histories. Who has not as a child been spellbound by the promise of adventure inherent in the lines "Once upon a time there was a girl named Cinderella, who had a wicked stepmother . . . ." We want to know what happens to Cinderella, just as we want to know what happens to Chaucer's knight who commits rape in the "Wife of Bath's Tale."

> And so it happened that King Arthur
> Had in his house a lively bachelor
> Who one day came riding from hawking
> And in his path he saw a maiden alone walking before him
> Whom he raped by force.
> There was such outrage against this crime and
> Such suing for justice to King Arthur
> That this knight would have been doomed to die
> By the course of law and should have lost his head
> For that was the punishement then
> Except that the queen and other ladies
> Begged the King to have pity
> Till the King relented and spared his life

And handed him over to the queen to decide
At her discretion whether she wanted to
Save or destroy him.[2]

But even in the fairly simple narrative forms where the interest obviously
centers on the unfolding of a series of events, some implicit arguments are
involved in the telling of the story. In the case of Cinderella, the narrative
has the implicit argument that if one is virtuous he will be rewarded. In the
case of the knight who commits rape, the Wife of Bath tells this story to rein-
force her argument that true happiness in marriage comes if the wife maintains
sovereignty over her husband. Very rarely does the narrative type of discourse
exist in pure form, with no other purpose but that of telling a story. But it
is always necessary to ask whether the primary aim of a discourse is to tell a
story or to present an argument. If it is to tell a story, then we do not expect
as much logical precision as we might otherwise; truth and falsity of premises
are not as significant. The Wife of Bath may indeed be wrong in believing that
a wife ought to maintain sovereignty over her husband. It is still questionable—with all due respect to the Women's Liberation Movement—whether
women would in fact be better rulers than men. But whereas the truth of the
evidence is important in an argument, it is not that important in a story.
We may not agree with the Wife of Bath, but her characterization and tale
are perennial sources of enjoyment.

Similarly, it is very unusual to find the *descriptive* type of discourse in as
pure a form as we find it in the following poem where the poet seems to have
no other purpose except to appeal to our visual sensations through his description of a wave.

The long-rólling,
Steady-póuring,
Deep-trenchéd
Green billów:

The wide-topped
Unbróken
Green-glacid,
Slow-sliding,
Cold-flushing,

---

2. G. Chaucer, *Canterbury Tales*, in *The Works of Geoffrey Chaucer* (F. N. Robinson,
ed.), Second Edition. Boston: Houghton Mifflin Co., 1957, p. 84. (This is our translation.)

—On—on—on—
Chill-rushing,
Hush—hushing,
... Hush—hushing. ...[3]

Thus the primary aim of descriptive discourse is simply to describe, to appeal to what is sensory in our experience through the employment of visual, auditory, gustatory, olfactory, tactile, and kinesthetic images. But descriptive writing, like any other kind of writing, is rarely pure in form. The following passage by James Baldwin describes his bitter, handsome father who preached "chilling" sermons and was cruel in his personal relations:

> ... It must be said that there was something else in him, buried in him, which lent him his tremendous power, and, even, a rather crushing charm. It has something to do with his blackness, I think—he was very black— with his blackness and his beauty, and the fact that he knew that he was black but did not know that he was beautiful. He claimed to be proud of his blackness but it had also been the cause of much humiliation and it had fixed bleak boundaries to his life.[4]

But this selection also seems to contain an implicit argument, which might be paraphrased as follows: "The blackness of a man's skin can make him look beautiful, powerful, and charming. My father was a black man. Therefore my father was beautiful, powerful, and charming." The descriptive vividness of Baldwin's style is most striking in the quoted passage. For this reason such writing is called descriptive, but a detailed analysis would also reveal an argument which equates blackness with beauty.

In still another example, a reporter's description of the scene outside the Chicago Democratic Convention of 1968 contains an implicit argument:

> The police lined up in front of the building, trying to keep the unruly mob from entering. The youthful defenders of freedom and peace threw beer cans at them, yelling, "Fascist pig, go home," and other assorted obscenities. The demonstrators had long hair, beards, and wore clothes from which such foul odors emanated that I had to hold my nose to keep

---

3. James Stephens, "The Main-Deep," in *Collected Poems.* Copyright 1925, 1926 by Macmillan Publishing Co. Inc., renewed 1953, 1954 by James Stephens. Reprinted with permission.

4. James Baldwin, *Notes of a Native Son.* Boston: The Beacon Press, 1955, p. 87.

from being nauseated. Some of them actually got close enough to hit the police, but they turned back when the police threatened to use their clubs.

The reporter who wrote this account does indeed provide a description of a given scene. But at the same time, by the use of certain words and sentences designed to arouse emotions, he is arguing that the demonstrators are bad because of their behavior, and that the police are the innocent victims of their violence. It would certainly seem that the aim of this report is to present an argument rather than merely to describe. Made explicit, the argument might read that the so-called "defenders of freedom" are not really defenders at all, but merely dirty, obscene, young people with long hair and beards who attack the forces of law and order and deserve to be threatened by the police. If a reporter is really concerned with presenting an argument, then the argument ought to be made explicit and examined in terms of its soundness.

Exercises

1. Which of the following are examples of narrative, descriptive, or argumentative discourse?

   a) I saw on that ivory face the expression of somber pride, of ruthless power, of craven terror—of an intense and hopeless despair. Did he live his life again in every detail of desire, temptation, and surrender during that supreme moment of complete knowledge? He cried in a whisper at some image, at some vision—he cried out twice, a cry that was no more than a breath—

   "The horror! The horror!"

   I blew the candle out and left the cabin. The pilgrims were dining in the mess-room, and I took my place opposite the manager who lifted his eyes to give me a questioning glance, which I successfully ignored. He leaned back, serene, with that peculiar smile of his sealing the unexpressed depths of his meanness. A continuous shower of small flies streamed upon the lamp, upon the cloth, upon our hands and faces. Suddenly the manager's boy put his insolent black head in the doorway, and said in a tone of scathing contempt—

   "Mistah Kurtz—he dead."

   Joseph Conrad, *Heart of Darkness*

   b) I know this fellow down the block who is not working. He looks strong and healthy, but he's on welfare. He told me himself he's better off on welfare than working for peanuts on some cruddy job. He says he's looking forward to that guaranteed income that the government is planning to give him.

c) Scientists have recently discovered that the offspring of rats who have had regular doses of marijuana have given birth to defective offspring. We must draw the obvious conclusion that this is a harmful drug that should not under any circumstances be legalized.

d) Fog everywhere. Fog up the river, where it flows among green aits and meadows; fog down the river, where it rolls defiled among the tiers of shipping, and the waterside pollutions of a great (and dirty) city. Fog on the Essex marshes, fog on the Kentish heights. Fog creeping into the cabooses of collier-brigs; fog lying out on the yards, and hovering in the rigging of great ships; fog drooping on the gunwales of barges and small boats.... The raw afternoon is rawest, and the dense fog is densest, and the muddy streets are muddiest, near that leaden-headed, old obstruction, appropriate ornament for the threshhold of a leaden-headed old corporation: Temple Bar. And hard by Temple Bar, in Lincoln's Inn Hall, at the very heart of the fog, sits the Lord High Chancellor in his High Court of Chancery.

    Never can there come fog too thick, never can there come mud and mire too deep, to assort with the groping and floundering conditions which this High Court of Chancery, most pestilent of hoary sinners, holds, this day, in the sight of heaven and earth.

Charles Dickens, Bleak House

2. Which of the following contain either implicit or explicit arguments, or no arguments at all? Where there are arguments, either explicit or implicit, formulate the premises and the conclusion.

a) Why is sexual intercourse very pleasant, and does it occur among living creatures because it is necessary or for another reason? Is the pleasure due to the fact that the semen is drawn from all parts of the body, as some say, or does it not come from all parts, but only through that part to which all the passages of the veins lead? As the pleasure from the friction is the same in both cases, it must pass through the whole body. Such friction is pleasant, as the vaporous moisture which is unnaturally enclosed escapes. But the act of generation is an emission of such matter for its own proper purpose. It is, therefore, pleasant both because it is necessary and also for another reason; necessary, because the passage out of semen for its natural purpose is pleasant, if it produces sensation, and also for another purpose, that there may be procreation of living creatures. For owing to the pleasure derived living creatures are more inclined to have intercourse.

Aristotle, Problems, IV, 15–20

b) Ten percent of all homicides in England are caused by guns whereas sixty percent of all homicides in the United States are caused by guns. Furthermore, an Englishman cannot buy a long gun without getting a certificate from the local police. In order to buy a handgun or a military rifle, a Frenchman has to have a police permit. In Sweden a person must prove that he needs a gun before he is allowed to purchase one. All handguns must be registered in Canada.

c) College students are spoiled. Living in an affluent society, they are accustomed to comfort and have never known what it is to go hungry. As a result they look for "causes" when the intellectual pressures at school become too overwhelming and the competition for academic success is keen. They get interested in the minority problem, in pollution, in any controversial issue that will enable them to rationalize their refusal to work hard to achieve a genuine college education.

d) Why has every man a conscience, then? I think that we should be men first, and subjects afterwards. It is not desirable to cultivate a respect for the law, so much as for the right. The only obligation which I have a right to assume is to do at any time what I think right. It is truly enough said that a corporation has no conscience; but a corporation of conscientious men is a corporation *with* a conscience. Law never made men a whit more just; and, by means of their respect for it, even the well-disposed are daily made the agents of injustice.

H. D. Thoreau, On the Duty of Civil Disobedience

e) The Vietnam War has cost us dearly as a nation in lives and money, and those who insisted that we could never win this war in any real sense were right. We should never have intervened in the internal civil struggle of that country. The notion that we did so to fight Communism there and in the rest of Asia was an absurd excuse. We cannot and should not play the role of World Policeman. We have embarked on a very perilous course in foreign policy in this country, and it will prove disastrous to us from both a moral and an economic viewpoint.

f) Chaucer's *Canterbury Tales* is a great poem, and it contains some delightful stories. However, the "Prioress' Tale" in the *Canterbury Tales* is often disliked by modern readers. It tells the story of a good young Christian boy who is murdered by evil Jews. Chaucer's sympathy is clearly with the young boy. Modern readers find his anti-Semitism distasteful, even though they may recognize that Chaucer was merely reflecting the typical views of his age. There is no question, however, that by failing to eschew the bigotry which was so characteristic of the medieval Christian world, Chaucer clearly did not rise above the spirit of his age.

g) Among beings there are some more and some less good, true, noble, and the like. But *more* and *less* are predicated of different things, according as they resemble in their different ways something which is in the degree of *most*, as a thing is said to be hotter according as it more nearly resembles that which is hottest; so that there is something which is truest, something best, something noblest, and consequently, something which is uttermost being; for the truer things are, the more truly they exist. What is most complete in any genus is the cause of all in that genus; as fire, which is the most complete form of heat, is the cause whereby all things are made hot. Therefore there must also be something which is to all beings the cause of their being, goodness, and every other perfection; and this we call God.

St. Thomas Aquinas, *Summa Theologica*

h) When H. L. Mencken said that "the essential traits and qualities of the male, the hallmarks of the unpolluted masculine, are at the same time the hallmarks of the numskull," he was, of course, employing his usual hyperbole for comic effect. But he was right when he claimed that "women, in fact, are not only intelligent but they have almost a monopoly of certain of the subtler and more utile forms of intelligence." Specifically, they have the special female ability to distinguish between truth and delusion.

SUPPLEMENTARY READINGS

Beardsley, Monroe C., *Aesthetics*. New York: Harcourt, Brace, and Co. 1958, Chapter 3, "The Literary Work."

Stein, Gertrude, "Parts of Speech and Punctuation," in Walker Gibson (ed.), *The Limits of Language*. New York: Hill and Wang, 1962.

Taylor, Paul W., *Normative Discourse*. Englewood Cliffs, N. J.: Prentice-Hall, 1961, Chapter 10, "Wittgenstein's Conception of Language."

Turbayne, Colin M., *The Myth of Metaphor*. New Haven, Conn.: Yale University Press, 1962, Chapter 1, "The Nature of Metaphor."

3

Fallacies

To identify reasons and conclusions is obviously not all that is required to show that a given argument is a good one. The supportive reasons must be established as true. And in learning to check the truth of statements that are given as reasons, certain fundamental difficulties must be recognized and eliminated. The words may be ambiguous; the sentences themselves may be open to different interpretations; the reasons may not be relevant to the conclusion; and finally, certain important logical rules may be violated in moving from evidence to conclusion. Later chapters will reveal what these logical rules are. Here we shall show how an argument can be made unsound because of (1) a defect in the words or the sentence structure that is employed or (2) the use of irrelevant premises to form arguments.

A person may know how to speak and write a language, yet his unawareness of subtle shifts in the meanings of words and even entire sentences could misguide him into thinking he has given a sound argument when in reality the argument is defective. Language is unquestionably a remarkable tool, yet, like all tools, it can be mishandled. A lack of understanding of how words and the structure of language function can result in ambiguity, which is usually one of the prime deterrents to effective inference. The first group of fallacies that we shall examine results from a lack of awareness of how words and sentences can cause confusion.

LANGUAGE FALLACIES (LEXICAL AND STRUCTURAL AMBIGUITY)

Lexical Ambiguity

Words are often deliberately used in an ambiguous fashion by writers who wish to achieve special imaginative or other effects. The idiosyncratic use of language is appropriate in certain contexts. William Empson has shown how the deliberate use of ambiguity plays a vital and significant role in literature. Its use in symbolic works like Kafka's *The Trial* has enriched our reading experience immeasurably. In poetry, ambiguous words produce an endless variety of images, associations, feelings, and thoughts. But even in practical affairs, it is sometimes wiser not to be precise. The politician who warns that his country will take "retaliatory measures" is less likely thereby to commit his country to war than is the politician who makes explicit the nature of these retaliatory measures. When a teacher calls a student an "underachiever" he may want to avoid stating the cruel truth—namely, that the student is not too bright.

Thus ambiguity is sometimes more effective and more desirable than clarity. But when the prime aim of discourse is to communicate clearly, and when words serve to obfuscate rather than to clarify, they are obviously not performing their most necessary function. Some of the more common types of ambiguous expression which hamper communication are listed below.

1. Inappropriate use of figurative language (metaphors, similes, analogies, symbols). In many contexts we deliberately compare things which are, at least on first analysis, quite different from one another. Such nonliteral or figurative language takes various forms. When a woman is a peach, a chick, or a red-hot tomato, when a hippie is an animal, and a policeman is a pig, *metaphor* is being employed. If the comparison is made more explicit through the use of *like* or *as*, as in "That man is strong as a bull," the *simile* is being used. The *analogy* is a more extended version of such comparison.[1] Here is an example: "The king wanted to know why his income diminished even though he increased the taxes of his people. One of his officials took a large piece of ice, passed it to other officials until it came into the hands of the king no larger than the size of a bean." This story in the form of an analogy tells us that taxes are like chunks of ice in the hands of corrupt officials. When the eagle is made to stand for the United States, the bear for the Russians, and the lion for the English, we have used words as *symbols* to compare disparate objects. These are all useful and imaginative means of revealing our attitudes towards persons, places, and things. If we say, "The man is like a robot," the simile "like a robot" tells us much more about the man than such literal descriptions as "He obeys orders without question," or "He behaves mechanically without thinking." Figurative language is an indispensable medium for all writers, and particularly for poets. Robert Frost once said that all poetry is metaphor. Imagine a poet who could not say, "My love is like a red red rose," or "Her eyes were shining stars."

However, nonliteral language is misused when it is assumed to be the equivalent of literal expression, or when it is used as a substitute for argument. Suppose that during the course of a speech, a disillusioned American applied Hamlet's famous description of life to the United States, calling the country "an unweeded garden that quickly grows to rank and seed." If the speaker uses this metaphor to make more vivid his view that the United States is decaying, then he is perfectly justified in using it. But if he is using the metaphor as evidence for an argument, then he is utilizing it in an unwarranted fashion. If he argues that the United States is decaying because it is like an unweeded garden and all unweeded gardens decay, then his metaphor is being used

---

1. For a discussion of the role of analogy in scientific inquiry, see Chapter 15, pp. 259–260.

incorrectly. To compare a country's decay with a garden's decay may be interesting, but a country is not a garden, and the fact that one decays does not prove or imply anything about the decay of the other. In fact, it is not at all clear whether the term *decay*, which can be appropriately applied to fruits, vegetables, and thus to gardens, is also applicable to nations. What may be regarded as decadent by one man may be wholesome to another. Thus in recent times one group considers the changing of sexual mores to be indicative of the moral decline of the United States, whereas another group considers it to be evidence of maturity. In brief, similes, metaphors, and analogies may stimulate us to think in different ways about things; they may even motivate us to look for arguments, but they are not arguments in themselves.

2. Misuse of abstract words. Words can mean different things to different people. But general words are probably the most common cause of ambiguity. *Love, duty, democracy, freedom* are troublesome terms because they can connote such a variety of meanings. Every term has some degree of ambiguity, but many words identify something concrete and thus are directly observable. To speak of a cat or a dog is to speak of something that can be seen or heard. On the other hand, no one actually sees or hears love, duty, democracy, or freedom. (Of course, one might say, "I saw my duty and I did it." But in this context *see* is not being used in the sense of observing something.) To say, "John Loves Mary" is not analogous to saying, "John runs to Mary." Running is an observable act, but love is never seen in the same way. We can see *evidence* for love; we can say, "John gave Mary his fraternity pin," and therefore this is evidence that he loves her. But there is no way of directly seeing something called love. For this reason, definitions of love have always required endless amounts of modification. Love is a feeling; ah, yes, but what kind of feeling? How can we differentiate it from mere physical attraction? Perhaps it is no more than physical attraction. But some people are physically attracted to one another and yet they hate each other. Then perhaps love is mutual respect; but surely people can respect one another and yet not love each other. And so it goes. Love seems to be too abstract a term to define.

Similar analyses can be made for duty, democracy, and freedom. Stalin's daughter, Svetlana, left the Soviet Union because she felt it was not a *free* country. She came to this country to be free, yet there are those in this country who call for a revolution because the United States is *not* free. The world has fought bloody wars in which each side has claimed to be fighting for freedom, but such a term turns out to be no more than an ambiguous abstraction. Hemingway's famous lines on the use of abstract words in relation to war are worth repeating in this connection:

> I was always embarrassed by the words sacred, glorious, and sacrifice . . .
> There were many words that you could not stand to hear . . . Abstract
> words such as glory, honor, courage, or hallow were obscene beside the
> concrete names of villages, the numbers of roads, the names of rivers,
> the numbers of regiments and the dates.[2]

However, practically speaking, abstract words do have an important function in a language. When they are used carefully to indicate specific things and
occurrences, they can be valuable. For example, sometimes we need a term that
will summarize various kinds of information. In mathematics, 7^3 is introduced
to stand for $7 \times 7 \times 7$ as a shorthand way of communicating information.
Similarly, scientists refer to *forces*, *masses*, and *gravitational pulls* which are
shorthand expressions for a variety of physical actions and reactions. Both the
mathematician and the scientist use abstract terms with an understanding of
the specific data to which they refer, and to this extent neither the mathematician nor the scientist has any difficulty with this use of abstract terms.
Thus when we are quite clear about the specific data to which an abstract
term refers, the term is then useful. It summarizes for us information that
would normally be too lengthy and too time-consuming to list. If we have a
clear understanding of what we mean when we use *democracy*, then it is
significant to be able to say that men fought for democracy during the First
and Second World Wars. In brief, if we know the *cash value* of an abstract term,
then and only then can we avoid the ambiguity of such a term.

Sometimes it is argued that abstract terms, except perhaps those employed
in mathematics, are open-ended in the sense that we never have a completely
sufficient definition for them. No matter how *atom* is defined, scientific information is always growing and thus the definition is continually changing.
There is always more information to be included in the definition of democracy,
since men and their institutions are always undergoing change. But the point
is that even though abstract terms are never fully defined, if they are to be used
at all, it is important that we have some understanding of their definition at the
time of use. Perhaps there will never be a completely adequate definition of
freedom. But if a man is ready to fight and to kill others with bombs and guns
in the name of freedom, then he should at least have thought out very carefully
what—specifically and concretely—it means to speak of a free man and a free
society. He ought to make sure that his fight for freedom is not simply a fight
for the totalitarianism he claims he is rejecting.

---

2. Ernest Hemingway, *A Farewell to Arms*. New York: Charles Scribner and Sons,
1953, p. 191.

3. Hypostatization or reification of abstract words. Hypostatization of abstract words occurs when they are regarded as if they refer to real entities or forces. Not only can these expressions never be verified, but also they provide their users with a false sense of security. Thus "Mankind can never be destroyed," "Goodness triumphs over all," "The meek shall inherit the earth," "My country can do no wrong," contain hypostatizations of mankind, goodness, the meek, and my country, because the terms supposedly signify some concrete reality which, like a Platonic form, is indestructible, immutable, and forever perfect. Actually we know only that human beings can be destroyed if the controls of war and disease are loosened; we know that good men very often do lose out to evil men; we know that there is no guarantee that the meek will inherit the earth; and we know that Hitler's Germany offers a clear example of the fact that one's own country is *not* always right. Similarly, in recent times attacks are made against "The Establishment" as if there is some specific vicious entity that can be destroyed by a bomb or a sniper. And the terrorist Weathermen have declared that they will destroy "The System" as if this is some distinct octopus entity that must be eliminated. But, of course, The Establishment and The System are not entities, but terms for laws, rules, moral codes, and various other kinds of beliefs that many people respect and find important. Using abstract terms such as Establishment and System makes it easier to avoid showing why certain laws, rules, and moral codes are valueless. It is far easier to argue that The System is bad than to argue that the Constitution, or the Bill of Rights, or various educational or economic bills are bad.

4. Equivocation. When the meaning of a word or expression is changed either knowingly or inadvertently during the course of a discussion, the result is equivocation. Consider the following statement: "Whenever there are laws, then there must be a lawgiver. Nature consists of laws; therefore there must be a lawgiver over nature." Equivocation is present here because whereas *law* in the first sentence refers to the societal laws which must make reference to some lawgiver, its meaning is changed in the second sentence to signify the laws of nature which made no reference to a lawgiver. It should be noted that equivocation is often deliberately used to achieve humorous effects, as in "Your argument is sound, nothing but sound," or in Ben Franklin's "If we don't hang together, we'll hang separately." The Czech underground was reported to have said the following about the Russian invasion: "The Russians said that they came in peace; let us hope they rest in it." Here the first use of *peace* refers to peaceful intentions; the second is used in the sense of *rest in peace*, an expression which refers to those who are dead. Note how Shakespeare, an inveterate punster, in the following scene from *Hamlet* uses the word *tender* to achieve a special kind of dramatic effect. Polonius warns his daughter Ophelia not to trust Hamlet's vows of affection...

Ophelia: He hath, my lord, of late made many tenders of his affection to me.

Polonius: Affection pooh! You speak like a green girl,
            Unsifted in such perilous circumstance.
            Do you believe his tenders, as you call them?

Ophelia: I do not know, my lord, what I should think.

Polonius: Marry, I will teach you. Think yourself a baby
            That you have ta'en these tenders for true pay
            Which are not sterling. Tender yourself more dearly,
            Or (not to crack the wind of the poor phrase)
            Tend'ring it thus you'll tender me a fool.

I.iii.99–109, *The Signet Classic Shakespeare*

The first two uses of *tender* mean *offers*. The third use, in the phrase "tenders for true pay," means *counters* or *chips*, i.e., money used in games. The fourth *tender* means *value* or *hold*. The fifth, *Tend'ring*, has been emended in many editions of the play to read *running*. The last *tender* contains the most equivocation. In saying, "You'll tender me a fool," Polonius may mean (a) Ophelia will *show herself* to him as a fool, (b) will *show him* as a fool, or (c) will *present* him with a baby (*fool* was an Elizabethan term of endearment for an infant).

5. Misuse of emotive words. It is very important to be sensitive to the nuances of word meanings. Two words may have the same general definition, but the emotions and attitudes they reflect and produce can be vastly different. It is one thing to speak of *policemen*, quite another thing to speak of *fuzz*. The former term is fairly neutral and not designed to arouse emotions, whereas the term *fuzz* aims to arouse strong feelings. A distinction is usually made between emotive and neutral, or at least, less emotive language. Emotive language consists of words and sentences which are deliberately designed to produce emotional and often irrational responses. *Black Power* is an expression to which people often react in either positive or negative fashion. Undoubtedly the words *Black Power* played some kind of role in influencing the attitudes of those in the Detroit riots. A generation ago some popular emotive terms were *Commie, Red, Wop, Kike, Aryan, G.I.* Today the evocative words include *Hippie, Digger, Shrink, Hawk, Dove, Pothead*, and many others.

It must be stressed at this point that words are often used effectively to arouse emotion. According to the expressionist theory of art, the primary aim of literature is to express feelings, and in this view emotive language would be indispensable to the literary artist. Also there are many occasions when the appeal to emotion serves a practical function. The fund solicitor for crippled children who vividly describes the plight of these young ones achieves a worth-while end if his speech inspires monetary aid for them. However, when emotive words are used under the pretense that they offer rational arguments, they are being misused. When terms are used primarily to evoke emotional responses and inflame the passions of the ignorant, they should be regarded with suspicion and rejected if the aim is rational discourse.

Structural Ambiguity

Certain kinds of sentence structure do not produce clear meanings. They result in the ambiguities of amphiboly and accent.

1. Amphiboly is caused by the ambiguous arrangement of words in a sentence. Many different amphibolies have been identified. Listed below are some of the more common types.

    a) *Dangling modifier.* "Walking along the street the Woolworth building came in sight." *Walking* is the dangling modifier because the subject that it modifies does not appear in the sentence. Obviously the Woolworth building is not doing the walking.

    b) *Squinting modifier.* "The swimming pool will be available to members only from Monday to Friday." *Only* is the squinting modifier because it looks in two directions. It can modify what precedes it—that is, *members*—or it can modify what follows it—that is, *from Monday to Friday.* In other words, it is not clear whether the club is open Monday to Friday to members only, or whether it is open to members only from Monday to Friday.

    c) *Elliptical construction.* "Serve the chicken when thoroughly stewed." The ambiguity results from the omission of the subject of the clause, namely, *it is.*

    d) *Faulty pronoun reference.* "Among the last to enter the airplane as it left the airport was Mrs. Jones. Slowly her huge nose was turned into the wind and then, like some enormous beast, she crawled along the grass runway." Whose nose, and who crawled? The pronoun *her* has two antecedents, the airplane and Mrs. Jones.

2. Misuse of accent. It is possible to apply an assortment of meanings to a single sentence by accenting different words, as in the following three examples:

a) *I* didn't plan to ask her to the party.

b) I didn't plan to ask *her* to the party.

c) I didn't *plan* to ask her to the party.

In (a) the meaning seems to be that the speaker personally had not intended to issue the invitation; in (b) the *her* of the sentence is clearly not in the good graces of the speaker; and in (c) the implication is that a woman probably crashed a party to which she was uninvited. When accent is employed either orally or in writing to clarify meaning, it is being used in a valid fashion. Unfortunately it is very often used for insidious purposes. Propagandists deliberately distort through accent to mislead audiences. For example, tabloid newspapers often use large type to attract the reader's attention:

WAR DECLARED

against pollution

The undiscerning reader who did not look at the small type would assume that a war had broken out and would rush to buy the paper to check the details.

Exercises

Identify the language fallacies in the following:

1. I know that many people will have to sell their homes to make way for the new highway. But after all, you can't make an omelet without breaking an egg.

2. We must all strive to attain the most important goal of civilization—the brotherhood of man.

3. Moving through the crowd, her big bosom appeared strikingly before me on the billboard.

4. Dick Gregory entered an Atlanta restaurant and sat at the counter. The waitress said, "I'm sorry, but we don't serve colored people here." "That's

okay," answered Gregory, "I don't eat colored people. Just bring me a chicken sandwich on toast."

5. She is some woman.

6. My family is revolting.

7. Intellectual A: Gad, what an ass!
   Nonintellectual B: Yeah, not bad.

8. It is un-American to trade with the Soviet Union.

9. Demonstrators at Harvard College prevented speakers who were defending the Government policy in Indo-China from addressing an audience that had come to hear them. The demonstrators claimed that free speech is only for those who really value freedom.

10. The following headline appeared in the *Cortland Standard*, April 13, 1972, page one:
    CSEA MEMBERS MAY BE STRIPPED OF PAY RAISES
    The first sentence underneath the headline stated: "State workers may be stripped of automatic pay raises for seniority. . ."

FALLACIES OF IRRELEVANCE

Rational discussion can fail through means other than the ambiguous use of language. Erroneous reasons may be used to draw conclusions. Some of these errors occur when a strict rule of logic is violated; these shall be identified and discussed when the rules of logic are examined in later chapters. Below we shall indicate certain violations that occur because the premises *seem* to be true, yet actually are either untrue or irrelevant to the conclusion.

1. Hasty generalization. A statement is called a hasty generalization when an insufficient number of instances are used as the basis for asserting its truth. Example:

All the people in this little Asiatic town are enemy soldiers. Let's shoot them all.

But this argument depends on the truth of the premise "All the people in this little Asiatic town are enemy soldiers." Is it true? Has someone gone into the town, inspected it carefully, and found only enemy soldiers? Or, as is probably the case, has someone seen one or two or even three enemies and then drawn the *hasty generalization* that "all the people in this little Asiatic town are enemy soldiers"? If the premise in this argument is accepted as true even though it is really only a hastily drawn generalization, the consequences could be disastrous. Lynchings, unauthorized assaults, and other kinds of violence have frequently occurred because general statements have been taken to be true although the evidence for them has been miniscule or even nonexistent. Are all Italians members of the Mafia? Are all Blacks members of the Panthers, all French women loose, or all professional army men bloodthirsty brutes? Think of how little evidence there really is for any of these generalizations.

2. Accident occurs when an accepted generalization is mistakenly assumed to be true without exception. Example:

> Everyone ought to have freedom of speech. Therefore this man shouldn't be persecuted just because he yelled "fire" in a crowded theater.

Everyone may believe in free speech, but obviously there are circumstances which might require the modification of such a belief if it led to harmful acts. Similarly, it might very well be taken as true that all Weathermen are committed to the use of violent tactics. This might not be a hasty generalization at all. But perhaps it might be wrong to infer from this that Joe Smith, a Weatherman, was so committed. Perhaps he joined inadvertently. Perhaps he believed only in the social goals and not in the tactics. This generalization is not necessarily always true without exception.

3. Division is based on the misconception that the characteristics of a whole are necessarily the same as the characteristics of each individual part. Example:

> He is a citizen of the United States of America, which is a democracy. Therefore he must have very democratic views.

It is well-known that America harbors not only people with democratic views, but also its share of Fascists and other groups who hate democracy. Thus what is true of the country as a whole is not true of each person in the country.

4. Composition (the converse of division) occurs when the characteristics of an individual part of a whole are assumed to be like the characteristics of the whole. Example:

> Each of the actors is very good. Therefore the presence of each one of them in the new movie is a guarantee that it will be excellent.

It is certainly possible to think of bad movies with good actors. The individual actor might play his role extremely well, but if the movie script is inferior, the movie as a whole could be mediocre.

5. Oversimplification is produced by the failure to consider all the complex issues involved in a problem. It is usually much easier to find a *quickie* explanation for an event than to go through all the trouble of analyzing various alternatives and considering the complexities. Example:

> The trouble with our civilization is that it really believes that God is dead.

The lack of religious belief may be causing problems in our civilization; but if so, it is only one of the possible causes such as poverty, war, injustice, and others which may be equally responsible for such problems. Very few issues are so simple that they can be dealt with in terms of one simple explanation. It might be argued in this connection that scientists seem to work with the simplest explanation when they attempt to formulate a solution to a problem. But scientists reject a simple answer if it does not turn out to be the correct one.

6. Bifurcation (also called the black-white fallacy, the either-or fallacy, or the fallacy of the false dilemma). This kind of thinking assumes that there are two and only two alternatives for the solution of a problem. The middle ground is ignored. Example:

> Either we abandon Southeast Asia or we renew aerial bombardment. But our promises of security to Southeast Asia make it impossible to leave it completely. Therefore we must renew aerial bombardment.

This argument lists only two alternatives for the solution of the Southeast Asia problem. There might be other possibilities. The United States might supply only military equipment without either renewing aerial bombardment or abandoning the area. The two alternatives given in the example are not the only ones that must be considered.

7. Argument of the beard. This is an argument that seeks refuge in the middle ground (and thus it may be viewed as the opposite of Bifurcation). Those who employ it refuse to see any real difference between two apparently opposing alternatives. Example:

> There really is no such thing as a bad boy. Boys are in varying degrees maladjusted and cannot ever be considered really evil.

At some point in judging the nature of a human being it might be necessary to characterize him as bad, for example, if he has killed several people. At certain times it might be wrong to avoid telling it like it is. In certain situations it might be erroneous to insist that the answer to a given question should be sought in some compromise view which rejects the notion of opposites. At one time some argued that Nazi Germany was not entirely bad; like all nations, they asserted, it had its good and its bad points. Thus we had no reason to fight against it. And today we say that students who bomb buildings are not really doing anything criminal; they are simply expressing their resentments. But Nazi Germany was indeed evil. And those who bomb buildings are indeed doing something criminal.

8. Extension involves the technique of exaggerating the views of an opponent so that they can be made to seem absurd. Example:

> Well, if Darwin wanted to believe his ancestor was a monkey, that is his prerogative, but I know darn well my grandfather was never a monkey!

It is one thing to criticize the Darwinian theory on relevant grounds; however, it is not justifiable to ridicule it by misrepresenting it. Darwin never said that anyone's grandparents were monkeys. This is an exaggeration of Darwin's views, used to ridicule the entire theory.

9. Special pleading results from the deliberate omission of relevant evidence during the course of an argument. It therefore constitutes one-sided reasoning. Example:

> This administration must be condemned for levying high taxes.

Perhaps the administration is to blame, but certain extenuating circumstances beyond its control might have forced it to levy the taxes. Perhaps the cost of health insurance and welfare had increased. If a critic of the government wishes to gain votes through criticism, he might use this kind of one-sided reasoning, ignoring the other side of the issue which could put the government's actions in a better light. But one-sided reasoning is indefensible.

10. Lifting out of context is related to special pleading in that it is a special way of deliberately omitting relevant evidence. By changing the content of a quotation through omission or misrepresentation of the context in which it appears, it is always possible to make a writer or speaker seem to have said what he did not actually say. Example:

> Dr. Morrison, in his recent report on Marijuana addiction, has said, "There is evidence on the basis of cases studied that this drug is no more harmful than alcohol."

This passage has been lifted out of context, and as a result its meaning has been changed. A preceding sentence has been omitted, namely, "Alcoholism is one of the great killers." Furthermore, words have been deleted from the quoted sentence, although no ellipses have been used to indicate the omission. The original version read: "There is evidence on the basis of an inadequate number of cases studied that Marijuana is no more harmful than alcohol."

11. Begging the question (also called petitio principio, circulus in probando, circumlocution) is a form of discussion which assumes at the outset something equivalent to what the argument is supposed to prove. Example:

> There's no question but that the deterioration in modern moral values is to be attributed to people's inability to distinguish between what is right and what is wrong.

Actually this sentence states that the deterioration in moral values is caused by the deterioration in moral values, because people's inability to distinguish between what is right and what is wrong has essentially the same meaning as *deterioration in moral values*. The reasoning is circular.

12. Complex question (also known as leading question or implicit assumption) is a question which is asked in such a way that a particularly significant—usually incriminating—belief or assumption has to be accepted as the basis for answering the question. Example:

> Exactly how did you feel when you murdered your wife?

If the poor fellow never murdered his wife, he would hardly know how he felt. The question assumes he committed this act. And a lawyer would ask such a question purposely to trap a defendant into making an implicit admission of his guilt. The late Senator Joseph McCarthy used to ask witnesses, "Have you finally left the Communist Party?" In this way he hoped to trap them into incriminating themselves without being explicitly aware of it. Either a *yes* or a *no* answer was sufficient to show the witness had been a member of the Communist Party.

13. Genetic fallacy involves rejecting or condemning an idea solely on the basis of its source of origin. Example:

Medicare won't work in this country because it is a Socialist plan.

The fact that Socialists may have originated the Medicare plan has nothing to do with its merits. To reject something solely on the basis of its source of origin is usually unwarranted. Sometimes the origin is relevant when it can be shown to imply something important about evidence. Thus if a man is shown to be a perennial liar then this could serve to discredit what he says.

14. Poisoning the wells can be regarded as a special type of genetic fallacy. To poison the wells is to discredit in advance without objective analysis the evidence that can be used to support or deny a conclusion. Example:

> I wouldn't pay any attention to Jim's statement that he heard someone walking in the house last night. He uses a hearing aid.

Jim's evidence should not be summarily rejected simply because he uses a hearing aid. Perhaps with the aid he hears more accurately than the person with normal hearing.

15. False cause results when a causal relationship is assumed to exist where none actually does. Two forms may be distinguished:

a) *Non causa pro causa:* Stating that to be a cause which is not actually the cause. Superstitions are prime examples of this type of fallacy. Example:

> I'm not surprised that he broke his leg today, since I saw a black cat walk in front of him.

Undoubtedly he broke his leg because he fell down a flight of stairs after slipping on a stone. We have to stop blaming that poor black cat for our misdeeds.

b) *Post hoc ergo propter hoc:* Assuming mistakenly that because phenomenon A precedes phenomenon B in time, such priority necessarily makes A the cause of B. Example:

> Smith must have committed the murder because I saw him enter the the house and immediately after that I heard Mrs. Smith's scream and the sound of a revolver.

Perhaps Mr. Smith did kill Mrs. Smith, but the fact that he entered the house just before she screamed and a shot was fired does not necessarily make him the murderer.

16. Diversion. Any means used to sidetrack the issue under discussion is a form of diversion. Special kinds are listed below.

a) Red herring. When the main topic is ignored during the course of a discussion and another issue is made the main focus for consideration, then a *red herring* has been utilized. Example:

> The President has recommended that Municipal Bonds be taxed. The Vice President disagrees with his view. I think the Vice President is very wrong to disagree with the President. A Vice President should support the position of the President and help him to achieve his goals.

The main issue concerns the taxation of municipal bonds. To suddenly bring up the matter of the role of the Vice President is to subvert the main topic by introducing a *red herring*, a diversionary topic.

b) Pettifogging. When the diversion from the main topic consists in dealing with trivial matters, it is called pettifogging. Example:

> The new museum is flawed. It is well-designed and shows off its paintings very effectively. However, the bathroom is very inadequate and the lunchroom is small and very prosaic looking.

Since the main purpose of a museum is to display paintings, the objection to the bathroom and lunchroom is a trivial one, and certainly sidetracks the main issue.

c) Humor (ridicule, sarcasm, etc.). To make people laugh is a noteworthy aim, but when humor is used to convert a serious issue into a ludicrous one, then it is an invalid form of diversion. Example:

> One of the candidates running for Mayor of New York stated that he believed in law and order and that he would do everything possible to make the streets safe so our wives could walk the streets at night. What, I ask you, does he want to do, make hookers out of our wives?

If the mayoralty candidate is seriously interested in the problem of law and order, then it is manifestly unfair for anyone to turn the whole subject into a dirty joke.

17. Appeal to the people (argumentum ad populum) is a fallacious appeal since it deals with important and controversial issues merely by appealing to the spirit of camaraderie of a group or mass of people. Example:

> America is a very powerful nation. But as members of this great nation we want to make it the most powerful nation in the world. We should therefore protect this country that we love by supporting every effort to protect our military might, and this obviously includes supporting the new ABM missile.

There may be valid reasons for supporting the ABM missile but none is offered in the preceding passage. Instead, the speaker is appealing to the chauvinistic emotions of his audience; they should all agree with him simply because he is and they are AMERICANS.

18. Argument to the man (argumentum ad hominem) is a fallacious kind of reasoning employed by the speaker or writer who is *solely* concerned with attacking his opponent rather than with the argument required to prove the truth of his conclusion. The *ad hominem* takes three forms:

a) *Abusive.* In this version, the conclusion is based on an opponent's supposed defects rather than on the argument itself. Example:

> Of course, Mr. John Smiles is against birth control; he has ten children and doesn't know any better. He's one of the ignorant ones.

Mr. Smiles may or may not be ignorant. But he might have intelligent reasons for opposing birth control and to call him ignorant is to avoid dealing with his reasons for opposing birth control. (Of course, if his reasons are unintelligible, then knowing that he has an I.Q. of 20 would be relevant. One would hardly want to elect him to a committee which opposed birth control.)

b) *Circumstantial.* On this form of the ad hominem, an individual gives reasons why his opponent should accept a conclusion rather than reasons which prove the conclusion to be true. Example:

> Priest: I do not believe that the state should provide public aid to parochial schools.
> Congressman: But you are a Catholic and your schools need money, and certainly your religion requires you to support the bill for financial aid to Catholic schools.

Instead of using valid arguments to justify his view, the congressman uses the personal circumstance of the priest's religion to coerce him into acceptance of the bill.

c) *Tu quoque* ("you're another"). In this form, a person accused of wrong-doing answers the charge by accusing his accuser of wrongdoing. Example:

> Student No. 1: I saw you copying the answer to the exam question from your math book.
> Student No. 2: At least it was my math book. Didn't you borrow John's term paper and hand it in as your own work?

Student No. 1 may have been plagiarizing, but this does not deal with the issue of whether Student No. 2 was actually cheating. The guilt of Student No. 1 does not exonerate Student No. 2.

19. Appeal to pity (argumentum ad misericordiam) makes an unwarranted appeal to obtain sympathy for the cause or demands of an individual or a group, Example:

> We must give the engineering position to Henry Jones. After all, he has six children to feed and clothe.

We are asked in this instance to feel pity for Mr. Jones, who has so many children to take care of. Obviously, if the job requires an experienced engineer and Mr. Jones is not really qualified, he should not get the job even if he has 20 children to feed. Who would want to use a doctor *simply* because he is not wealthy. However, sometimes the appeal to pity in our society is viewed as warranted because humanitarian rather than logical considerations are involved. Thus underprivileged children with substandard grades are sometimes admitted to colleges because administrators feel compassion for those with environmental handicaps. In such cases the appeal to pity is judged to be warranted because of special concern.

20. Appeal to force (argumentum ad baculum) is used when the threat of punishment or force of some sort is substituted for warranted reasons. Example:

> Professor Allen told his students, "There's no official rule about cutting classes, but I will always call the roll. I want to know how many times you have been absent when I give you your final mark."

Implicit in the teacher's statement is a warning to the wary student that he will be penalized for his absence. The teacher is threatening punishment in the form of poor marks. Thus the appeal to force does not necessarily have to involve a physical threat, such as "If you don't do this, I will hit you." Anyone who tries to force you to accept his views or actions by threatening dire consequences rather than offering valid reasons is guilty of using the *ad baculum*.

21. Appeal to authority (argumentum ad verecundiam) constitutes an illegitimate appeal to the opinions of an expert. The appeal is unwarranted when the expert is mistakenly assumed to be knowledgeable about a particular issue. Example:

> I think this theory of education is sound. After all, General MacArthur approved of it.

MacArthur was an authority on military matters and an appeal to his authority on that subject would be legitimate, but this does not mean that one should espouse his views on all other subjects. He was not an expert on education. The most reliable authorities on education could more relevantly serve to bolster a theory to be tested.

22. Appeal to ignorance (argumentum ad ignorantiam) signifies that the lack of evidence has been used as evidence in an argument. Example:

> You may not believe in ghosts, but tell me, has anyone ever been able to prove definitely that they do not exist?

The argument about the existence of ghosts is based in this context upon an appeal to our ignorance rather than our knowledge. The fact that we cannot definitely prove that they do not exist does not conversely prove their existence.

Exercises

Identify the fallacious types of reasoning in the following examples. (In many cases, more than one fallacy is present.)

1. A man must face the consequences of his actions. If he lives a good life, he will find his reward in heaven; but if he lives a life of sin, the black pit of hell awaits him.

2. Let's get one thing straight. This country guarantees the freedom of all

of its citizens through the constitution. No one has the right to stop someone from taking LSD if he wants to take it.

3. I think anyone who is against the new state Constitution is really ignorant
   of the issues involved. Only someone who wants to stir up religious conflict would be against it.

4. Americans are very materialistic and value split-level houses, electrical
   appliances, and swimming pools above all else.

5. Vietnam is really a very complex issue. Both the Hawks and the Doves
   are wrong in taking extreme positions. There probably is no simple solution to be found.

6. The President is going to stop Americans from going to Europe in order
   to improve the American economy. If we don't watch out, he'll be telling us what we can eat for breakfast and when we can go to the
   movies.

7. Beauty is that which arouses in us feelings of appreciation for the beautiful.

8. People who make fun of the theory that God exists can never really prove
   that He doesn't exist.

9. We have been having record cold weather, and when the temperature
   goes down to 50 degrees below zero you can be sure that atomic explosions
   have upset climatic conditions all over the world.

10. Since no one can prove that marijuana is harmful to a person, it should
    be made legal.

11. I am against Jane's marrying Bob Dolan. In fact, I'm going to do every-
    thing I can to stop the marriage. He comes from a terrible family. His
    father was convicted of petty larceny and you know how his mother spends
    her evenings.

12. People have the right to express their opinions freely in this country and
    it is deplorable that the President refused to allow the head of the Ameri-
    can Fascist Society to speak in the college. It's about time someone came
    to tell us the real truth about the Jewboys in America.

13. The department decided to hire the student with the Harvard degree
    because he is obviously the one with the superior education.

14. The interior decorator bought six beautiful antique pieces of furniture
    and, combined, they will make the living room look exquisite.

15. The Black Power boys tell me that if something isn't done soon for the

blacks, this summer will see riots in the major cities that will be the worst they have ever experienced.

16. Without LSD no one can know who he really is. LSD is a religion that will transfigure man's soul and make the world a more beautiful place.

17. To make progress, you have to break the mold. Conformity is the greatest evil of our age.

18. Dr. Spock is a very famous doctor, and his counseling of young men to refuse to be drafted should make all of us aware of what a great humanitarian he is.

19. Three airplanes just crashed, killing a total of seventy people. I've always said that if God intended man to fly, he would have given him wings.

20. This...is one of the greatest movies ever filmed...Stupendous.

21. I can't understand why you don't like Fred. He's very wealthy and has a magnificent physique.

22. Southerners can't get used to the idea that their children will go to school with blacks. They object to the cost of busing the children to schools.

23. We are against the passing of a gun law in this country, because as Americans we know that such a law is an infringement on the personal freedom of all of us.

24. During a demonstration, students sent the following message to the Dean of Ashwash College: "These are our nonnegotiable demands. You know the consequences if you do not meet them."

25. Commissioner Jones claims that the welfare system is corrupt, but he is really corrupt himself when he uses the poverty issue for the political purpose of gaining the votes of those who are against welfare.

SUPPLEMENTARY READINGS

Bacon, Francis, *Novum Organum*. Aphorisms 45–51, "The Four Idols," 1620.

Mill, J. S., "Fallacies of Observation," *A System of Logic: Ratiocinative and Inductive*, Vol. II, Ninth Edition. London: Longmans, Green, Reader, and Dyer, 1875.

Peirce, Charles Sanders, "The Fixation of Belief," in J. H. Randall, J. Buchler, E. V. Shirk (eds.), *Readings in Philosophy*. New York: Barnes and Noble, 1946.

4

Sentences

THE DEFINITION OF SENTENCE

We have established the fact that there are rules of logic which govern—or should govern—the relationship of premises to conclusion. But what are these rules? It is sometimes argued that they are no more than the rules of grammar. All grammar books contain sections on the relationship between sentences called premises and those called conclusions. Therefore one might be led to think that logical rules are no more than certain kinds of grammatical rules. Just as some of the rules of grammar tell us how to construct a sentence, it might be argued that other rules of grammar tell us how to construct a logical argument. But if the rules of logic are no more than rules of grammar, then certain curious consequences follow. Grammarians and linguists have often told us that languages are conventional in the sense that yesterday's grammatical rules need not be today's. And, of course, it is well-known that different languages have completely different ways of structuring their sentences. English-speaking people tend to think in terms of nouns, verbs, adjectives, and so on, but it does not necessarily follow that the languages of tomorrow will contain such categories, or that all the languages that are in use today classify their terminology this way. We have only to compare Anglo-Saxon to contemporary English to see the changes that can and do take place in sentence structure. Thus it might be justifiable to claim that if the rules of logic are derived from, or are in some way dependent upon, grammar then these very rules themselves are subject to continual change. Under these conditions an argument that is logical at one time might be illogical at another. And if this is so, then the rules of logic that we will present in this book may be outmoded before the book is even printed. But fortunately, rules of logic are not quite the same as the rules of grammar. It may well be that there are strong ties between logic and grammar, but even though grammar may change radically from one century to the next—again, compare Anglo-Saxon to modern English—rules of logic change very slowly. In fact, for hundreds of years Aristotle's rules of logic governed logical argumentative procedures and changed very little. Only in recent times has Aristotle's logic been modified as a result of additional knowledge and analysis; but the essential rules remain the same. We shall see that the rules of logic, like those of mathematics, are not mere arbitrary conventions which change from year to year; indeed there is some question as to whether certain fundamental rules could *ever* be changed without seriously impairing our whole view of rational argumentation. Anglo-Saxon is no longer used, but the Anglo-Saxon equivalent of "Either I go walking or I do not go walking" was as true for the Anglo-Saxons as the modern English version is for us today. Thus one man's reasoning is not necessarily as good as another's, and objective rules can show how one man's way of reasoning is correct while another's is not.

The first and most important element to understand in the investigation of logical reasoning is the notion of the *sentence*. The least we should be able to say about complex arguments is that the premises and the conclusion are sentences. "Socrates is rational" can be derived from "All men are rational" and "Socrates is a man." But nothing can be derived from "Are is a man" and "Socrates rational are." We expect arguments to contain sentences. But are we sure that we know what a sentence is? Would we always be able to distinguish it from a nonsentence? The following are undoubtedly sentences:

a) John loves Mary.

b) The snow is white.

c) All metals are conductors.

But what are the next two constructions?

d) Colorless green ideas sleep furiously.

e) Tha horster ruggled veerily.

Examples (d) and (e) *look* like sentences; (d) seems similar to the easily recognizable sentence, "Restless red roans run furiously," while (e), even though each of the parts are meaningless, seems to be comparable to "The horse struggled wearily." But even though (d) and (e) look like sentences, are they really? On first analysis it would seem to be odd to call them sentences since they consist either of expressions which are meaningless, or of meaningless combinations of expressions. Clearly, if making correct inferences requires us to employ sentences, then we ought to make sure we know something about such linguistic structures.

Let us begin the study of sentences by turning first to the grammarian's definition. Traditionally, he has defined the sentence as a group of words consisting of a subject and predicate, and expressing a complete thought or a complete state of affairs. But this definition assumes that the expressions *subject*, *predicate*, and *complete thought* or *complete state of affairs* can be given a clear explication. Perrin's *Writer's Guide and Index to English* is a standard grammar text which describes the *subject* as being that which is "the starting point of the statement [i.e., declarative sentence]; the verb predicate advances the statement [i.e., declarative sentence].”[1] These remarks might be useful if it were made clear what the starting point of a sentence is and how an expression makes it advance. Is the *starting point* the first or second word of the sentence? Is it the first descriptive term? And when a sentence is advanced, what is taking place? The *Gorrell and Laird Modern English Handbook*, another standard grammar text, offers the more usual definition: “The subject of the sentence usually is what we are thinking about and propose to talk about. The verb [predicate] tells something about this subject; that is, it asserts, postulates, or declares about this subject.”[2] However, note the difficulty involved in this explanation. A person might be thinking about or proposing to talk about Mary and he might write “John loves Mary.” But in this sentence *Mary* is part of the predicate and not a subject at all. Furthermore, in terms of this definition, *John loves* could easily be taken as the predicate of “John loves Mary,” since it does tell us something about Mary, namely, that John loves her.

To be fair to the grammarians, we should note that they usually discuss these aspects of a sentence in connection with structural pattern. For example, a word is viewed as a subject not only because it names something, but also because of its position in the noun-verb-object word-order pattern supposedly characteristic of a typical English sentence. Thus in the sequence “John loves Mary” the word order tells us that (a) *John* is the subject, (b) *loves* is the verb, and (c) *Mary* is the object—the verb and object comprising the predicate. In brief, word order must also be considered when we are dealing with subjects and predicates. In a later chapter, more will be said about the form of sentences, especially the distinction between logical and grammatical form. But at this point the following observations are relevant. Word order is a convention of language. Many years ago the Anglo-Saxons, who spoke the language that was to evolve into modern English, could have said,

Lufað Johannes and Marian

instead of “John loves Mary.” The ending of each word—which we have deliberately italicized—would indicate its function in the sentence. *Johannes* would have to be the subject, *lufað* the verb, and *Marian* the object.

---

1. Porter G. Perrin, *Writer's Guide and Index to English*, Revised Edition. Chicago: Scott Foresman and Co., 1950, p. 248.

2. Robert M. Gorrell and Charlton Laird, *Modern English Handbook*, Second Edition. Englewood Cliffs, N. J.: Prentice Hall, Inc., 1956, p. 197.

Today the English language relies much less on endings and far more on word order. Of course, it is possible that the subject-verb-object pattern will not be adhered to in the future, just as the reliance on inflection (that is, word ending) was modified in the past. Indeed, our poets, novelists, and dramatists deliberately experiment with different word orders to achieve special artistic effects, and undoubtedly they influence the process of change in language. But it should be recognized that word order does not determine the subject and predicate of a sentence. On the contrary, we first decide upon the subject and predicate, and then we place them in their proper order in a linguistic sequence. If, for example, I know beforehand that *John* rather than *Mary* is to be the subject, I would write "John loves Mary" rather than "Mary loves John." My prior knowledge that John is to be the subject permits me to place *John* first in the sequence of words rather than last. Furthermore, the same subject and predicate are identified even when the usual word order is changed in a context. Thus in the sentence "Mary John Loves," *John* is still the subject even though it is not part of the usual subject-predicate pattern. Here the subject does not appear as the first word. Thus it is doubtful whether the introduction of form helps the grammarian's definition of subject and predicate.

Finally, even if the terms *subject* and *predicate* could be adequately defined, their presence in a linguistic sequence does not guarantee the formation of a sentence. For example, *when I run to the store* might be said to contain a subject and predicate, but it is obviously not a sentence. Grammatically speaking, it is a *subordinate clause*, which does not have the sense of unity and completeness characteristic of a sentence. For this reason the third part of the definition of a sentence is usually introduced: namely that a sentence expresses a complete thought. This notion of a complete thought as a means by which a sentence can be identified has been very popular with traditional grammarians. But such a notion is not without its problems.

What does it mean to say that a given cluster of words "expresses a thought"? Is a thought some entity that I happen to possess and which my words are meant to designate? At least some philosophers have argued that my thoughts are private in the sense that no one can ever actually experience or encounter them, since they reside only in my brain, inaccessible to anyone but me. If a sentence is defined as something that expresses a thought, then I alone can understand what I am talking about, since I alone have access to my own thoughts. But the fact remains that I do talk to someone else who does understand me. It might be maintained that communication occurs because my words serve to stimulate similar thoughts in the mind of another person. But since I can never inspect anyone else's thoughts, I cannot know whether they are similar to mine. A private entity can never be compared to another private entity. Thus there is no way, on this analysis, to discover whether I am really communicating with anyone.

Even if it were possible to escape the difficulty of defining what a thought is, we would still have to determine what makes a thought complete. Why is the image or idea or other psychological phenomenon evoked by the word *rose* any less complete a thought than that produced by the sentence "There is a rose in the garden"? Some efforts have been made to show that the difference can be explained in terms of certain feelings. Somehow we feel a sense of unity in "There is a rose in the garden," whereas we do not feel it in the mere utterance of the word *rose*. Such reference to feeling, however, is not only vague, but also lacking in significant purpose. How is it possible to refute the contention of a person who claims that he receives a strong feeling of unity and completeness from *rose* but not from the sentence that contains this word? Surely, in this connection, one man's feeling is as good as another's.

In the light of these objections it might be wiser to explain a sentence in terms of something other than a person's feelings or ideas or other mental phenomena. For this reason the *complete thought* part of the grammarian's definition has sometimes been replaced by *a given state of affairs*, or simply *a fact*. This does eliminate referring to personal and private ideas with the attendant ambiguities, but it does not provide us with an adequate definition. Why couldn't the single word *rose* refer to a state of affairs? It might be said that a state of affairs is not like a single object and ought not to be confused with one. But what exactly *is* a state of affairs? While it is possible to point to an object, it is not possible to point to a state of affairs.

An additional problem is that both definitions, the one concerning the complete thought and the other concerning the state of affairs, cannot account for false sentences. False sentences apparently do not refer to anything at all, yet they are considered sentences. If I wrongly say, "There is an automobile at the curb," even though I am mistaken and not referring to anything at all, I am still expressing a sentence.

But what exactly do such sentences refer to? Is it possible to speak of false ideas, false states of affairs, or false complete thoughts? If so, then what else is a false sentence but a glaring example of the rhetorical device known as the *oxymoron* which juxtaposes contradictory words such as *cruel kindness*, or *false truth*? But while a rhetorical expression which contains a contradiction may be usefully employed in a literary context, it is hardly of any real value in a logical one. How can something exist—that is, be a state of affairs, an idea, or a complete thought—yet be false at one and the same time?

The notion of a state of affairs leads directly into the most obvious circularity. If I say, "There is an automobile at the curb," and you ask me why this is a sentence, I might reply, "Because it refers to a given state of affairs." But when you ask, "Which state of affairs?" I can only reply, "The one in which there is an automobile at the curb." In other words, there is no way of finding out whether a given group of words is a sentence unless I have already used it as a sentence.

The grammarian's analysis of a sentence, therefore, has too many ambiguities to give us an adequate definition. But the philosopher has also been very concerned with defining a sentence, and a few words ought to be said about his investigation. Some philosophers have argued that sentences must be defined in terms of certain entities called *propositions*. Propositions are the *meanings* which are expressed by sentences regardless of the language used. Thus consider the following:

1. Il pleut.

2. Es regnet.

3. It is raining.

The first sentence is in French, the second in German, and the third, of course, in English. All of them are different, yet they all express the same proposition, namely, that it is raining. Thus it is often claimed that a group of words is a sentence if and only if it is expressing a proposition. Otherwise we merely have a conglomeration of words. It is because "Il pleut" expresses a proposition that it can legitimately be called a French sentence. A similar analysis can be made for (2) and (3). However, serious objections can be raised against this view.

For one thing, it presents the same problem encountered with ideas, facts, and states of affairs. What are the propositions that sentences are said to express or to be the vehicles for expressing? Are we to say the furniture of the world consists of chairs, tables, houses, and human beings, as well as propositions? About a given room we can ask whether there are any chairs in the room. Can we also ask whether there are any propositions in the room? Surely this is rather strange. Furthermore, the same problem arises in regard to false sentences. If true sentences refer to propositions, then do false sentences also refer to propositions, although they happen to be false? Just as we have yet to see a negative fact, we have yet to see a negative proposition.

Those who argue for the existence of propositions, however, claim that one must not confuse truth with meaning. If I say, "It is raining," then I must know the meaning of this sentence before I can go on to check its truth or falsity, and this meaning is the proposition. "Pegasus is the winged horse of

Bellerophon" does not refer to any existent entity or state of affairs, but surely, regardless of its truth or falsity, it is meaningful. Thus the sentence must incorporate or express a meaning, and this meaning is the proposition. But can we account for the so-called meaning of a sentence without having to posit some strange entity called a proposition? Perhaps the meaning of a sentence is no more than its function in a given discourse? For example, if I want to know the meaning of a sentence in a foreign language, I watch what people do when this sentence is said; I observe their actions with one another and with their environment. If a man, Jacques, says "Garachi" to me and he does this only when he is eating apple pie, then I can begin to hypothesize that "*Garachi*" means "I am eating applie pie," or "I like apple pie." (Presumably we could construct situations in which we could discern whether "*Garachi*" means "I am eating apple pie," or "I like apple pie." For example, we could find someone else besides Jacques—say, Andre who dislikes apple pie, and see whether he would say "*Garachi*." If he did then we would know that the expression does not mean "I like apple pie," but probably means "I am eating apple pie.") Thus sentences would obtain their meanings by associations with the occurrence of various kinds of human activities and certain specific objects.

But the desire to retain propositions is still not quenched. Surely there are some meaningful sentences which do not relate to objects or to human behavior in any usual sense. "Two plus two is four" is meaningful, but no objects like chairs or tables are referred to by this sentence. Nor is any human behavior relevant. Who cares how Jacques and Andre behave—two plus two still equals four! Here would seem to be a need to posit a kind of an abstract referent that gives "Two plus two equals four" its meaning, and this abstract referent is what is meant by a proposition.

We could continue to pursue the problems philosophers have with propositions, but for our purposes we need simply indicate that philosophers are still wrestling with these intricate issues, and that it is not yet clear whether propositions must also be added to the population of things in the world. Thus the philosopher's attempt to define the sentence is no more successful than the grammarian's.

More recently some linguists, among them Chomsky, have attempted to give a strict linguistic definition of a sentence which is "independent of meaning."[3] Chomsky defines a sentence as a chain of linguistic symbols con-

---

3. N. Chomsky, *Syntactic Structures*. Hague, Netherlands: Mouton and Co., 1957, p. 17.

sisting of a "noun phrase plus a verb phrase."[4] But, of course, this assumes that a noun phrase and a verb phrase can be defined without reference to meaning (traditionally, nouns designated objects and verbs designated properties or relations). More important, even if we made the appropriate modifications and stipulated that the chain of linguistic symbols must consist of a name and a verb in that order, we still might not have a sentence. "John runs" is not a sentence if it is no more than the word *John* followed by the word *runs* for then "John runs" would be equivalent to *John, runs,* which is surely not a sentence. Only when something further is added to the two words, i.e., if the two words are regarded as expressing some situation, do we begin to regard "John runs" as a sentence. (This does not mean that "expressing some situation" is any more satisfactory than "expressing some proposition" in defining a sentence. But the point is that it is not possible to rely on a rule which refers only to the combination of certain symbols.)

In speaking of sentences, then, we are left to our own devices. What we shall do is approach the matter of sentences from the aspect of inference. Instead of attempting to define a sentence, we shall ask what a language must be like if it is capable of inference. And one of the requirements of an inference-producing language is that some parts of it can be labeled as either true or false. It does not matter, for purposes of inference, how we determine which groups of expressions are to be labeled true and which are to be labeled false—this may be done in terms of the amount of available evidence. What is important is that some groups of *symbols* should be regarded as true or false. This does not mean that in all cases we can actually determine the truth of falsity of a given sentence. Perhaps in our lifetime we may never be able to determine whether "There is life on Pluto" is a true or a false sentence, but we are able to say that this combination of words is indeed either true or false, and to this extent it is to be regarded as a sentence. There may very well be languages that are extremely different from our own in terms of linguistic structure, but they can be said to contain sentences inasmuch as they are equipped to speak of some linguistic segment as true or false. Whatever they can affirm as true or as false will, for inference purposes, be taken as sentences.

It might be relevant to ask at this point whether questions, commands, and exclamations are to be rejected as sentences, since these are not regarded as true or false. It does not seem possible to consider "Are you going to the movies?" or "Close the window!" as true or false. However, some logicians

---

4. *Ibid.,* p. 26.

have indeed sought to construct logics in which questions and commands can be taken to have properties somewhat analogous to true or false. Perhaps other kinds of linguistic segments besides true and false ones might be called sentences. But our concern is with the fundamental logic which deals with whatever linguistic elements are taken to be true or false. Whatever these elements are, we call them sentences. Perhaps other elements are also called sentences, but they will not be dealt with here.

Exercises

1. Some grammarians claim that all sentences, including questions and commands, can be shown to be of subject-predicate form. Identify the subject and predicate in each of the following:

   a) It is raining.

   b) There really are no ghosts.

   c) What a ring!

   d) Don't do that.

   e) I have ten books to read.

   f) It is a pleasure to meet you.

2. Which of the following would be considered sentences? Discuss.

   a) what have I done to have been given children like these Benjamin was punishment enough and now for her to have no more regard for me her own mother I've suffered for her dreamed and planned and sacrified I went down into the valley

      William Faulkner, *The Sound and the Fury*

   b) I could hear my watch whenever the car stopped, but not often they were already eating *Who would play a* Eating the business of eating inside of you space to space and time confused

      William Faulkner *The Sound and the Fury*

   c) As we there are where are we are we there from tomtittot to teetootom-totalitarian. Tea tea too oo.

      James Joyce, *Finnegans Wake*

   d) Evolution is an integration of matter and concomitant dissipation of motion; during which the matter passes from a relatively indefinite incoherent homogeneity to a relatively definite coherent heterogeneity;

and during which the retained motion undergoes a parallel transformation.

Spencer, Principles of Biology

e) Live wake falls fruit nearby.

f) All metals are vegetables.

g) A rose is a rose is a rose.

3. The following are sentences in the African language, Bimoba, as listed and translated by John T. Bendor-Samuel in his "Problems in the Analysis of Sentences and Clauses in Bimoba," *Word*, **21** (1965), p. 454.

a)   a won   wuur   gbenn   ti   won
   he   yesterday washed   finished   we   yesterday

   jcob   tɔ   sanjok
   took   our   road

   Yesterday as he finished washing, we started on our way.

b) m i   bo   i biak i sãã   saa Naliatùk l ϶
   I if immediate again   future   go Nalerigu it

   bo   siiʒa.
   immediate   better

   If I were to go to Nalerigu again, it would be better.

Each language has its own forms. But what has the translator of these passages had to do in order to make sense out of them? What does this seem to reveal about the nature of language forms? Would we be able to understand a language that could not be translated into our language forms?

4. What is the difference between the grammarian's and the logician's notion of a sentence?

5. Scientists now speak of both negative and positive matter. Therefore why can't we speak of negative and affirmative states of affairs?

6. Discuss: Propositions are the ideas people get in their minds when they hear a sentence.

A PROBLEM CONCERNING TRUE OR FALSE

The point might be made that since all beliefs are merely probable, the rules of logic which deal only with true and false statements[5] are irrelevant for any kind of significant inquiry. In fact, philosophers such as John Dewey have argued that *true* and *false* are words which should be dropped from the language, not only because final truths or falsehoods do not exist, but also because these words lead us to believe statements can be formulated which will always remain true or false. But the search for absolutes is illusory and would be discontinued if the use of true or false were eliminated. Moreover, these philosophers contend that in all instances more adequate and less troublesome words can be substituted; for example, *honest* friend instead of *true* friend; *deceitful* friend instead of *false* friend. It should be apparent that even in the expression *true facts*, *true* is an unimportant word; *true* is clearly redundant since a fact is by definition taken to be true. Furthermore, if it is very important to be able to speak of a true fact, then it must also be very important to speak of a false one. But false facts are like false propositions or false ideas. They embody contradictions. The following expression contains a redundancy, but it makes some sense: "It is raining out there, and this is true." But it is clearly contradictory, if not nonsensical, to say, "It is raining out there, but this is false." Thus instead of having to deal with the odd phenomenon of false facts, it might be better to eliminate the notions of truth or falsity altogether.

Nor are philosophers the only ones who are sometimes skeptical about the need to speak of *truth*. Most sociologists, anthropologists, and natural scientists believe in the relativity of knowledge. Perhaps in the past, during Aristotle's time or during the medieval period when men supposedly believed in absolutes, a logic dealing with truth and falsity was appropriate. But what meaning can it have in an age that views all beliefs as probable, statistical, confirmable, or disconfirmable?

To answer these objections it might be noted that some statements are always taken to be true or false. Consider the following:

Nothing can be both red and green at one and the same time and in the same respect.

If A is the father of B, then B is the child of A.

Time will never stop.

Motion exists.

$2 + 2 = 4$.

---

5. Some philosophers distinguish between *sentences* and *statements* on the grounds that the former is a strictly grammatical form whereas the latter is a grammatical form with meaning. But in our analysis we will take these terms to be synonymous.

All of these examples are surely true and their negations are surely false. Nor have many doubted the old Cartesian view that each individual is certain of his own existence although he cannot really be certain of the existence of anyone else. And if someone is not lying when he says, "I have a pain," then he must be telling the truth. Furthermore, if all our knowledge is merely probable, then we should be able to state it as a *truth* that all our knowledge is probable. Thus even if the vast majority of beliefs are no more than probable, some statements are indeed either true or false.

Certain statements are taken to be, *for all practical purposes,* either true or false. I might be wrong when I state that "Hydrogen gas combined in a certain proportion with oxygen produces water." But ordinarily it is assumed that all the evidence has been tabulated and that therefore it is true to say that hydrogen combined with oxygen will produce water. Similarly, I might be wrong to assert that a typewriter is before me now and I am typing this manuscript with it. I could be dreaming. But again I would certainly accept this belief as true. In brief, for the practical purposes that primarily guide our use of language, many statements are taken to be assuredly true or false.

Finally, even though all the criticism directed against the use of *true* and *false* might be correct, these two terms can be shown to have an important function and should not be rejected. The operation of true and false can be compared to the operation of numbers in a language. Physics and chemistry reveal that things are simultaneously losing and gaining atoms. Thus no perfect measurement can ever actually be given. Yet we do not hesitate to say that a room is ten feet long. Precise mathematical measurements were utilized to build the room. Mathematical specifications would also be necessary if we wished to order carpeting and furniture for such a room. To describe it merely as *fairly large* or *fairly small* would not suffice. Once a number is mentioned in relation to an object, mathematical knowledge of the most advanced kind can be employed to attain the highest degree of accuracy in solving problems. The use of *true* and *false* can be compared to the use of numbers. Once a sentence is labeled *true* or *false* rather than *fairly certain* or *nearly true* or *unlikely*, then a whole system of logic and logical inference can begin to operate. Inferences can be drawn that would otherwise not be easily discernible. Probably few readers of this book at this time know that if it is true to say, "I will pass this course," then it is also true to say, "If I do not pass this course, then I will receive the car my father promised me." And if it is true to say, "I am swayed by reason rather than emotion, and also I will oppose injustice with arms if necessary," then it is false to say, "If I am swayed by reason rather than emotion, then I will not oppose injustice with arms if necessary." These are complicated inferences which are quite easy to justify once sentences are designated as *true* or *false* and rules of logic are applied to them. But to justify inferences by simply thinking about them is exceedingly difficult.

Thus the notions of *true* and *false* will be accepted by us with the understanding that a sentence will be any combination of words to which it would be legitimate to apply *true* or *false*. But the references to true and false sentences will not involve any commitment to the notion of absolute truths or absolute falsehoods. Certain linguistic segments are labeled *true* or *false* simply because we are interested in the construction of arguments whose logic can be tested.

Exercises

1. Discuss the following:

   a) It is absolutely true that the Vietnam war was wrong.

   b) There is no such thing as *the* correct grammar. All grammar is relative.

   c) Can you think of any rules in a language that seem to be inviolate? For example, does a sentence have to have a subject and predicate?

   d) There is no such thing as the correct kind of reasoning. All reasoning is relative to one's culture.

   e) The following is absolutely true: "America is now decadent."

2. Can you think of any sentences, aside from those mentioned in the text and in these exercises, which you do not think can be falsified? If so, try to think of how such sentences could be falsified.

3. Analyze the meaning of *true* or *false* in the following:

   a) He's true blue.   b) Be true to me.

   c) Yours truly, John Jones.   d) The truth will set you free.

   e) This sentence is false.   f) He's a false person.

SUPPLEMENTARY READINGS

Ewing, A. C., "Truth," in E. Nagel and R. B. Brandt (eds.), *Meaning and Knowledge.* New York: Harcourt, Brace, and World, 1965.

Frege, Gottlob, "The Thought," in G. Eiseminger (ed.), *Logic and Philosophy.* New York: Appleton-Century-Crofts, 1968.

Waismann, F., *The Principles of Linguistic Philosophy.* New York: St. Martin's Press, 1965; Chapter 14, "What is a Proposition?"

5

Connector Expressions-- Or, Not, and And

ATOMIC AND MOLECULAR SENTENCES

Arguments depend upon sentences which can be regarded as true or false. Especially in the case of sound arguments, premises must be true and not merely speculative or highly questionable. But an argument does not contain only sentences.

Let us look carefully at the following:

1. Either he goes by car or he goes by bus. He goes by car. Therefore he does not go by bus.

2. If Smith leaves and Jones enters, then Jones is the killer. Jones enters and Smith leaves. Therefore Jones is the killer.

These two arguments contain such true or false sentences as "He goes by car," "He goes by bus," "Smith leaves," "Jones enters," and "Jones is the killer." But these words and sentences do not exhaust all the words in the arguments. Also present are other expressions, words such as *therefore, either, or, if, then,* and *and* which obviously serve to connect one sentence to another. Not only must we understand what sentences are and how they function if we are to clarify what legitimate arguments are, but also we must understand how these *connector* expressions function.

The connector expressions *and, either, or, if—then,* and *therefore* are not descriptive. We do not check to see what is designated by *and,* or by *or,* or by *therefore.* As in ordinary language, these words do not signify anything extra-linguistic. Given object A and object B in the same room, there is no third entity signified by *and.* If there were, then an infinite regress would ensue, for if *and* referred to a third entity, then a fourth entity would have to be posited which would unite *A, B,* and *and,* and so forth *ad infinitum. Connector expressions link sentences in accordance with certain rules in order to form molecular sentences.*

Every grammar book distinguishes between a sentence that does not contain other sentences as parts and one that does. For example, there is a difference between the number of sentences present in "The tree is brown" and the number in "The tree is brown or the rose is red." The latter can be broken down into two sentences: "The tree is brown," and "The rose is red." These distinctions should be familiar enough since grammar books also distinguish between *compound* sentences and their parts. Compound or what we have termed *molecular* sentences are made up of two or more *component* sentences which are themselves either compound or *atomic,* i.e., sentences that cannot be broken down into more basic ones. Thus "The tree is brown or the rose is red" is a compound sentence consisting of two atomic ones. "Either she stays home and she sews, or she goes to the theater and she enjoys herself" is a compound sentence consisting of two component sentences: "She stays home and she sews" and "She goes to the theater and she enjoys herself." The component sentences are themselves compound and consist of the atomic sentences "She stays home," "She sews," "She goes to the theater," and "She enjoys herself."

These connector terms are important because they enable us to determine whether or not an argument is valid. If I say, "If Ruth goes to the movies, then she buys popcorn, and Ruth has gone to the movies," it is because of the rules that govern *if—then* and *and* that I can correctly infer "Ruth buys popcorn" rather than some other conclusion. I must note the connector terms and then ask whether the rules governing these terms permit us to call the argument valid. And if an argument does not explicitly give its connector terms, or if it uses synonyms, then we are responsible for making the appropriate translation. Consider the following example:

Since he went to the store, he saw his friend. He did not see Mary. Presumably he did not see his friend.

To determine whether the conclusion can be logically inferred it would be necessary to change this to:

If he went to the store then he saw his friend. And he did not see Mary. Therefore he did not see his friend.

We would be required to make explicit the *if—then* construction and add *and* and *therefore*. Then we would be able to ask whether the conclusion does or does not follow from the premises. In other words, the key to logical inference rests on an understanding of how the connector expressions operate in relation to atomic and molecular sentences. Whenever an argument is encountered, the following questions should be asked: (1) What atomic and molecular sentences does the argument contain? (2) Are all the connector expressions explicitly given?

Sentences which are supposed to comprise an argument must be so structured that either (1) they cannot be further subdivided into more than one sentence, or (2) they are combinations of atomic sentences connected by connectors. Thus "John is friendly" cannot be further divided into two or more sentences. On the other hand, "John who is my neighbor is friendly" can be subdivided, and therefore should be considered as "John is my neighbor and he is friendly,"—resulting in two sentences connected by *and*. In any argument these atomic sentences can be connected to one another only by the basic connector words, *and, therefore, if—then, or,* and *if and only if.* What this means is that if in an argument two or more sentences are connected by some other expressions, as for example, in "I went to the store, but I did not buy sugar," where *but* is the connecting expression, the molecular sentence *must* be rephrased so that (1) only the acceptable connector terms are used, and (2) no loss of meaning is incurred in the rephrasing. It is easy to make the necessary changes in the aforementioned example. "I went to the store but I did not buy sugar" can be changed to "I went to the store and I did not buy sugar." No serious loss in meaning has resulted from the rephrasing. Similarly, "The book which is on the table does not belong to me" can be made to read, "A book is on the table and it does not belong to me."

Sometimes changing a sentence can be a rather tricky procedure. For example, how should the following be treated?

"He goes unless I stop him."

Usually logicians translate this into "If he does not go, then I stop him." But does this translation adequately convey the meaning of "He goes unless I stop him"? The main point to remember about any translation is that it must result in little if any loss of meaning. Sometimes, as in the aforementioned example, it is not possible to be sure that in changing the wording of a sentence, the exact meaning of the original wording has been retained. We said that "I went to the store but I did not buy sugar" means the same as "I went to the store and I did not buy sugar." *And* is equated with *but* in this example. Are they really the same? It might very well be argued that *but* seems to have as a part of its meaning the notion of something having been neglected. *And* has no such implicit meaning; it simply connects two sentences. The same kind of objection probably could be offered in relation to other translations. But whatever the limitations of a certain change, some translation into atomic sentences and connectors must be agreed upon if the validity of an argument is to be tested. It may require special effort to find the appropriate translation; but if the sentence is to play a role in logical inference, it must have the appropriate structure and be connected to other sentences by the stipulated connectors and no others. Most sentences can be changed without any loss of meaning. As we proceed, we shall show how various translations are made and how some very significant sentences have proved to be refractory to the whole process of translation.

Exercise

1. Change the following into appropriate atomic or molecular form; make explicit any implicit connector expressions.

a) Should he come through that door, I will shoot him.

b) He who hesitates is lost.

c) Although he tried and failed, he won the battle.

d) I shall not fire unless he runs.

e) I will go only if you go.

f) Leave if you want to.

g) He cried, but I did not care.

h) I will fight although my heart is not in it.

i) The lady next door, who happens to be my mistress, is not too bright.

SENTENTIAL CONSTANTS AND VARIABLES

Now that the notions of atomic and molecular sentences as well as connector expressions have been introduced, we shall make our first venture into the realm of pure logic. Hopefully, the venture will not be too painful. Alphabetical letters will be used instead of the expressions *this* sentence or *that* sentence. Thus instead of saying, "Either John stays or Mary goes," it is simpler to say *J* or *M*, where *J* stands for the entire sentence "John stays" and *M* stands for the entire sentence "Mary goes." Any letter can be used so long as the sentence for which it stands is clearly identified. It is, of course, possible to continue to refer to specific sentences without ever using any letters at all. But it simplifies matters for inference purposes to be able to deal with alphabetical letters rather than with specific sentences. Letters enable us to make abbreviations of all sentences. Thus "John stays and Mary goes" becomes "*J* and *M*"; "If John stays, then Mary goes" becomes "If *J* then *M*"; "John stays or Mary goes" becomes "*J* or *M*," and so forth for all atomic and molecular sentences.

Any letters can be used to stand for particular, that is specific, sentences. *S* and *G* or any other shorthand devices could have been used instead of *J* and *M*. All such letters will be called *sentential constants*. They stand for one and only one specific sentence. But sometimes we want to consider not one and only one specific sentence, but any sentence of a certain form: for example, any molecular sentence that has *or* as its connective—"Bill is happy or Mary is unhappy," "Jane goes to the movies or she visits her friend." In such cases we are not referring to a specific sentence but rather to a specific *kind* of sentence. That is to say, a molecular sentence might have the form "... or ———," where "..." and "———" serve as placeholders in which various atomic sentences can be placed. The placeholders "..." and "———" can be used for any sentence. But the use of such marks would be rather clumsy especially when a large number of placeholders are required. Thus a molecular sentence containing three atomic sentences would be symbolized as "... or −−− or × × ×." What we shall do is use certain letters instead of dots and dashes and crosses, and call them *sentential variables*. Specifically, the letters *p*, *q*, *r*, and *s* will be the sentential variables, i.e., placeholders for atomic sentences. Thus *p or q* will stand for any one of an indefinite number of molecular sentences which have the form of two atomic sentences connected by *or*, e.g., "I go or you stay," "John is happy or Mary is sad."

The introduction of sentential constants and variables should not frighten those who have some special fear of mathematical or symbolic devices; *p* and *q* simply stand for any atomic sentences. If I say *p* and *q*, I am simply saying consider any two sentences connected by the word *and*. Jones might think of two sentences *A* and *B*; Smith might think of two sentences *C* and *D*. Then *p* and *q* would stand for both sets of sentences as well as for an indefinite number of other sets.

Exercises

1. Using sentential variables, symbolize the exercises in the preceding section.

2. Using sentential constants, symbolize the following:

    a) Either you go and he stays, or I call the police.

    b) If John runs or Mary walks, then I walk and John leaves.

    c) John is happy; Mary is also happy.

    d) Mary is happy if and only if John makes love to her and tells her she is beautiful.

ALTERNATION

Molecular sentences are formed by using such connectors as *or*, *if—then*, *and*, and *if and only if*. These connectors are used for different purposes. The difference between alternation expressed as *p or q* and conjunction expressed as *p and q* can be discerned by observing how *or* and *and* are actually used in a language. Given any molecular sentence *p or q*, if *p* is true, then regardless of whether *q* is true or false, *p or q* is true. For example, if I say, "Either I will go to the movies or I will stay home," this molecular sentence is surely true if I should go to the movies and not stay home—that is, if *p* is true and *q* is false. And surely "Either I will go to the movies or I will stay home" would be regarded as true if it turns out that I do not go to the movies, but I do stay at home—that is, if p is false and q is true. In brief, connector terms are the means of revealing certain kinds of truth relationships among sentences. Specifically, when *or* appears in a sentence it indicates that if the truth or falsity of the component parts of that sentence are known, then the truth or falsity of the sentence as a whole can be determined. This is why *or* sentences are called *truth-functional*. In an *or* molecular sentence, if either of the component parts is true, then the whole sentence is true. Thus the molecular sentence "He goes to the movies or sees his girl, Pearl" is true under any one of the following conditions.

1. "He goes to the movies" is true; "He sees his girl, Pearl" is true.

2. "He goes to the movies" is true; "He sees his girl, Pearl" is false.

3. "He goes to the movies" is false; "He sees his girl, Pearl" is true.

However note that this molecular sentence is false when

4. "He goes to the movies" is false; "He sees his girl, Pearl" is false.

Thus it is evident that the truth or falsity of an *or* sentence is determined by the truth or falsity of its component sentences. If "He goes to the movies" and "He sees his girl, Pearl" are both true, then we know automatically that the molecular sentence, "Either he goes to the movies or he sees his girl, Pearl" is also true. The various relationships between *or* sentences and their parts can be summarized in the following table.

| | Column | | |
| | 1 | 2 | 3 |
	p	q	$p \ or \ q$
Row 1	T	T	T
Row 2	T	F	T
Row 3	F	T	T
Row 4	F	F	F

This *truth table*, as it is usually called, tells us that given any sentence p as T (true) and another sentence q as T, then the alternation $p \ or \ q$ is T. This is the information given in Row 1. Similarly, the information in Row 2 tells us that given a sentence p as T and another sentence q as F (false), then $p \ or \ q$ is T. Row 3 tells us that if p is F, and q is T, then $p \ or \ q$ is T. And finally, Row 4 informs us that if p is F and q is F, then p or q is F. The first two columns exhaust all the possible ways in which T and F can be attributed to p and q. The third column summarizes what specific *truth value*, either T or F, is to be attributed to p or q.

We have been using letters as symbols for words—the sentential variables p and q to symbolize atomic sentences, and T and F to symbolize *true* and *false*. The justification for using these symbols is that they serve to simplify logical inference. With them it is easy to show why one inference is legitimate and another is not. This is our excuse for gradually introducing symbolic devices. And it now becomes necessary to introduce still another symbol, ∨, which stands for *or*. Although any other symbol could have been used, we shall use the letter ∨ to stand for *or*. Thus the sentence p or q will appear as $p \vee q$. Since $p \vee q$ is now a completely symbolized sentence (i.e., all the English words have been replaced by symbols), it is called a *formula*. But the reader is reminded that if he is disturbed by this use of symbolism, he can always work backwards and think of some actual sentences to substitute for p and q, and then go on to substitute *or* for ∨.

The truth table for the formula of alternation $p \vee q$ now reads as follows:

	Column		
	I	2	3
	p	q	$p \vee q$
Row I	T	T	T
Row 2	T	F	T
Row 3	F	T	T
Row 4	F	F	F

This table reiterates what has been stated previously, namely, that if one or both of p and q is true, then $p \vee q$, i.e., p or q, is true; otherwise if both p and q are false, then $p \vee q$ is false.

It is important to recognize that truth tables can be constructed no matter how many sentential variables are involved. Thus for the formula $p \vee q \vee r$ it is possible to work out a truth table in the same way that one was formulated for two variables. But instead of four lines of T and F, eight lines will be used since it takes eight lines to exhaust all the possible ways in which T and F can be attributed to p, q, and r. The truth table for three variables connected by *or* becomes:

	Column			
	1	2	3	4
	p	q	r	$p \lor q \lor r$
Row 1	T	T	T	T
Row 2	T	T	F	T
Row 3	T	F	T	T
Row 4	T	F	F	T
Row 5	F	T	T	T
Row 6	F	T	F	T
Row 7	F	F	T	T
Row 8	F	F	F	F

Note how this table is constructed. Columns 1, 2, and 3 are obtained through the following procedures:

A. The number of T's and F's in any column is given by the formula 2^n where ^{n} is the number of sentential variables. Thus given $p \lor q \lor r$, consisting of three sentential variables, we know that each column will have 8 rows since 2^3 is equal to 8 (that is, $2 \times 2 \times 2 = 8$). If the formula were $p \lor q \lor r \lor s$, consisting of four sentential variables, then each column under p, q, r, and s would have 16 rows since 2^4 is equal to 16.

B. Choose any variable (in this example we arbitrarily choose r), and in its column place T followed by F followed by T followed by F, and so on. Then choose another variable, q, and in its column place TT followed by FF followed by TT followed by FF, and so on. Then in the column of the next variable p place $TTTT$ followed by $FFFF$ followed by $TTTT$ followed by $FFFF$, and so on.

   In other words, each successive variable *doubles* the group of T's and the group of F's that follow one another. Thus if we had a fourth variable, s, then in the column of s, 8 T's would have been followed by 8 F's. Once columns 1, 2, and 3 have been set up, it is easy to account for the last column. In alternation, if at least one of the component atomic parts is true, then the sentence is true. Since all rows except Row 8 have at least one T in the p, q, or r columns, T's are therefore listed in the last column except in row 8, which has an F because all the component parts of Row 8 (i.e., all the truth values of p, q, and r) are F's.

These truth tables for alternation account for all those combinations of sentences in which the alternation would be true if one or all of the atomic parts were true. This is called *inclusive* alternation. Both atomic parts—or alternants—of "I will either go to the movies or I will see my friends" could be true. I could go to the movies and also see my friends. On the other hand, *or* could be used in such a way that both component sentences could not be true, as in "Either he will stay home tonight or he will go to the movies." Since it is impossible for a person both to stay home and go to the movies, this molecular sentence is false not only if both component parts are false, but also if both are true. This information can be summarized in a truth table for *exclusive* alternation where a new sign ‡ is introduced to symbolize this different form of alternation:

I	2	3
p	*q*	*p ‡ q*
T	*T*	*F*
T	*F*	*T*
F	*T*	*T*
F	*F*	*F*

(Note: Henceforth the numbering of rows and the word "column" will be omitted.)

Thus *or* can be used inclusively or exclusively, and the exclusive sense of *or* could always be given by ‡. However the introduction of ‡ is not necessary. We shall simply stipulate that *or* is always to be regarded in its inclusive sense, that is, in the sense that is expressed by the truth table for ∨. But this does not mean that the exclusive sense of *or* has simply been legislated out of existence. In the section on conjunction (p. 85), it will become apparent that once we have symbolized and given the truth tables for the connector terms *and* and *not*, the exclusive sense of *or* will be explained merely by using ∨ and the symbols for *and* and *not*. The exclusive *or* will then be stated as *p or q, and not both*. Here the *or* is inclusive, while the *and* and the *not* serve to restrict it. Hence we can obtain the meaning of the exclusive *or* without introducing a new symbol for it.

Or, or alternation, has several other interesting characteristics besides its particular truth table interpretation. It is *associative, commutative,* and *idempotent.* Alternation is *associative* in that the variables can be regrouped without any change of truth value. In *p ∨ q ∨ r ∨ s*, with the use of parentheses to indicate groupings, *p ∨ q* can be grouped to form *(p ∨ q) ∨ r ∨ s* or *q ∨ r* can be combined to form *p ∨ (q ∨ r) ∨ s* or any other groupings, and yet they would all be equivalent to each other. Alternation is *commutative* in that the order of variables can be rearranged without any loss of truth value. *P ∨ q ∨ r ∨ s* can be changed to $q \vee r \vee p \vee s$ or $s \vee r \vee p \vee q$ or any other possible arrangement and these would all be equivalent to one another. Alternation is *idempotent* in that, if the variables are the same, they can be reduced down to the one variable involved. Thus $p \vee p$ as well as $p \vee p \vee p$ are all equivalent to p.

But what does it mean to say that two formulas are "equivalent"? The answer is that two formulas are equivalent if the last columns of their respective truth tables are the same. Thus consider why $p \vee q$ is taken to be equivalent to $q \vee p$. Let us examine the truth tables for each:

I	2	3		I	2	3
p	q	$p \vee q$		p	q	$q \vee p$
T	*T*	*T*		*T*	*T*	*T*
T	*F*	*T*		*T*	*F*	*T*
F	*T*	*T*		*F*	*T*	*T*
F	*F*	*F*		*F*	*F*	*F*

In both examples, whatever assignment is made of *T* or *F* to p and q, the truth values in the last column remain the same. Thus assigning *F* to both p and q gives us *F* in the last column in both examples. If *T* is assigned to p and *F* to q, *T* is obtained in the last column in both examples. This applies as well to the other two possible assignments. *Thus when the truth values of the last columns are the same, the formulas are taken to be equivalent.* This rule holds no matter how few or how many formulas are involved. Thus p can be shown to be equivalent to $p \vee p$ by simply noting the sameness of their final truth table columns:

I	2		I	2
p	p		p	$p \vee p$
T	*T*		*T*	*T*
F	*F*		*F*	*F*

Since no q is involved in either formula, a new column for q is not needed. Both final columns are the same; therefore the formulas are equivalent. Similarly we can show by truth tables that $s \vee (q \vee r) \vee p$ as well as $(p \vee q) \vee r \vee s$ and $r \vee p \vee (q \vee s)$ are all equivalent even though they are grouped—that is, associated—differently and have their variables arranged differently. We construct truth tables from them and compare their final columns:

I	2	3	4	5	6	7
p	q	r	s	$(q \lor r)$	$s \lor (q \lor r)$	$s \lor (q \lor r) \lor p$
T	T	T	T	T	T	T
T	T	T	F	T	T	T
T	T	F	T	T	T	T
T	T	F	F	T	T	T
T	F	T	T	T	T	T
T	F	T	F	T	T	T
T	F	F	T	F	T	T
T	F	F	F	F	F	T
F	T	T	T	T	T	T
F	T	T	F	T	T	T
F	T	F	T	T	T	T
F	T	F	F	T	T	T
F	F	T	T	T	T	T
F	F	T	F	T	T	T
F	F	F	T	F	T	T
F	F	F	F	F	F	F

This truth table has been constructed in the following way: All the possible combinations of p, q, r, and s have been listed in accordance with procedures (A) and (B) given on page 73. This truth table has four sentential variables and since 2^4 equals 16, this means each column will have 16 truth values. In accordance with rule (B), choose a sentential variable, s, and place in its column T followed by F followed by T followed by F, and so on. Then take any other sentential variable and double the number of T's and F's following one another. This is what happens under r. We again double the number of T's and F's under q so that four T's are followed consecutively by 4 F's until under column p, 8 T's are followed by 8 F's. We obtain the fifth column, $(q \lor r)$, by listing the truth values that result if the columns of q and r are in alternation. Then the fifth column of truth values is placed in alternation with the fourth column, s. This gives us the truth values for this sixth column, $s \lor (q \lor r)$. Finally, the values of the sixth column are placed in alternation with those of the first column, p. This gives us the final column of truth values.

Following similar procedures, we construct the tables for $(p \lor q) \lor r \lor s$ and $r \lor p \lor (q \lor s)$.

1	2	3	4	5	6	7
p	q	r	s	$(p \lor q)$	$(p \lor q) \lor r$	$(p \lor q) \lor r \lor s$
T	T	T	T	T	T	T
T	T	T	F	T	T	T
T	T	F	T	T	T	T
T	T	F	F	T	T	T
T	F	T	T	T	T	T
T	F	T	F	T	T	T
T	F	F	T	T	T	T
T	F	F	F	T	T	T
F	T	T	T	T	T	T
F	T	T	F	T	T	T
F	T	F	T	T	T	T
F	T	F	F	T	T	T
F	F	T	T	F	T	T
F	F	T	F	F	T	T
F	F	F	T	F	F	T
F	F	F	F	F	F	F

1	2	3	4	5	6	7
p	q	r	s	$(q \lor s)$	$p \lor (q \lor s)$	$r \lor p \lor (q \lor s)$
T	T	T	T	T	T	T
T	T	T	F	T	T	T
T	T	F	T	T	T	T
T	T	F	F	T	T	T
T	F	T	T	T	T	T
T	F	T	F	F	T	T
T	F	F	T	T	T	T
T	F	F	F	F	T	T
F	T	T	T	T	T	T
F	T	T	F	T	T	T
F	T	F	T	T	T	T
F	T	F	F	T	T	T
F	F	T	T	T	T	T
F	F	T	F	F	F	T
F	F	F	T	T	T	T
F	F	F	F	F	F	F

When the final columns of these three truth tables are checked, all of them are found to be the same. For this reason the three formulas are equivalent.

As an exercise, the reader should be able to show how the truth tables for $(p \lor q) \lor r \lor s$ and $r \lor p \lor (q \lor s)$ were constructed.

Exercise

1. Show by use of truth tables which of the following equivalences hold and which do not.

   a) $p \lor (q \lor r)$ is equivalent to $(q \lor r) \lor p$.

   b) $p \lor (s \lor r) \lor q$ is equivalent to $s \lor (p \lor q) \lor r$.

   c) p is equivalent to $p \lor (p \lor p) \lor p$.

   d) $q \lor s \lor p$ is equivalent to $(q \lor s) \lor p$.

   e) $p \lor q \lor r \lor s$ is equivalent to $r \lor p \lor (q \lor s)$.

   f) $p \lor q \lor r$ is equivalent to $(p \lor q) \lor (r \lor s)$.

   g) $(p \lor q) \lor (r \lor s)$ is equivalent to $(p \lor s \lor q) \lor r$.

NEGATION

We shall shortly be examining other connector expressions, such as *and*, *if—then*, and *if and only if*. But before we continue with our explanation of connector terms, we ought to stop and introduce negation terms, e.g., *not*, *it is false that*, and others, since these are closely tied to the functioning of all other connector terms. In every instance of the use of a connector term we want to be able to deny that the connection holds, and also deny any atomic sentence. Thus, just as we might want to say, "Either John or Mary goes to the movies," we would also want to be able to say "Either John does not go, or Mary stays"; or, "It is false that both John and Mary went to the movies." Negation, therefore, is one of the most essential of the connector signs.

But even though *not* seems like a fairly simple word, it is probably one of the most difficult terms to explain in any language. It is usually classified as a connector term, but it is not really comparable to such connector terms as *or*, or *and*, and *if—then*. These expressions have fairly clear functions; they tell us the truth conditions for the two or more sentences which they connect. But *not* is hardly a sentence connector. We do not place two sentences on either side of *not*, and then ask what it tells us about truth conditions. Furthermore, "The tree is not brown" would seem to be as much an atomic sentence as "The tree is brown." In fact, negative statements are used as often as affirmative ones to form molecular sentences such as "Either I will go or I will not go." But the presence of *not* in any atomic statement poses a problem.

Since an atomic sentence signifies a given occurrence, "The tree is brown" signifies the extralinguistic occurrence that a given tree is brown. But a negative atomic sentence seems to state that an occurrence is negative. And what can this mean? We can see something that is there, but can we ever see something that is not there? We can see something having the property of brown, but can we see something having the property of nonbrown? It may well be that both matter and antimatter exist, but this does not mean that both properties and nonproperties exist. However, it is still important to be able to say that something does not have a given property.

The reader might object to this analysis of negative sentences. He might argue that he is not committing himself to negative properties when he makes a negative sentence. He is simply stating that a given object *lacks* a certain property. He is not attributing anything to the object. But let us examine what it means to say something is lacking a certain property. It means something can be attributed to the thing, specifically that it lacks rather than possesses a given property. But what can it mean to say something has a certain lack? We know what it means to say something has the property of black, or has a particular crack—these can be directly observed—but it is not possible to observe a lack of color in the same way it is possible to observe color itself. A lack signifies absence, the failure to exist at a given place and time. But how can one observe what is not present or does not exist? Thus the commonsense view of negation does not hold up under close scrutiny.

Another solution might be to avoid altogether the use of *not* by substituting affirmative for negative sentences. It would take us too far afield to investigate this matter with any degree of thoroughness. But let us consider a simple example. Can the same information in "John is not in the room" be expressed without the negative? To say, "Bill and Frank are in the room" is not the same as saying, "John is not in the room." To know that both Bill and Frank are in the room does not tell us that John is not in the room. He might be there also. Perhaps a better alternative would be to state, "Only Bill and Frank are in the room." This would seem to offer the information that John is not in the room, without employing any negative. But is not the negative implicit in *only*? To say, "Only Bill and Frank are in the room" surely means that Bill and Frank are in the room and *no one* else is there. In other words, we might be able to disguise the fact that we are using some variant of *not* by using *only* or by employing negative prefixes, as in "I am unhappy" instead of "I am not happy." In all these instances the negative is still present. It has also been suggested that the information given in "The table is not green" can be expressed by omitting references to *green* and by simply listing the colors that the table can have: "The table is either blue or red or purple or yellow." But to list all the alternative colors we must know that we have a *complete* list of colors, that no color has been excluded. Once again the negative form cannot be avoided.

Obviously, negation has a very significant place in language. While it is possible in a very precise and scientific language to substitute certain signs for others and avoid the use of some of them, negation cannot be eliminated. Indeed, to some existentialist philosophers negation is the most primary and the most profound concept in philosophy. Some theological existentialists, for example, have maintained that a true analysis of the word *nothing* will lead to an all-inclusive theory proving the existence of God and man's relationship to Him. Things must have come into existence from a state in which nothing existed. Thus how something can come out of nothing is one of the key problems in theology. But this means that a clear explanation of negation must be made available. However, a more detailed discussion of these matters would lead us too far afield from the ordinary problems of logical inferences.

What we shall do is treat *not* as a special connector term which, unlike other connectors, relates to the truth conditions of one and only one sentence, regardless of whether that sentence is atomic or molecular. Whereas the truth or falsity of "John loves Mary or John hates Mary," i.e., $p \vee q$, is determined by the truth or falsity of the component parts, the truth or falsity of "John does not love Mary," i.e., *not-p*, is determined by the truth or falsity of the one component part, "John loves Mary." If p is true in *not-p*, then *not-p* is false; if p is false in *not-p*, then *not-p* is true. Thus a truth table can be formulated for negation. But three conditions must be met if the truth table is to function properly: (1) Every implicit negative sentence must be made explicit; for example, "That is unsatisfactory" must be changed to "That is not satisfactory." (2) The negative sign must be extracted from the sentence and placed before it. Thus the statement, "The tree is not brown," is to have the form "Not (the tree is brown)." (3) Just as sentential variables use the sign $\vee$ to stand for *or*, the sign $-$ will stand for negation. Thus $\bar{p}$ will stand for the negation of an atomic sentence. But for the negation of a molecular sentence, the negation sign will be placed outside the entire sentence, e.g., $-(p \vee q)$. The truth table for negation follows:

1	2
p	$\bar{p}$
T	F
F	T

The table indicates that if any sentence p is taken as true or false, then $\bar{p}$ is respectively false or true.

The truth table for negation can be combined with the truth table for alternation to form truth tables for more complex formulas. Thus to obtain the truth table for $\bar{p} \vee q$, simply add another column for $\bar{p}$ as in the following, and then use the rules of alternation to obtain 4:

| 1 | 2 | 3 | 4 |
p	$\bar{p}$	q	$\bar{p} \vee q$
T	F	T	T
T	F	F	F
F	T	T	T
F	T	F	T

The truth values for the last column are obtained by taking the alternation of columns 2 and 3. Thus the first row in columns 2 and 3 consists of p as F and q as T and this combination in the truth table for alternation gives us a T in the last column. In the second row of columns 2 and 3 the combination of F and F in the truth table for alternation gives us an F for the last column, and so on for the last two rows.

With the truth table for negation, it becomes possible to construct a truth table for such a complicated formula as $- - (\bar{p} \vee \bar{q})$. The truth table can be constructed by merely adding the columns for $\bar{p}, \bar{q}, \bar{p} \vee \bar{q}, - (\bar{p} \vee \bar{q})$ and $- - (\bar{p} \vee \bar{q})$, and then using the basic tables for negation and alternation accordingly. Thus the truth table for $- - (\bar{p} \vee \bar{q})$ becomes:

| 1 | 2 | 3 | 4 | 5 | 6 | 7 |
p	$\bar{p}$	q	$\bar{q}$	$\bar{p} \vee \bar{q}$	$- (\bar{p} \vee \bar{q})$	$- - (\bar{p} \vee \bar{q})$
T	F	T	F	F	T	F
T	F	F	T	T	F	T
F	T	T	F	T	F	T
F	T	F	T	T	F	T

Here also we see how we use columns 2 and 4, the negations of p and q, to obtain column 5; and since column 6 is no more than a negation of column 5, simply reverse all the values of 5 to obtain 6. Finally since column 7 is a negation of column 6, the values of 6 are reversed to produce column 7. Observe how double negation in logic is similar to double negation in grammar. The negation cancels out.

Exercises

1. Give the truth table for:

   a) Either he stays or I do not go.
   b) It is false that I do not stay or he does not go.
   c) It is not false that I do not stay or he does not go.
   d) How true it is that Presidential candidates do not keep their promises after they are elected, or else they find sneaky ways of pretending that they have kept their promises.

2. Give the truth tables for:

   a) $- (\bar{p} \vee q \vee \bar{r})$.
   b) $\bar{p} \vee q \vee - (\bar{p} \vee \bar{r})$.
   c) $- (p \vee q) \vee (\bar{p} \vee \bar{r})$.
   d) $- (p \vee q \vee q \vee q \vee r)$.

3. Show by truth table whether or not the following pairs are equivalent.

   a) $\bar{p} \vee q \vee r$ and $r \vee q \vee \bar{p}$.   d) $- (p \vee q \vee r)$ and $\bar{p} \vee \bar{q} \vee \bar{r}$.
   b) $\bar{p} \vee (\bar{q} \vee r)$ and $(r \vee \bar{q}) \vee \bar{p}$.   e) $- (\bar{p} \vee \bar{q} \vee \bar{r})$ and $p \vee q \vee r$.
   c) $(\bar{p} \vee \bar{q} \vee \bar{r}) \vee \bar{r}$ and $\bar{p} \vee (\bar{q} \vee \bar{r})$. f) $- - (\bar{p} \vee \bar{q} \vee \bar{r})$ and $\bar{p} \vee \bar{q} \vee \bar{r}$.

4. Discuss the following:

   a) There are negative things in the world. What about antimatter, negative electrons, and unhappy (that is, not happy) people, as well as negative attitudes.

   b) It is possible to construct a language without negative signs. For example, the sentence "It is not raining" can always be changed to read "It is cloudy or it is sunny," where the negation sign does not appear.

   c) It would seem that just as it is perfectly meaningful to say, "There is something," it is also perfectly meaningful to say, "There is nothing." But how do we translate "There is nothing" into some set of nonnegative sentences?

5. Suppose that a room had twenty objects in it. Could you describe it by simply naming the objects? Or would you also have to include the following final statement: "There are no more than twenty objects in this room"?

CONJUNCTION

And, like *or*, is usually explained truth-functionally; that is, it is explained by reference to true or false atomic sentences. If "John went to a good movie and saw Greta Gable" is true, then "John went to a good movie" is true and "He saw Greta Gable" is true. In fact, if *and* is used truth-functionally, the resultant molecular sentence is true only when all of its component parts are true. Otherwise it is false. Thus in an extended sentence, such as "John went to a good movie and he saw Greta Gable, and he ate popcorn and he enjoyed the movie," if one of the atomic parts is false, then the whole sentence is false.

Sometimes *and* does not operate truth-functionally, as in "Richard Nixon and Edward Kennedy are contemporaries." This sentence cannot be made truth-functional by the revision "Richard Nixon is a contemporary and Edward Kennedy is a contemporary," since this changes the sense of the original statement which means that Nixon and Kennedy are contemporaries of one another. In this kind of sentence *and* can be eliminated by changing it to read: "Nixon is a contemporary of Kennedy." Thus words that are usually connectors can sometimes be used nonconnectively.

Ordinarily, a number of words are used as equivalents of *and*. None of the following sentences is explicitly an *and* statement.

1. I will go, but you will stay.
2. I will go; you will go.
3. He tried, although he failed.
4. He tried. He failed.

However, the words *but*, *although*, the semicolon in (2), and the period in (4) serve the same function as *and*. Of the three examples only (3) seems to need some explanation. The equating of *although* with *but* and *and* might well be questioned. In grammar *although* has a different meaning and function from *and*; they are classified differently. *And* is a *coordinate conjunction*, while *although* is a *subordinate conjunction*. In the sentence "Although he was a bright student, he failed the course," *although* leads us to expect that he should have passed the course. On the other hand, in "He was a bright student and he failed the course," *and* does not convey any sense of expectancy. This is an example of how the grammarian seems to make a finer distinction than the logician, who takes *although* for all practical purposes to be equivalent to *and*. But we shall continue to translate *although* into *and* on the grounds that, at the very least, *although* means *and*. In "Although he was a bright student, he failed," the very least that is being said is "He was a bright student and he failed." In other words, while *although* may have several different nuances of meaning, it must always have the sense of *and*. Whatever is meant by "Although he was a bright student, he failed," certainly it must be true that he was a bright student and he failed.

Of course, if one still insists on the sense of expectancy in *although*, "Although he was a bright student, he failed" can be changed to "He is a bright student, and he was expected to pass, and he failed." But this translation still requires the changing of *although* into *and*.

Just as symbols are used for negation and alternation, so a symbol will stand for *and* insofar as it is used truth-functionally. The period sign will be used to signify *and*. Thus $p \cdot q$ means that p is conjoined to q by the connector *and*. The truth table for conjunction will summarize what has been stated about *and*, namely, that any conjunction of sentences is true only if each conjunct—that is, component sentence of conjunction—is true; otherwise the conjunction is false.

1	2	3
p	q	$p \cdot q$
T	T	T
T	F	F
F	T	F
F	F	F

Conjunction has many characteristics which are similar to alternation. It is commutative; $p \cdot q \cdot r$ is equivalent to $r \cdot p \cdot q$ and $q \cdot r \cdot p$. It is also associative; $p \cdot (q \cdot r)$ is equivalent to $(p \cdot q) \cdot r$ and $p \cdot (r \cdot q)$. Finally, it is also idempotent; $p \cdot p$ is equivalent to p. (All of these equivalences can, of course, be checked simply by constructing truth tables and then observing whether the final columns are the same.) However, it is important to stress that these characteristics hold only when the same connector appears throughout the formula. In other words, the formula must consist either solely of conjunction connectors, as in $p \cdot q \cdot r$, or solely of alternation signs, as in $p \vee q \vee r$. But the characteristics of commutation, association, and idempotence do not apply when a formula has mixed signs, as in $(p \vee q) \cdot r$; $(p \vee q) \cdot r$ is not equivalent to $p \vee (q \cdot r)$. This lack of equivalency can be readily observed, since $(p \vee q) \cdot r$, as a conjunction of the two conjuncts $(p \vee q)$ and r, requires r to be true if this molecular sentence is true, whereas the truth of $p \vee (q \cdot r)$ as an alternation does not require r to be true. If p is true, then it would not matter what value r has. This lack of equivalence is more clearly seen by simply combining the truth tables for conjunction and alternation, and checking whether the last column of the truth tables for $(p \vee q) \cdot r$ is the same as the last column of the truth table for $p \vee (q \cdot r)$. The truth tables turn out to be:

1	2	3	4	5	6	7	8	9	10
p	q	r	$p \vee q$	$(p \vee q) \cdot r$	p	q	r	$(q \cdot r)$	$p \vee (q \cdot r)$
T	T	T	T	T	T	T	T	T	T
T	T	F	T	F	T	T	F	F	T
T	F	T	T	T	T	F	T	F	T
T	F	F	T	F	T	F	F	F	T
F	T	T	T	T	F	T	T	T	T
F	T	F	T	F	F	T	F	F	F
F	F	T	F	F	F	F	T	F	F
F	F	F	F	F	F	F	F	F	F

The truth tables are constructed by giving all the possible combinations of truth values in columns 1, 2, 3, 6, 7, and 8 by using the procedures of truth-table construction. In column 4 appear the results of combining 1 and 2 by alternation (in the lefthand truth table). In column 9 appear the results of combining columns 7 and 8 by conjunction (in the righthand truth table). Column 5 results from combining columns 3 and 4 by conjunction. Column 10 results from combining columns 6 and 9 by alternation. In this way it is possible to see that the final columns 5 and 10 are not the same. Therefore $(p \vee q) \cdot r$ is not equivalent to $p \vee (q \cdot r)$.

Using the truth table for conjunction, we can now give a truth table for the exclusive sense of *or* without introducing some special table for this kind of *or*. The exclusive sense of *or* means that at least one sentence must be true, but it is further stipulated that both cannot be true. In symbols, the *or* of exclusion states:

$$(p \vee q) \cdot - (p \cdot q)$$

This can be expressed by using the regular truth tables of conjunction and alternation.

I	2	3	4	5	6
p	q	$p \vee q$	$p \cdot q$	$- (p \cdot q)$	$(p \vee q) \cdot - (p \cdot q)$
T	T	T	T	F	F
T	F	T	F	T	T
F	T	T	F	T	T
F	F	F	F	T	F

The formation of this truth table should be apparent to the reader.

Exercises

1. Give the truth tables for the following:

   a) He went to the store and saw either Mary or Jean.

   b) He stays or I go and get the police.

   c) I did not see the movie although he did and he did not like it.

   d) $(p \vee \bar{q}) \cdot \bar{r}$.

   e) $p \cdot (q \vee \bar{r}) \cdot q$.

   f) You can either study or join the radicals; but you cannot do both.

2. By truth table show whether or not the following are equivalent:

   a) $(\bar{p} \vee \bar{q})$ to $- (p \cdot q)$.

   b) $- (p \vee q)$ to $\bar{p} \cdot \bar{q}$.

   c) $p \vee - (q \cdot r)$ to $p \vee \bar{q} \vee \bar{r}$.

   d) $p \vee - (q \cdot r)$ to $(p \vee \bar{q}) \cdot (p \vee \bar{r})$.

   e) $(q \cdot r) \vee s$ to $(q \cdot r) \vee (q \cdot s)$.

   f) $- - (\bar{p} \, \bar{q} \, \bar{r}) \vee r$ to $(\bar{p} \vee r) \cdot (\bar{q} \vee r) \cdot (\bar{r} \vee r)$.

   g) $\bar{q} \vee q$ to $\bar{r} \vee p \vee s \vee r$.

SUPPLEMENTARY READINGS

Taylor, Richard, "Negative Things," *Journal of Philosophy*, XLIX (1952), 433–449.

Urmson, J. O., *Philosophical Analysis*. London: Oxford University Press, 1966. Part I, "Philosophical Analysis and Logical Atomism."

6

Connector Expressions-- If-Then and If and Only If

THE CONDITIONAL (IF—THEN)

One of the most interesting sentences in the English language is the conditional *if—then* such as, "If I drop this piece of chalk, then it will fall 32 feet per second per second." It is especially significant in the formulation of scientific laws and hypotheses, since these are usually stated in the form "If this occurs, then that will occur." Also, every inference can be placed in the form "If this evidence is reliable, then the following conclusion is legitimate." Thus the *if—then* construction is quite essential.

As we have noted, *or* and *and* are commutative. For example, $p \vee q$ is equivalent to $q \vee p$, and $p \cdot q$ is equivalent to $q \cdot p$. But this is not true for the conditional. "If I see *Oh! Calcutta* this afternoon, then I will see nude players on the stage this afternoon" is not equivalent to "If I see nude players on the stage this afternoon, then I will see *Oh! Calcutta* this afternoon." The *if* part of this sentence—known as the *antecedent*—could be true, while the *then* part of the sentence—known as the *consequent*—could be false. I might be seeing nude players on the stage this afternoon and yet they might not be in *Oh! Calcutta*. I could be seeing *Hair*, which also has its fair share of nude players. In other words, *if p then q* is not equivalent to *if q then p*.

The sign that shall be used to stand for the *if—then* construction is the inverted horseshoe $\supset$. Thus $p \supset q$ symbolizes "If I see *Oh! Calcutta* this afternoon, then I will see nude players on the stage this afternoon." Also $p \supset q$ is not commutative; nor is it associative. For example, $p \supset (q \supset r)$ is not equivalent to any other arrangement, such as $(p \supset q) \supset r$ or $r \supset (p \supset q)$. Nor is it idempotent; $p \supset p$ is not equivalent to p. "If I see nude players on the stage this afternoon, then I see nude players on the stage this afternoon" is obviously not the same as saying, "I see nude players on the stage this afternoon." However, once we have constructed the truth table for $\supset$, then we shall be able to show quite explicitly that these equivalences do not hold.

The construction of the truth table for the conditional poses some problems. Ordinarily, a conjunctive or alternation sentence is false if its component parts are false. But now let us look at what is regarded by logicians as the truth table for the conditional:

1	2	3
p	q	$p \supset q$
T	T	T
T	F	F
F	T	T
F	F	T

The first row offers no real difficulty. It pretty well jibes with the ordinary use of *if—then*. The statement "If I see *Oh! Calcutta* this afternoon, then I see nude players on the stage this afternoon" is obviously true if it turns out that I do see *Oh! Calcutta* this afternoon and I do see nude players on the stage at the same time. The second row is also easily explained. If I see *Oh! Calcutta* this afternoon, and I do not see nude players on the stage, then it is false to say "If I see *Oh! Calcutta* this afternoon, then I see nude players on the stage this afternoon." It is possible—perhaps the heating system broke down—that I saw *Oh! Calcutta*, but all the players were clothed. (It is not clear, however, whether *Oh! Calcutta* could still be *Oh! Calcutta* if all the actors were dressed.) So much, then, for the first two rows of the truth table. But now consider the last two rows. They are really interesting, because what they state is that if the antecedent of an *if—then* statement is false, then, *regardless of what the consequent is—either true or false*—the conditional is always true. According to this principle, if I do not see *Oh! Calcutta*, then the conditional is true regardless of whether or not I saw nude players on the stage. In other words, if a conditional has a false antecedent, then it is true no matter what consequent follows it. Does it not seem odd to say that if I do not see *Oh! Calcutta* this afternoon, then the following sentences are true?

1. If I see *Oh! Calcutta* this afternoon, then I will see nude players on the stage this afternoon.

2. If I see *Oh! Calcutta* this afternoon, then I will not see nude players on the stage this afternoon.

3. If I see *Oh! Calcutta* this afternoon, then pink elephants will appear.

How are we to account for this seemingly strange portion of the truth table for *if—then*? The truth table might be changed to read:

1	2	3
p	q	$p \supset q$
T	T	T
T	F	F
F	T	F
F	F	F

But this truth table is equivalent to $p \cdot q$ and surely, "If I stay home, then I do my homework" is not the same as saying, "I stay home and I do my homework." Also, if this change is made, then certain sentences which are usually taken to be equivalent to *if p then q* lose their equivalency. Thus, for example, "If I see *Oh! Calcutta* this afternoon, then I will see nude players on the stage this afternoon" is usually taken to mean the same as "If I do not see nude players on the stage this afternoon, then I do not see *Oh! Calcutta*." In brief it is usually assumed that $p \supset q$ is equivalent to $\bar{q} \supset \bar{p}$. If the usual truth table is used where a false antecedent makes the whole sentence true, then the equivalence does indeed hold, as the following two truth tables show us:

1	2	3		1	2	3	4	5
p	q	$p \supset q$		p	q	$\bar{p}$	$\bar{q}$	$\bar{q} \supset \bar{p}$
T	T	T		T	T	F	F	T
T	F	F		T	F	F	T	F
F	T	T		F	T	T	F	T
F	F	T		F	F	T	T	T

The final columns here are identical. Thus $p \supset q$ is equivalent to $\bar{q} \subset \bar{p}$. But now consider what happens if the revised truth table for $p \subset q$ is accepted.

1	2	3		1	2	3	4	5
p	q	$p \supset q$		p	q	$\bar{p}$	$\bar{q}$	$\bar{q} \supset \bar{p}$
T	T	T		T	T	F	F	F
T	F	F		T	F	F	T	F
F	T	F		F	T	T	F	F
F	F	F		F	F	T	T	T

On this analysis $p \supset q$ is not equivalent to $\bar{q} \supset \bar{p}$, since the final columns are not the same. Finally, if the revised truth table is accepted then a most fundamental truth disappears. "If I see *Oh! Calcutta* this afternoon then I see *Oh! Calcutta* this afternoon" is obviously true, but it is surely not the same as saying, "I see *Oh! Calcutta* this afternoon." *If* I see *Oh! Calcutta* this afternoon, then, of course, I see it. But I need not see it all. In other words, "If I see *Oh! Calcutta* this afternoon, then I do see it" is surely not equivalent to "I see *Oh! Calcutta* this afternoon." But now let us see what happens when truth tables for both of these sentences are constructed in accordance with the revised truth table for $\supset$, and their final columns are checked.

I	2
p	$p \supset p$
T	T
F	F

I	2
p	p
T	T
F	F

If the revised truth table for $\supset$ is used, we find that $p \supset p$ is equivalent to p since their last columns are the same. In other words, on this analysis I would be seeing *Oh! Calcutta* every time I said that if I see it, then I see it.

It can be shown without much effort that if the conditional truth table were revised in other ways, for example as:

I	2	3
p	q	$p \supset q$
T	T	T
T	F	F
F	T	F
F	F	T

the same problems involving the violation of some fundamental truth would arise. Thus, even though it might seem odd to say that if an antecedent is false, then the statement is true regardless of what the consequent is, it would be odder and lead to some extreme paradoxes not to accept this. Perhaps it is best to think of $p \supset q$ as expressing the fact that the conjunction of p and $\bar{q}$ is false. Whatever else we may mean by $p \supset q$, this is the minimal meaning that is always involved. Thus the least I mean by "If I see *Oh! Calcutta* this afternoon, then I see nude players on the stage this afternoon" is "It is false both that I see *Oh! Calcutta* this afternoon and I do not see nude players on the stage this afternoon." In other words, we shall simply stipulate that $p \supset q$ is to be taken as equivalent to $- (p \cdot \bar{q})$. What we will do is simply obtain the truth table for $- (p \cdot \bar{q})$ and then observe its last column, since whatever the last column is it will be the one for $p \supset q$ as well. The truth table for $- (p \cdot \bar{q})$ is:

I	2	3	4	5
p	q	$\bar{q}$	$p \cdot \bar{q}$	$-(p \cdot \bar{q})$
T	T	F	F	T
T	F	T	T	F
F	T	F	F	T
F	F	T	F	T

And lo and behold! the last column for $- (p \cdot \bar{q})$ does turn out to be identical to the last column for $p \supset q$. For this reason we permit it to stand that a false antecedent always makes $p \supset q$ true.

The *if—then* sentence which can be formulated in terms of the accepted truth table is called a *material* conditional and is often expressed in other ways besides *if—then*. The following are all equivalent ways of saying *if p then q*:

p only if q   *q in case p*

q if p   *p hence q*

q provided that p   *since p then q*

q on condition that p

It is possible to argue that sentences with the form of *q provided that p*, *q if p*, etc., contain somewhat different shades of meaning. But they shall be treated in the same way as the other connector terms *and*, *but*, and *although*, which also vary in meaning but still retain the general sense of *and*. Under normal conditions *if—then* is equivalent in meaning to the above variant forms, but whenever any question arise about them, additional sentences can be supplied to obtain the desired sense.

Perhaps *p only if q* deserves special attention, since it is sometimes difficult to understand why this is equivalent to *if p then q*. An example might clarify the nature of this equivalence. Consider the following:

This match burns only if it is not wet.

Surely this does not mean that if this match is not wet, then it will burn. Obviously many dry matches do not burn, either because they are not scratched or their sulphur content is inadequate. Thus what the sentence must mean is that if the match does burn, then we can be sure that it was not wet. In other words, *p only if q* is equivalent to *if p then q*.

Exercises

1. Give the truth table for each:

   a) If I go to the movies and see my friend, then I will not be home early.

   b) Either he stays indoors or goes outside or he will be caught. But he will not go outside.

   c) If he goes to the theater and does not see Bridget Bardahl, then he will be unhappy.

   d) $(\bar{p} \supset \bar{q}) \vee (q \cdot \bar{r})$.

   e) I will go on condition that he does too.

   f) He sees *Hamlet* only if he gets free tickets.

2. a) Show that "If I go to the store, then I see Fats Waller" is equivalent to "Either I do not go to the store, or I see Fats Waller."

   b) Would the equivalence of (a) hold if $p \supset q$ had the following truth table?

1	2	3
p	q	$p \supset q$
T	T	T
T	F	F
F	T	T
F	F	F

3. By truth-table analysis show whether or not the following are equivalent:

   a) $p \supset (q \cdot r)$ and $(p \supset q) \cdot (p \supset r)$.

   b) $\bar{p} \vee (q \supset r)$ and $(\bar{p} \vee q) \supset (\bar{p} \vee r)$.

   e) $--\,(p \vee q \vee r)$ and $-\,(\bar{p} \vee \bar{q} \vee \bar{r})$.

SUBJUNCTIVE CONDITIONALS

The *if—then* sentence which can be formulated in terms of the accepted truth table is called a *material* conditional. It must be sharply distinguished from a special type of conditional for which a truth table cannot be formulated, namely, the *subjunctive* conditional. As we have seen, the antecedent of the material conditional can be either true or false, but in the subjunctive conditional the antecedent is usually false. The subjunctive form of the verb is used to indicate a hypothetical, imagined, or contrary-to-fact situation, as in the sentence "If you were the last man on earth, then I might marry you," where the antecedent is expected to be taken as false. (It is highly unlikely that you will ever be the *last* man on earth!) Compare this with the material conditional form, "If he runs fast, then he will catch the train," where the antecedent is probably expected to be true. (He probably will run fast, and he will catch the train.) We would not be asserting the conditional if we considered the antecedent to be false, since this would make the conditional trivial. The difference between the two conditionals might be made clearer by pointing out the following: In the material conditional the antecedent is usually regarded as true. A false antecedent makes the conditional trivially true. On the other hand, in the subjunctive conditional the antecedent is usually false. But the falsity of the antecedent does not make the conditional trivial; sometimes the conditional is false, sometimes it is true. Thus the following subjunctive conditional is true:

> If I were to jump out of this window (but of course I never will), then I would fall thirty-two feet per second per second.

But the following is false:

> If I were to jump out of this window (but of course I never will), then I would fall three hundred feet per second per second.

If both of these sentences were treated as material conditionals, then one would be just as true as the other since the antecedents of both are false. But obviously the first is surely true and the second surely false.

Subjunctive conditionals, therefore, are some of the most difficult sentences to use in logical systems, and some additional comments on them are required.

Even though the antecedent of the subjunctive conditional is false, the sentence may be true or false. On the other hand, in the ordinary material or truth-functional conditional, the sentence is *always* true if the antecedent is false. The question then arises as to what can be done with the subjunctive conditional if it is to play a role in logical inference. If logic is truth-functional in that the truth value of all molecular sentences can be mechanically given by the truth value of their parts, then how can we use molecular sentences the truth values of which are not determined by their parts?

First of all, it might be possible to deny the existence of any subjunctive conditionals by claiming that all subjunctives are really parts of narrative rather than argumentative writing, in that they allude to some nebulous imaginary circumstances that can never be seriously considered. Thus if I say, "If I were king, then there would be no beggars," I am simply expressing some belief that cannot really be considered a part of any serious discourse. Since it is ridiculous to think I ever could be king, my statement is no more than a disguised wish that means "I wish I were rich enough to help the poor." Similarly, if I were to say, "Ah, if I were only twenty years younger, I could conquer the world," I am simply making an emotional statement that might be better expressed in the form "I wish I were young again," rather than in the form of a conditional. Thus subjunctives, on this analysis, can simply be relegated to narrative discourse where inference is not important. But this view is wrong. Subjunctives are needed in order to explain some of the most crucial scientific beliefs. Thus I do wish to say, in scientific inquiry, that some object is magnetic or that something is soluble in water, even though that thing is not at the moment magnetizing nor is it being dissolved in water. In other words, I want to be able to say of a magnetic or a soluble object: "If this object were placed under certain conditions (although it is not now under such conditions and perhaps might never be placed under such conditions, since this could cause a disaster of some sort), then it would magnetize or it would dissolve." A subjunctive statement is necessary in order to speak of such properties as magnetism and solubility. Similarly, psychologists frequently refer to the abilities of animals and human beings. But what else is an ability but a hidden subjunctive? "Jones has the ability to play the piano" means "If Jones were to sit down at the piano now (but he is not doing it and does not intend to do it), then he would be able to play it." Thus subjunctive conditionals seem to be required in most important discourses. In fact, there is also a strong suspicion that no scientific law can be properly explained without reference to a subjunctive conditional. If I say, "All metals are conductors," I do not merely mean that I came across a given number of metals and found them all to be conductors. I seem to mean that not only did I come across a given number of metals and find them all to be conductors, but also that if I were to encounter still another metal (even though I may never encounter another metal), then it also would be a conductor. Again, a subjunctive conditional cannot be avoided.

A second alternative is to view the antecedent and the consequent of the subjunctive as being connected in a certain peculiar way. The antecedent *entails* the consequent. We mean by *entails* that if someone understands the meaning of the antecedent, then he will also understand that the consequent *necessarily* follows from the antecedent. In ordinary material conditionals such necessity is not present. In "If I go to the theatre, then I will see Sophia Toothless playing Lady Macbeth," the consequent surely does not necessarily follow from the antecedent. There is nothing about my going to the theatre that makes it necessary for Sophia Toothless to be present or to be playing Lady Macbeth. I may hope for it, dream of it, and even demand it at the box office, but no guarantee can be forthcoming. On the other hand, if I say, "If I were to jump out of this twentieth-story window, then I would be killed or seriously wounded," there would seem to be a necessary connection between the antecedent and the consequent. Anyone who understands what it means to jump from a twentieth-story window would also understand that it would mean being killed or seriously wounded. Thus, on this view, the subjunctive describes certain necessary relationships that exist in the natural world. To put the matter more bluntly, subjunctives describe certain necessary truths about the world. They seem to tell us that certain events, say A and B, are connected to one another so that if at some time and at some place A occurs, then B will necessarily occur. This seems to be undeniable.

Unfortunately, it *is* deniable. Someone might jump from a twentieth-story window and not be killed. He might land on a parapet; or if he were an acrobat, he could jump from the window and grab a wire or rope that would save him. It does not *necessarily* follow that if someone jumps from a twentieth-story window, he will be killed or seriously wounded. Thus the subjunctive conditional does not express some kind of *necessary* connection between the antecedent and the consequent. Furthermore, it is highly dubious whether any physical event can necessitate any other.

Ever since David Hume (1711–1776), the empiricist philosopher, offered his famous (or infamous) criticism, it has been difficult to affirm that there are any necessary relationships among things or events. There is no guarantee, Hume argued, that because one thing happens, therefore some other thing *must* happen. We cannot be sure of anything, since, search as we may, we never find any hidden glue in the universe that ties one event to another. The sun has always risen on the following day. But there is nothing in this universe that makes it absolutely necessary that the sun will rise again tomorrow. Everything is merely a matter of probability. In fact, Hume believed that not even probability should be trusted, since theories of probability apparently assume that the future will at least in some ways be like the past. But who can guarantee this? One good hydrogen bomb in the right or the wrong place can ensure that very little of the future will be like the past. Thus whatever the subjunctive does, it certainly does not express some necessary causal relations, since there are no such things.

However, the subjunctive conditional does have one very interesting characteristic. Its truth or falsity very often seems to be related to some general scientific or commonsensical principle. We accept the statement "If I were to jump through this twentieth-story window, then I would either be killed or seriously wounded" because we believe in the general principle that if *anyone* jumps through a twentieth-story window, and nothing stops his fall, he is seriously wounded or killed. On the other hand, "If I were to jump through this twentieth-story window, then I would fly gently to the ground" is taken to be both false and silly, simply because it is not connected to some general statement such as, "If anyone were to jump through this twentieth-story window, then he would fly gently to the ground." No known instances confirm this statement. Thus subjunctive conditionals are taken to be true or false in accordance with whether they can be regarded as instances of some accepted generalization.

Subjunctives can be treated in the following way: if the subjunctive can be changed into a generalization which would be acceptable to either scientific or commonsense knowledge, then both the antecedent and the consequent will be taken as true. If, on the other hand, such a generalization would not be acceptable to either scientific or commonsense knowledge, then the antecedent will be regarded as true and the consequent as false. Hence, on this analysis, the sentence

If I were to drop this chalk, then it would fall 32 feet per second per second.

is to be regarded as a sentence consisting of a true antecedent and a true consequent, since it states what would be scientifically acceptable if it were generalized into "If anyone drops this chalk, then it will fall 32 feet per second per second. On the other hand,

If I were to drop this chalk, then it would fall 50 feet per second per second.

is to be regarded as a sentence consisting of a true antecedent and a false consequent, since it would produce a generalization that is unacceptable, namely, "If anyone drops this chalk, then it will fall 50 feet per second per second."

Similarly, other subjunctives can be analyzed in terms of whether or not they rely upon acceptable commonsense knowledge. Thus the sentence

If I were president, then I would eliminate poverty.

is to be taken as a true sentence with a true antecedent and consequent since it could very well be the case that any person who is president could eliminate poverty. But the sentence

If I were president, then I would stop the moon from moving.

would be regarded as a false subjunctive consisting of a true antecedent and a false consequent, since clearly the fact that one is president does not give him the power to stop the moon.

But now consider this sentence:

If I were you I would stay home.

How is this subjunctive to be treated? Here again, the truth or falsity of the subjunctive would depend upon how willing we were to argue that anyone in "your circumstances" or "in your boots" would stay home rather than go out. We would still be looking for some underlying commonsense generalization which could be taken as true. If such a generalization could be found, if there was sufficient evidence that anyone in the same or a very similar situation would stay home, then the subjunctive is to be taken as true with a true antecedent and true consequent. On the other hand, if no such generalization can be upheld, if circumstances do not warrant saying that anyone in your situation stays home, then the subjunctive is to be taken as a false one with a true antecedent and a false consequent.

Of course, this is not by any means an entirely satisfactory solution of the subjunctive problem. More analysis would require us to examine the exact nature of scientific and commonsense generalizations. Is such a distinction legitimate? Furthermore, what does it mean to say that circumstances do or do not warrant making certain generalizations? These are important questions that are dealt with in the philosophy of science.

Exercises

1. Discuss the following statements.
   a) Subjunctive conditionals are merely tricks of language. We can always eliminate the subjunctive tense. Thus, for example, "If I were to go to the movies, then I would see Sophia Toothless" means no more than "I will not go to the movies and I will not see Sophia Toothless."
   b) Scientific laws are not implicit subjunctive conditionals. They are simply statistical statements telling us what percentage of a certain group of objects has a given property.
   c) Hume was wrong. There are certain necessary relations. For example, if A is to the right of B, then B must be to the left of A. This surely holds in every universe.

2. Which of the following are true subjunctive conditionals and which are false?

a) If I were president, I would vote everyone a bonus.

b) If hydrogen were combined with oxygen, then water would occur.

c) If Cleopatra had had a longer nose, Rome might not have fallen.

d) If Jones were to go to the movies, then he would see Sophia Toothless.

e) If this chalk were dropped, then it would fall 33 feet per second per second.

PARENTHESES, BRACES AND BRACKETS

We have distinguished $(p \lor q) \cdot r$ from $p \lor (q \cdot r)$ by the use of parentheses. In ordinary language and especially in mathematics, parentheses as well as brackets [] and braces {} are frequently employed to clarify a context and render it free of ambiguity. If the above example did not contain parentheses and it was written simply as $p \lor q \cdot r$, then it would not be clear whether $p \lor q$ is conjoined to r, or only q is to be conjoined to r. In other words, we would not know which connective sign is to be taken as the most binding one, $\lor$ or $\cdot$. Parentheses serve to make this distinction. In our examples they tell us that $\cdot$ is the main sign in $(p \lor q) \cdot r$ while $\lor$ is the main sign in $p \lor (q \cdot r)$. We shall make use of parentheses, braces, and brackets whenever possible ambiguity might be present in the grouping of symbols, or when we wish to make explicit which connective terms are stronger and which are weaker. Consider the following example:

I go to the movies or I watch television and cook a meal and sew some clothes, then I will feel rested or I will be bored and miserable.

Here the main sign will obviously be $\supset$ since this symbolizes the *if—then* construction of the sentence as a whole. Thus the initial step in symbolizing this sentence is:

I go to the movies or I watch television and cook a meal and sew some clothes $\supset$ I will feel rested or I will be bored and miserable.

But now the antecedent and consequent clauses of the $\supset$ sign must be symbolized. Let us begin with the antecedent. What is the main sign here? Do I want to say (1) "I go to the movies *or* watch television and cook a meal and sew some clothes," where the main sign is *or*; or (2) "I go to the movies or I watch television *and* cook a meal and sew some clothes," where the main sign is *and*? There is no real way of deciding this. One speaker might want to make *or* the main sign; another might want *and*. In a real argument it would be necessary to ask which one the speaker intended, since it would make a great deal of difference in terms of truth-table analysis whether *and* is taken to be the main sign or *or* is. Let us arbitrarily decide that *or* is to be the main sign of the antecedent. Thus the sentence now has the following symbolization.

I go to the movies ∨ I watch television and cook a meal and sew some clothes ⊃ I will feel rested or I will be bored and miserable.

But now to make sure that the main sign is ⊃ and not ∨, simply place the parentheses around the antecedent:

(If I go to the movies ∨ I watch television and I cook a meal and I sew some clothes) ⊃ I will feel rested or I will be bored and miserable.

Still dealing with the antecedent, substitute dots for *and*:

(I go to the movies ∨ I watch television · I cook a meal · I sew some clothes) ⊃ I will feel rested or I will be bored and miserable.

Now, in order to make sure that ∨ is definitely seen as the main sign in the antecedent, insert parentheses around the conjuncts:

(I go to the movies ∨ (I watch television · I cook a meal · I sew some clothes)) ⊃ I will feel rested or I will be bored and miserable.

In order to distinguish the parentheses around the entire antecedent from those on the inside of the antecedent, we change the former to brackets. Thus we have:

[I go to the movies ∨ (I watch television · I cook a meal · I sew some clothes.)] ⊃ I will feel rested or I will be bored and miserable.

The same procedure is now used with the consequent. Here also we must decide whether *or* or *and* is the main connective. But the choice is made easier by the telescoping of the implicit sentence after "I will be bored." That is, "I will be bored and miserable" is a telescoping of "I will be bored," and the implicit sentence "I will be miserable." In normal language usage this kind of telescoping eliminates *and* as a main connective, unless it is the *only* connective, as in "I feel sad and tired." Thus *or* becomes the main connective. Then by replacing all sentences by sentential variables we obtain

$$[p \lor (q \cdot r \cdot s)] \supset [t \lor (u \cdot w)]$$

where p stands for "I go to the movies," q for "I watch television," r for "I cook a meal," s for "I sew some clothes," t for "I will feel rested," u for "I will be bored," and w for "I will be miserable."

Of course, here we are assuming that $\vee$ is the main sign of the antecedent and the consequent respectively. But a speaker might have intended the sentence to be understood in such a way that $\cdot$ was the main sign instead of $\vee$— at least in the antecedent. Then the symbolization of the sentence would be:

$$\left[(p \vee q) \cdot (r \cdot s)\right] \supset \left[t \vee (u \cdot w)\right]$$

Which is the *proper* symbolization? It would have to be decided either by investigation of the context or by arbitrary stipulation.

Although we shall use parentheses, braces, and brackets, it is important to note that the use of these marks in some sentences might prove to be more confusing than clarifying. Consider, for example, the following symbolization:

$$\left\{\left[(p \vee q) \supset (r \cdot s)\right] \vee \left\{\left[(p \supset q) \vee r\right] \supset s\right\}\right\} \supset \left[(p \vee q) \cdot (r \supset s)\right]$$

Here not only parentheses, braces, and brackets are employed but also larger and smaller braces, $\{\{$. It might also be a bit confusing to determine which are the main connective signs. If we were going to deal with highly complicated formulas, additional rules would be necessary to eliminate many of the parentheses, braces, and brackets that are normally used. But the formulas in this book will not reach such a degree of complexity, and it will be possible to make free use of braces, parentheses, and brackets.

Exercises

In the following, use sentence variables, parentheses, brackets and braces where necessary.

1. $p \supset q \cdot r$ (Conjunction is the main connective.)

2. $p \vee q \supset r \cdot s \vee t \supset q$ (Conjunction is the main connective; alternation is the main connective in each conjunct.)

3. $p \cdot q \vee r \supset s \cdot t \vee u$ (Conditional is the main sign; alternation is the main connective in the antecedent and the consequent.)

4. If I stay home and watch the late show, I will either do my homework or eat sandwiches and neck with my boyfriend all night.

5. He loves me, but I will respond only if he brings me a ring or has a talk with my father, who happens to be a justice of the peace.

6. If the Reptiles reelect a President, then the Demons will be out for four more years and the Panthers will neither be happy nor successful.

THE BICONDITIONAL

Let us recall how two formulas are tested for equivalence. The formulas for the truth tables are constructed and then the final columns are checked to determine whether they are alike. However, the equivalence could have been tested in another way. The biconditional or *if and only if* truth table could have been used. *If and only if*, like *or*, *and*, and *if—then*, is a truth-functional expression because a knowledge of the truth of the individual sentences comprising the biconditional will give us the truth of the sentence as a whole. The sign $\equiv$ shall be used to stand for *if and only if*. The truth table for it follows:

I	2	3
p	q	$p \equiv q$
T	T	T
T	F	F
F	T	F
F	F	T

What this truth table tells us is that two sentences are equivalent—that is, materially equivalent—if both have the same truth value. Otherwise they are not equivalent. Thus to test whether one sentence is equivalent to another, we would construct the truth table for each sentence, place an equivalence sign between them, and then check whether T is the only value that appears in the final column; T appears only when both sentences have the same truth value. This can be seen more clearly in the following example. To test whether $p \supset q$ is equivalent to $\bar{p} \vee q$, the knowledge of the truth tables for $\vee$, $\supset$, and $\equiv$ is used to obtain the following:

I	2	3	4	5	6
p	$\bar{p}$	q	$p \supset q$	$\bar{p} \vee q$	$(p \supset q) \equiv (\bar{p} \vee q)$
T	F	T	T	T	T
T	F	F	F	F	T
F	T	T	T	T	T
F	T	F	T	T	T

In column 4, $p \supset q$, appear the ordinary truth values for the conditional. Column 5, $\bar{p} \vee q$, is the result of combining the values of column 2, $\bar{p}$, with column 3, q, by alternation. Then the last column, $(p \supset q) \equiv (\bar{p} \vee q)$, receives its values by combing the truth values of columns 4 and 5 by means of equivalence. The final column tells us that $p \supset q$ does indeed equal $\bar{p} \vee q$, since both are simultaneously true or simultaneously false.

It should be noted that *p if and only if q* must be distinguished from other somewhat similar expressions such as *p only if q* and *p if q*. As we have seen previously, "Plutonium produces neutrons only if it is bombarded by other neutrons," is the same as saying "If Plutonium produces neutrons, then it is bombarded by other neutrons." In other words, if plutonium produces neutrons, then other neutrons are certainly bombarding it. But it might be the case that neutrons are bombarding plutonium and no neutrons are being produced. Thus *p only if q* simply says $p \supset q$ but not necessarily $q \supset p$. On the other hand, *p if q* simply says *if q then p*; i.e., $q \supset p$. It follows then that *p if and only if q* combines both $p \supset q$ and $q \supset p$. For this reason $p \equiv q$ means the same as $(p \supset q) \cdot (q \supset p)$.

Exercises

1. By truth tables show which of the following are equivalent.

   a) $(p \supset q) \equiv -\,(p \cdot \bar{q})$.

   b) $(\bar{p} \vee \bar{q}) \equiv -\,(\bar{p} \cdot \bar{q})$.

   c) $(\bar{p} \equiv q) \equiv \left[(\bar{p} \supset q) \cdot (q \supset \bar{p})\right]$.

   d) $(p \equiv q) \equiv \left[(\bar{q} \supset \bar{p}) \cdot (\bar{q} \vee p)\right]$.

   e) $(p \equiv r) \equiv \left[(p \equiv q) \cdot (q \equiv r)\right]$.

   f) $-\,\{\left[\bar{p} \vee (q \cdot r)\right] \vee \bar{p}\} \equiv \left[(p \cdot q) \supset \bar{r}\right]$.

2. Give the truth tables for:

   a) I will permit you to take a make-up exam if and only if you promise to study every night.

   b) Either John passes the course, or he passes the course if and only if the teacher likes me but not John.

   c) If and only if John wins will he be permitted to compete.

SUPPLEMENTARY READINGS

Mitchell, David, *Introduction to Logic*. London: Hutchinson and Co., 1962, Chapter 3, "The Logic of Propositions."

Ryle, Gilbert, "Formal and Informal Logic," in Ronald Jager (ed.), *Essays in Logic*. Englewood Cliffs, N.J.: Prentice-Hall, 1963.

Strawson, P. F., "Truth-Functional Constants and Ordinary Words," in Gary Iseminger, *Logic and Philosophy*. New York: Appleton-Century-Crofts, 1968.

7

Validity, Consistency, Contradiction, Implication

TRUTH-TABLE CONSTRUCTION

Through truth tables we have now learned to make explicit the kind of truth conditions implicit in the use of such terms as *and, or, if–then, not,* and *if and only if.* Except for some perplexing portions of the *if–then* truth table, these tables generally reveal everything that is essential about connector terms. Now, in the light of these truth tables, the following observation can be made:

> Given any line of reasoning consisting of true or false sentences connected by truth-functional connective expressions, it is possible to determine by strictly mechanical procedures whether the conclusion does or does not follow from the premises.

In other words, if an argument can be translated into truth-functional terms, then purely mechanical tests can be employed to show whether or not the conclusion does indeed follow from the premises. We hardly need to point out the significance of this statement. Consider the results if all sentences could be converted into a form whereby truth-functional procedures could be used with them. This would mean that finally—after centuries of verbal outpourings from diplomats, politicians, economists, scientists, and other important leaders—we could test, once and for all, whether what they say is logical or illogical. The words of our illustrious leaders could be examined to determine whether they offer rational solutions to the problems at hand. The results might be embarrassing, but embarrassment is preferable to ill-conceived wars, and other social, political, and economic blunders. (Although we must face the sad fact that a totally logical person could prove to be overwhelmingly obnoxious. Imagine a parent's response to a child who reasons perfectly or a man's response to a woman who reasons better than he does!)

Truth tables, then, provide a *decision procedure,* that is, a technique for determining whether a given conclusion follows from a certain set of premises. In the following example it is possible to determine whether the conclusion is assertible on the basis of the reasons, or premises, merely by *thinking about* or *intuitively grasping* the relationship of the premises to the conclusion:

1. If Hamlet intended to kill Polonius, then he was a murderer at heart. (first premise)
2. Hamlet was not a murderer at heart. (second premise)
3. Therefore he did not intend to kill Polonius. (conclusion)

But with the introduction of the truth-table technique, conclusions can be justified without reliance on such vague notions as *intuitions* and *bursts of insight* or *thinking.*

The truth-table procedure requires first that all arguments be translated into symbolic form consisting of sentential variables and connective terms. Thus the Hamlet argument would be symbolized as follows: p for "Hamlet intended to kill Polonius" and q for "Hamlet was a murderer at heart."

1. $p \supset q$ (material conditional)
2. $\bar{q}$ (negation of the consequent, the *then* clause, of the first premise)
3. $\bar{p}$ (negation of the antecedent, the *if* clause, of the first premise)

This argument has two premises, (1) and (2). But an argument might have many premises, and no matter how many are involved, they are always in conjunction with one another and therefore the conjunction symbol can be used. Thus (1) and (2) in this example could be written as the conjunction:

$$(p \supset q) \cdot \bar{q}$$

Furthermore, an argument always has the *if–then* form as primary. That is to say, an argument always states that if the premises are true, then the conclusion follows. Thus the example could have been given as "if (1) and (2), then (3)." In other words, the example could be fully symbolized as

$$\left[(p \supset q) \cdot \bar{q}\right] \supset \bar{p}$$

Once the sentences of an argument are symbolized, and the argument is placed into an *if–then* form, then the next step is to test whether the conclusion follows from the premises. Proceed by constructing a truth table.

The example is:

$$\left[(p \supset q) \cdot \bar{q}\right] \supset \bar{p}$$

To obtain the truth table for this formula, the basic tables for the conditional, conjunction, and negation are used; they are summarized below:

I	2	3	4	5	6
p	q	$p \supset q$	$p \cdot q$	$\bar{p}$	$\bar{q}$
T	T	T	T	F	F
T	F	F	F	F	T
F	T	T	F	T	F
F	F	T	F	T	T

Since the symbolized argument uses negation, conjunction, and the conditional, only these truth tables are required. (Of course, if the argument had also employed alternation and the biconditional, it would be necessary to use the truth tables for these connective expressions as well.)

Using these basic truth tables, we obtain the following table for our argument:

1	2	3	4	5	6	7
p	q	$p \supset q$	$\bar{q}$	$(p \supset q) \cdot \bar{q}$	$\bar{p}$	$[(p \supset q) \cdot \bar{q}] \supset \bar{p}$
T	T	T	F	F	F	T
T	F	F	T	F	F	T
F	T	T	F	F	T	T
F	F	T	T	T	T	T

This table was constructed in the following way: all the possible arrangements of true and false for p and q are given in columns 1 and 2. Column 3 gives the respective truth values when p and q are combined by $\supset$. Column 4 simply lists the negation of column 2. Column 5 shows the result of the conjunction of columns 3 and 4. Column 6 merely lists the negation of column 1. Finally, in column 7, the results of combining 5 and 6 by $\supset$ are obtained.

Once the truth table for a formula is given, we have on hand all the information for determining whether a conclusion does or does not follow from the reasons or evidence given.

Exercises

1. Symbolize the following arguments; give their truth tables.

   a) If I stay home and watch television, then either I will pass the test or neither watch television nor stay home.

   b) Jones stays, but Mary leaves. If Mary leaves although her friend stays, then Jones will not stay. Therefore Mary leaves.

2. Discuss:

   Robots are better than human beings since robots reason perfectly.

VALIDITY, CONSISTENCY, CONTRADICTION

Let us try to consider what kind of crucial information is given by the truth table. To begin with, it tells us under what conditions an argument does or does not hold. For example, look again at the truth table for the Hamlet argument given in the preceding section.

1	2	3	4	5	6	7
p	q	$p \supset q$	$\bar{q}$	$(p \supset q) \cdot \bar{q}$	$\bar{p}$	$\left[(p \supset q) \cdot \bar{q} \right] \supset \bar{p}$
T	T	T	F	F	F	T
T	F	F	T	F	F	T
F	T	T	F	F	T	T
F	F	T	T	T	T	T

It indicates that if p is true and q is true, then we will obtain T in the first row of column 7. This means that the conclusion legitimately follows. That is to say, if it is true that Hamlet intended to kill Polonius, p, and it is also true that Hamlet is a murderer, q, then the conclusion that Hamlet did not intend to kill Polonius, $\bar{p}$, follows. The truth table also tells us that even if p and q were both false, the conclusion is still legitimately asserted: the last row of column 7 is T even if p and q are both false. Similar analyses can be made in the cases where p is F and q is T, and where p is T and q is F. In other words, given any argument in which the truth or falsity of the premises are given, then the legitimacy of the argument can be determined by a purely mechanical procedure. The last column of the truth table tells us whether a T or an F is present. If a T appears, then the conclusion does follow: if an F is present, then the conclusion does not follow.

The truth table provides us with even more information. Sometimes the conclusions of arguments follow only under certain conditions, for example, consider:

John stays home.
Either John stays home or he leaves.
Therefore John leaves.

Here we find that the conclusion follows only under certain conditions pertaining to the truth or falsity of the premises. Again, let us first provide the truth table for this argument, which is symbolized as $\left[p \cdot (p \vee q) \right] \supset q$: ($p$ stands for "John stays home," and q for "he leaves".)

I	2	3	4	5
p	q	$p \lor q$	$p \cdot (p \lor q)$	$[p \cdot (p \lor q)] \supset q$
T	T	T	T	T
T	F	T	T	F
F	T	T	F	T
F	F	F	F	T

Compare this truth table to the one concerning Hamlet. In the Hamlet argument, the last column of the truth table contains *only* T's, while in the present argument T is found in three out of the four rows. In the row where p is T and q is F, the last column contains F. Thus some arguments give us all T's in the last column, others give us some T's and some F's, and still others give us all F's in the final column. An example of this final one would be any argument symbolized as $(p \lor \bar{p}) \supset (q \cdot \bar{q})$. The truth table is:

I	2	3	4	5	6	7
p	q	$\bar{p}$	$\bar{q}$	$p \lor \bar{p}$	$q \cdot \bar{q}$	$(p \lor \bar{p}) \supset (q \cdot \bar{q})$
T	T	F	F	T	F	F
T	F	F	T	T	F	F
F	T	T	F	T	F	F
F	F	T	T	T	F	F

Now if we keep in mind that the final columns of truth tables can contain only T's or only F's or a combination of the two, we can give precise definitions to certain kinds of logical relations that occur between premises and conclusion. Thus it is possible to explain what we mean by saying an argument is *valid*, or as it is sometimes called, *tautological*. In casual talk to say that a person's point is valid means that in some sense his concluding view follows necessarily from his evidence. On the basis of the truth table, a valid argument can be defined as any argument whose truth table contains only T's in the final column. Thus in the *Hamlet* truth table only T's were found in the final column. For this reason the argument is valid; no matter what the truth or falsity of the individual premises, T and only T always appears in the last column.

Again, by looking at the truth table we can determine whether or not an argument is *contradictory*. If the truth values in the final column are all *F*, then the argument is contradictory. In the truth table of $(p \vee \bar{p}) \supset (q \cdot \bar{q})$ given above, all the values in the final column are *F*'s; for this reason the argument is a contradiction. But it should be indicated that contradictions are not so easily recognizable as one might think. If I say, "John is going to the movies and John is not going to the movies," then I can intuitively recognize that this is a contradiction. But would the reader be able to recognize intuitively that the following argument is a contradiction?

It is certainly untrue that if Dixon and McGumphrey are nominated, then it follows that either Wallskie will not support the Democratic Party or McGumphrey will be nominated.

Now this argument is a contradiction, but unless someone has particularly strong intuitions he can not easily recognize it. However, with the technique of truth tables it is not necessary to rely on intuition. Instead, the argument is symbolized and then translated into a truth table. Using sentential variables we obtain:

$$-\big[(p \cdot q) \supset (\bar{r} \vee q)\big]$$

where *p* stands for "Dixon is nominated," *q* for "McGumphrey is nominated," and *r* for "Wallskie will support the party." Since the argument deals with three sentential variables, the truth table will have three columns of eight rows of *trues* and *falses*. A fourth column will be needed for $\bar{r}$, a fifth for $p \cdot q$, a sixth for $\bar{r} \vee q$, a seventh for $(p \cdot q) \supset (\bar{r} \vee q)$, and finally an eighth for $-\big[(p \cdot q) \supset (\bar{r} \vee q)\big]$. This truth table follows:

I	2	3	4	5	6	7	8
p	q	r	$\bar{r}$	$p \cdot q$	$\bar{r} \vee q$	$(p \cdot q) \supset (\bar{r} \vee q)$	$-\big[(p \cdot q) \supset (\bar{r} \vee q)\big]$
T	T	T	F	T	T	T	F
T	T	F	T	T	T	T	F
T	F	T	F	F	F	T	F
T	F	F	T	F	T	T	F
F	T	T	F	F	T	T	F
F	T	F	T	F	T	T	F
F	F	T	F	F	F	T	F
F	F	F	T	F	T	T	F

Here again the various columns are obtained by using the basic truth tables. What is important to note is what has occurred in column 8. The values in column 8 result from negating 7. Only *F* appears here. When this occurs we have a complete proof that the argument is contradictory. The table tells us that regardless of what values are placed for *p*, *q*, and *r*, the argument will always have *F* in the final column. Thus, despite its appearance, the argument is a contradiction, and whenever an argument can be shown to be contradictory, then we know the argument is inadequate.

But now let us consider the following argument: "If I go to the theater and I see the Beatles, then I shall feel happy." This is symbolized as

$(p \cdot q) \supset r$

where *p* stands for "I go to the theater," *q* for "I see the Beatles," and *r* for "I shall feel happy." The truth table for this argument is:

1	2	3	4	5
p	*q*	*r*	*p · q*	*(p · q) ⊃ r*
T	T	T	T	T
T	T	F	T	F
T	F	T	F	T
T	F	F	F	T
F	T	T	F	T
F	T	F	F	T
F	F	T	F	T
F	F	F	F	T

Note that in the final column—column 5—both false and true appear. Therefore this argument is taken to be neither valid nor contradictory, but *consistent*. At least one interpretation of *p*, *q*, and *r* turns out to be true; this is all that is required to show that an argument is consistent. Had all the values in column 5 been true, then the argument would be not only consistent but also valid.

It should also be noted that if a valid argument is denied, then a contradiction results, since all the *T*'s that appear in the last column of a valid argument would then be changed into *F*'s. Similarly, if a contradiction is denied, then a valid argument is obtained since all the *F*'s in the last column would be changed to T's. On the other hand, it is important to be aware that the negation of a consistent formula may or may not result in a consistent formula. Thus if we negate the final column in the above truth table, we are still left with some T's and some F's; the second F becomes T and all the other T's become F's. But if our final column had consisted solely of T's, then the negation of this column would have resulted in a contradiction.

A precise definition of *inconsistency* can now be given. As we have seen, an argument is consistent if there is at least one T in the final column of its truth table. It is inconsistent if there is not at least one T in the final column. In other words, inconsistency means no more than contradiction.

Another important term, *implication*, can be given some degree of explanation by means of truth tables. A traditional philosophical problem concerns the question of whether the occurrence of any given thing or event implies that some other event or thing must occur. Prior to the important analysis of David Hume, it was thought that there were certain necessary connections among various kinds of events. If it thundered, then it could be inferred that lightning would also occur; or if a billiard ball was struck by a cue in a certain way, then we would think it would surely move in a certain prescribed direction. Thus it was held that the occurrence of some events could be taken to imply—that is, to make necessary—the occurrence of certain other events. But Hume's analysis shattered this view. He argued that the universe did not contain any glue by virtue of which one thing had to be connected to some other thing. We believe thunder will be accompanied by lightning simply because it has happened this way in the past. But we have no guarantee that this is the way things *must* be. There are no absolute assurances about how things will behave.

But while we cannot speak of implication among events, we can speak of implication among sentences. Thus to say "p implies p or q" is not to say that the given event described by p implies—that is, is necessarily connected to—some other complex event, p or q. It simply means that given any truth-functional sentence, such as p, then p in alternation with any other sentence, q, can be logically inferred. Implication for our use involves only a relation among sentences and not among things or events. On this basis implication is now clearly definable. Premises imply a conclusion if the relation between the two is valid; that is, if it is asked whether $p \cdot q$ implies p, a conditional sign is substituted for *implies* and then a test for validity is made. We test whether the final column of the resulting truth table contains only T's.

It is sometimes claimed that contradiction is not necessarily a bad feature in argumentation. The contradiction enables us to infer everything. (Remember the truth table for $p \supset q$. If p is false, the conditional holds no matter what q is.) Since we can infer both the conclusion we might want, as well as the one we would not want, it is easy to understand why the contradiction would be looked upon with great favor in some quarters. For example, if we have a false antecedent—and a contradiction is, of course, false—then by the truth table for material implication, regardless of what the consequent is, the implication is always true. Thus one can draw any inference he wishes from a contradiction. But this really means no conclusion can ever be drawn. For it is just as legitimate to infer a statement $\bar{p}$ from a contradiction as it is to infer p. No argument is then more justified than any other. Thus those who feel there is nothing wrong with a contradiction are mistaken. However, the fact that from a contradiction no specific conclusion can be drawn ought not to be taken to mean that contradictions do not play an important role in determining the *validity* of arguments. If an argument is known to be a contradiction, then we know that the negation of this contradiction is valid. Thus if $p \cdot \bar{p}$ is contradictory, then we can be sure $-(p \cdot \bar{p})$ is valid. Also, as we shall see in the next section, contradiction plays an important role in the *reductio ad absurdum* method of proving validity.

Again it should be stressed that a *valid* argument is not necessarily a *sound* one. The validity of the following arguments can be determined by truth-table analysis.

1. If the sun is blue, then the rose is green.
   The sun is blue.
   The rose is green.

2. John is 40 feet tall and Rose is 30 feet tall.
   Therefore John is 40 feet tall.

However, these are not sound arguments. A valid argument means that the argument is an example of a certain type of formula that always has T in the final column of the truth table. But this can occur even if one or more of the premises are false, as in (1) and (2) above. A sound argument, on the other hand, is not only valid; its premises are true. Thus normally we ask, "If such-and-such is true, then what follows?" We ask what conclusion follows validly from a given set of true premises. Usually we are not concerned with what validly follows if the premises are false (although we might say, "I know p and q are false, but assume, for the sake of argument, that they are true.")

Exercises

1. Test for consistency, contradiction, and validity.

   a) If I decide to go, then you cannot go.

   b) If John loves Mary, then Mary loves John implies that if Mary does not love John, then John does not love Mary.

   c) I may or I may not go.

   d) The table is partly brown and partly not brown.

   e) Either Nixon wins or Wallace wins. But Nixon does not win. Therefore Wallace wins.

   f) If Bill wins the race, then he will make a great deal of money. If he makes a great deal of money, then he will retire. Therefore either he does not win the race or he will retire.

   g) The movie was good and bad.

   h) He is both happy and unhappy about leaving his family and going to Europe.

   i) $\left[p \supset (q \vee r) \right] \supset \left[(\bar{q} \cdot \bar{r}) \supset \bar{p} \right]$

   j) $(\bar{p} \cdot r) \supset \bar{p}$

   k) $- \left[(p \cdot r) \supset p \right]$

2. Which of the following implications hold:

   a) If Mary loves both John and Bill, then she loves neither.

   b) If this is a metal, then it is a conductor.

3. Discuss:

   a) But perhaps there could be a society in which contradictions are true. Then, in such a society, contradiction would be good, not evil.

   b) Of course there are some things that must necessarily happen. If I jump out of a window on the top floor of the Empire State building, you can bet your bottom dollar that I'll be crushed flatter than a mackerel.

SOME SHORT CUTS

To test for validity in some instances, an entire truth-table analysis is not required. For example, assume that we wish to know whether "John is not a considerate person" can be inferred from the two premises "If John is a considerate person, then he is a good human being" and "John is not a good human being." In other words, can $\bar{p}$ be inferred from $p \subset q$ and $\bar{q}$? In terms of truth tables, the question is whether $\left[(p \supset q) \cdot \bar{q}\right] \supset \bar{p}$ always has *true* in its final truth-table column. But a material implication can be false only if the antecedent is true and the consequent false. Since $\left[(p \supset q) \cdot \bar{q}\right] \supset \bar{p}$ is a material implication, we can ask whether the antecedent can be made true and the consequent false. The procedure is to substitute some value in $\bar{p}$, the consequent, that will make it false and then substitute the same value in the antecedent to see whether the antecedent, namely $(p \supset q) \cdot \bar{q}$, can be made to be true. In brief, *true* is substituted for p; this makes the consequent false, and the same substitution in $(p \supset q) \cdot \bar{q}$ gives us $(T \supset q) \cdot \bar{q}$. Can $(T \supset q) \cdot \bar{q}$ be made true? If T is substituted for q, then $(T \supset T) \cdot F$ is obtained. But any conjunction with false as a component is false. Let us now try to substitute false for q. This gives us $(T \supset F) \cdot T$. But again $(T \supset F)$ is false and the conjunction is false. Thus the antecedent cannot be made true, and the implication $\left[(p \supset q) \cdot \bar{q}\right] \supset \bar{p}$ holds; that is, from "If John is a considerate person, then he is a good human being" and "John is not a good human being," we can infer "John is not a considerate person."

But now consider the following formula:

$$(p \lor q) \supset (p \cdot q)$$

Is this valid? If the short-cut method is used, then we must ask whether the consequent $(p \cdot q)$ can be made false and the antecedent $(p \lor q)$ made true. If we choose false for p and false for q, then the consequent does indeed become false, but the antecedent also becomes false. If we stopped here, then the formula could be taken as valid since a substitution of false for p and q does not make the antecedent true. But what is required is that the consequent be made false in all the ways that it can be false. Then if it turns out that *none* of these ways makes the antecedent true, the formula is valid. So in our example, even though false for both p and q makes the consequent false and the antecedent false, the formula is still not valid, for if false is substituted for p and true for q, then a false consequent is indeed obtained, but now the antecedent is true. Thus the general rule is: Given any material implication, if in all cases in which the consequent is false, the antecedent is also false, then the implication is valid.

The rule can also be stated in terms of the truth of the antecedent: If in all cases in which the antecedent is true, the consequent is also true, then the implication is valid. Thus, for example, in

$$p \supset (p \lor q)$$

the antecedent p is true only if it is itself true and, of course, this is the only possible way in which it can be made true. We substitute T for p throughout the formula and check whether it is possible for $T \vee q$, the consequent, to turn out false. But since a T in an alternation always makes the alternation true, we see that no matter what is substituted for q, the consequent $T \vee q$ must also be true. Thus the formula is valid.

Another short-cut method is *reductio ad absurdum*: If the consequent is denied, and if this denial is placed into conjunction with the antecedent, then a contradiction will appear in the antecedent if the conditional is valid. Using the *reductio ad absurdum* method with the conditional $(p \cdot q \cdot r) \supset p$, we change p to $\overline{p}$. Then we place $\overline{p}$ into conjunction with the antecedent $p \cdot q \cdot r$ to obtain the conjunction $\overline{p} \cdot p \cdot q \cdot r$. But $\overline{p} \cdot p$ gives us a contradiction. This shows that the conditional $(p \cdot q \cdot r) \supset p$ is valid.

The above methods of testing for validity are short cuts in that they do save time, especially in those cases where the consequent is false in one and only one way—e.g., $(p \cdot q) \supset p$—or where the antecedent can be true in one and only one way—e.g., $p \supset (p \vee q)$. But of course, if time is not of the essence, a full truth-table analysis can always be employed.

Exercises

Test by using the simplifications mentioned:

1. If the Republicans do not win, then it is untrue that the Republicans win and the Democrats do not.
2. If the Republicans win, then it is untrue that the Republicans win and the Democrats do not.
3. If Maddox is nominated, then I shall vote for Nixon. But fortunately, Maddox was not nominated. Therefore I shall not vote for Nixon.
4. $\left[p \cdot (q \vee r) \right] \supset (p \supset r)$
5. $(p \cdot q) \supset (r \vee q)$
6. $\left[(r \cdot q) \vee \bar{p} \right] \supset (p \supset q)$
7. $p \supset \left[(p \vee q \vee r \vee s) \cdot \bar{t} \right]$
8. $\left\{ (p \vee m) \supset \left[(\overline{n} \cdot - (s \cdot t)) \vee (u \cdot n) \right] \right\} \supset \left[(m \cdot \overline{u}) \supset \overline{n} \right]$

SUPPLEMENTARY READINGS

Engels, Friedrich, "The Negation of the Negation," in I. M. Copi and J. A. Gould (eds.), *Readings on Logic*. New York: Macmillan, 1964.

Hook, Sidney, *Reason, Social Myths, and Democracy*. New York: The Humanities Press, 1940, Chapter 9, "The Laws of Dialectic."

Hume, David, *An Inquiry Concerning Human Understanding*, Section IV. 1748.

Will, F. L., "Will the Future be like the Past?" in Paul Edwards and Arthur Pap (eds.), *A Modern Introduction to Philosophy*, Revised Edition. New York: The Free Press, 1965.

8

Conditional and Equivalent Valid Forms

VALID FORMS

To be very precise during the course of argumentation, truth tables and/or some of the short cuts introduced in the last chapter could be used to determine validity. But this could be a cumbersome time-consuming activity. Imagine how long it would take to test by truth tables the validity of an argument consisting of four or five sentential variables, especially when the short cuts are not easily applicable. Fortunately, some steps can be taken to shorten the process of checking for validity.

It is possible to list a number of formulas which have been proven valid by truth-table analysis; when an argument is shown to be an instance of one of these formulas, it can be considered valid. No additional truth tables are required. In other words, assume that the list of formulas contains the following:

$$[(p \supset q) \cdot p] \supset q$$

This means that whenever an argument can be shown to have two premises having the form

$$p \supset q$$

$$p$$

then it can be assumed that q follows validly from the premises. We need not go to the trouble of working out a truth table. As we shall shortly see, the acceptance of the validity of a certain basic set of formulas will enable us to test the validity of rather complicated and cumbersome arguments.

Listed below are the formulas whose validity shall be taken for granted. (Of course, if any question arises about the validity of any formula, the formula can be tested by changing *therefore* to $\supset$ and using the truth-table technique.)

Conditional Valid Forms

1. $(p \supset q) \cdot p$ therefore q Modus Ponens

2. $(p \supset q) \cdot \overline{q}$ therefore $\overline{p}$ Modus Tollens

3. $p \cdot q$ therefore p Simplification
   $p \cdot q$ therefore q

4. p therefore $p \vee q$ Addition

5. $(p \supset q) \cdot (q \supset r)$ therefore   Hypothetical Syllogism
   $(p \supset r)$

6. $(p \vee q) \cdot \bar{p}$ therefore q Disjunctive Syllogism
    $(p \vee q) \cdot \bar{q}$ therefore p

7. $(p \supset q) \cdot (r \supset s) \cdot (p \vee r)$ there-   Constructive Dilemma
    fore $(q \vee s)$

8. p , q therefore $p \cdot q$ Conjunction

Equivalent Valid Forms

9. $- (p \cdot q) \equiv (\bar{p} \vee \bar{q})$ DeMorgan's First Theorem

10. $- (p \vee q) \equiv (\bar{p} \cdot \bar{q})$ DeMorgan's Second Theorem

11. $(p \vee q) \equiv (q \vee p)$ Commutation of Alternation

12. $(p \cdot q) \equiv (q \cdot p)$ Commutation of Conjunction

13. $\left[p \vee (q \vee r) \right] \equiv \left[(p \vee q) \vee r \right] \equiv$ Association of Alternation
    $(p \vee q \vee r)$

14. $\left[p \cdot (q \cdot r) \right] \equiv \left[(p \cdot q) \cdot r \right] \equiv$ Association of Conjunction
    $(p \cdot q \cdot r)$

15. $\left[p \cdot (q \vee r) \right] \equiv \left[(p \cdot q) \vee (p \cdot r) \right]$ Distribution of Conjunction

16. $\left[p \vee (q \cdot r) \right] \equiv \left[(p \vee q) \cdot (p \vee r) \right]$ Distribution of Alternation

17. $p \equiv \bar{\bar{p}}$ Double Negation

18. $(p \supset q) \equiv (\bar{q} \supset \bar{p})$ Transposition (or Contraposition)

19. $(p \supset q) \equiv (\bar{p} \vee q)$ Material Implication (using *or* and *not*)

20. $(p \supset q) \equiv - (p \cdot \bar{q})$ Material Implication (using *and* and *not*)

21. $(p \equiv q) \equiv \left[(p \supset q) \cdot (q \supset p) \right]$ Material Equivalence (using *and* and *conditional*)

22. $(p \equiv q) \equiv \left[(p \cdot q) \vee (\bar{p} \cdot \bar{q}) \right]$ Material Equivalence (using *and*, *negation*, and *or*)

23. $p \equiv (p \vee p)$ Idempotency with *or*

24. $p \equiv (p \cdot p)$ Idempotency with *and*

25. $\left[(p \cdot q) \supset r \right] \equiv \left[p \supset (q \supset r) \right]$ Exportation

26. $\left[p \vee (r \cdot q \cdot \bar{q}) \right] \equiv p$ Contradiction with Alternation

There are several points that ought to be made in regard to these 26 formulas. In the conditional formulas 1 through 8, validity occurs only in one direction. That is, formula 5, for example, states that given $(p \supset q)$ and

$(q \supset r)$, then $(p \supset r)$ can be inferred. But this does not mean that given $(p \supset r)$, we can infer $(p \supset q)$ and $(q \supset r)$. On the other hand, the equivalent formulas are two-directional. That is, formula 15, for example, states that given $\left[p \cdot (q \vee r) \right]$ then $\left[(p \cdot q) \vee (p \cdot r) \right]$ can be validly inferred from it. But it also says that the converse is valid. From $\left[(p \cdot q) \vee (p \cdot r) \right]$ it is legitimate to infer $\left[p \cdot (q \vee r) \right]$.

Note also that equivalence in truth-value logic operates like equivalence in mathematics or in grammar. If $2 + 2 = 4$, then $2 + 2$ can be substituted wherever 4 appears, and 4 can be substituted wherever $2 + 2$ appears. This does not mean that 4 is identical to $2 + 2$. Obviously 4 is not the same sign as two 2's combined with $+$. But they are *mathematically* the same; this means that if one is substituted for the other, no mathematical calculations are affected. If $4 + 8 = 12$, then so will $(2 + 2) + 8 = 12$; if $(2 + 2) - 3 = 1$, then so will $4 - 3 = 1$, and so on. Similarly, in grammar if "John loves Mary" is the same as saying "Mary is loved by John," then one sentence can be substituted for the other without any change in the truth or falsity of the given discourse. Thus if "John loves Mary, and he will marry her" is true, then also it will be true to say, "Mary is loved by John. And he will marry her."

Sometimes it is argued that in some contexts mutual substitution is not allowable, even though one sentence or formula is taken to be equivalent to another. For example, consider someone who is weak in mathematics who says:

I believe $4 - 3 = 1$.

It would seem to be justified to claim that this sentence is the same as:

I believe $(2 + 2) - 3 = 1$.

But not necessarily. If one is weak in mathematics, he might say he believes $4 - 3$ equals 1, but he might also say he does not believe $(2 + 2) - 3 = 1$ even though $(2 + 2)$ is equivalent to 4. In other words, in sentences whose verbs relate to believing, substitution of 4 for $2 + 2$ would not be legitimate. Sentences with verbs such as *think, know, believe, imagine,* etc., are prone to cause these odd difficulties concerning substitution. These *oblique* sentences, as they are called, are not truth-functional, however; that is, their truth value is not determined by the truth or falsity of their component sentences. Thus the truth or falsity of "I think $(2 + 2) - 3 = 1$" does not depend upon the truth value of the component sentence "$(2 + 2) - 3 = 1$." Someone could legitimately claim that even if this mathematical formula were false, he might still have thought it was true. In short, the oblique sentence must be regarded as outside the realm to which truth-functional logic is applicable. In more advanced logics, e.g., those dealing with possibilities, such sentences may be capable of being dealt with successfully. But since our concern here is with truth-functional logic, we will not become involved with such sentences.

Equivalent formulas or sentences, then, are mutually substitutable in any context. Since $(p \supset q)$ is equivalent to $(\bar{p} \lor q)$ by virtue of formula 19 above, this means that the former can always be substituted for the latter formula. Thus in such an argument as

$$[p \supset - (p \cdot q)] \supset (q \lor r)$$

$(\bar{p} \lor \bar{q})$ can be substituted for $-(p \cdot q)$, following formula 9, to obtain

$$[p \supset (\bar{p} \lor \bar{q})] \supset (q \lor r)$$

which is equivalent to the original argument. Similarly, even if a simple formula is given, such as

$$- (p \lor q)$$

then it can be changed into

$$\bar{p} \cdot \bar{q}$$

by referring to formula 10, DeMorgan's First Theorem.

But this wholesale kind of substitution is not available in relation to conditional valid formulas. One side of the conditional formula can not be substituted for the other. Given

$$(p \cdot q) \supset - (\bar{p} \lor \bar{q})$$

it is not possible to assert

$$q \supset - (\bar{p} \lor \bar{q})$$

on the grounds that formula 3, Simplification, permits a valid inference from $p \cdot q$ to q. When we are concerned with conditional valid formulas only, the whole argument and not its parts can be considered. Thus if the argument is

$$p \cdot q$$

then q can be validly inferred from it.

Exercises

1. Using the symbols p, r, and s, give the formulas for the following valid forms.

    a) Modus Ponens

    b) Modus Tollens

    c) Simplification

    d) Addition

    e) Hypothetical Syllogism

    f) Disjunctive Syllogism

    g) Constructive Dilemma

    h) Conjunction

2. Using the symbols p, r, and s, give the formulas for the following equivalent valid forms.

    a) DeMorgan's First Theorem

    b) DeMorgan's Second Theorem

    c) Commutation of Alternation

    d) Commutation of Conjunction

    e) Association of Alternation

    f) Association of Conjunction

    g) Distribution of Conjunction

    h) Distribution of Alternation

    i) Double Negation

    j) Transposition

    k) Material Implication (using *and* and *not*)

    l) Material Equivalence (using *and* and *conditional*)

    m) Material Equivalence (using *and*, *negation*, and *or*)

    n) Idempotence with *and*

    o) Exportation

    p) Contradiction with Alternation

3. Refer to the list of conditional valid forms, and show that the following are valid. Use truth tables to check your answers.

    a) $(\bar{p} \lor q) \cdot p$ therefore q

    b) $-(p \cdot \bar{q}) \cdot \bar{q}$ therefore $\bar{p}$

    c) $(p \lor q) \cdot \bar{p}$ therefore q

    d) $(\bar{p} \lor q) \equiv (\bar{q} \supset \bar{p})$.

e) $\left[(p \supset q) \cdot (q \supset p) \right] \equiv \left[(p \cdot q) \vee (\bar{p} \cdot \bar{q}) \right]$

f) $(p \equiv q) \equiv \left[(\bar{p} \vee q) \cdot (q \supset p) \right]$

RULES OF SUBSTITUTION

In the previous section, some indication has been given as to how equivalent forms can be substituted for one another. But substitution can be used in other ways when we are dealing with the valid forms. It is important to be aware that the occurrence of valid or contradictory formulas, i.e., formulas whose truth tables have either all T's or all F's in their final columns, means that an infinite number of valid or contradictory formulas are now possible. In other words, if $p \supset (p \vee q)$ is valid, then it also follows that any formula which substitutes some other letter or even some other formula for the p's and q's in this formula will also be valid. Thus since $p \supset (p \vee q)$ is valid, so are the following:

$r \supset (r \vee q)$

$s \supset (s \vee p)$

$(p \cdot q) \supset \left[(p \cdot q) \vee q \right]$

$\left[(r \cdot s) \equiv p \right] \supset \left\{ \left[(r \cdot s) \equiv p \right] \vee m \right\}$

etc.

Similarly, since $p \cdot \bar{p}$ is a contradiction, so also will the following be contradictory:

$q \cdot \bar{q}$

$(p \supset q) \cdot - (p \supset q)$

$\left[(r \cdot s) \vee q \right] \cdot - \left[(r \cdot s) \vee q \right]$

etc.

The only restriction in these substitutions is that a substitution for a given letter must be made for the same letter throughout the formula. For example, s could not be substituted only for the first p in $p \supset (p \vee q)$ and still retain validity, for then the formula would become $s \supset (p \vee q)$, and this is easily rendered false by making s true and p and q false.

An important rule of substitution, therefore, is that substitution of letters or formulas for letters in a contradictory or in a valid formula (regardless of whether it is a conditional or an equivalent valid form) retains contradictoriness or validity respectively. But two points must be noted. The substitution is made only for single letters. It does not follow that validity or contradictoriness will be retained if substitution is employed for molecular formulas. Thus if s is substituted for $p \vee q$ in $p \supset (p \vee q)$, the resultant formula $p \supset s$ is clearly not valid, since p can be made true and s false to give us a false in the final column of its truth table. Also substitution in consistent formulas need not necessarily retain consistency. Substitution in consistent formulas can result in either validity or contradiction. Thus $p \supset q$ is consistent, but it becomes valid if $r \cdot \bar{r}$ is substituted for p to obtain $(r \cdot \bar{r}) \supset q$. Since $r \cdot \bar{r}$ is always false, the antecedent in this formula is always false; and since a false antecedent makes a conditional true, this conditional must always have trues in the final column of its truth table. Hence it is valid. Similarly, if, in $p \supset q$, $r \cdot \bar{r}$ is substituted for q and $r \vee \bar{r}$ is substituted for p, then we obtain a formula which is always false, i.e., is a contradiction. Thus consistent formulas can change their truth value when substitution occurs.

Another important rule of substitution noted in the previous section states that equals can always be substituted for equals. But such substitution is not made only for single letters and need not take place throughout the formula as in the case of the substitution for letters. Thus, for example, one of the logically equivalent formulas is $(p \supset q) \equiv (\bar{p} \vee q)$. On this basis $\bar{p} \vee q$ can be substituted in $(p \supset q) \vee \left[(r \cdot s) \cdot (p \supset q) \right]$ either in both instances of $p \supset p$ or simply in one. In this situation the same substitution need not be made throughout as in the case of single letters.

Exercise

1. On the basis of the substitution rules and the valid forms, show that the following are valid:

a) $\left[p \supset (q \vee r) \right] \cdot - (q \vee r)$ therefore $\bar{p}$

b) $\left[(p \cdot q) \supset (r \cdot q) \right] \cdot \left[(s \cdot p) \supset (r \cdot s) \right] \cdot \left[(p \cdot q) \vee (s \cdot p) \right]$ therefore $(r \cdot q) \vee (r \cdot s)$

c) $-(p \vee p) \equiv (\bar{p} \cdot \bar{p})$

d) $\left\{ \left[(p \vee r) \cdot s \right] \supset (m \cdot q) \right\} \equiv \left\{ (p \vee r) \supset \left[s \supset (m \cdot q) \right] \right\}$

e) $\left[\bar{s} \vee -(\bar{q} \vee \bar{r}) \right] \equiv \left[(\bar{s} \vee q) \cdot (\bar{s} \vee r) \right]$

f) $\left[-(\bar{p} \vee \bar{q}) \supset s \right] \equiv \left[\bar{p} \vee (\bar{q} \vee s) \right]$

USE OF THE CONDITIONAL AND EQUIVALENT VALID FORMULAS

It should be stressed again that the 26 valid formulas are not accepted merely on the basis of intuition. A truth-table analysis can be provided in every case; the last column of the resultant truth table would be found to contain only T's.

Using the two lists of valid forms, we can now go on to check the validity of fairly complicated arguments without requiring a truth-table analysis. Consider the following argument:

"Either Smith will receive a raise or else if he obtains a job offer from Jones, he will leave here. But he does not receive a raise and he does not leave here. Therefore he has not obtained a job offer from Jones."

This argument is symbolized as:

$p \lor (q \supset r)$ premise
$\bar{p} \cdot \bar{r}$ premise
Therefore $\bar{q}$ conclusion

where p is "Smith will receive a raise," q is "he obtains a job offer from Jones," and r is "he will leave here."

To construct a truth table, it would be necessary to state the argument as $\{[p \lor (q \supset r)] \cdot (\bar{p} \cdot \bar{r})\} \supset q$, and then check whether the resultant final column of the truth table gives us only T's. But by using the two lists of valid forms we can simplify the procedure. First, each line of the aforementioned argument is to be numbered.

1. $p \lor (q \supset r)$ premise

2. $\bar{p} \cdot \bar{r}$ premise/∴ $\bar{q}$

Note that the conclusion $\bar{q}$ is placed alongside the last premise.

Lines can now be added to show how the conclusion can be reached if the list of valid forms is applied to the premises. But how are the valid forms applied? We might begin by showing how the valid forms permit us to draw certain inferences from the premises. Thus notice the second premise, $\bar{p} \cdot \bar{r}$. Now there is a form, namely form 3—Simplification—that tells us the following: given any formula that consists strictly of a conjunction of formulas, then any one of the conjuncts can be derived. Thus from $p \cdot q$, according to form 3, p can be derived or, for that matter, q also. This same procedure can be used with the second premise, since it is a conjunction of formulas. Hence from $\bar{p} \cdot \bar{r}$, by means of the reasoning involved in valid form 3, $\bar{p}$ is derived. (We shall shortly see that $\bar{r}$ is also derived in the same way.) Thus the principle expressed in valid form 3 is used to draw an inference from the premises of the given example. To show this derivation, another line is added to the original argument. Thus instead of two numbered lines as above, the argument now shows three lines:

1. $p \lor (q \supset r)$ premise

2. $\overline{p} \cdot \overline{r}$ premise/$\therefore \overline{q}$

3. $\overline{p}$ 2, Simplification

Let us again explain what is signified by line 3. The formula $\overline{p}$ on line 3 states that this formula has been derived from one or more of the lines that preceded it. The "2, Simplification" on the right-hand side of line 3 states that $\overline{p}$ is derived from premise 2 and the simplification formula, which tells us that given any conjunction of letters (or formulas), we can infer any one of them. Thus from $\overline{p} \cdot \overline{r}$ we can infer $\overline{p}$. Henceforth $\overline{p}$ can be regarded as another premise added to the ones we have. We can now proceed to the next step for showing how the conclusion follows from the premises.

The examination of the argument started with the second premise, because by means of this premise it was easy to show how the valid forms could be applied so that a new inference could be drawn, that is, another formula could be derived. But we could as well have begun with the first premise. What is important to remember is that we want to use our valid forms with our premises in such a way that finally the conclusion will be derived. In this case the conclusion is $\overline{q}$. What we will do is to keep making all the derivations we can until this conclusion is reached. Using the valid forms to show the validity of an argument is like working through a cross-word puzzle. If you are a bit lucky and you keep practicing, gradually you will learn the little clues which will enable you to fill in all the words. Similarly, if you are a bit lucky and you practice enough, then you will *see* just what valid forms are needed to derive the conclusion. But it will take time to be able to *see* that this premise can be connected to that valid form. Remember the following rule: *Make as many inferences as you can whenever you can.* Then sooner or later you will reach the point where you will recognize the valid form whose application will make the conclusion inferable.

Turn now to the first premise and ask whether anything can be derived from it. Well, not in any obvious way, as in the previous case of $\overline{p} \cdot \overline{r}$. But now note the following: Any set of premises can be combined by conjunction. This is what valid form 8 tells us. So let us combine $p \vee (q \vee r)$ with the newly derived premise, $\overline{p}$. We thus obtain a fourth step:

1. $p \vee (q \supset r)$ premise

2. $\overline{p} \cdot \overline{r}$ premise/$\therefore \overline{q}$

3. $\overline{p}$ 2, Simplification

4. $[p \vee (q \supset r)] \cdot \overline{p}$ 1, 3, Conjunction

Again, "1, 3, Conjunction" to the right on line 4 simply tells us that by use of valid form 8, Conjunction, we are allowed to combine $p \vee (q \supset r)$ and $\bar{p}$, i.e., lines 1 and 3.

But now consider line 4. Is there any valid form that is somewhat comparable to it? Yes. Notice valid form 6, Disjunctive Syllogism. This tells us that if an alternation, i.e., $p \vee q$, is conjoined with a denial of one of the alternants, i.e., $\bar{p}$, then the other alternant, i.e., q can be derived. And, of course, the rules of substitution tell us that this will hold no matter what is substituted for p or for q. Well, in that case if $q \supset r$ is substituted for q, then we can derive $q \supset r$. And this is precisely what happens with line 4. Apply valid form 6 to line 4, but with $q \supset r$ substituted for q; and line 5 can be inferred, namely $q \supset r$. Thus the argument now becomes:

1. $p \vee (q \supset r)$ premise

2. $\bar{p} \cdot \bar{r}$ premise/$\therefore \bar{q}$

3. $\bar{p}$ 2, Simplification

4. $\left[p \vee (q \supset r) \right] \cdot \bar{p}$ 1, 3, Conjunction

5. $q \supset r$ 4, Disjunctive Syllogism.

Again, as in previous lines, the justification for line 5 appears at the right-hand side. The "4, Disjunctive Syllogism" tells us that $q \supset r$ was derived from line 4 with the use of form 6, Disjunctive Syllogism, which tells us that any conjunction consisting of an alternation and a denial of one of the alternants permits us to infer the alternant that is not denied. In line 4, $\bar{p}$ is a denial of the alternant p; thus we can infer the other alternant, $q \supset r$.

The next step is to derive $\bar{r}$ from line 2. This is done in the same way we obtained $\bar{p}$, by means of Simplification, form 3. We can infer $\bar{r}$ just as previously we could infer $\bar{p}$. The argument now reads:

1. $p \vee (q \supset r)$ premise

2. $\bar{p} \cdot \bar{r}$ premise/$\therefore \bar{q}$

3. $\bar{p}$ 2, Simplification

4. $\left[p \vee (q \supset r) \right] \cdot \bar{p}$ 1, 3, Conjunction

5. $q \supset r$ 4, Disjunctive Syllogism

6. $\bar{r}$ 2, Simplification

But now we are almost in the position of deriving the conclusion for which we are searching, namely $\bar{p}$. By means of the principle of Conjunction, valid form 8, let us combine lines 5 and 6. The argument then becomes:

1. $p \vee (q \supset r)$ premise

2. $\overline{p} \cdot \overline{r}$ premise/$\therefore \overline{q}$

3. $\overline{p}$ 2, Simplification

4. $\left[p \vee (q \supset r) \right] \cdot \overline{p}$ 1, 3, Conjunction

5. $q \supset r$ 4, Disjunctive Syllogism

6. $\overline{r}$ 2, Simplification

7. $(q \supset r) \cdot \overline{r}$ 5, 6, Conjunction

But line 7 is almost a duplicate of valid form 2, Modus Tollens, which states that given any conditional, i.e., $p \supset q$, if the consequent, $\overline{q}$, is denied, then the denial of the antecedent, namely $\overline{p}$, can be inferred. Thus applying valid form 2 to line 7, the next line, line 8, can be inferred.

1. $p \vee (q \supset r)$ premise

2. $\overline{p} \cdot \overline{r}$ premise/$\therefore \overline{q}$

3. $\overline{p}$ 2, Simplification

4. $\left[p \vee (q \supset r) \right] \cdot \overline{p}$ 1, 3, Conjunction

5. $q \supset r$ 4, Disjunctive Syllogism

6. $\overline{r}$ 2, Simplification

7. $(q \supset r) \cdot \overline{r}$ 5, 6, Conjunction

8. $\overline{q}$ 7, Modus Tollens

And this turns out to be the very conclusion we have been trying to derive, $\overline{q}$, namely, "he has not obtained a job offer from Jones."

We have now given what can be called a *formal proof* for the validity of an argument. What this means is that with a finite number of steps, using formulas from the valid list of formulas, we have been able to reach the conclusion.

A very interesting kind of argument sometimes arises when the conclusion is in conditional form. For example, "If the doctor is late, then he is ill. Therefore if the doctor is late, then he is late and he is also ill" is symbolized as:

1. $p \supset q$ premise/$\therefore p \supset (p \cdot q)$

To prove this argument, the list of valid forms would not be adequate. From $p \supset q$ we cannot, by the application of the formulas, obtain $p \supset (p \cdot q)$. (But you, the reader, are perfectly free to try!) How then can we show that the conclusion does actually follow? (It really does!)

We proceed by applying valid form 25, the rule of Exportation, to the conclusion rather than to the premise of the argument. If we look at valid form 25, we should quickly see that the rule tells us the following: If a conclusion is in the form of a conditional, we can always extract the antecedent, add it as a premise to the other premises, and then treat the consequent alone as the conclusion. Thus if the argument can be stated as $p \supset (q \supset r)$, where $q \supset r$ is the conclusion, the rule tells us we can extract the antecedent of the conclusion, namely q, add it as another premise with the premise p, and then treat the entire argument as if it were $(p \cdot q) \supset r$. Proof of validity of $(p \cdot q) \supset r$ would be equivalent to proof of validity of $p \supset (q \supset r)$.

Thus whenever a conditional appears as the conclusion of an argument, the antecedent of the conditional can be extracted and placed in conjunction with the premises. Consider, then, an argument such as the one given above:

1. $p \supset q$ premise/$\therefore p \supset (p \cdot q)$

On the basis of our analysis concerning conclusions that are conditional in form, we can immediately extract the antecedent of the conclusion and insert it as another premise.

1. $p \supset q$ premise/$\therefore p \supset (p \cdot q)$
2. p 1, additional premise by Exportation

Step 2 tells us that p, the antecedent of the conclusion, has been extracted from 1 and added as an extra premise. But the conclusion that is left is $p \cdot q$, and this is what must now be proved, rather than the original $p \supset (p \cdot q)$. Thus the argument now becomes:

1. $p \supset q$ premise/$\therefore p \supset (p \cdot q)$
2. p 1, additional premise by Exportation/$\therefore p \cdot q$

Now this new conclusion is easy to prove by means of the list of valid forms:

1. $p \supset q$ Premise/$\therefore p \supset (p \cdot q)$
2. p 1, additional premise by Exportation/$\therefore p \cdot q$
3. $(p \supset q) \cdot p$ 1, 2, Conjunction
4. q 3, Modus Ponens
5. $p \cdot q$ 2, 4, Conjunction

Once we prove $p \cdot q$, we have also proved the original argument, namely, $p \supset q$ therefore $p \supset (p \cdot q)$.

The same principle holds even if there is more than one conditional sign in the conclusion. Thus if $p \supset (q \supset r)$ were a conclusion in an argument, we could extract both p and q and change them into additional premises, and then prove the conclusion r. This would be the same as proving $p \supset (q \supset r)$.

A formal proof has many advantages because it enables us to check the validity of a given conclusion without having to construct a huge truth table. But even though it takes time to construct such a table, eventually we could reliably determine whether the last column contains all T's, all F's, or some T's and some F's. On the other hand, constructing a formal proof could be just as time-consuming, if we are required to go through every valid formula in order to see if it applies. The success of the method of formal proof rests on our being able to *see* within a reasonable length of time that certain valid formulas are very similar to those of the premises and can be applied, while certain others cannot. This kind of *seeing* is not a simple process; therefore in the case of formal proofs there is good reason for heeding the advice that practice can certainly improve, even if it cannot really make perfect.

Exercises

1. The following are formal proofs of arguments. Fill out the right-hand sides of each line by stating which valid forms and other lines were used to derive it.

a) 1. $p \supset (q \vee r)$ premise

   2. p premise/$\therefore$ $q \vee r$

   3. $[p \supset (q \vee r)] \cdot p$

   4. $q \vee r$

b) 1. $p \supset (q \supset r)$ premise

   2. $p \cdot q$ premise/$\therefore$ r

   3. $(p \cdot q) \supset r$

   4. $[(p \cdot q) \supset r] \cdot (p \cdot q)$

   5. r

c) 1. $\bar{p} \vee (q \cdot r)$ premise

   2. $\bar{q} \vee s$ premise

   3. p premise/$\therefore$ s

   4. $(\bar{p} \vee q) \cdot (\bar{p} \vee r)$

   5. $\bar{p} \vee q$

6. $p \supset q$

7. $q \supset s$

8. $(p \supset q) \cdot (q \supset s)$

9. $p \supset s$

10. $(p \supset s) \cdot p$

11. s

d) 1. $p \cdot (q \vee r)$ premise

2. $(p \cdot r) \supset (s \cdot t)$ premise

3. $(\bar{s} \vee \bar{t}) \supset -(p \cdot q)$ premise/ $\therefore s \equiv t$

4. $-(s \cdot t) \supset -(p \cdot q)$

5. $(p \cdot q) \neg (s \cdot t)$

6. $\left[(p \cdot q) \supset (s \cdot t)\right] \cdot \left[(p \cdot r) \supset (\bar{s} \cdot \bar{t})\right]$

7. $(p \cdot q) \vee (p \cdot r)$

8. $\left[(p \cdot q) \supset (s \cdot t)\right] \cdot \left[(p \cdot r) \supset (\bar{s} \cdot \bar{t})\right] \cdot \left[(p \cdot q) \vee (p \cdot r)\right].$

9. $(s \cdot t) \vee (\bar{s} \cdot \bar{t})$

10. $s \equiv t$

e) 1. $\bar{L} \supset (\bar{M} \vee L)$ premise

2. $\bar{M} \supset (\bar{L} \vee M)$ premise/ $\therefore -(L \cdot M) \supset (\bar{L} \cdot \bar{M})$

3. $\bar{\bar{L}} \vee (\bar{M} \vee L)$

4. $L \vee (\bar{M} \vee L)$

5. $(\bar{M} \vee L) \vee L$

6. $\bar{M} \vee (L \vee L)$

7. $\bar{M} \vee L$

8. $M \supset L$

9. $\bar{\bar{M}} \vee (\bar{L} \vee M)$

10. $M \vee (\bar{L} \vee M)$

11. $(\bar{L} \vee M) \vee M$

12. $\bar{L} \vee (M \vee M)$

13. $\bar{L} \vee M$

14. $L \supset M$

15. $-(L \supset M) \cdot (M \supset L)$

16. $L \equiv M.$

17. $(L \cdot M) \vee (\overline{L} \cdot \overline{M})$

18. $- (L \cdot M) \supset (\overline{L} \cdot \overline{M})$

2. Check the validity of the following:

a) If John wins, then Mary will be happy. If Fred wins, then Sadie will be happy. If Bill wins, then Sadie will be happy, and if Paul wins, then Mary will be happy. Either Sadie will not be happy or Mary will not be happy. And either Fred does not win or Bill does not win. Therefore either Bill does not win or Paul does not win; and either Fred does not win or John does not win.

b) Either the carburetor does not work or the valves are sticking. But if the valves are sticking, then the oil is poor. Therefore it is untrue that the carburetor works and the oil is not poor.

c) If the book is well written, then if I read it, I will enjoy it. If I enjoy it, then either I will keep it or loan it to a friend. The book is well written and I do read it but I do not keep it. Therefore I will loan it to a friend.

d) $-(p \cdot \overline{q})$, $\overline{r} \supset \overline{q}$, $\overline{r} \vee s$. *Therefore $\overline{p} \vee s$.*

e) $\overline{p} \vee \overline{q} \vee r$, $(\overline{p} \vee r) \supset s$, $q \supset t$. *Therefore $q \supset (s \cdot t)$.*

f) $(p \vee q) \cdot (r \vee s)$. *Therefore $(p \cdot r) \vee (p \cdot s) \vee (q \cdot r) \vee (q \cdot s)$.*

SUPPLEMENTARY READINGS

Carroll, Lewis, "What the Tortoise Said to Achilles," in I. M. Copi and J. A. Gould (eds.), *Readings on Logic*. New York: MacMillan, 1964.

Feigl, H., "De Principiis non Disputandum," in Y. H. Krikorian and A. Edel (eds.), *Contemporary Philosophic Problems*. New York: Macmillan, 1959.

Hahn, Hans, "Logic, Mathematics, and Knowledge of Nature," in M. Weitz (ed.), *Twentieth Century Philosophy: The Analytic Tradition*. New York: The Free Press, 1966.

9

Words,
Extensions,
Intensions

LINGUISTIC FORM

The basic requirement for the logic of truth tables has been the acknowledgment of some linguistic segment that could be regarded as true or false. Such linguistic segments have been called *sentences*, and thus far it has not been necessary to examine the internal structure of these segments. Anything was a sentence if it made sense to attach "it is true that" or "it is false that" to it. For example, in the case of $(p \cdot q) \supset p$ we only require that p and q be replaceable by T or F in order to know that the formula is valid. Very little need be known about the actual linguistic structure to which T or F can be applied. Unfortunately the application of T or F is not always sufficient to show us whether a given argument is valid or not. Consider the following argument:

> All blondes are rather interesting.
> Chicita is a blonde.
> Therefore Chicita is rather interesting.

This argument is valid, but its validity cannot be shown merely by reference to truth tables. In a truth-table analysis this argument would be symbolized as

$$(p \cdot q) \supset r$$

where p stands for "All blondes are rather interesting," q for "Chicita is a blonde," and r for "Chicita is rather interesting." The truth table for $(p \cdot q) \supset r$ would reveal that this formula is *not* valid. Remember that on our analysis of validity an argument is valid if and only if the final column of the resultant truth table contains only T's, or if validity can be shown by using the formal proof method. But all we have to do is to replace p by T, q by T, and F by r, and $(p \cdot q) \supset r$ turns out false in the last column. But we do know that the argument is valid! Thus some further additions or modifications must obviously be made to the truth-table technique if the validity of arguments such as these are to be demonstrated. To discover what these additions and modifications are, it becomes necessary to examine in greater detail these linguistic segments to which true or false apply. For it is because these segments have a certain kind of *form* that the test of their validity is made possible. We shall now explicate more thoroughly the notions of *form* and *validity* which were briefly mentioned in the first chapter.

What is meant by *form*? One has only to look at any dictionary to become aware of the vast number of diverse meanings attributed to this word. But perhaps the meaning of form can be made clear if we examine ways in which form becomes recognized. Examine the following linguistic segments:

1. John runs.

2. Mary goes.

3. Susie remains.

Note that they have several characteristics in common:

a) They consist of words.

b) They each contain a word that is taken to refer to an individual and is usually labeled by grammarians as a subject, e.g., *John, Mary,* and *Susie.*

c) They each contain a word that is taken to refer to some behavioral or physical characteristic of an individual and is usually labeled by grammarians as a predicate or a verb, e.g., *runs, goes, remains.*

On the basis of this analysis there is nothing strange about saying that even though (1) through (3) are different sentences, they all have the same form, namely:

Subject (proper name or noun)—predicate (verb).

Probably most students, in their regular English classes, have parsed sentences. But parsing means that the grammatical form of the sentence is being indicated: the subject and the predicate are identified.

Logicians are also concerned with the forms of sentences. But their view of form varies considerably from that of the grammarian. In fact, we will distinguish grammatical from logical form, and then one of our major tasks will be to show that there are many sentences whose grammatical form is not at all similar to its logical form. For example, "All men are mortal" is regarded by the grammarian as a subject-predicate form where *men* is the subject, *mortal* is the predicate, and *all* is an adjective. But the logician cannot even begin to recognize what form is present in this sentence until he has converted it to read: "If anything is a man, then it is mortal." That is, he must change the sentence into one that uses the conditional construction.

We shall, of course, have much more to say about these matters. But now let us begin our examination of some of the notions that play an important role in the understanding of the logical as distinct from the grammatical form of sentences. Perhaps the easiest way to begin is with a study of words. Whatever logical form turns out to be, it will in some way be connected to words. This seems almost trivially obvious, since logical—like grammatical—form must finally reveal itself in sentences, which, in the final analysis, are made up of no more than words. But are we sure we know what a word is? Even though everyone uses words, few people can really explain what they are. Thus let us turn to an investigation of what these things called *words* are.

Only certain groupings of alphabetical letters can form words; for example, *bad* is a word, but *bcd* is not. Why? Some linguists claim that certain combinations of alphabetical letters are not permissible. For example, a word cannot be made up entirely of consonants. Thus *bcd* is not a word because it is not an allowable combination. But many groupings of letters which cannot form modern English words do form words in other languages, as for example, in the following Czech sentence:

Put	the finger	through	the throat
Strč	*prst*	*skrz*	*krk*

None of the groupings of letters *strč, prst, skrz,* or *krk* is to be found in English words, which use vowels to break up combinations of consonants. But in the Czech language such arrangements are permissible. Nor does English employ the peculiar combination of consonants and vowels to be found in the Welsh name of a town near Caernarvon, Wales:

Llanfairpwllgwyngyllgogerychwyrndrobwllllantyssyliogogogoch.

However, many allowable combinations of letters, such as *brosch* and *falanik*, do not necessarily form words.

Linguists have told us that certain combinations of letters are not used because they are difficult to pronounce. Try to say *bcd* or *qxr*. Rather difficult (although, apparently, not so difficult for the Czech). If our language had only a written form, if it were never spoken at all, then pronunciation would not be a factor to consider in the formation of words, and any combination of letters could become a word. But our language is spoken. Thus we must ask again what it is that makes certain select groups of letters *words*.

Another possible answer states that a group of letters becomes a word when a *meaning* is attached to it. But the nature of meaning, like the nature of propositions, constitutes one of the most difficult philosophical and linguistic problems. Letters that take on meaning are transformed in some way, but what this transformation involves has been one of the most elusive issues in the history of human inquiry. It has been argued that letters attain meaning when they are accompanied by ideas, thoughts, or concepts. But as we have already mentioned, ideas, thoughts, and concepts have not been clearly analyzed. If the presence of an idea changes a group of letters into a word, then what is the nature of this presence? Is an idea present in the same way that a person is present in a given room? Obviously an idea cannot be found in the way a person can be found in a given room. It is usually said that ideas are in the head, but so far no one has been able to look into a human skull and say, "Ah, there is the idea we have been looking for!" And even if it were possible to invent a machine that could look directly into a human skull, it is dubious that such a machine could help us find ideas in the skull. A great many neurons, dendrites, and other physical materials do seem to float around in the human brain, but so far no one has been able to reach out and catch an idea. We have yet to read a medical paper in the *Journal of Neurology* which describes a recent operation on James Jones, from whose brain several fine specimens of ideas were extracted which are now on display in Montefiore Hospital preserved in formaldehyde. Similar comments are applicable to the use of thoughts or concepts as comprising the factors that can turn groups of letters into words.

It might also be maintained that letters are changed into words when they are viewed differently. Thus as we concentrate on some letters they gradually seem to change into an ideogram, into a small picture. Undoubtedly this sometimes does happen when we look at segments of the alphabet. To someone *doob* might look like two eyes set between two ears, but it would be preposterous for him to insist that therefore *doob* means "two eyes set between two ears." (How it ever came to mean *Bermuda grass* we leave to the reader's ingenuity to discover.)

At this point we could get involved with the various psychological and philosophical theories which are used when meaning is analyzed. But perhaps there is a way of avoiding this complicated procedure. If someone asked an engineer what an automobile is, he could answer by discussing the engine, the valves, and other technical matters. But he could also explain what an automobile is simply by listing the uses human beings have for it. Thus even though meaning can be analyzed in very profound and esoteric terms, it can also be dealt with by referring to the uses a group of letters have when they are functioning as words.

If we were examining how language is actually employed by human beings, we would probably find that for them words operate for the most part in three different ways:

1. As connector signs

2. As expressive signs

3. As descriptive signs

Connector signs have already been adequately analyzed. They are to be understood in terms of truth tables. They tell us, in other words, the allowable ways in which one sentence can be inferred from or connected to another.

Expressive signs have also been discussed. They are ways of indicating a feeling or a desire. Thus I might say, "That painting is beautiful," where *beautiful* means that I am getting a certain favorable feeling. Similarly I might say, "I have a pain," where the word *pain* is a way of indicating to someone else that I am very uncomfortable and would like some help. It should be noted that *pain* does not refer to some internal thing which is a pain. I cannot pick up a pain and place it under a microscope. Having a pain is not like having a martini. A martini I can see and drink, and avoid if I have had one too many. But clearly pains cannot be examined in any such way. Nor is having a pain like having a tumor. A tumor can be cut out and examined for its size, weight, and color. But this cannot be done to a pain. (What color could a pain possibly be?) To say, "I have a pain," is to point out that I am very uncomfortable because of some physical or psychological condition. But it is not to refer to some entity in the way *dog* might be said to refer to an entity. "I have a pain" operates like *ouch* as a way of expressing verbally a felt discomfort and also alerting others to the fact that I have such discomfort. Similarly "He has a pain" means that if he could communicate, he would say, "I have a pain," whereby he would be indicating a degree of physical or psychological discomfort.

Other curious problems arise in relation to such expressive signs as *pain* and *love* when they appear in sentences. First of all, there is a peculiar distinction to be made between a first person pain sentence and a third person pain sentence. For example, consider the difference between John's saying, "I have a pain," and my saying of John, "He has a pain." These two sentences would seem to be identical since both *I* and *he* obviously refer to the same person. But they are not identical. If I am John and I say, "I have a pain," I clearly could not be mistaken. It would be ridiculous for me to say, "Wait a minute. Let's see now if I really have that pain or not. Perhaps I'm mistaken. Perhaps I only think I'm in pain, but I'm not." Such a conversation would be very odd. If I have a pain, then I have it. It is impossible to think that I could be mistaken. But now consider someone who, referring to me, says, "He has a pain." This sentence could obviously be incorrect. To say of anyone that he is in pain is surely not to state something absolutely certain. Someone may look as if he is in pain, but I might still be mistaken if I said that he was in pain. He could be feigning pain. I might be misinterpreting what I see and therefore mistakenly think that certain facial characteristics presuppose that pain is occurring. Thus, whereas "I have a pain" seems to be highly difficult to falsify, "He has a pain" is clearly falsifiable. Yet since *I* and *he* refer to the same person, both sentences are apparently identical, and one would therefore think that whatever characterizes one sentence also characterizes the other. But oddly enough this is not the case.

A second problem concerning pain sentences is that it is not quite clear how "He has a pain" becomes meaningful. Everyone undoubtedly agrees that it is meaningful to say of someone that he is in pain. But of course, so far as we know, no one has ever really felt anyone else's pain. Having a pain is a highly personal matter. If I have a dog, then many people can pat it and feed it dog food. But my *pain* is strictly my own. Others might sympathize with me; but no one can have my pain, and I cannot have anyone else's. Furthermore, I can never tell whether my pain is in any way similar to anyone else's. What might be a pain in the head to me could be a pain in the neck to you. Thus your pain is always a mystery to me. But then what can I mean when I say of you, "He has a pain"? The answer apparently is that the word *pain* seems to operate in two different ways. When it is used with first person singular sentences as in "I have a pain," then it refers to some highly personal state of physical or psychological discomfort I am presently experiencing and for which I am seeking help. On the other hand, when I say, "He has a pain," I am only referring to the fact that he has certain physical and behavioral characteristics which are similar to mine when I am undergoing pain. But I can never experience his pain. Thus when I say, "He has a pain," I am in the odd position of talking about something I can never possibly experience.

Pain sentences are perplexing and interesting to analyze. But just as interesting and problematical are the descriptive signs in a language. Descriptive signs are probably the most frequently used in scientific contexts since they attempt to communicate information about the world and its inhabitants. Thus the expressions *is a dog* or *runs to* refer to certain kinds of animals or certain kinds of activity. However, descriptive signs which refer to the world ought not to be confused with those which simply refer to other words. Thus *dog* in the sentence "*Dog* is spelled *d-o-g*" refers to the word itself. As long as we take care to use either quotes or italics when we are using the word as a word, we shall have little difficulty. But at times the quotes are ignored, and then a question does arise as to whether the word is being *used*, i.e., has a regular extralinguistic reference, or whether it is merely being *mentioned*, i.e., is functioning solely as a word without reference to anything other than words. Confusion results in some contexts where no rules are given for the use of quotes. In "Melanie is beautiful," is Melanie the person beautiful, or is the name *Melanie* beautiful-sounding? Thus care must be taken in regard to the use and mention of an expression. But even with this warning, descriptive signs require further analysis, since sometimes they seem to refer, yet what they refer to does not exist—for example, *unicorn* or *Hamlet*.

Exercises

1. What are some of the theories on how letters become words?

2. Which of the following groups have the same form? State what the form is.

    a) All men are mortal; all metals are conductors; all students are bright; all children are careless.

    b) No men are cowards; no rabbits are animals; no metals are conductors; none of the students was present.

    c) Some students are bright; some students are not bright; some children are spoiled.

3. Identify the descriptive, connector, and expressive signs in the following sentences.

    a) He hit the tree with his car. Consequently he was arrested.

    b) If he refuses to marry her, then she will sue him.

    c) I hate Joe Smith. But I love his art work.

    d) Boy, she's lovely!

    e) That steak is delicious.

    f) The soul of man will endure.

4. In the following sentences, indicate which descriptive words are being used and which are merely being mentioned.

    a) Cat is spelled c-a-t.

    b) Melanie is a beautiful name.

    c) I christen you Joanna.

    d) Paradise Lost is a great epic.

    e) She saw Diane and yelled Diane!

    f) Mary refers to Mary which in turn is the name of Mary.

    g) Friendship has different meanings to different people.

5. What is the difference between a word and a sentence? In "John loves Mary," if I know the meaning of each word, does this mean I know the meaning of the sentence?

6. Discuss: "Of course I know other people have pain. They act just like I do when I have a pain."

EXTENSIONS AND INTENSIONS

Descriptive signs can usually be recognized by the fact that they perform two functions: (1) They refer to some object or group of objects; that is, they have an *extension*. (2) They designate one or more properties of such objects; that is, they have an *intension*. Thus the extension of *dog* is a certain class of animals whose individuals can be pointed out and whose existence can be affirmed by some acknowledged test. The intension of *dog* consists of certain properties of this class of objects, such as *being able to bark, having a wagging tail,* and *having four legs and a snout*. In scientific contexts, of course, a more precise listing of these properties would be forthcoming, for example, *having a certain kind of blood composition and blood structure*. The important point to note is that descriptive signs usually have both an extension and an intension.

Extensions are dependent upon context in the sense that a word might be taken to refer to one set of objects in one context and another set in some other context. The extension attributed to *atom* by a layman might be far different from the extension attributed to it by a physicist. The layman might take *atom* to refer to one or more particles surrounded by still smaller particles. But many physicists today have far different views of what it means to speak of atoms. Thus Eddington rejected the notion of a material atom and spoke of certain "ghost-particles" which are defined by certain wave vectors rather than by traditional notions of mass and size. And some of Einstein's followers speak of atoms as "relational fields of energy." Thus when we ask for the extension of a term, we must also give some indication of the context involved. Extensions, however, are less context-dependent than intensions. In most cases if we disagree about what the extension of an expression is, there are at least some external elements to which we can refer. I can show you what objects I intend to designate by *dog*. But intensions of words can and often do involve personal feelings and attitudes. Thus two people might agree about the extension of *cat*. But one might regard cats as vicious, the other as friendly. It becomes necessary to think of intensions in terms of the following classification:

1. Subjective intension
2. Objective intension
3. Conventional intension

The subjective intension of an expression consists of the properties that an individual personally attributes to an object. If he thinks of women as beings who are created primarily for the purpose of making men happy, then for him the subjective intension of *women* will be *created primarily for the purpose of making men happy*. On the other hand, the objective intension of an expression consists of all the characteristics—that is, properties—that can actually and verifiably be attributed to an object with the subjective element eliminated. Thus the objective intension of *dog* would designate all the possible objective properties that can be predicated of a dog, that is, *having a tail, being four-legged*, and so on.

However, from a practical viewpoint, both subjective and objective intensions are generally inadequate for inference and communication purposes. If words were used solely in terms of subjective intensions, it would be difficult for human beings to communicate, since each person could give an infinite number of personal meanings to any word. A child might speak in ameliorative language of a mouse, regarding it fondly as a plaything, whereas his mother might use pejorative terminology, regarding it as a dirty diseased animal. As the Father states in *Six Characters in Search of an Author*, we do not really understand one another because of "words, words. Each one of us has . . . his own special world. . . . [H]ow can we ever come to an understanding if I put in the words I utter the sense and value of things as I see them; while you who listen to me must inevitably translate them according to the conception of things each one of you has within himself?"[1] Subjective intensions obviously serve a purpose, particularly in the realm of literary writing, but they are not adequate means of attaining the goals of communication with precision and clarity.

Objective intensions are also troublesome. They not only require us to avoid any subjective allusions, but they also require that *every* objective characteristic of a particular object be enumerated. But just imagine how much time it would take to list every characteristic of a man! Biologists still have to present us with an exhaustive list of the components of a tiny cell. Thus, while a communicable meaning is unattainable with these two types of intension, a third type, the *conventional intension*, is for practical purposes the most satisfactory. This kind of intension consists of a selection of properties which would under normal conditions lead to an identification of an object. A certain number of objective characteristics or properties are taken for granted when reference is made to some object. You might like dogs and I might hate them,

---

1. L. Pirandello, *Six Characters in Search of an Author*, in *Naked Masks*. New York: E. P. Dutton, 1952, p. 224.

but we would still agree that something is a dog if it has four legs, a bushy tail, barks, and—perhaps—eats dog food. Of course, both of us could still be wrong since other animals, namely wolves, have these characteristics. But in a given context of discourse it would only be necessary to list a few of the characteristics of the objective intension in order to be certain that we are attaching the same meaning to the same word. For most purposes of communication and inference, we use the conventional intension of terms. From this point on, whenever intensions are mentioned, they are of the conventional kind.

Some interesting relations exist between intensions and extensions. We often tend to think that the primary way of identifying an object is through its extension. What is a dog? Why, merely point to this object, that object, and another; that is, give the extension of *dog* and it has been identified. But this is wrong. Pointing, by itself, can indicate an indefinite number of things. Try to point to some object and you will find that it would be easy for someone to mistake what you are pointing at. It is only as we are told "A dog is that which is furry, has a bushy tail, barks, and so on "; that is, only when the intension is given can we identify the extension. Discovering the extension of a term therefore depends upon our knowledge of the intension.

Proper names seem to be the only terms that are not so readily amenable to the extension-intension analysis. It is possible to speak of the extension of a proper name, e.g., *John Smith*, as referring to that one individual who is John Smith. But the intension usually consists of properties applicable to more than one individual. Hence it is often argued that no set of properties can ever identify the one and only one individual designated by a proper name. In other words, no matter how large an intension may be, it might always be applicable to A rather than to B. This is a major problem in many criminal investigations. A witness claims he saw a man with black hair and a scar on his cheek, running from the scene of the crime. But this description, no matter how detailed, can fit more than one individual.

Sometimes it is argued that if spatio-temporal properties were attributed to an individual, then even proper names could be given an intension by means of which the extension could be identified. Thus I might say, "John Smith is the individual with bushy hair, brown eyes, and a scar on his left cheek, and also one who is now two feet in front of me." Surely, attributing the space-time property of "being now two feet in front of me" would, in conjunction with other listed properties, be sufficient to identify John Smith. However, even with this information, mistakes might result. Detectives are often involved with cases in which A is seen and identified by B as John Smith, and yet it turns out that B was mistaken. Similarly, fingerprints can indeed identify a man; but as any good amateur sleuth knows, fingerprints can be altered and in some cases even completely erased.

Thus proper names are said to have an extension but no intension. However, in Chapter 14, we shall examine another way of dealing with proper names and consider a means by which some series of properties can be taken as the intension of a proper name.

Another interesting feature of intensions and extensions is that often the intension of a term is increased when its extension is decreased; and when the intension is decreased, the extension is increased. If a term has the intension of being furry, then its extension would be *dogs, wolves, hamsters,* and the like. But if the intension is increased by adding another property, such as *capable of being domesticated,* then instead of *dogs, wolves, hamsters,* the extension would be required to exclude wolves since even though wolves may be furry, they cannot be domesticated. If another property is added, namely *barking,* then the extension is diminished further since hamsters, which are furry and can be domesticated but which do not bark, must be excluded. Thus this example shows that as the intension is increased, the extension becomes smaller. Similarly if the intention is decreased, the extension increases. If *capable of being domesticated* and *barking* are eliminated, and only *being furry* remains as the intension, then we have the largest extension, namely *dogs, wolves, hamsters,* and the like. However, there are exceptions to this rule, as in the case where the properties both appear in exactly the same class or group of objects. Thus we can add *rational* to *human being,* but this would not decrease the extension, since everything that is rational is also a human being and everything that is a human being is also rational—at least this is what many people believe.

A third interesting aspect of intensions and extensions is that if a term is remiss in either intensions or extensions, then certain interesting questions arise. If, for example, it is not possible to indicate an intension or an extension for *Xerxx,* then we call it a nonsense term and reject it. Furthermore, if we cannot give the extension of a term, then it might still have an intension, e.g., *dinosaur,* but we surely deny that the term refers to something existent. But now consider *being an angel.* We can describe an angel, but so far no one has ever been able to give an extension to this phrase, although there seems to be sufficient evidence that at one time one could give the extensions of *Jesus* and *Luther.* We cannot find angels in the same way we might find elephants or human beings. Thus what are we to say? Do angels exist or do they not? If they do, then how is this possible if no extension can be given for the expression *being an angel.* If they do not exist—well, we shall leave this question with the theologian and the reader.

Exercises

1. Give the extension as well as the conventional and subjective intension of the following:

   a) dog

   b) Nazi

   c) Communist

   d) book

   e) baby

2. Discuss the following:

   Some terms are meaningful and yet they have neither extensions nor intensions. For example, *idea* has no extension since no one has ever seen an idea. Nor can we speak of the objective or conventional characteristics of an idea. It is certainly not possible to speak of a large idea, or a blue idea, or a kind idea. Yet it is perfectly meaningful to say, "Your idea was the best one." Similarly, it makes sense to say, "You are in a bad mood today." What is the extension and intension of *mood*? No one has ever observed a mood; therefore how can anyone ever speak of its characteristics?

3. Arrange the items in order of increasing intension:

   a) American

   b) John Smith

   c) Christian

   d) animal

   e) human being

SUPPLEMENTARY READINGS

Russell, B., *An Inquiry into Meaning and Truth*. London: Allen and Unwin, 1940. Chapter 1, "What is a Word?"

Sapir, E., *Language. New York*: Harcourt, Brace, and Co., 1921. Chapter 2, "The Elements of Language."

Wittgenstein, L., "Pain and Private Language," *Philosophical Investigations*, translated by G. E. M. Anscombe. Oxford: Basil Blackwell, 1953, pp. 88e−104e.

10
Predicates

The most significant category of descriptive terms is that consisting of *pre-dicates*. As we shall see, even proper names can be defined in terms of some series of predicates. But it is important to distinguish the grammarian's notion from that of the logician. For the grammarian, a predicate is everything in the sentence exclusive of the subject. Thus in "John runs to the store," the entire phrase *runs to the store* is the predicate. But for the logician, the predicate of a sentence has a much more specialized function. Let us consider a few sample sentences and then see how the logician differs from the grammarian in analyzing them.

    1. John is pale.

    For the grammarian, *John* is the subject and *is pale* is the predicate. The predicate can then be subdivided with *is* as a linking term and *pale* as an adjective. But the predicate is still definable as that part of the sentence which is exclusive of the subject. For the logician, the predicate is only that expression which is taken to refer to some property or to some relation. Thus for him, *pale* is the predicate with *is* operating as a term indicating that the object referred to by a given name does indeed purportedly have the property referred to by *pale*. In this instance the difference between the grammarian and the logician is not every noticeable. But now let us examine the next example:

    2. John runs to the store.

    The grammarian and the logician analyze this sentence in different ways. The grammarian takes *John* as the subject and *runs to the store* as the predicate. The predicate is then taken to consist of the verb *runs* and the prepositional phrase *to the store*. But the logician makes a different distinction. He always identifies the predicate as that which refers to a property or a relationship. By a property is meant some characteristic or some particular feature that a thing may have. Thus in (1), *pale* is a predicate referring to a property of the boy. A relationship also refers to a characteristic or a feature, but in this case the characteristic is shared by two or more objects, for example, *taller than*, which requires two objects if it is to function at all in a language. It is not enough to say "John is taller than"; it is necessary to say, "John is taller than Philip." We must surely supply a second term if *taller than* is to function.

    As for sentence (2), let us ask what the logician considers to be its predicate. The answer is that *runs to* is the predicate since it is the expression which refers to the relationship connecting John to the store. Thus only *runs to* functions as a predicate for the logician. Both *John* and *the store* are the two terms needed to permit the relation to function in the language. We can arbitrarily decide to call the term on the left-hand side of the relationship the subject, and the term on the right-hand side the object. Or if we wish to omit all reference to either subjects or objects, we could simply speak of left-hand side and right-hand side terms that are required if relational terms are to exist in a language.

For the logician then, predicates are special terms that cannot simply be explained as that portion of the sentence exclusive of the subject. Predicates are the designators of properties and relationships, a very important distinction for the purposes of logical inference.

This analysis of predicates makes it possible to go on to differentiate between *monadic* and *polyadic* predicates. The monadic predicate needs only one object in order to be applicable. Thus in "The hat is blue," *blue* or, technically, *is blue*, is a monadic predicate since only one object is needed in order for it to become applicable; that is, I can say of a single given object that it is blue. (Sometimes predicates are indicated by the addition of dots. Thus . . . *is blue* is a monadic predicate; the dots signify that a term referring to some individual object, e.g., the hat, must be implicitly understood as replacing the dots of . . . *is blue* if the predicate is to function at all.)

On the other hand, the polyadic predicate requires two or more objects in order to become applicable. Thus in the example "John runs to the store," *runs to* or, if we wish to show the polyadic predicate more explicitly, . . . *runs to* . . . , requires two objects before it can be applied; that is, I cannot say of one single object that it has the property of running to. Two objects are required, in this case John and something which is a store. When a polyadic predicate requires only two objects in order to complete it, that is, in order to make it function, then we call it a *dyadic* predicate; . . . *runs to* . . . is a dyadic predicate. But sometimes polyadic predicates require three or more objects for completion. Thus in such a sentence as "John gives the letter to Bill," the phrase . . . *gives* . . . *to* . . . is a *triadic* predicate in that it takes three objects to complete it, namely *John*, *the letter*, and *Bill*. There can also be *quadratic* predicates, as in "John traded his penknife to Frank for a wristwatch." Here . . . *traded* . . . *to* . . . *for* . . . is the predicate and *John, his penknife, Frank*, and *a wristwatch* are the expressions which complete the predicate. However, for the most part we shall be concerned with either monadic predicates or those polyadic ones that are either dyadic or triadic.

Monadic predicates are in one sense the easiest kind of descriptive term to understand. They simply refer to a property that an individual object may be said to have. In most cases the presence of such properties is observable or at least capable of being tested. Thus if I say an object is blue, I can observe that it is blue, or if it is magnetic, I can test it for its magnetism. But there is another sense in which the understanding of monadic predicates is no easy matter.

Consider the predicate *blue*. I say that *blue* refers to a property of some given object, say, X. Thus X is blue. Then I say that some other objects, Y, is also blue. But what does this mean? Do both X and Y have the same property? Taken literally this is impossible. X cannot have the same property that Y has, just as a person could not have the same hat that another person is wearing. He can have a similar hat, or he can share the same hat at different times. But at one and the same time no two persons can be wearing the same hat. Similarly, two objects cannot have the same property. Thus what must be intended here is that X and Y have similar, but not identical properties. Well, then let us call the properties similar. Now, what is it that makes the two properties similar? What is it that makes the blue of X similar to the blue of Y? Or, in other terms, what is it that permits the application of the same monadic predicate to two different objects? The question here might seem to be analogous to what one might ask about the two hats. What makes them similar? Our answer could be that they are similar simply because they have the same color. But then what makes the color of one hat identical to the color of the second hat? And here is the fundamental problem again. Sooner or later in the analysis of what makes two objects similar, a point must finally be reached where similarity itself must be accounted for, and this is what occurs when colors are considered. What is it that makes two blues similar?

We might answer this question by claiming that the colors are similar because they are both instances of the same color. This seems satisfactory until one asks what is this color that both blues are instances of? In other words, there is this curious situation that whenever two objects are taken to have the same property, then there must also be reference to a third property that is itself never observable. Thus in the case of the two objects, X and Y, if they are both called *blue*, then it must be because both objects have the same color. But how can they both have the same color? They can both *share* the same color or be instances of the same color. But they cannot both have the same color. It is as if we said that two men are wearing the same hat, but then recognized that two men may be wearing hats of the same style. But they cannot be wearing the same hat. Thus when two objects are said to be blue, it is meant that they are instances of the same color, and not that they both have the same color. But the problem remains. Where can we observe that of which the blue objects are instances? In the case of hats, a die or a cast can be shown from which some set of hats has been created and which gives them the same style. But this analogy is not satisfactory when applied to colors. No die or cast can be found. Thus sometimes philosophers will posit a third kind of entity, e.g., blueness, which all instances of blue exhibit. This kind of basic analysis of what a monadic predicate is has led some philosophers to believe that there exist abstract kinds of things which can never be directly observed—e.g., *blueness*—and yet to which one must be committed if knowledge is to occur. Sometimes they are called Platonic forms, in honor of the Greek philosopher, Plato; sometimes they are called concepts; sometimes just ideas. But whatever they are, they are taken to be abstractions which are not ever directly observable, yet are part of the furniture that makes up our world.

In more recent times it has sometimes been argued that we should not ask whether two properties or two objects are identical. Instead we can ask how we know when two words are synonyms. Thus instead of asking how the blue of one object can be identified with the blue of another object, we simply ask whether *blue₁* is synonymous with *blue₂*. But the problem of explaining the nature of synonymy is a difficult one. One explanation frequently offered is that a term *A* is synonymous with another term *B* if and only if, given any sentence in which *A* appears, *B* can replace *A* without changing the truth value of the sentence. Thus given the sentence "X is blue," where *blue₁* refers to some specific color, we ask if *blue₁* can be replaced by *blue₂*, where *blue₂* refers to another specific color, without any change in truth value of the sentence. Then consider other sentences employing *blue₁* and ask the same question. If the reply is the same about every sentence in which *blue₁* appears, then *blue₁* is taken to be synonymous with *blue₂*. But there are serious objections to this approach.

The question of abstract entities again arises. One must ask how it is known that in any given sentence "X is blue₁," it is legitimate to replace *blue₁* by *blue₂*? If I look at one object and say, "A is blue₁," why is it legitimate for me to say, "A is also blue₂"? Why should a color of one object be regarded as identical to a color of another?

Another objection is that it is not at all clear whether it is sensible to say two terms are synonymous if one can be substituted for the other in every sentence in which one appears. Think of all the possible sentences in which *blue₁* can appear! Perhaps the number might not be infinite, but it would surely be great—much greater than anyone can think of enumerating. Thus we can never really check whether or not *blue₁* can be substituted for *blue₂* in every sentence. It might be argued that we need simply check a large sample of sentences. But no matter how large the sample, it is still always possible that some sentence outside the sample might not permit the substitution of *blue₁* for *blue₂* and conversely.

Still another objection is that there are always some sentences in which *blue₁* can never be substituted for *blue₂*. Consider the following: "*Blue₁* is spelled *b-l-u-e₁*." We cannot substitute *blue₂* here for *blue₁*. Similarly, if one asks, "Is *blue₁* identical to *blue₂*?" he is not asking "Is *blue₁* identical to *blue₁*?" or "Is *blue₂* identical to *blue₂*?"

It would seem then that we are required to accept the existence of abstract entities whenever we wish to say that one thing is the same as or similar to another. But at the same time it is really difficult to believe that such things exist. Usually when something is taken to exist, then I can see it or feel it or taste it. But I have never seen or felt or tasted an abstract entity. What is this abstract thing that I must accept and yet which by its very nature cannot be experienced?

It has been pointed out that numbers exist, yet these cannot be seen or felt or tasted. We can see the written symbol, e.g., 2, but we cannot see what this symbol stands for. We grasp its meaning in some kind of intellectual act. Thus some abstract things must exist. The reply might be given that mathematics simply involves playing a game with some set of written marks and that therefore it is not necessary to ask whether or not numbers exist. But in any event the reader can now get some understanding of some of the philosophical problems arising in the analysis of monadic predicates.

Polyadic predicates pose even more troublesome philosophical dilemmas than do monadic predicates. The traditional problem of polyadic predicates involves the question: How is it even possible to have such predicates? Consider the dyadic predicate, *is above*, in

1. My right hand *is above* my left hand.

Assume that I do what this sentence states. I place my right hand above my left hand. Now what has happened here? I know that I have two hands before me. But where is the relation *is above* that is between them? Does some third entity exist between my right hand and my left hand when one is above the other? Similar remarks can be made about such relations as *is to the right of*, *is to the left of*, and *is below*. But if such relations cannot be said to exist in the same way that objects such as my hands do, what exactly are they? Again, as in the case of monadic predicates, we must ask whether a relation is an objective occurrence, a psychological concept—or what?

Bertrand Russell once summarized the curious problem of a relation when he said, "It is neither in space nor in time, neither material nor mental; yet it is something."[1] But what kind of something it is simply eludes us. Mathemati-

---

[1] Bertrand Russell, *The Problems of Philosophy*. London: Oxford University Press, 1912, p. 98.

cians have often defined a relation as a class of ordered pairs (or ordered triples, if the relation is triadic rather than dyadic). Thus *A is above B* would be defined as the class of pairs such that A is ordered in certain way to B. But *ordered in a certain way* is no more than a synonym for *being related in a certain way*, and thus we still cannot avoid asking exactly what relations are and whether they exist or not.

Perhaps one of the most fascinating aspects of both monadic and polyadic predicates concerns the problem of how objects are related to either properties or relations. A monadic predicate has been defined as one referring to a property of an object. Thus *blue* is the monadic predicate referring to a given object's property of being blue. But what is this object that has properties? As soon as we begin to discuss it, we simply begin to list more predicates. Thus we ask, "What is it that is blue?" Well, it is that which is large and has windows. We simply supply more predicates. But what then is this *it* that has properties? Shall we accept the view that it is some odd entity which is never open to observation, which is always the underlying uninspectable *it* which philosophers have at various times called *substance* or *thing-in-itself* or *thing-we-know-not what*? Of course, it is possible to maintain that there is no *it*; things are no more than clusters of properties stuck together. For some reason, properties cluster together to make up this chair or, for that matter, to make up me. But what is it that keeps them clustered together? Furthermore, some properties seem to be more necessary than others. Thus it would seem to be necessary for a human being to be rational, but it is not necessary for him to be bald. But some philosophers have claimed that there is a cause for everything, so that if a man is bald, he had to be bald because of an endless chain of circumstances. Thus even those properties that would seem to be unnecessary would, on closer analysis, be found to be necessary. But if all properties are necessary, if everything that can characterize any individual is really absolutely necessary, then what happens to freedom? A strict determinism seems to explain the causation of events. We are led to the famous (perhaps infamous) doctrine of *internal relations* which states that every property and relation is necessary; nothing occurs accidentally. Thus the study of predicates, if pursued further, would ultimately lead us to a discussion of freedom and determinism.

Although these questions concerning the existence (or nonexistence) of relations are of profound concern to the philosopher, the logician can fortunately avoid them. He need simply maintain that his job is to show how sentences with monadic or polyadic predicates function in logical arguments. He does not have to become involved in the philosophical issues. In other words, the logician need only say: "People use sentences which they take to be true or false and which consist of proper names, predicates, connector terms, and certain other kinds of words. My job is to show how and under what circumstances these sentences produce contradiction, consistency, or validity. This I can do without becoming involved in the philosophical problems." But of course, in the final analysis it is philosophical inquiry which tells us about the kind of universe to which we are applying the logic.

Exercises

1. What is the difference between the logician's and the grammarian's view of a predicate?

2. Identify the logical predicates in the following sentences. Which are monadic and which are polyadic? Which are dyadic, triadic, or quadratic?

   a) John is happy.

   b) John is happier than Jim.

   c) Jim is friendly.

   d) John is friendlier.

   e) Muskie and Nixon are contemporaries.

   f) Jim gives a gift to John.

   g) Mary sold her watch to Joan for twenty dollars.

3. Discuss:

   a) It is ridiculous to think we are committed to some strange abstract entity when we say A is similar to B. When we say one thing is similar to another, we mean only that they both look alike or behave in the same way. Nothing abstract is needed to explain this.

   b) Of course, there are things that are abstract and can never be observed, such as relations. In *A is to the left of B*, we can observe both *A* and *B*, but where is *to the left of*?

   c) *Dog* means something; *house* means something; *five* means something. *Dog* and *house* have an extension, namely, some object or set of objects signified by the word. Now what is the extension of *five*; what is the object or set of objects signified by the word?

   d) In the case of man we know what the *it* is which holds together all his properties—the soul, or the ego, or the self.

e) Of course, we know when two terms are synonyms. When A is used in the same way as B, then A and B are synonyms.

4. Discuss:

a) A man is a set of properties held together by something. When he dies, the properties disappear, but the something that binds these properties together does not die or disappear.

b) A man is like an onion. If you keep peeling away the properties of an onion, you are finally left with nothing at all. Similarly, if a man's properties disappear, then so does the man.

c) Newton's Third Law states that to every action there is a direct and opposite reaction. Thus everything affects everything else. Therefore everything is determined.

SUPPLEMENTARY READINGS

Frege, G., "The Concept of Number," in W. E. Kennick and M. Lazerowitz (eds.), *Metaphysics*. Englewood Cliffs, N.J.: Prentice-Hall, 1966.

Hempel, C. G., "On the Nature of Mathematical Truth," *American Mathematical Monthly*, Lii (1945), pp. 543–556.

Loux, M. J., "The Problem of Universals," in M. J. Loux (ed.), *Universals and Particulars*. New York: Doubleday, 1970.

Russell, B., *The Problems of Philosophy*. London: Clarendon Press, 1912. Chapter 11, "The World of Universals."

11

Quantification, Universal and Particular Sentences

UNIVERSAL AND PARTICULAR SENTENCES

With a clearer though perhaps not utterly comprehensible view of what the logician means by a predicate—especially the monadic predicate which will be the only kind of predicate discussed in the next few chapters—we are almost ready to consider the rules of logic dealing with the internal parts of sentences and not merely with sentences. However, one more technical notion must be introduced, namely the *quantified* sentence. Quantified sentences are simply those sentences that begin with *all, some,* or *no,* as in "All women are sex objects," "Some women are sex objects," or "No women are sex objects." These sentences are important for two main reasons. First, they involve rules of validity that are not to be found among the rules given or derived in the preceding chapters. If I say, "All women are sex objects. Mary is a woman. Therefore Mary is a sex object," I am presenting a valid argument. Even intuitively I can probably recognize this. But, as we have already indicated, if this argument is symbolized simply with the devices referred to in preceding chapters, it will read

$$(p \cdot q) \supset r$$

where p stands for "All women are sex objects," q for "Mary is a woman," and r for "Mary is a sex object." If a truth-table analysis is applied to this argument, it turns out to be invalid since at least one interpretation can make this formula false, namely, if p and q are true and r is false. Thus to account for arguments involving *all* or *some* or *no,* it becomes necessary to introduce further notions concerning validity.

A second reason for our interest in these quantified sentences, particularly sentences beginning with *all,* is that they are crucial for all important inquiries, especially scientific ones. In a science the search is not merely for the accumulation of factual data, but for the organization of this data in such a way that generalizations can be made. It is not sufficient to be able to say that such-and-such an object falls 32 feet per second per second or that such-and-such an object is both a metal and a conductor. We want to be able to say that *all* objects will fall 32 feet per second per second under given circumstances, and that *all* metals are conductors. Only by the use of generalizations can predictions be made about new and future occurrences. Thus the word *all* or its equivalent, *every,* is necessary if any scientific inquiry is to become possible.

However, before we proceed to show how *all* sentences and their corresponding *some* and *no* sentences operate in a logical context and how they are to be symbolized for logical purposes, there are a few interesting observations to be made. Sentences containing either *all* or some of the other quantifier words are not so easily understood as the sentences in preceding chapters which do not contain quantifier words. If I say, "John is pale," there is a sense in which I can explain most of the meaning of this sentence, by pointing to someone called *John*, i.e., giving the extension of *John*, and then indicating by various behavioristic or other techniques the extension and intension of *is pale*. But now let us turn to the sentence "All men are rational." It should be clear that *all* is not an adjective in the same way *pale* would be an adjective if I said, "Pale men are rational." It makes some sense to point to a pale man, but I cannot, except in certain idiomatic expressions—e.g., "He is all man!"—speak of an *all* man. I cannot point to an *all* man. What next suggests itself is that *all* is a kind of abbreviatory device in the same way that such devices are sometimes employed in mathematics. If I use the term 10^4, I mean no more than $10 \times 10 \times 10 \times 10$. Similarly I might argue that if I say, "All men are insecure," I mean no more than "John Smith is insecure, Fred Jones is insecure, Robert Doe is insecure," and so on. *All* serves merely to abbreviate a whole series of simple sentences referring to individuals having a given property. The same argument can be applied to *some*. The *some* in "Some men are insecure" is not an ordinary adjective. We do not compare some men to sad men. (But again, we can have an idiomatic expression that changes *some* into an adjective as in "He is some man!") I might feel unhappy if I met a sad person, but I do not know how I would feel if I were introduced to a *some* person. However, whereas *all* is an abbreviation for a *conjunction* of sentences (e.g., "John Smith is insecure, *and* Fred Jones is insecure, *and* Robert Doe is insecure ..."), *some* is used as an abbreviation for a *disjunction* or *alternation* of sentences (e.g., "John Smith is insecure, *or* Fred Jones is insecure, *or* Robert Doe is insecure ... ").

This kind of analysis of *all* and *some* would be satisfactory if it were not for one disturbing factor—the question of whether or not the universe is made up of a finite or an infinite number of objects. It might seem rather incredible that from the fairly simple analysis of words such as *all*, we are suddenly led to the profound and awe-inspiring question of whether the universe contains an infinite or a finite number of objects. Yet the relevance of this question is very real. The sentence "All objects, starting from a state of rest, will fall 32 feet per second per second," can be taken as either true or false, but since it is no more than an abbreviation, its truth or falsity depends upon the truth or falsity of what it abbreviates. In other words, if this sentence means no more than "Object 1, starting from the state of rest, will fall 32 feet per second per second; object 2, starting from a state of rest, will fall 32 feet per second per second; object 3 . . . and so on," then it will be true if and only if all the conjuncts are true (this is our definition of conjunction) and it will be false if one of the conjuncts is false. To check for falsity is quite simple. As soon as one false conjunct is discovered—for example, if we encounter an object that does not, starting from a state of rest, fall 32 feet per second per second—then the *all* sentence is false. But how can we ever determine whether a statement is true if the universe contains an infinite number of objects? No matter how many true conjuncts are found, there are always more to be tested, and some of these could be false. Hence if we are dealing with an infinite number of objects, we can never determine whether the *all* sentence is true, and therefore we can never legitimately call such a sentence true. But if, as we noted at the beginning of this book, we are going to deal only with true and false sentences, then either we must say that *all* sentences cannot be treated as true or false or that some other analysis must be made.

The exception to this view of the *all* sentence arises when the sentence is changed into a definition. For example, if it is arbitrarily stipulated that *penny* is to be taken to mean *a form of currency*, then of course it follows by definition that "All pennies are forms of currency" is true. Similarly, if the meaning of *bachelor* is taken to be *unmarried man*, then it follows by the very meaning that has been attached to *bachelor* that "All bachelors are unmarried men" is true. In mathematics, numbers might be defined so that whenever a number ending in 2, 4, 6, 8, or 0 appears, then it can be divided by 2. Thus the sentence "All numbers which end in 2, 4, 6, 8, or 0 are divisible by 2" is true. Here it is the definition that has been given of number that makes the *all* sentence true. Unfortunately, in most cases the *all* sentences are true or false in terms of what we discover in the world and not simply in terms of what we arbitrarily stipulate. "All metals are conductors" is not *defined* to be true. Its truth or falsity rests on what is found in the world, namely, that whenever a metal has been encountered it turns out to be a conductor. But in this case the problem of infinite numbers does arise.

The same problem—except, of course, in connection with definitions— arises with *some* when we are dealing with an infinite set of objects. But whereas it is easy to determine the truth of a *some* sentence, it is not possible to determine its falsity. If "Some men are rational" is the same as saying "John Smith is rational or James Jones is rational or Robert Doe is rational . . . ," and an infinite number of past and future entities is involved, then the truth is easily determinable. If it were to turn out that "James Jones is rational" is a true sentence, then by the definition of alternation the whole sentence is true. On the other hand, since an alternation can be false only if all the disjuncts are false, and we can never check all the disjuncts, we can never determine the falsity of "Some men are rational." Thus again either *some* sentences are not to be allowed in the logic which deals solely with true-or-false sentences, or some separate provision must be made for them.

It should be indicated that the problem of *all* becomes even more serious in relation to such sentences as the following:

1. All numbers have successors.
2. All bodies that do not have forces operating upon them will continue in a straight line.

In the case of (1), which is not to be viewed as an arbitrary definition, there is not even the possibility that we may perhaps be dealing with a finite number of entities, so the ordinary abbreviatory view of *all* cannot be upheld without difficulty. Numbers automatically project us into the realm of the infinite, since it would seem to be undoubtedly true that for every number there is a succeeding one. (But it should be pointed out that the intuitionist in mathematics challenges the validity of this generalization. After all, since no one has ever encountered *all* numbers, how is it possible to be sure that all of them must have successors? But presumably most mathematicians are not intuitionists, and therefore sentences such as (1) do allude to an infinite number of numbers.)

In the case of (2), an *all* sentence would seem to be abbreviatory of nothing at all since, so far as is known, there are no bodies that do not have forces operating upon them. This law—Newton's second law—is most enigmatic for logicians, precisely because there is no way of thinking that it merely means "This body does not have a force operating upon it and continues in a straight line, and this body does not have a force operating upon it and continues in a straight line, and ...". No abbreviation at all seems to be involved here.

Philosophers have been very concerned with the question of whether the universe contains a finite or an infinite number of objects. Those who are aware of the logical problems will immediately recognize that the validity of some important proofs for the existence of God—those of Aristotle and Aquinas, for example—rests, among other things, upon whether the universe is to be regarded as having a finite or an infinite number of entities. But logicians can simply sidestep this issue. They can arbitrarily postulate the existence of an infinite number of entities and then proceed to show the logic of quantified sentences in such a universe. They can also arbitrarily postulate a finite number of entities, or perhaps no entities at all, and then proceed to show the kind of logic of quantified sentences which could be constructed about such a universe.

Thus whatever the status of the entities in the universe, we can presumably give the logic of the sentences describing such a universe. The existence of an infinite number of objects is postulated even if these objects are merely numbers (of which there are surely an infinite number). Of course neither the mathematician nor the physicist is compelled to accept this view; the notion of an infinite is merely being assumed.

Exercises

Discuss the following:

1. Of course there are an infinite number of objects in the universe. Aren't there an infinite number of numbers?

2. We have been fooled by the *all* sentence. It looks like a declarative sentence, but it is really a command. Thus if I say, "All metals are conductors," I mean "Given any metal, take it also to be a conductor." Thus there really is no problem about *all* sentences.

3. We can easily account for *all* sentences by distinguishing *essential* from *accidental* properties. An *essential* property is one that a thing must have. Thus if I say, "All metals are conductors," I mean that a metal must be a conductor if it is to be called a metal. Being a conductor is essential rather than accidental to being a metal.

4. All *all* sentences are simply definitions. Thus when I say, "All metals are conductors," I mean no more than that *metal* means *being a conductor*.

5. Does it make sense to speak of an empty universe? Aren't we then thinking of the universe as a big empty box? But can the universe be thought of in this way?

THE SYMBOLIZATION OF ALL

Perhaps the best way of dealing with such terms as *all*, *some*, and *no* is to think of them in relation to the problems involving *true* and *false*. We justified the use of *true* and *false* sentences on the gounds that these expressions function like mathematical terms. Mathematics is employed even though it may well be incorrect to say that an object has a specific final measurement. The very fact that all objects take in and lose atoms every second means that *the* mathematical number which gives *the* measurement of an object can never be obtained. But of course we still do decide that an object is of such-and-such a size and has such-and-such a weight, for only in this way can we go on to make the kind of inferences we wish to make. If I say a table is three feet by six feet, then I can be fairly confident that a tablecloth five feet by eight feet would fit perfectly. The mathematics involved in the addition of natural numbers would suddenly come into use. Analogously, as we have already seen, sentences are called *true* or *false* even if no sentences can ever be called absolutely true or absolutely false. A similar kind of reasoning is applicable to *all*. When *all* is used with an infinite number of objects, it is not possible to tell whether each object does or does not have a given characteristic. But we still do make this jump from the finite number—that is, the sampling we do have—to the infinite number, which is unattainable. And our rationale for doing this is: (1) all the logical tools for *all* and *some* and *no* can be brought into play, and (2) the inferences made turn out to be more, rather than less successful. If the view is accepted that all metals are conductors, then we can be fairly certain that if a given object is called *metal*, then it will also be called *conductor*. In brief, extending the use of *all* from finite groups to infinite ones is justified by the successful inferences which then become possible.

Once we acknowledge that it does make sense to speak of sentences beginning with *all*, and that we shall indeed take them to be *true* or *false* even though there may be an infinite number of objects in the universe, we can begin to show how such sentences are used in the process of inference. To begin, let us try to state clearly our commitment when we assert an *all* or, as it shall sometimes be called, a *universal affirmative* sentence.

Consider the sentence "All metals are conductors." It is clear that this sentence does not mean that all things are metals and conductors. Obviously, many things are neither. Nor do we mean all conductors are metals. This might indeed be true, but the original sentence simply tells us that whenever we have a metal it is a conductor, and not that whenever we have a conductor it is a metal. There is nothing odd about saying that all metals are conductors, but there are some conductors that are not metals. Nor do we mean that there are metals and they are conductors. It might seem as if this is what is meant until we ask whether we would still claim that all metals are conductors even if, suddenly, all metals disappeared from the earth. The answer is that even if all metals disappeared from the earth, it would still be the case that if a metal does appear somewhere at some time, then it will be a conductor. In other words, the sense of "All metals are conductors" is:

1. Given any object, if it is a metal, then it is a conductor.

This does not commit us to saying that there are metals which are conductors. It simply tells us that if an object which is a metal is encountered at some time and in some place, then it will be a conductor. The important point to notice about an *all* sentence is that it really contains a disguised conditional. It tells us that if such-and-such is the case, then something else is the case.

With this understanding of a universal affirmative sentence, it is possible to fit such a sentence into the logical truth-functional system developed in previous chapters. How is a universal affirmative to be symbolized? An *all* sentence is really conditional in form. It tells us if *this*, then *that*; if *this* is a *conductor*, then it is a *metal*. So with (1) as our example, the initial symbolization of (1) becomes

2. Given any object, it is a metal ⊃ it is a conductor.

The sign of the conditional ⊃ is introduced to stand for the *if–then* part of the sentence. But now let us introduce a new symbol, namely (*x*). This symbol will stand for *all* or for any phrase, such as *given any object*, which is a paraphrase of *all*. Sentence 2 becomes:

3. (*x*) it is a metal ⊃ it is a conductor.

But now note that the *it* in the antecedent and the *it* in the consequent both refer to the same object that might be selected from (*x*). In other words, (3) states: "Given any object, if that object is a metal then it (the same object) is a conductor." Thus the *it* refers to any particular object selected from (*x*). In the language of the logician, both *its* are within the *scope* or under the control of the *universal quantifier* (*x*). Instead of using *it* we shall use *x*, and then enclose the entire conditional by parentheses to show that the *x* in both the antecedent and the consequent are under the scope of the universal quantifier. This is symbolized as:

4. (*x*) (*x* is a metal ⊃ *x* is a conductor).

The *x*'s following (*x*) are called *individual variables*, which means that they are replaceable by one or more proper names or other terms that refer to individual entities. Thus (4) really states: "If this object is a metal, then it is a conductor; if that object is a metal, then it is a conductor, etc. The individual variable *x* stands as a kind of place-holder for an indefinite list of names or other terms designating specific entities.

This is the first step in symbolizing *all* sentences. *All* has been eliminated and replaced by (*x*) and the implicit *if–then* is indicated by the horseshoe sign of material implication. Parentheses have been placed around "*x* is a metal ⊃ *x* is a conductor" in order to make sure that these *x*'s are controlled by

(x). Had the parentheses been placed merely around "x is a metal," then the x in "x is a conductor" would not be under the control of (x). In such a case (4) would have read, "If everything is a metal, then something or other is a conductor." We would have lost the meaning we want, namely, that every metal is also a conductor and not that only some of them are.

But what shall be done with the phrases *is a metal* and *is a conductor?* These are monadic predicates and they will be replaced by *predicate letters*. A predicate letter is simply an alphabetical letter that stands for a particular monadic predicate phrase. *F* is substituted for *is a metal*, and *G* is substituted for *is a conductor*. The full symbolization of (4) then becomes:

$$(x) \, (xF \supset xG)$$

But since most contemporary logic books tend to place the predicate terms before the individual variable, we shall follow this practice and write the symbolization as

5. $(x) \, (Fx \supset Gx)$

Any letters can be used as individual variables and any letters can be used as predicate terms so long as they are consistently applied as variables and as predicate terms. In order to avoid any possible confusion, we shall simply stipulate that the small letters w, x, y, and z will always play the role of individual variables, while capital letters F, G, H, I, etc., will always play the role of predicate terms. Also for the sake of simplification, all combinations of predicate letters with individual variables will be called *sentential functions*. Thus Fx, Gx, and Hx are all sentential functions which become sentences when the variables are replaced by names and the predicate terms by predicates.

With the use of individual variables, monadic predicates, and material implication, the vast majority of *all* sentences can now be symbolized. This same technique is also applicable to any other sentences which are synonymous to *all* sentences. Thus all the following can be symbolized as $(x) \, (Fx \supset Gx)$:

a) If anything is an *F*, then it is a *G*.

b) *F*'s are *G*'s.

c) Every *F* is a *G*.

d) Each *F* is a *G*.

The symbolization of the *all* sentence also gives us a way of symbolizing the *no* sentence such as "No metals are conductors." The *no* sentence, or *universal negative* sentence says no more than:

6. Given any object, if it is a metal, then it is not a conductor. (Compare this formulation to (1) on p. 165.)

Thus the *no* sentence is exactly like the *all* sentence except that it negates the consequent. In other words, the symbolization of "No metals are conductors" becomes:

7. $(x)(Fx \supset \overline{Gx})$

Here also (7) can be used to symbolize any of the following universal negative sentences:

a) If anything is an F, then it is not a G.

b) F's are not G's.

c) Nothing which is an F is a G.

Thus two important kinds of sentences can be symbolized.

Universal Affirmative: $(x)(Fx \supset Gx)$

Universal Negative: $(x)(Fx \supset \overline{Gx})$

And along with these kinds of sentences we can also symbolize any such sentences which are combined by $\lor, \cdot, \equiv,$ or $\supset$. Thus the symbolization of "All men are rational or all men are fools" is

$(x)(Mx \supset Rx) \lor (x)(Mx \supset Fx)$

Exercises

1. Symbolize the following:

a) All men are rational.

b) Either no students are radicals or all professors are wrong.

c) No one is perfect.

d) If everyone goes to the party, then no one will be unhappy.

e) An animal is a strong beast.

f) To each his own.

g) No man is above the law.

h) The lion is a noble animal.

i) Students are not cowards.

j) Only men are allowed.

PARTICULAR SENTENCES

The preceding section dealt with *all* or *universal* sentences. Just as important in a language are *some* or *particular* sentences, such as "Some metals are conductors" or "Some human beings are insecure." The *some* sentence can also be analyzed in the same way as the *all* sentence in terms of individual variables and monadic predicate terms. However, whereas the material implication sign is the main connective in the *all* sentence, the conjunction sign is the main connective in the *some* sentence. Whereas a special sign (x) is used to signify *all*, another sign $(\exists x)$ will be used to signify *some*. But all of this will become clearer as a given *some* sentence is analyzed. For example:

Some jewels are precious.

One important distinction is to be made between an *all* sentence and a *some* sentence. In the analysis of the universal sentence, it was made clear that a reference to *all* does not mean that existence is being claimed for anything. If I say, "All metals are conductors," I am saying, "If any object is a metal, then it is a conductor." But this does not mean that there are any metals. It would be as if I said, "If anything is a dinosaur, then it is very large"; this does not mean that dinosaurs exist. On the other hand, if I say, "Some jewels are precious," I am claiming that I have encountered or someone has encountered at least one jewel which is precious. In other words, the *some* sentence does claim that something exists. Thus "Some jewels are precious" is usually taken to mean:

1. There are jewels and they are precious.

It is sometimes argued that *some* sentences are not so easily identifiable as existential ones, whereas *all* sentences are readily identifiable as material implications. Note, for example, the following *some* sentences.

2. Some dinosaurs were vegetarians.
3. Some unicorns were friendly to men.
4. Some of Hamlet's friends were deceitful.

Obviously no dinosaurs, unicorns, or friends of Hamlet exist. Yet this does not mean that sentences 2, 3, and 4 are meaningless or that they must be taken to be false. In the case of (2) there is no genuine difficulty since the use of *were* merely requires changing the *time* of existence. Sentence 2 means "There were dinosaurs at some specific time and they were vegetarians." Sentences

3 and 4 cannot be handled in this way for there never were any unicorns and Hamlet's friends are strictly fictitious. Yet it would seem odd to call (3) and (4) false. Some unicorns were indeed friendly to men; and as all dramatists know, some of Hamlet's friends were deceitful. How are such sentences to be treated?

The answer is to be sought in the fact that no one really attributes existence to unicorns or to Hamlet's friends, but rather such beings are thought of in terms of some written context—mythological works in the case of unicorns, Shakespeare's tragedy in the case of Hamlet's friends. In these contexts, statements are true or false in accordance with the way the mythologist or the tragedian introduces them. The statement about Hamlet's friends refers to *contextual existence*, that is, the terms and expressions are used as if they refer to what exists, even though they do not. Thus (3) and (4) will be translated in the following way:

3. There exists contextually (in the context of mythology) at least one unicorn that was friendly to man.

4. There exists contextually (in the context of Shakespeare's play, *Hamlet*) at least one friend of Hamlet who was deceitful.

In this way *some* can be used as a way of indicating existence even though in several instances *some* will indicate contextual existence, or *as–if* existence.

Following the procedure utilized in the previous analysis of *all*, we shall symbolize the expressions in terms of predicate terms, individual variables, and one new expression which will be called an *existential quantifier* in analogy with the universal quantifier. The existential quantifier will be symbolized as $(\exists x)$ and will take the place of *some*. Where *some* is used with an expression that has only contextual existence, the subscript c will be introduced into the existential quantifier as $(\exists x_c)$. Thus (1), (2), (3), and (4) become:

1. $(\exists x) (Jx \cdot Px)$; J stands for *is a jewel*; P stands for *is precious*.

2. $(\exists x) (Dx \cdot Vx)$; D stands for *is a dinosaur*; V stands for *is a vegetarian*.

3. $(\exists x_c) (Ux \cdot Fx)$; U stands for *was a unicorn*; F stands for *friendly to man*.

4. $(\exists x_c) (Fx \cdot Dx)$; F stands for *was a friend of Hamlet;* D stands for *was deceitful*.

Just as there are affirmative and negative universal sentences, there are affirmative and negative particular sentences. And negative particular sentences can also be symbolized merely by using the existential quantifier and the negative sign over the second conjunct. Thus "Some jewels are not precious" would be symbolized as:

5. $(\exists x)\,(\mathcal{J}x \cdot \overline{Px})$

Just as universal sentences can be understood in different ways, so can particular ones be interpreted in a number of ways. All of the following would be examples of a particular affirmative sentence such as $(\exists x)\,(Fx \cdot Gx)$:

Something is an F and a G.

There is at least one thing that is an F and a G.

Some F is G.

There exists at least one F that is G.

Similarly, $(\exists x)\,(Fx \cdot \overline{Gx})$ would symbolize the following kinds of sentences:

Something is an F and not a G.

There is at least one thing that is an F and not a G.

Some F is not G.

There exists at least one F that is not G.

Note also that the parentheses play an important role in defining the scope of the existential quantifier. Thus $(\exists x)\,(Fx \cdot Gx) \cdot Hx$ should be sharply distinguished from $(\exists x)\,(Fx \cdot Gx \cdot Hx)$. In the latter case something is an F, a G, and an H. In the former case something is an F and a G, but since the x of Hx is not under the scope of the quantifier, the same thing need not also be an H. Thus care must be taken to place the parentheses correctly.

Just as universal sentences can be combined by $\lor$, $\cdot$, $\equiv$ and $\supset$ to produce such a sentence as

$(x)\,(Fx \supset Gx) \supset (x)\,(Gx \cdot \overline{Rx})$

so also can such combinations be made with existential sentences. Thus "If some men are rational, then some men are not fools" can be symbolized as

$(\exists x)\,(Mx \cdot Rx) \supset (\exists x)\,(Mx \cdot \overline{Rx})$

In fact, we can now combine both universal and existential sentences. A sentence such as "If all men are rational, then some men are fools" can be symbolized as

$(x)\,(Mx \supset Rx) \supset (\exists x)\,(Mx \cdot Fx)$

Existence has been related rather loosely to existential quantification. But one might ask why *exists* cannot be treated as a predicate in the same way that *cries* and *laughs* are treated as predicates. "Some babies cry" is symbolized as

$$(\exists x) \ (Bx \cdot Cx)$$

and "Some students laugh" is symbolized as

$$(\exists x) \ (Sx \cdot Lx)$$

Why then can't "Some dinosaur eggs exist" be symbolized as

$$(\exists x) \ (Dx \cdot Ex)$$

where *E* stands for *exists* and *D* for *dinosaur eggs?*

It is interesting that if *exists* could be treated as a predicate, then the possibility of producing a very interesting proof for the existence of God presents itself. (The proof is not ours but belongs to Anselm [1033–1109] and to Rene Descartes [1596–1650].) The argument briefly states that God is by definition One who has every property that the world has and probably He has many more. If God lacked a property that appears in the world, He would be limited and not ominpotent. One of the properties things have in this world is that they exist. Therefore God must exist. It is not our purpose to examine the pros and cons of this argument. It is sufficient to say that both philosophers and theologians still are concerned with this argument even today. But its importance rises or falls in accordance with whether *exists* is accepted as a predicate. Can *exists* be treated as a predicate?

If one says, "Babies cry," then it also makes sense to say, "Babies do not cry." If one says, "The apartment has the property of being warm," then it is also sensible to say (even though it may be false), "The apartment does not have the property of being warm." An object may or may not have a certain property, but it still makes sense to speak of that object. A cold apartment can be criticized just as a warm one can be praised. But what can it mean to say of an object that it does not have the property of existing? I cannot point to an object and say of it that it is like that blue one over there, only it so happens that it does not exist. It is meaningful to say that I made a light object heavy or painted a blue object some other color. But can I say of something that I left all its properties but took away the one of existing? Very odd.

Another difficulty is that if *exists* is treated as a predicate, then some things must exist in a way far different from anything we can imagine. For instance, all of us know that "Pegasus does not exist" is true. But if this sentence is true, then it must be meaningful. But if it is meaningful, then *Pegasus* must refer to something. If it refers to nothing, the sentence would be meaningless.

It would be as if we said "*Xexxis* does not exist," which would be nonsense since *Xexxis* refers to nothing at all. Thus we must say that *Pegasus* does refer to something, but what it is must exist in a way different from the chairs, table, and other articles with which we are ordinarily acquainted. It must exist in some different way—in the domain of concepts, perhaps, or in some other strange domain. But what is this group of objects that exist in a way that none of us can really understand? In other words, even though we have previously spoken of contextual, i.e., mythological existence, this is by no means a clear conception.

Logicians usually argue that the only intelligible way to treat *exists* in the English language is by means of existential quantification. Thus if I say, "Men exist," I really mean "Something is a man" and symbolize it accordingly as $(\exists x)\ Mx$. Similarly, if I wish to say, "Diseases exist," I mean "There are diseases" or, in symbols $(\exists x)\ Dx$. In these instances the existential quantifier can be employed without difficulty for the simple reason that the predicates are clearly identifiable. We can give the extensions or intensions of *a man* and *diseases*. But even in this connection certain ordinary sentences are troublesome to logicians and philosophers.

1. John exists.

Probably this means no more than

2. John lives

which is an ordinary atomic sentence or even, as we shall see later, a universal affirmative sentence that does not even require the introduction of an existential quantifier. If we were not quite sure of what is meant by *lives*, we could always translate it into such clearly descriptive predicates as *has a heart beat, is breathing*, and so on. But now how are we to deal with

3. God exists.

Exists here, unlike the *exists* of (1) cannot be taken to be translatable into "God lives," where *lives* is then translatable into the clearly descriptive predicates such as *has a heart beat, is breathing, contains chlorophyll*, or any of the other kinds of predicates that might be used to define *lives*.

Therefore *exists* cannot be eliminated in favor of the word *lives*. Are we now to treat *exists* as existential quantification? If we use existential quantification for "Man exists," we mean "There is something which is a man." But can the same be said of (3), "God exists"? It seems obvious that we cannot say, "There is something which is a god." In (3), *God* is a proper name and is therefore parallel with *John* in (1), "John exists." We do not think of *God* as a predicate of something else in the way that *blue* might be a predicate of some object. As we noted in our previous discussion of extension and intension, terms become meaningful because they have either an extension or an intension or both. But even if *God* could be changed into *is a god*, that is, even if *God* were treated as a predicate, there would be a serious question about what the extension and the intension of such a predicate would be. *Is a god* is not reducible to descriptive predicates whose extensions and intensions can be given by reference to observation or some scientific test. (Although in I Kings 18:17, God is at least partly identified with fire and water.) To claim that "God exists" means "There is something which is a god," is to admit the possibility that there could be more than one god, since predicates are such that it is always theoretically possible for them to be applicable to more than one object. Thus (3) is an interesting problem still without adequate explication.

Finally, let us note the following sentences:

4. Something exists.

5. Nothing exists.

On the face of it, these are perfectly meaningful sentences. In fact, for many contemporary existentialists the prime issue of theology is why something rather than nothing exists. But regardless of how this issue is finally settled, the logician has the additional task of determining how these sentences are to be formulated in the language of quantification. Since *exists* is identified as the existential quantifier, it cannot be treated as a predicate on the same level as *blue* or *is a man* or *is larger than*. Thus (4) and (5) cannot be symbolized as:

6. $(\exists x)\ Ex$

7. $-(\exists x)\ Ex$

Furthermore, if, in spite of the difficulties previously indicated, *exists* were treated as a predicate, this would involve us in a more serious kind of issue. Then we ought to be able to say "Something does not exist," which, oddly enough, becomes symbolized as:

8. $(\exists x)\ \overline{Ex}$

that is, "There is something that does not exist," which seems to be an obvious contradiction. How can there be (exist) something that does not exist?

How then are we to treat (4) and (5)? Another existential quantifier might be substituted for *exists* to obtain for (6) and (7):

9. *(∃x) (∃x)*

10. *−(∃x) (∃x)*

But these are no longer sentences, since true or false are not applicable to them. One cannot ask whether the following are true or false: "There is an x which there is an x which," or "It is false there is an x which there is an x which." Thus (4) and (5) have the curious status of apparently being two crucial sentences for many philosophers, but they seem to defy any translation into the language of logical inference, at least a language with the kind of logical tools we have introduced.

What we shall do is to treat "Something exists" and "Nothing exists" as statements *about* a language and not statements about the world itself. In other words, "Something exists" and "Nothing exists" are sentences in a *metalanguage*, a language which refers to some other language rather than to the world itself. What they tell us is that the language being referred to does contain expressions with extensions, that is, expressions which refer to objects in the world. In brief, "Something exists" becomes "There are expressions with extensions in a given language"; "Nothing exists" becomes "There are no expressions with extensions in a given language." At least these translations will be adequate for us until someone does discover a way of showing us that (4) and (5) are really sentences about the world and can be symbolized in a language of logical inference.

Exercises

1. Discuss: *Some* sentences can be true but they need not refer to anything that exists. Consider the following:

   a) Some numbers are even. (But can we say that numbers exist in the same way as chairs?)

   b) Some possibilities are more realistic than others. (Do possibilities exist?)

   c) Some goals are worth realizing. (Do goals exist? If they do, then all of them have already been realized and therefore one cannot strive to realize a goal.)

2. Symbolize:

   a) Some metals are not conductors.

   b) If some students are extremists, then all professors are responsible.

   c) Either no students have rights or all of them have.

   d) Everything exists.

   e) Nothing exists.

   f) There exists at least one man who is faithful.

   g) If there is at least one person who is not evil, then none of us will be destroyed.

3. Discuss:

   a) God exists, but He exists in a way different from the way we do.

   b) Of course there are different levels of existence. The world of objects, including humans, is one level. The world of fictitious things, including Hamlet, is another level; and the world of angels, including Gabriel, is still another level.

SUPPLEMENTARY READINGS

Moore, G. E., "The Notion of Infinity," *Some Main Problems of Philosophy.* New York: Macmillan, 1953, Chapter 10.

Nielsen, Kai, "St. Anselm and the Ontological Argument," *Reason and Practice.* New York: Harper and Row, 1971, Chapter 14.

St. Anselm, *Proslogium,* S. N. Deane (trans). LaSalle, Ill.: Open Court Publishing Co., 1903, Chapters 2, 3, 4.

12

Syllogisms

VENN DIAGRAMS

With a knowledge of quantification, we can now begin to investigate how arguments with quantified sentences can be tested. It has been shown that the test for validity cannot be given for such sentences merely by the use of a truth-table analysis or by the formal method of proof. How then can arguments with quantified sentences be tested for validity?

Certain kinds of quantified arguments can be tested for validity by traditional methods, that is, by methods which originated with Aristotle. In this chapter, we shall show what these arguments are and how they have been analyzed traditionally. But what will also be revealed is the fact that these traditional methods are limited because they cannot be used for a great number of arguments.

There are four basic kinds of quantified sentences.

1. $(x)(Fx \supset Gx)$ — Universal Affirmative sentence, or briefly A-form.
2. $(x)(Fx \supset \overline{Gx})$ — Universal Negative sentence, or briefly E-form.
3. $(\exists x)(Fx \cdot Gx)$ — Particular Affirmative sentence, or briefly I-form.
4. $(\exists x)(Fx \cdot \overline{Gx})$ — Particular Negative sentence, or briefly O-form.

All of these forms involve two monadic predicate terms, F and G, in such a way that the group of objects described by one predicate is included or excluded from the group of objects described by the second predicate. For example, $(x)(Fx \supset Gx)$ is a symbolization of a sentence such as "All metals are conductors" or "Given any object if it is a metal, then it is a conductor." But another way of expressing this sentence is "The group of objects which are metallic, or are described as being metals, is included in the group of objects which are conductors." Similarly, $(\exists x)(Fx \cdot Gx)$ symbolizes a sentence such as "Some metals are conductors," which can also be expressed as "There is at least one of the group of metals that is included in the group of conductors." The O-form $(\exists x)(Fx \cdot \overline{Gx})$ can also be expressed as "Some metals are not conductors" or "There is at least one of the group of metals that is excluded from the class of conductors." In other words, the A, E, I, and O forms can always be represented as relating one group or some of a group to another, either by inclusion or exclusion. Thus the A, E, I, O forms can be described in the following way:

A Every F is included in G.
E Every F is excluded from G, or No F is included in G.

I   Some *F* is included in *G*.

O   Some *F* is excluded from *G*, or some *F* is not included in *G*.

F and *G*, then, can be regarded as two groups related to one another in different ways. These different relationships can be pictorialized by inscribing two overlapping circles, each one of which represents either the group of *F* or the group of *G* respectively.

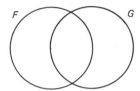

On the basis of these two overlapping circles—Venn diagrams, as they are commonly known—each of the four quantified forms can be pictorially represented. Thus the *A* form, all *F* is *G*, is completely represented as:

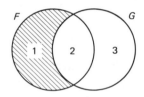

This diagram tells us that everything which is an *F* is included in *G*. Using the numbers in the diagram as aids in referring to the different parts of the circles, we can see that part 1 must be blocked out since the *A* form states that if anything is an *F*, it must be included in *G*—that is, there can be no *F*'s excluded from *G*. Thus to make sure that the information in the *A* form is truly represented, part 1 is blocked out and as a result every *F*, that is, everything in part 2, is included in *G*.

The *E* form is fully symbolized as:

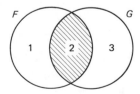

The *E* form tells us that all of *F* is totally excluded from *G*. Thus *F*'s and

G's cannot overlap. For this reason part 2 is blocked out, for it does have both F and G overlapping. To be certain that the information of the E form is truly represented, namely, that F's are excluded from G's, it is important to recognize that neither the A nor the E form claims that anything exists. The fact that sections 2 and 3 in the A form and sections 1 and 3 in the E form are not blocked out does not mean that these sections are assumed to have existent entities. An unblocked-out section simply means that perhaps it contains existent entities but perhaps it does not. On the other hand, the I and O forms, unlike those of A and E, tell us something does exist. Thus the asterisk, *, will be used as a means of indicating that there actually is at least one existent entity in a given part. The I form is fully represented as:

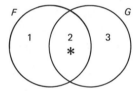

The asterisk in part 2 indicates that there exists at least one object that belongs to both group F and group G, which is the information given to us by the I form. But nothing here is blocked out, since we are not told anything else about whether or not there are any objects in part 1 or part 3; in other words, we are not told whether there are or are not F's that are not G's or G's that are not F's.

The Venn diagram for the O form follows:

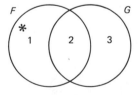

Here also the meaning of the O form is clearly depicted, namely, that there is at least one thing which is an F but is not a G. Thus the asterisk is placed in part 1, but parts 2 and 3 are left untouched since the O forms tell us nothing about whether there also exist objects in parts 2 or 3.

The diagrams for the quantified forms can now be summarized:

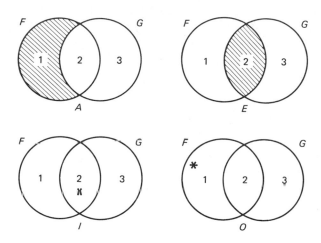

A third overlapping circle is required in order to show how these diagrams can be used to test the validity of certain special arguments called *syllogisms*. But before this is done, some interesting observations and inferences can be drawn merely by examining the above four diagrams.

First of all, the *A* diagram and the *O* diagram are such that both could not simultaneously be true or false. The *A* diagram shows part 1 to be empty, that is, blocked out. On the other hand, the *O* diagram shows part 1 to contain at least one entity. Thus if *A* is true, then *O* must be false, since *A* tells us that there can be no member in part 1 while *O* tells us that there must be a member in part 1. Similarly if *O* is true, then *A* must be false. If *A* is false, then *O* must be true; and if *O* is false, then *A* must be true. This relationship between the diagrams is called contradiction. *A* is the contradictory of *O* and conversely.

A similar analysis can be made when the *E* and *I* diagrams are compared. In the *E* form, section 2 has no members. But the *I* form says section 2 has at least one member. Thus if *E* is true, then *I* must be false and conversely. The *E* and *I* forms are also to be taken as contradictories.

Now instead of comparing diagrams, let us concentrate on them individually. The *E* diagram is taken to be a representative of "No *F* is *G*," or "The group of *F* is excluded from the group of *G*." But if the group of *F* is excluded from the group of *G*, then of course the group of *G* is excluded from the group of *F*. In other words, the circles can be read from left to right or from right to left. The diagrams for "No *F* is *G*" and "No *G* is *F*" would be exactly the same.

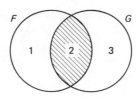

Since the diagram remains the same regardless of whether *F* and *G* are inter-changed, "No *G* is *F*" is equivalent to "No *F* is *G*."

A similar analysis can be made for the *I* diagram. If it is read from right to left, as "Some *F* is *G*" rather than as "Some *G* is *F*," the diagram remains exactly the same in terms of where the asterisk is placed. Thus "Some *F* is *G*" is equivalent to "Some *G* is *F*."

Note, however, that the terms in the *A* form and the *O* form can not be reversed. If the *A* diagram is read from left to right, the familiar *A* diagram listed above is obtained.

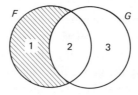

This is the diagram for "All *F* is *G*." Now let us read the diagram from right to left to obtain "All *G* is *F*." Then it would be necessary to shade out part 3 rather than part 1 as in the previous diagram, since all the *G*'s that are not *F*'s would have to be excluded. Thus the diagram would become:

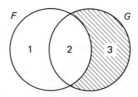

The fact that the diagram changes when *F* and *G* are reversed in "All *F* is *G*" means that "All *G* is *F*" is not equivalent to "All *F* is *G*."

In the *O* form we find the same lack of equivalency if the descriptive terms *F* and *G* are reversed. Read from left to right, the *O* form becomes diagrammed as:

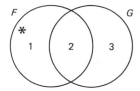

But if this is read from right to left, it is necessary to place the asterisk in part 3 and not in part 1. Since the diagram changes when the descriptive terms are reversed, "Some F is not G" is not equivalent to "Some G is not F." It becomes:

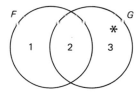

Several other less obvious inferences can be derived from an investigation of the Venn diagrams. If F were empty, that is, contained no members at all, then both parts 1 and 2 of the Venn diagram would have to be blocked out:

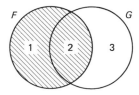

What this diagram reveals is very interesting. Since part 1 is shaded out, the diagram represents an A form. But since part 2 is also shaded out, the diagram represents an E form as well. Thus, oddly enough, if there were no F's, then "All F is G" would be true as well as "No F is G." This seems curious for it means that since, for example, there are no unicorns, then it is true to say "All unicorns are very large," and it is also true to say "No unicorns are very large." Where both groups do have existent entities, then we cannot have as true both the E and the A forms. Thus if "All metals are conductors," and there are metals, then it is false that "No metals are conductors," as can be seen in the following diagram:

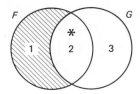

However, in a group without members, the *A* form cannot be differentiated from the *E* form. We might consider this from two points of view. From the ordinary point of view, since there are no unicorns in the universe, then one thing being said about them is just as true as any other thing being said about them; these claims can never be tested. From a formal point of view, it is easy to see why a universal sentence about nonexistent things must always be true. "All *F* is *G*" becomes, in terms of the symbols of quantification, *(x) (Fx ⊃ Gx)*. But if there are no *F*'s, then *Fx* would always be false. However, by the rules of the truth table governing ⊃, a false antecedent always makes the entire sentence true, regardless of what the consequent is. Thus *Fx ⊃ Gx* would always be true because of its false antecedent, and therefore *(x) (Fx ⊃ Gx)* must always be true since the antecedent is always false. Similarly, "No *F* is *G*" becomes, in terms of the symbols of quantification, *(x) (Fx ⊃ $\overline{Gx}$)*. But if there are no *F*'s, then *Fx* is false, and the conditional is true. Thus when there are no *F*'s both the *A* and *E* forms are true.

Exercises

1. Diagram by means of Venn diagrams:

   a) A few men are immoral.

   b) No man is an island.

   c) Everybody is unhappy about the war.

   d) Some women are some women.

   e) Each man is sacrosanct.

   f) Everything is atomic.

   g) No unicorns are happy.

   h) At least one man has told the truth.

   i) Elephants are big.

2. If there are no *F*'s but there are *G*'s, show by using Venn diagrams which of the following must be true:

a) Some *G* is not *F*.

b) Some *F* is not *G*.

c) No *F* is *G*.

d) No *G* is *F*.

e) All *F* is *G*.

f) All *G* is *F*.

3. If there are *F*'s and there are *G*'s, show which of the following must be true:

a) Some *F* is *G*.

b) Some *G* is not *F*.

c) Some *F* is not *G*.

d) All *F* is *G*.

4. Would the answers to Exercise 3 change if there are things that are *both* *F* and *G*?

SYLLOGISMS

One kind of argument has traditionally been very important. In fact, at one time some logicians believed that all arguments were reducible to this basic form. This kind of argument is called the *syllogism*. Three examples of the syllogism are listed below:

1. All women's liberationists are weirdos.
   All weirdos are hippies.
   Therefore all women's liberationists are hippies.

2. All metals are conductors.
   All conductors are magnetic.
   Therefore all metals are magnetic.

3. No students are extremists.
   Some extremists are violent persons.
   Therefore some violent persons are not students.

These three arguments have certain basic characteristics. They consist of two noncontradictory premises and a conclusion, each one of which is either an *A*, *E*, *I*, or *O* sentence, containing two and only two different descriptive terms. In each argument there are three and only three descriptive terms, each of which appears twice and only twice. Thus, for example, in (1) there are three descriptive terms: *women's liberationists, weirdos,* and *hippies. Women's liberationists* appears in the first premise and in the conclusion. *Weirdos* appears in the first and second premises. *Hippies* appears in the second premise and the conclusion. Similar analyses can be made for the descriptive terms of (2) and (3). Any argument is a syllogism if it has these two characteristics, namely, if it consists of *A, E, I,* or *O* sentences as the two premises and the conclusion, and contains three descriptive terms, each of which appears twice and only twice.

By using a modification of the Venn diagrams, we can easily determine the validity of such syllogistic arguments. This modification introduces a third circle which overlaps the other two. The resultant diagram enables us to show the validity of syllogisms:

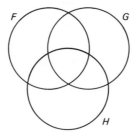

Another circle, *H,* is added in order to account for the third descriptive term introduced in the syllogism, whereas the original Venn diagram with its two circles depicted two and only two descriptive terms. Again all of this can be made clear by a few examples. Let us then see how the three-circle diagram is used in order to test the validity of (1):

All women's liberationists are weirdos.
All weirdos are hippies.
Therefore all women's liberationists are hippies.

First a three-circle diagram is drawn and each part is numbered.

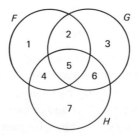

Each letter of the diagram stands for one specific descriptive term of the argument. Thus F stands for *women's liberationists*; G for *weirdos* and H for *hippies*. The next step is the most important one.

Take each premise and draw into the three-circle diagram the particular Venn diagram that the premise represents. Thus the first premise is "All women's liberationists are weirdos" or, rather, "All F is G." Dealing now strictly with the F and G circles as if no third circle were present, we introduce the particular shading of the Universal Affirmative, since this is what the first premise is.

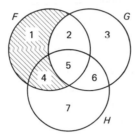

We shade out parts 1 and 4, as we would if we only had the two circles F and G.

Now turn to the second premise, "All weirdos are hippies" or, using the letters, "All G are H." Again dealing with the G and H circles as if no other circle were present, we proceed to shade in the information of this Universal Affirmative premise. The diagram now becomes:

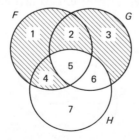

Parts 2 and 3 are shaded out as they would be if there were only two circles, G and H.

Once the two premises have been diagrammed upon the three circles, *nothing more is to be added to the circles*. This is very important. We do not go on to diagram the conclusion as well as the premises. On the contrary, *if the argument is valid, then diagramming the two premises should automatically present us with the conclusion diagrammed as well.* Nor is it difficult to see why the conclusion must not be drawn in.

In the truth-table analysis of validity, it was made clear that what was meant by validity was that, given the premises, the conclusion could be shown to follow necessarily. The conclusion was already implicit, so to speak, in the premises. The truth-table analysis merely made this explicit. Similarly, once the premises of an argument have been drawn into the Venn diagrams, then if the conclusion is indeed implicit in the premises—i.e., if the argument is valid—it should automatically appear. (If the conclusion were drawn in, then of course *every* argument would turn out to be valid.) The conclusion in (1) is "All women's liberationists are hippies," or "All *F* are *H*." What we do is ask whether by drawing in both premises we have automatically also drawn in the conclusion. Checking the final three-circle diagram above, we ask whether "All *F* are *H*" also appears within it. Indeed it does. Part 4 has been shaded out. But all that is left of circle *F*, namely part 5, is still in *H*. "All *F* are *H*" has been automatically inscribed when the premises were inscribed. Hence (1) is valid.

We can now summarize how we test the validity of a syllogism. Using the three-circle diagram, draw in the premises. If the conclusion also is shown to be drawn in, then and only then is the syllogism valid. Using this rule, analyze example 3:

No students are extremists.
Some extremists are violent persons.
Therefore some violent persons are not students.

Again begin by drawing a three-circle diagram with its parts numbered:

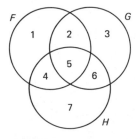

Then arbitrarily take *F* to stand for *students, G* for *extremists,* and *H* for *violent persons.* On the basis of the first premise, "No students are extremists," shade out parts 2 and 5 to obtain:

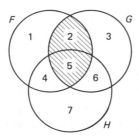

Now turn to the second premise, "Some extremists are violent persons," or "Some *G* are *H*." This premise tells us that an asterisk, *, is to be placed in the section in which *G* and *II* overlap, namely in parts 5 and 6. But since part 5 has already been shaded out by the first premise, the asterisk can only be placed in part 6. Thus the three-circle diagram becomes:

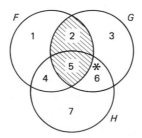

We now ask whether the conclusion "Some violent persons are not students," or "Some *H* are not *F*," has automatically been inscribed in the circles. For this to occur, an asterisk must appear in either part 6 or 7, since the conclusion is an *O* form. An asterisk does appear in part 6. Therefore the argument is valid.

It is possible to begin the diagramming with any premise. Thus in the above example the second premise, "Some extremists are violent persons," could be diagrammed first. The asterisk would be placed on the line between 5 and 6. To diagram the first premise the asterisk would be moved from the line between 5 and 6 to 6. To avoid this small inconvenience it is advisable to begin the diagramming with the universal premise.

Finally, let us examine the validity of the following:

Some children are fast readers.
Some fast readers are slow thinkers.
Therefore some children are slow thinkers.

This becomes symbolized as:

Some *F* are *G*.
Some *G* are *H*.
Therefore some *F* are *H*,

where *F* stands for *children*, *G* for *fast readers* and *H* for *slow thinkers*. (Note that the terms of the syllogism need not consist of single words. *Fast readers* and *slow thinkers* can serve as terms just as *men* and *mortal* can.)

Now draw the circles, and draw in the first premise, "Some *F* are *G*."

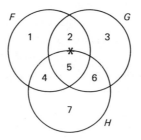

Note carefully where the asterisk is placed. It is placed on the line between parts 2 and 5. Let us recall what information is given in the *I* form. It tells us that there is *at least* one *F* that is *G*. Thus it could be that there is only one existent entity in the overlapping area—parts 2 and 5—of *F* and *G*. This means that this existent entity could be solely in part 2 or it could be solely in part 5 or, if there is more than one entity, there could be entities in both part 2 and part 5. In order to account for all these possibilities, we place the asterisk directly on the line between parts 2 and 5. This tells us explicitly that one or more entities are somewhere in parts 2 and 5, but exactly where is not specified. Part 2 might have an entity, but not part 5; part 5 might have an entity, but not part 2; or both parts 5 and 2 might contain entities.

Now draw in the second premise, "Some *G* are *H*."

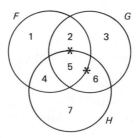

Again place the asterisk directly on the line between parts 5 and 6 since the premise tells us there is at least one entity present in parts 5 and 6, but we are not told exactly where it might be located or whether there is more than one located in both parts. But now has the conclusion "Some F are H" automatically been inscribed in the three circles?

We might think that it has, since "Some F are H" requires an asterisk somewhere within parts 4 and 5 and there are asterisks on the perimeters of part 5. But the fact that the asterisks are on perimeters means that there *might* be an existent entity in part 5 and not that there actually is one. Part 5 could be empty if there is only one entity within parts 2 and 5 and it is only in part 2, and if there is only one entity within parts 5 and 6 and it is only in part 6. Thus part 5 *could* be empty. And since it could be empty, this means that the conclusion "Some F are H" is *not* automatically inscribed once we have inscribed the two premises, and therefore the argument is invalid.

Now let us consider the following example:

All students are bright.
John is a student.
Therefore John is bright.

Is this a syllogism? On first examination it is not, since the second premise, "John is a student," and the conclusion, "John is bright," are not either A, E, I, or O sentences. Although some problems arise in connection with proper names, and we shall deal with them later, for our purpose sentences in the syllogism such as "John is a student" and "John is bright" will be treated as A forms. What will be meant by "John is a student" is that John is a whole class in himself and this class which consists solely of John is included in the class of students. A similar analysis can be made for "John is bright." In other words, "John is a student" will mean "Any person who is John is a student"; "John is bright" will mean "Any person who is John is bright." Thus every sentence of the form "H is F" where H is a proper name (or any expression that refers to a single individual, e.g., *that man*) and F is a predicate is to be treated as in the form "All H is F."

Once proper names can be translated into A, E, I, or O forms, the validity of the above argument is easily determined. "All students are bright" becomes:

All F is G.

"John is a student" becomes:

All H is F.

"John is bright" becomes:

All *H* is *G*.

We then test by Venn diagrams. First, the first premise is drawn in:

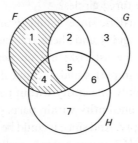

Then the second premise is drawn in:

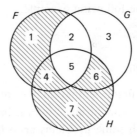

Then is "All *H* is *G*" automatically drawn in? Yes. All that is left of the *H* circle is in *G*. Thus the argument is valid.

Also note the following argument:

All men are rational.
All rational beings are well adjusted.
Therefore some men are well adjusted.

When this argument is diagrammed, it turns out to be invalid. Treating *men* as *F, rational being* as *G,* and *well-adjusted (persons)* as *H,* we obtain:

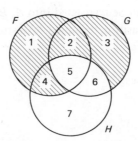

The conclusion "Some men are well adjusted" is not diagrammed, and therefore the argument is not valid. But it is *almost* valid. If the premise "There are men" were added, then 5 would contain an asterisk, and this would mean "Some men are well adjusted" was diagrammed. Thus if we are permitted to make a slight modification in the syllogistic form and add a third premise that states that there are objects referred to by *men*, then the argument is valid. But without the third premise, the argument is invalid.

It is important to reiterate a previous point; if a conclusion is indeed found to follow logically from a given set of premises—that is, if an argument is found to be valid—this does not necessarily mean that the conclusion is true. A distinction must be made between the validity and the soundness of an argument. When we say an argument is valid, we mean that the premises are so related to the conclusion that the conclusion must follow from the premises even if the premises are false. Thus the following is valid:

> All monkeys are rational beings.
> All rational beings are warmongers.
> Therefore all monkeys are warmongers.

In this instance the premises as well as the conclusion are false. Yet if this argument were tested by Venn diagrams, it would prove to be valid. Thus either one or both premises of valid arguments can be false with either a true or false conclusion. However, if an argument is valid and its premises are true, then the conclusion also must be true. And this kind of argument—one that is valid and contains true premises—is what is often called *sound*. Ideally, a sound argument is what we should always strive to attain. But it is important not to confuse validity with soundness.

Exercises

1. Test for validity by Venn diagrams.

   a) No Democrats are liberal.
      Every liberal is a Republican.
      Therefore no Democrats are Republicans.

   b) Some McCarthyites are disillusioned.
      Some Republicans are disillusioned.
      Therefore some McCarthyites are Republicans.

   c) Some men are not rational.
      Other men are kind.
      Therefore some who are kind are not rational.

d) If everyone is entitled to vote and everyone is capable of reading, then whoever is entitled to vote is capable of reading.

e) Some men are strong.
John is not strong.
Therefore John is not a man.

f) Only x is y.
Some x is z.
Therefore some z is y.

2. Show whether or not Venn-diagram techniques can be applied to test the validity of the following:

a) All metals are conductors.
There are no conductors.
Therefore all conductors are metals.

b) Metals as well as everything else exist.
Automobiles exist.
Therefore unicorns exist.
(*Hint*: Be prepared to place an asterisk outside the circles.)

c) No metals exist.
Therefore all metals are conductors.

IMPLICIT SYLLOGISMS

If an argument can be formed into a syllogism, it can be tested by Venn diagrams to show validity or lack of validity. Sometimes an argument is not explicitly a syllogism but is implicitly a syllogism. Note the following:

Every bright child passes the exams.
Therefore all his children pass exams.

At first glance this does not seem to be a syllogistic argument, since only one premise is used. But actually it does contain an implicit premise, namely, "All his children are bright." This premise, added to the one explicitly given, permits the use of the Venn-diagram method. Such partial syllogisms are called *enthymemes,* and they are most frequently used by those who would prefer to leave out a part of the argument which, when made explicit, might show the argument to be unsound. Thus, for example, one might simply say, "Democrats favor intensive investigation of the Watergate affair. Therefore Democrats are out to destroy the president." This is an abbreviated kind of argument which might be more palatable to some people than the fully explicit argument that would require the acceptance of the truth of the dubious premise "All who favor intensive investigation of the Watergate affair are out to destroy the president." Thus enthymemes are occasionally used to conceal a premise which might not be acceptable if made explicit.

Sometimes the enthymeme is expressed in one word. Imagine an irate, conservative father who sees his daughter going out with a guitar-strumming, long-haired hippie, and he (the father) says:

SHIT!

The father's colorful remark might be interpreted as an argument of the following sort:

Any girl who goes out with a nut such as this must have her head examined.

My little Gloria is going out with a nut such as this.

Therefore my little girl, Gloria, must have her head examined.

This argument can then be treated as the syllogism:

All A is B.

All B is C.

Therefore all A is C.

Where A stands for "girl who goes out with a nut such as this," B for "one who must have her head examined," and C for "my little girl, Gloria." (Those of you who may be a bit upset by this argument must recognize that a Venn-diagram analysis does show it to be valid.)

Another form of implicit syllogism is called a *sorites*, and is no more than a series of syllogisms telescoped together. The following is a sorites:

All children are emotional.

All those who are emotional are deficient in reason.

All those who are deficient in reason are untrustworthy.

Therefore all children are untrustworthy.

At first glance this argument does not seem to be a syllogism since it consists of three, rather than two, premises. But if we analyze it carefully, we find that two syllogisms have been telescoped here. If we take the first two premises and ask what conclusion could be drawn from them to present a valid syllogism, we would be required to add the conclusion "All children are deficient in reason." This conclusion is not given. But it is implicit in the first two premises. Then this conclusion is used as a premise and combined with the third premise, "All those who are deficient in reason are untrustworthy," from which the given conclusion "Therefore all children are untrustworthy" is inferred. In order to check the validity of a sorites it is necessary to extract all the implicit syllogisms and then test each one individually. If all the syllogisms are valid, then the sorites is valid. But if any one is invalid, then the sorites as a whole is invalid.

Exercises

1. Test by Venn diagrams:
   a) All metals are conductors.
      All conductors are magnetic.
      All magnetic objects are dangerous.
      Therefore all metals are dangerous.
   b) Hippies are homosexual.
      Therefore they are security risks.
   c) Hippies are not good clean-cut Americans.
      Therefore let us arrest them.
   d) Some of her friends wore mini skirts.
      Therefore some of her friends must be real swingers.
2. Which of the above arguments are sound?
3. Interpret the following as possible implicit syllogistic arguments. Then test for validity:
   a) A college student says lecherously to his girlfriend while they are watching a particularly sexy movie: "Now that's a mature and enlightened movie." (*Hint*: Is he really interested in evaluating the movie, or does he have some ulterior motive for equating a *sexy movie* with *enlightened* attitudes?)
   b) A big cigarette ad shows a woman smoking a Chesterfield and getting ready to kiss a tall, dark, handsome, muscular, rich-looking man.
4. Think of some radio, television, and billboard advertisements that could be implicit syllogisms.

THE DISTRIBUTION METHOD

A traditional alternative to the Venn diagrams is the use of what is usually known as the *Distribution Method*.

This method is derived from the fact that the descriptive terms of the syllogism sometimes refer to everything as having a certain property and sometimes they do not. Perhaps the best way to understand this is with a few examples. Consider the sentence "All Americans are industrious." What this sentence says is that every American—fat, short, tall, skinny, sexy, oafish—every American is industrious. Thus reference is being made to anybody to whom the property *American* can be attributed. On the other hand, this is not the case with *industrious*. No reference is being made to every industrious person. Nothing is being said about industrious Russian people or about any other industrious non-American. Thus the term *American* is taken to be *distributed*, that is, the term is taken to apply to every American, while *industrious* is *undistributed*, that is, it does not apply to every industrious person.

Now consider an *E* form, "No Americans are industrious." This sentence tells us that every American—regardless of whether he is fat, short, tall, skinny, sexy, or oafish—every American is excluded from being industrious. Similarly, the *E* form tells us that every industrious person—regardless of whether he is fat, short, tall, skinny, sexy, or oafish—every industrious person is excluded from being an American. Thus in the *E* form *both* descriptive terms are distributed.

In the *I* form both terms are undistributed, since neither one is intended as a reference to all of a certain group. "Some Americans are industrious" does not mean that if anyone is an American, then he is industrious. Perhaps all skinny ones are, but perhaps not all fat ones are. Thus *Americans* is undistributed. Similarly, *industrious* is undistributed since no mention is being made of all industrious persons. Some Americans are being designated as industrious; but this does not refer to Russians or Chinese people as industrious.

Finally, in the *O* form, some *F* is not *G*, *F* is undistributed and *G* is distributed. Again the reason for this is that in *F* no mention is being made of everyone who has *F*. If our example is "Some Americans are not industrious," obviously no mention is made of everyone who happens to be an American. But *industrious* is distributed since we are saying that whatever group happens to be industrious—namely, those who are industrious and thrifty, or industrious and skinny and sexy, or industrious and skinny and sexy and ugly, and so on—that group automatically excludes some number of Americans. The following chart gives us the various distributions of terms in the *A*, *E*, *I*, and *O* forms.

A   All *F* is *G*; *F* distributed, *G* undistributed.
E   No *F* is *G*; *F* distributed, *G* distributed.

I   Some *F* is *G*; *F* undistributed, *G* undistributed.

O   Some *F* is not *G*; *F* undistributed, *G* distributed.

With this introduction of distributed and undistributed terms, we can construct rules by means of which any syllogistic form with descriptive terms such as *F* and *G* and *H*, which are taken to designate specific properties, can be tested. If such a syllogism does not violate any of the following rules, it is valid; otherwise it is invalid:

1. If a term is distributed in the conclusion, then it must be distributed in the premises.

2. The term that appears in both premises (*The Middle Term*, as it is usually called) must be distributed at least once.

3. At least one premise must be affirmative, i.e., *A* or *I*.

4. If a premise is negative, i.e., *E* or *O*, then the conclusion must be negative.

5. If the premises are both affirmative, then the conclusion cannot be negative.

6. If the premises are both universals, i.e., *A* or *E*, then the conclusion cannot be particular, i.e., cannot be *I* or *O*.

Now let us test a few syllogistic forms for validity by using these rules.

All *F* is *G*.
All *H* is *G*.
Therefore all *F* is *H*.

By checking the rules for distribution, we can easily determine why this syllogistic form is invalid. Both premises are universal sentences and the Middle Term *G* is undistributed in both instances. Rule 2 tells us that the syllogistic form is invalid.

Now consider the following:

Some *F* is *G*.
All *G* is *H*.
Therefore some *F* is not *H*.

Here both premises are affirmative, but the conclusion is negative. This violates Rule 5 and therefore this syllogism is invalid. The argument is also shown to be invalid by the fact that *H* is distributed in the conclusion but not in the premise. This is a violation of Rule 1.

Finally, consider this argument:

No Y is X.
No X is Z.
Therefore some Y is Z.

Here three rules are violated; the violation of any one of them would have been sufficient to make the argument invalid. Rule 3 states that at least one premise must be affirmative. But in this argument neither premise is affirmative. Rule 4 states that if a premise is negative, then the conclusion must also be negative. But in this argument the premises are negative while the conclusion is affirmative. Finally, Rule 6 states that if the premises are both universals, then the conclusion cannot be particular. But here the premises are both universal negatives while the conclusion is a particular affirmative.

The Venn diagrams and the distribution rules are the best-known rules for testing certain kinds of arguments. But as we shall shortly see, some arguments cannot be handled by the diagrams or by the rules of distribution. In fact, if we pursued the matter in greater detail we would find that the Venn diagrams and the distribution rules are not altogether free of problems even in their application to elementary syllogistic arguments.[1]

Exercise

Use distribution rules to test the validity of the arguments on pp. 193–194, 196.

SUPPLEMENTARY READINGS

Mill, J. S., "Of Reasoning," *A System of Logic: Ratiocinative and Inductive*, Vol. I, Ninth Edition. London: Longmans, Green, Reader, and Dyer, 1875, Chapters 1, 2, and 3.

Oliver, J. W., "Formal Fallacies and other Invalid Arguments," *Mind*, 76 (1967), 463–478.

Russell, B., "Aristotle's Logic," *A History of Western Philosophy*. New York: Simon and Schuster, 1945, Part II, Chapter 22.

---

1. J. W. Oliver, "Formal Fallacies and Other Invalid Arguments," *Mind*, 76 (1967), 463–478.

13

The Canonical Method of Validation

SUBSTITUTIONAL VALIDITY AND EQUIVALENCE

This chapter is perhaps the most difficult portion of the book. The sections on truth tables are by no means child's play, but at least they are somewhat tolerable because the symbolism in them is held down to a minimum. Now, unfortunately, if we are to realize our aim of giving the reader some insight into contemporary logic, a more involved concern with symbolic techniques is required. However, the reader who accepts the intellectual challenge of this section will, we hope, find the result rewarding.

The techniques of the Venn diagrams and the Distribution Method are satisfactory for some arguments that have the special syllogistic form or are in some way translatable into the syllogistic form. But not all arguments have the syllogistic form. How, for example, would the Venn diagrams or the Distribution Method be employed to test the validity of the following?

All teachers are critical thinkers.

If no critical thinker is a conscientious objector, then no extremist is a critical thinker.

Therefore if some extremists are teachers, then some critical thinkers are conscientious objectors.

Perhaps with a bit of ingenuity we might design diagrams that could be used to check the validity of this argument. But it would be a very difficult task. Furthermore, we have a general method of validation that will account for this argument as well as the ordinary syllogistic ones. We turn now to an explanation of this new technique, the Canonical Method of Validation introduced by W. V. Quine.[1]

The new Method will deal with quantified sentences insofar as they can be symbolized by the sentential functions such as Fx, Gx introduced earlier. To refresh our memories, the A, E, I, and O forms are symbolized in the following way:

A $\quad$ $(x)\ (Fx \supset Gx)$

E $\quad$ $(x)\ (Fx \supset \overline{Gx})$

I $\quad$ $(\exists x)\ (Fx \cdot Gx)$

O $\quad$ $(\exists x)\ (Fx \cdot \overline{Gx})$

For the sake of easy reference, let us use certain labels. First, any such forms

---

1. W. V. Quine, *Methods of Logic*, Third Edition. New York: Holt, Rinehart, and Winston, 1972. See also the Second Edition.

as (x) $(Fx \supset Gx)$ or $(\exists x)$ $(Fx \cdot Gx)$ or Fx, or $Fx \vee Gx$, and the like, are also to be called formulas. Even such a complicated form as (x) $(Fx \supset Gx)$ $\vee$ $(\exists x)$ $(Fx \cdot Gx)$ is a formula. On the other hand, there are some formulas which lack quantifiers in front of them. These are called *free* formulas. Thus Fx is a free formula; so is $Fx \vee Gx$. But $(\exists x)$ $(Fx \cdot Gx)$ is a *bound* formula, since every x in $Fx \cdot Gx$ is under the control of $(\exists x)$. In other words, every formula with an individual variable which is not controlled or under the scope of a quantifier is a free formula. Otherwise the formula is bound.

Sometimes it becomes necessary to refer to a part of a bound formula and to treat it separately. In such instances the part is referred to as a formula in its own right and also can be regarded in itself as free or bound, whatever the case may be. Thus in (x) $(Fx \supset Gx)$, $Fx \supset Gx$ is the free part of the formula, whereas in (x) $(\exists x)$ $(Fx \supset Gx)$, the part $(\exists x)$ $(Fx \supset Gx)$ is itself the bound part, which has $Fx \supset Gx$ as a free part.

We should not further that the various rules for $\supset$, $\cdot$, $^-$, $\vee$ and $\equiv$ given previously are applicable here as well. The only difference is that whereas previously these expressions were used with sentential variables such as p, q, and r, here they shall be used with either free or bound formulas or with free parts of formulas. Thus, for example, if $p \supset q$ is equivalent, either by use of the table of logically valid forms or by a truth-table analysis, to $\bar{p} \vee q$, then it can be said that $Fx \supset Gx$, whether it appears as a free formula or as a free part of a formula, is also equivalent to $\overline{Fx} \vee Gx$ for the same reasons. Similarly, if $p \cdot \bar{q}$ is equivalent by truth-table analysis to $-(p \supset q)$, then it can also be asserted that $Fx \cdot \overline{Gx}$ is equivalent to $-(Fx \supset Gx)$.

It follows from this that whenever free formulas or free parts of formulas are our concern, the various sentential functions can be treated as the truth-functional symbols, p, q, r, s. Thus if the question arises whether $Fx \supset Gx$ is equivalent to $\overline{Gx} \supset \overline{Fx}$, the answer is affirmative since $Fx \supset Gx$ is treated as if it were $p \supset q$. Then by the rule of Transposition (valid form 18 in the list of valid forms), $p \supset q$ equals $\bar{q} \supset \bar{p}$; hence $Fx \supset Gx$ is equivalent to $\overline{Gx} \supset \overline{Fx}$. Free parts of formulas are treated in a similar way. Thus (x) $(Fx \supset Gx)$ is equivalent to (x) $(\overline{Gx} \supset \overline{Fx})$ because the free part $Fx \supset Gx$ is merely replaced by its equivalent $\overline{Gx} \supset \overline{Fx}$.

Similarly, we can substitute bound formulas for p and q and still retain the original equivalence. Thus $(\exists x)Fx \supset (\exists x)Gx$ is equivalent to $-(\exists x)Fx \vee (\exists x)Gx$ again because $p \supset q$ is equivalent to $\bar{p} \vee q$, and we have simply made appropriate substitutions for p and for q. Substitutions can, of course, be made not only in logically equivalent formulas but also in logically valid ones. Thus since form 1 of the logically valid forms tells us that

$$[(p \supset q) \cdot p] \supset q$$

is valid, then the following is also valid:

$$\{[(x)Fx \supset (\exists x)Gx] \cdot (x)Fx\} \supset (\exists x)Gx$$

since we have merely substituted $(x)Fx$ for p and $(\exists x)Gx$ for q.

Also, it was noted earlier that substitution in a contradictory formula retained the contradiction. Thus by truth-table analysis it can be determined that $-\{[(p \supset q) \cdot p] \supset q\}$ will always give us F in the final column of the truth table. Hence whatever is substituted for p or for q in this formula will produce a contradictory formula. If $(\exists x)Fx$ is substituted for p and $(x)(Gx \supset Rx)$ for q, then we will obtain

$$\{[(\exists x)Fx \supset (x)(Gx \supset Rx)] \cdot (\exists x)Fx\} \supset (x)(Gx \supset Rx)$$

This formula is contradictory. Why? Simply because it is a substitution instance of another formula that could be shown to be a contradiction by truth-table analysis. Thus substitution instances of valid truth-functional formulas are also valid, even if they contain quantifiers. Similarly, substitution instances of contradictory truth-functional formulas are also contradictory even if they contain quantifiers. But we must remember that such substitution is not allowable with merely consistent truth-functional formulas. By truth-table analysis, $p \cdot q$ is consistent. But if $- (\exists x)Fx$ is substituted for p, and $(\exists x)Fx$ is substituted for q, we get a contradiction. Consistency is not necessarily retained when substitution occurs in consistent formulas. Finally, care must be taken that the same formula is substituted for the same letter throughout.

By using the substitution rules we have a way of testing for the validity of certain kinds of arguments containing quantified sentences. Given any such argument we should always ask: Is this argument a substitution instance of some formula that is valid by virtue of a truth-value analysis? If the answer is affirmative, then the argument is valid.

Thus at this initial point in the discussion of quantification, nothing really new has been introduced. No matter how complicated an argument with quantifiers may look, no one really needs to be concerned so long as it can be shown that the argument is no more than a substitution instance of an argument which has been proved valid or contradictory strictly by the use of the list of valid and equivalent forms, or by truth-table analysis. However—and this is where the problem lies—if the argument is not a substitution instance of a valid form, it does not necessarily follow that the argument is invalid. Examine the example given at the beginning of this chapter:

All teachers are critical thinkers.

If no critical thinker is a conscientious objector, then no extremist is a critical thinker.

Therefore, if some extremists are teachers, then some critical thinkers are conscientious objectors.

This is not a substitution instance of any of the logically valid forms; nor is there a way of showing it to be a substitution instance of some other form that is valid by truth-value analysis. Yet it is indeed valid. The Canonical Method, which will be explicated in the following pages, is designed primarily to test for the validity of those arguments which cannot be shown to be valid by any procedures dealt with previously.

Exercises

1. What is the difference between a bound and a free formula? Give an example of each.

2. Could there be a free formula that contains bound formulas? Give an example.

3. Using the truth tables and/or the list of valid formulas, show that the following are valid.

   a) $[(x) (Fx \supset Hx) \cdot (\exists x)Gx] \supset (x) (Fx \supset Hx)$

   b) $[-(x) (Fx \supset Hx) \supset (\exists x) (Gx \cdot Rx)] \supset [-(\exists x) (Gx \cdot Rx) \supset (x)(Fx \supset Hx)]$

   c) $(x) [Fx \supset (Gx \cdot Hx)] \equiv (x) [(Fx \supset Gx) \cdot (Fx \supset Hx)]$

4. The following are formal proofs of arguments. Fill out the right-hand side of each line by stating which valid forms and other lines were used to derive it:

   Part I

   1) $(\exists x) (Fx \cdot Gx) \supset [(x) Fx \supset - (\exists x) (Fx \cdot Gx)]$　　　　Premise

   2) $(\exists x) (Fx \cdot Gx) \equiv (x) Fx$　　Premise/$\therefore$.　$- (\exists x) (Fx \cdot Gx) \cdot - (x)Fx$

   3) $(\exists x) (Fx \cdot Gx) \supset [-- (\exists x) (Fx \cdot Gx) \supset - (x) Fx]$

   4) $(\exists x) (Fx \cdot Gx) \supset [(\exists x) (Fx \cdot Gx) \supset - (x) Fx]$

   5) $[(\exists x) (Fx \cdot Gx) \cdot (\exists x) (Fx \cdot Gx)] \supset - (x) Fx$

   6) $(\exists x) (Fx \cdot Gx) \supset - (x) Fx$

   7) $-(\exists x) (Fx \cdot Fx) \vee - (x)Fx$

8) $- \left[(\exists x) (Fx \cdot Gx) \cdot (x) Fx \right]$

9) $\left[(\exists x) (Fx \cdot Gx) \cdot (x) Fx \right] \vee \left[- (\exists x) (Fx \cdot Gx) \cdot - (x) Fx \right]$

10) $- (\exists x) (Fx \cdot Gx) \cdot - (x) Fx$

Part 2

1) $\left[(\exists x) Rx \vee - (x) Gx \right] \supset \left[(\exists x) Sx \cdot - (x) Hx \right]$ Premise

2) $- (\exists x) Sx$ Premise/ $\therefore$ $(x) Gx$

3) $- (\exists x) Sx \vee (x) Hx$

4) $- \left[(\exists x) Sx \cdot - (x) Hx \right]$

5) $- \left[(\exists x) Rx \vee - (x) Gx \right]$

6) $- (\exists x) Rx \cdot (x) Gx$

7) $(x) Gx \cdot - (\exists x) Rx$

8) $(x) Gx$

CONVERSION AND DISTRIBUTION OF QUANTIFIERS

We have used both existential and universal quantifiers. However, it is always possible to eliminate one in favor of the other. Even in ordinary language, universally quantified sentences are frequently replaceable by existentially quantified ones. Thus the obviously true sentence "All men are perfect" surely means the same as "It is false that there is a man who is not perfect"; and "Some students are great lovers" is taken to mean the same as "It is false that no students are great lovers." In each of these examples a universal and an existential quantifier is replaced by an existential and a universal quantifier respectively. One quantifier can be converted into another simply by proceeding with the following rule:

To change one quantifier into another, first change the signs on both sides of the quantifier to their opposites. Then change the quantifier sign itself to the opposite quantifier sign. A few examples will make this rule clear. Consider the formula $(\exists x) \overline{Fx}$. Following the rule, first change the signs on both sides of the quantifier; that is, $(\exists x)$ becomes $-(\exists x)-$. The right-hand negation sign is placed on top of $\overline{Fx}$; thus the formula is converted to $-(\exists x)\overline{\overline{Fx}}$.

Then change the quantifier itself to its opposite, namely, (x):

$$- (x) \overline{\overline{Fx}}$$

Since two negation signs cancel one another out, the final transformation is

$$- (x) Fx$$

Thus $(\exists x)\overline{Fx}$ is equivalent to $- (x)Fx$.

Let us try to change $(x)(Fx \supset Gx)$ into a form that has an existential quantifier instead of a universal one. Following the rule, first change the signs on both sides of the quantifier to their opposites. Thus $(x)(Fx \supset Gx)$ becomes $- (x) - (Fx \supset Gx)$. The next part of the rule tells us to replace the quantifier by its opposite, and hence we obtain

$$- (\exists x) - (Fx \supset Gx)$$

Thus $(x)(Fx \supset Gx)$ is equivalent to $- (\exists x) - (Fx \supset Gx)$. Since truth-table analysis tells us that $- (p \supset q)$ is equivalent to $p \cdot \overline{q}$, we can, if we so desire, change $- (Fx \supset Gx)$ to $Fx \cdot \overline{Gx}$ converting $- (\exists x) - (Fx \supset Gx)$ into $- (\exists x)(Fx \cdot \overline{Gx})$. For purposes of using the Canonical Method, this last change becomes very important, as we shall soon see.

The results concerning quantifier conversion can be summarized as follows:

1. (x) is equivalent to $- (\exists x) -$.

2. $- (x)$ is equivalent to $(\exists X) -$.

3. $- (x) -$ is equivalent to $(\exists x)$.

4. $(x) -$ is equivalent to $- (\exists x)$.

The reader might check these equivalences to see how each one follows the rule for quantifier conversion.

Along with quantifier conversion we should also be acquainted with quantifier distribution. If I say, "Something is either red or green," I am saying the same as "Something is red or something is green." In other words, I can always distribute the existential quantifier if I have only alternation signs. Thus $(\exists x)(Fx \lor Gx)$ is equivalent to $(\exists x)Fx \lor (\exists x)Gx$. The existential quantifier can always be distributed over the free part that it controls, in this case $Fx \lor Gx$, if the only main sign is alternation. Nor does it matter how many alternation signs are involved; $(\exists x)(Fx \lor Gx \lor Hx \lor etc.)$ would still be distributed into $(\exists x)Fx \lor (\exists x)Gx \lor (\exists x)Hx \lor etc.$ On the other hand, if I say, "Something is green and large," it is not the same as saying "Something is green and something is large," since something can be green and something can be large, but it does not follow that therefore something is both green and large. Thus we can assert $(\exists x)(Fx \cdot Gx) \supset [(\exists x)Fx \cdot (\exists x)Gx]$, but not the converse.

Universal quantifiers can also be distributed under certain conditions. "Everything is red and everything is large" means the same as "Everything is red and large." In other words, the following equivalence holds:

$$(x)(Fx \cdot Gx) \equiv \left[(x)Fx \cdot (x)Gx\right]$$

This kind of distribution of universal quantifiers occurs no matter how many conjunctions are used. Thus $(x)(Fx \cdot Gx \cdot Hx$ etc.$)$ is equivalent to $(x)Fx \cdot (x)Gx \cdot (x)Hx \cdot$ etc. On the other hand, where the free formula has an alternation sign as its main sign, then the distribution of quantifiers is modified. I can say

$$\left[(x)Fx \vee (x)Gx\right] \supset (x)(Fx \vee Gx)$$

but the antecedent is not equivalent to the consequent; $(x)(Fx \vee Gx)$ does not imply $(x)Fx \vee (x)Gx$. A simple example illustrates this point. If "Everything in this box is green or everything is red," then it does indeed follow that "Everything in the box is either red or green." But if "Everything in this box is either red or green," it does not follow that "Everything in it is red or everything in it is green." There can be both red and green objects in the box.

Thus note the two conditional and the two equivalent formulas involving the distribution of quantifiers:

1. $(\exists x)(Fx \vee Gx) \equiv \left[(\exists x)Fx \vee (\exists x)Gx\right]$
2. $(\exists x)(Fx \cdot Gx) \supset \left[(\exists x)Fx \cdot (\exists x)Gx\right]$
3. $(x)(Fx \cdot Gx) \equiv \left[(x)Fx \cdot (x)Gx\right]$
4. $\left[(x)Fx \vee (x)Gx\right] \supset (x)(Fx \vee Gx)$

And just as in the case of the other valid forms, the rules of substitution hold here as well. Thus since (2) is valid, so are all the following:

$$(\exists x)(\overline{Fx} \cdot Gx) \supset \left[(\exists x)\overline{Fx} \cdot (\exists x)Gx\right]$$
$$(\exists x)\left[Fx \cdot (Gx \vee Rx)\right] \supset \left[(\exists x)Fx \cdot (\exists x)(Gx \vee Rx)\right]$$

In each of these cases, substitutions for the original valid forms have been made.

Similarly, by substituting $Fx \supset Rx$ for Gx in (3), the following is valid:

$$(x)\left[Fx \cdot (Fx \supset Rx)\right] \equiv \left[(x)Fx \cdot (x)(Fx \supset Rx)\right]$$

Two points must be carefully noted regarding quantifiers which are preceded by negation signs. First, negative quantifiers are never distributed. Thus $- (x)(Fx \cdot Gx)$ is not distributed as $- (x)Fx \cdot - (x)Gx$. The negative sign extends over the entire formula so that technically it is not possible to speak of a negative quantifier. What we do is treat the quantifier itself and then the negative sign simply negates whatever results. Thus in the example $- (x)(Fx \cdot Gx)$, distribute the universal quantifier to obtain:

$$- \left[(x)\,Fx \cdot (x)\,Gx \right]$$

The use of the brackets indicates that the negation extends over both bound formulas. Now it is possible to eliminate this extended negative sign. Since the formula has the form of $- (p \cdot q)$, which, as valid form 9 (DeMorgan's First Theorem) tells us, is equivalent to $\bar{p} \vee \bar{q}$, we can use this to obtain:

$$- (x)\,Fx \vee - (x)\,Gx$$

Thus $- (x)(Fx \cdot Gx)$ is equivalent to $- (x)Fx \vee - (x)Gx$.

A second point to note is that we ought to be quite clear about how far a negative sign extends. In the formula

$$- \left[(x)Fx \cdot (x)Gx \right]$$

brackets are used to show that the negation sign extends over both bound formulas. This will be the means used to show that the negation sign extends over more than a single whole formula. Thus if the brackets had been omitted in the above example, to obtain the formula

$$- (x)\,Fx \cdot (x)\,Gx$$

the negation sign would automatically be taken to extend only over $(x)\,Fx$.

Exercises

1. On the basis of the equivalent and conditional formulas given on pp. 120–121 and of quantifier distribution, explain whether or not the following are valid:

   a) $(\exists x)(\overline{Fx} \cdot \overline{Gx}) \equiv \left[(\exists x)\overline{Fx} \cdot (\exists x)\overline{Gx} \right]$

   b) $- (x) - (Fx \cdot Gx) \equiv \left[(\exists x)\overline{Fx} \vee (\exists x)\overline{Gx} \right]$

   c) $(x)\left[(\exists x)(Fx \cdot Rx) \cdot (\exists x)Gx \right] \equiv \left[(x)(\exists x)(Fx \cdot Rx) \cdot (x)(\exists x)Gx \right]$

   Hint: Treat the existential quantifications as simple substitutions.

   d) $- (x)(Fx \cdot Gx) \equiv - \left[(x)Fx \cdot -(x)Gx \right]$

2. In the following exercises, change all universal quantifiers to existential ones:

   a) $(x)(Fx \supset Gx)$

   b) $(x)(Fx \vee Gx) \supset (x) - (Gx \equiv Rx)$

   c) $(x)\,Fx \vee - (x)(Gx \supset Rx)$

d) $- (x)\overline{Fx} \vee - (x) - - (Fx \cdot Gx)$

3. On the basis of quantifier distribution, the list of valid forms, and substitution rules, determine which of the following are valid:

a) $(x)(Fx \supset Gx) \equiv (x)\overline{Fx} \vee (x)Gx$

b) $(\exists x) - (\overline{Fx} \cdot \overline{Gx}) \equiv (\exists x)Fx \vee (\exists x)Gx$

c) $(x) - (\overline{Fx} \vee Gx) \equiv - (\exists x)\overline{Fx} \cdot - (\exists x)Gx$

THE NORMAL FORM

In the first section of this chapter, we have seen that very often it does not matter that we are dealing with quantificational forms so far as validity and contradiction are concerned. We know that $\left[(\exists x)Fx \cdot (x)Gx\right] \supset (\exists x)Fx$ is valid not because of any new rules regarding the use of the existential or universal quantifier, but simply because it is an instance of simplification, namely, $(p \cdot q) \supset p$. Soon we shall see that the Canonical Method by which complicated arguments can be tested is also based on the use of substitution in a certain special kinds of form. This special kind of form is usually called a *Normal Form*.

Connector signs can always be eliminated in favor of other connector signs. For example, by using material implication we can change $p \supset q$ into an equivalent form that does not have the $\supset$ sign. Material Implication tells us that $p \supset q$ can be changed into $\overline{p} \vee q$ where the $\supset$ sign has been replaced by the negation and alternation signs. Similarly, by using Material Implication we can change $p \supset q$ to $- (p \cdot \overline{q})$, in which the conditional sign has been replaced by conjunction and negation signs. These changes can be made with any form. Thus, if we wished to change

1. $p \supset (p \supset q)$

into a form with only negation and alternation signs as its connectors, we could begin by eliminating the main implication sign in favor of alternation. By Material Implication we know that $p \supset p$ is equivalent to $\overline{p} \vee q$; and we also know that the equivalence will hold regardless of what we substitute for p or q. If, for example, we substitute $\left[p \supset (q \cdot r)\right]$ for q, then $p \supset \left[p \supset (q \cdot r)\right]$ is equivalent to $\overline{p} \vee \left[p \supset (q \cdot r)\right]$. Thus if we substitute $p \supset q$ for q in the Material Implication form, we obtain (1) and this then becomes equivalent to

2. $\overline{p} \vee (p \supset q)$

Applying the same valid form to $p \supset q$ of (2) and dropping the parentheses (which we can do according to the rule of Association of Alternation), we obtain

3. $\bar{p} \vee \bar{p} \vee q$

where the implication sign of (1) has been eliminated in favor of negation and alternation signs as the sole connectors. By using the rule of Idempotency, $p \equiv (p \vee p)$, and substituting $\bar{p}$ for p, we change (3) into:

4. $\bar{p} \vee q$

With this understanding of how formulas can be transformed, we can state what a Normal Form is. A Normal Form is any one of the following:

a) A single propositional letter with or without a negation sign, e.g., $p, q, \bar{r},$

b) A conjunction of single propositional letters without negation signs or with negation signs only over single letters, e.g., $p \cdot q$, $p \cdot q \cdot r$, $p \cdot \bar{q} \cdot \bar{r} \cdot s$, with no letter appearing more than once.

c) Any alternation of (a) or (b), e.g., $p \vee \bar{r}$, $(p \cdot q) \vee (r \cdot s \cdot p)$, $(\bar{p} \cdot \bar{q} \cdot r) \vee p \vee (q \cdot \bar{r} \cdot s)$, simplifying wherever we can in accordance with the rule of Idempotency. $\left[\text{Thus } (\bar{p} \cdot \bar{q}) \vee (\bar{p} \cdot \bar{q}) \text{ simplifies to } \bar{p} \cdot \bar{q}. \right]$

Hence (4) above is a Normal Form, but (1), (2), and (3) are not Normal Forms because they contain conditional signs or have not been simplified by the rule of Idempotency. Note how the following complicated formula would be changed to Normal Form:

5. $\left[p \supset - (q \cdot r) \right] \supset \left[q \cdot (\bar{p} \vee r) \right]$

First, eliminate the main implication sign. We do this by noting that (5) has the outward form of $p \supset q$ where p stands for $\left[p \supset - (q \cdot r) \right]$ and q for $\left[q \cdot (\bar{p} \vee r) \right]$. Again using our old friend, Material Implication, which eliminates the conditional in favor of alternation, and negation (5) is changed to

6. $- \left[p \supset - (q \cdot r) \right] \vee \left[q \cdot (\bar{p} \vee r) \right]$

Now we eliminate the remaining implication sign by using the same valid form and thus (6) becomes

7. $- \left[\bar{p} \vee - (q \cdot r) \right] \vee \left[q \cdot (\bar{p} \vee r) \right]$

All implication signs have been eliminated in favor of negation and alternation. But (7) is not a Normal Form since it has two negation signs, the first and the third, extending over more than one letter. Second, $\left[q \cdot (\bar{p} \vee r) \right]$

is not a conjunction of single propositional letters, but rather a conjunction of q with a disjunction $\bar{p} \vee r$. Thus before we can have a Normal Form, we must take care of these two matters. Let us begin by dealing with the two extended negation signs of $- \left[\bar{p} \vee - (q \cdot r) \right]$.

The outward form of $- \left[\bar{p} \vee - (q \cdot r) \right]$ is $- (\bar{p} \vee \bar{q})$ where q has been replaced by $q \cdot r$. But according to DeMorgan's Theorem, $- (p \vee q) \equiv (\bar{p} \cdot \bar{q})$, we can always shorten a negation sign extending over an alternation to negation signs extending over single letters. Thus if we substitute $\bar{p}$ for p and $\bar{q}$ for q, then $- (\bar{p} \vee \bar{q})$ is equivalent to $\bar{\bar{p}} \cdot \bar{\bar{q}}$ which by the rule of double negation becomes $p \cdot q$. Thus $- \left[\bar{p} \vee - (q \cdot r) \right]$ becomes $p \cdot (q \cdot r)$. And since, by the rule of Association of Conjunction, parentheses can be ignored in a formula where the only connector sign is conjunction, (7) becomes

8. $(p \cdot q \cdot r) \vee \left[q \cdot (\bar{p} \vee r) \right]$,

in which negation now extends only over one letter. Now we must deal with $\left[q \cdot (\bar{p} \vee r) \right]$. Again we try to find some valid form that can be used to provide a Normal Form. The rule of Distribution of Conjunction, $\left[p \cdot (q \vee r) \right] \equiv \left[(p \cdot q) \vee (p \cdot r) \right]$ is the necessary form that tells us a letter in conjunction with an alternation can always be distributed. Thus in $\left[q \cdot (\bar{p} \vee r) \right]$ we can distribute q to obtain: $\left[(q \cdot \bar{p}) \vee (q \cdot r) \right]$; (8) then becomes: $(p \cdot q \cdot r) \vee \left[(q \cdot \bar{p}) \vee (q \cdot r) \right]$. But since the rule of Association of Alternation allows brackets to be omitted where the main connector sign is solely alternation, (8) becomes

9. $(p \cdot q \cdot r) \vee (q \cdot \bar{p}) \vee (q \cdot r)$

and (9) is the Normal Form of (5).

It is important to remember that in making changes to attain a Normal Form, we choose the valid forms which enable us to eliminate the conditional and the equivalence sign in favor of conjunction, alternation, and negation signs that extend only over one letter. For this reason such valid forms as $(p \supset q) \equiv (\bar{p} \vee q)$, $- (p \vee q) \equiv (\bar{p} \cdot \bar{q})$, $- (p \supset q) \equiv (p \cdot \bar{q})$, and $(p \equiv q) \equiv \left[(\bar{p} \cdot \bar{q}) \vee (p \cdot q) \right]$ play crucial roles in the conversion to Normal Forms. Similarly, the valid rules of Distribution such as $\left[p \cdot (q \vee r) \right] \equiv \left[(p \cdot q) \vee (p \cdot r) \right]$ play an important role when we want to change the main sign of conjunction to alternation.

One last point should be made concerning contradictions. Since in a Normal Form none of the components can have a letter repeated, contradictions are simply dropped from the form. Thus if we obtain $(p \cdot q) \vee (q \cdot \bar{q})$, we derive the Normal Form by simply dropping $q \cdot \bar{q}$. The Normal Form is then $p \cdot q$. The justification for dropping $q \cdot \bar{q}$ in this way is given in valid form 26,

Contradiction with Alternation, which permits a contradiction to be dropped in an alternational form. And if the Normal Form reduces to a contradiction such as $q \cdot \bar{q}$, then we simply consider the formula to be false.

Exercises

1. Give the Normal Forms of the following:

   a) $(p \supset q) \equiv (\bar{q} \supset \bar{p})$

   b) $(p \vee \bar{q}) \equiv (p \cdot q)$

   c) $[p \supset (q \cdot r)] \vee (p \equiv r)$

   d) $- (p \cdot q) \supset - [p \supset (q \cdot r)]$

CANONICAL FORM

With our understanding of Normal Form, we can now state what a Canonical Form is. Given any formula consisting of quantificational forms, the following changes in it will result in a Canonical Form:

   a) *Change all universal quantifiers to existential ones.*

   b) *Treating Fx, $\overline{Gx}$, and so on as p, $\bar{q}$, and so on, change all free parts of formulas to Normal Form.*

   c) *Treating $(\exists x)Fx, - (\exists x)(Gx \cdot Rx)$, and so on as p, $\bar{q}$, and so on, change the formula as a whole to Normal Form.*

   A few examples will give us a clear understanding of how these rules operate. Consider

1. $(x)Fx$

   Its Canonical Form is simple to construct. We merely change the universal quantifier to an existential one; (1) then becomes

2. $- (\exists x)\overline{Fx}$

which satisfies both (b) and (c) of the rules of change to Canonical Form. We see that (b) is satisfied because the one free part, $\overline{Fx}$, is itself a substitution instance of the Normal Form $\bar{p}$ and thus is in Normal Form.

   Since the whole formula $- (\exists x)\overline{Fx}$ is itself Normal as a substitution instance of $\bar{p}$, (c) is satisfied.

   But now let us take a more complicated formula:

3. $(x)(Fx \supset Gx) \supset - (\exists x) - (Gx \supset Rx)$

Again we begin the conversion of (3) to Canonical Form by changing all universal quantifiers to existential ones. Using the by-now familiar rule for changing universal into existential quantifiers, (3) becomes

4. $- (\exists x) - (Fx \supset Gx) \supset - (\exists x) - (Gx \supset Rx)$

Now proceed to change all free parts, namely $- (Fx \supset Gx)$ and $- (Gx \supset Rx)$, to Normal Forms. Both of these have the form of $-(p \supset q)$, which, by using valid form 20 with $p \supset q$ replaced by $- (p \supset q)$, is equivalent to $- (p \cdot \overline{q})$ and hence, by the double negation rule, to $p \cdot \overline{q}$. Thus (4) becomes

5. $- (\exists x)(Fx \cdot \overline{Gx}) \supset - (\exists x)(Gx \cdot \overline{Rx})$

The free parts of (4) are now Normal Forms, so proceed to the next step, which consists of treating (5) as a whole with each quantified formula treated as p, q, and so on; (5) has the outward form of $\overline{p} \supset \overline{q}$, where p stands for $(\exists x)(Fx \cdot \overline{Gx})$ and q for $(\exists x)(Gx \cdot \overline{Rx})$. Now simply obtain the Normal Form of $\overline{p} \supset \overline{q}$, replace p and q by the quantified formulas they stand for, and this will be the Canonical Form of (3).

By the Rule of Transposition, with p replaced by q and q replaced by p, $\overline{p} \supset \overline{q}$ is equivalent to $q \supset p$. By Material Implication, with p replaced by q and q by p, $q \supset p$ is equivalent to $\overline{q} \vee p$. This formula is the normal form of $\overline{p} \supset \overline{q}$. Substituting $(\exists x)(Fx \cdot \overline{Gx})$ for p and $(\exists x)(Gx \cdot \overline{Rx})$ for q in $\overline{q} \vee p$, we obtain

6. $- (\exists x)(Gx \cdot \overline{Rx}) \vee (\exists x)(Fx \cdot \overline{Gx})$

Equation 6 is the Canonical Form (or briefly, the C form) of (3).

Exercises

1. Describe how a Canonical Form is obtained from a given formula.

2. Which of the following are C forms? Explain.

   a) $(\exists x) - (Fx \vee Gx)$

   b) $- (\exists x)Fx \cdot (x)Gx$

   c) $- (\exists x)(Fx \cdot Gx) \vee - (\exists x)(\overline{Fx} \cdot \overline{Gx})$

   d) $(\exists x)(Fx \vee Rx) \cdot - (\exists x)(Gx \cdot Fx)$

3. Convert the following into C forms or to T or F.

   a) $(x)(Fx \supset Gx)$

   b) $(x)\big[(Fx \cdot Gx) \supset (Hx \cdot Gx)\big]$

   c) $(x)(Gx \cdot Rx) \supset (x)Gx$

d) $\left[(x)Fx \vee -(x)Fx \right] \supset (\exists x)(Fx \cdot \overline{Fx})$

e) $-(x)(Fx \supset Fx) \supset (\exists x)(Fx \vee \overline{Gx})$

f) $\left[(\exists x)(Fx \cdot Gx \cdot \overline{Fx}) \cdot (x)(Fx \supset Gx) \right] \supset (x)\left[(Gx \cdot Rx) \supset Fx \right]$

g) $(x)Fx \supset \left[(x)(Gx \cdot Fx) \vee (x)(Fx \cdot Gx) \right]$

CONSISTENCY

Normal Forms can be of six different types:

1. A single positive letter such as p, q, r.

2. A single negative letter such as $\overline{p}$, $\overline{q}$, $\overline{r}$.

3. A conjunction of positive letters such as $p \cdot q$, $p \cdot q \cdot r$, $p \cdot q \cdot r \cdot s$.

4. A conjunction of negative letters such as $\overline{p} \cdot \overline{q}$, $\overline{p} \cdot \overline{q} \cdot \overline{r}$, $\overline{p} \cdot \overline{q} \cdot \overline{r} \cdot \overline{s}$.

5. A conjunction of both positive and negative letters such as $p \cdot \overline{q}$, $p \cdot \overline{q} \cdot \overline{r}$, $p \cdot q \cdot \overline{r} \cdot \overline{s}$.

6. Any alternation of (1) through (5) such as $(p \cdot q) \vee (r \cdot s)$, $(p \cdot \overline{q} \cdot r) \vee (r \cdot s)$, $(\overline{p} \cdot \overline{q} \cdot \overline{r}) \vee (p \cdot \overline{q} \cdot \overline{r} \cdot \overline{s}) \vee (p \cdot q \cdot r)$.

Paralleling the list of Normal Forms is a list of Canonical Forms:

A. A single positive quantified form such as $(\exists x)Fx$, $(\exists x)Gx$, $(\exists x)(Gx \cdot \overline{Fx} \cdot \overline{Rx})$.

B. A single negative quantified form such as $-(\exists x)Fx$, $-(\exists x)\overline{Gx}$, $-(\exists x)(Gx \cdot \overline{Fx} \cdot \overline{Rx})$.

C. A conjunction of positive quantified forms such as $(\exists x)Gx \cdot (\exists x)Fx$, $(\exists x)(Gx \vee Hx) \cdot (\exists x)(Gx \cdot \overline{Rx} \cdot \overline{Hx})$, $(\exists x)\left[Gx \vee (\overline{Rx} \cdot Hx) \right] \cdot (\exists x) \left[(Gx \cdot Rx) \vee Hx \right]$

D. A conjunction of negative quantified forms such as $- (\exists x)Fx \cdot -(\exists x)Gx$, $-(\exists x)\left[(\overline{Gx} \cdot Fx) \vee (\overline{Fx} \cdot Hx) \right] \cdot -(\exists x)(Gx \cdot Hx \cdot Fx)$, $-(\exists x)(Fx \cdot \overline{Gx} \cdot \overline{Rx} \cdot Sx) \cdot -(\exists x)\left[(Fx \cdot Gx) \vee Hx \right] \cdot -(\exists x)(Fx \cdot \overline{Gx})$.

E. A conjunction of both positive and negative quantified forms such as $(\exists x)Fx \cdot -(\exists x)Gx$, $-(\exists x)(Fx \cdot Gx \cdot \overline{Rx}) \cdot (\exists x)Gx \cdot -(\exists x)\overline{Fx}$, $-(\exists x)\left[(Fx \cdot Gx) \vee (Hx \cdot Rx) \right] \cdot (\exists x)(Fx \vee Gx) \cdot (\exists x)\left[(Fx \cdot Gx) \vee Hx \right]$.

F. Any alternation of any of the forms (A) through (E) such as $\left[-(\exists x)(Fx \vee \overline{Gx}) \cdot (\exists x)(\overline{Fx} \cdot Hx) \right] \vee -(\exists x)Gx$, $\left[(\exists x)\overline{Fx} \cdot (\exists x)Gx \right] \vee (\exists x)(Gx \cdot Fx)$, $\{ -(\exists x)\left[(Fx \cdot \overline{Gx}) \vee Hx \right] \cdot (\exists x)(Gx \cdot \overline{Rx} \cdot Hx \} \vee (\exists x)(\overline{Fx} \cdot Gx) \vee -(\exists x)(Fx \cdot \overline{Gx} \cdot \overline{Rx})$.

Listings (A) through (F) exhaust all the possible kinds of Canonical Forms.

Thus if we can find a test of consistency for (A) through (F), then we will have a test for consistency for *any* argument that is reducible to Canonical Form.

Before we examine (A) through (F), one comment is necessary. We are assuming a universe that is not empty. What this means is that formulas are to be taken as applicable to the actual world and not to one that is postulated as devoid of any entities. Otherwise any sentence such as $(\exists x)Fx$ would turn out false, and every sentence such as $(x)(Fx \supset Gx)$ would turn out true, since Fx would always be false. We do, however, want such sentences to be applicable to a world of objects, and in this way they have the capacity to be either true or false.

In dealing with sentential variables such as p, q, and r, we saw that the consistency of any formula made up of these letters and the logical connectives could be tested merely by observing the results of the final column of the constructed truth table. Thus, for example, to show that $p \lor q$ implies p—i.e., that $(p \lor q) \supset p$ is consistent—simply construct a truth table.

p	q	$p \lor q$	$(p \lor q) \supset p$
T	T	T	T
T	F	T	T
F	T	T	F
F	F	F	T

Since there is at least one T in the final column, this assures us that the formula is consistent. In brief, if it is possible to give at least one interpretation of a formula that turns out to be true, then it is consistent. With this understanding of how the consistency of a formula is checked, let us inspect the six different groups of C forms listed above. Any quantified argument will be reducible or convertible into one of the six C forms. If we can show how tests for consistency are made for all of these six forms, we will have shown how to test for consistency of any quantified argument which contains only C forms.

Let us work with an example of group A of the C forms, $(\exists x)Fx$. In words this tells us "Something has the property F". It is obvious that a given property could easily be selected to make this sentence true. If F is replaced by *green*, then the sentence is obviously true. This same analysis can be made for any of the other formulas such as $(\exists x)\overline{G}x$ and $(\exists x)(Gx \cdot \overline{Fx} \cdot \overline{Rx})$. Thus formulas of group A are usually consistent except for the one such as $(\exists x)(Fx \cdot \overline{Fx})$ where the open part, $Fx \cdot \overline{Fx}$, is inconsistent. Therefore consistency in the case of (A) is determined by the consistency of the open part. We can now state the rule for all forms of group A:

Given any Canonical Form of group A, drop the quantifier and test truth functionally for consistency.

By this rule $(\exists x)\overline{Gx}$ and $(\exists x)(Gx \cdot \overline{Fx} \cdot \overline{Rx})$ are consistent. When the quantifiers are dropped and the open parts, $\overline{Gx}$ and $Gx \cdot \overline{Fx} \cdot \overline{Rx}$, are treated as if they were $\overline{p}$ and $p \cdot \overline{q} \cdot \overline{r}$, a quick truth-table test shows that there is always at least one T in the final column (For example, if in the case of $\overline{p}$ we take p to be F, then $\overline{p}$ is T. Similarly, if in the case of $p \cdot \overline{q} \cdot \overline{r}$ we take p as T and q and r as F, then $p \cdot \overline{q} \cdot \overline{r}$ turns out T in the final column.)

Now let us look at sentences with the C form of group B. For example, $- (\exists x)Fx$ tells us "Nothing has the property F," and again we ask whether it would be possible to replace G by a property that nothing has. And of course this is possible. Since there are no dinosaurs, nothing has the property of being a dinosaur. Thus $- (\exists x)Gx$ can, on a given interpretation, be shown to be true. But if instead of Fx we had had $Fx \vee \overline{Fx}$ for the open part of the example, then the example would have turned out to have the value false. Since the formula $(\exists x)(Fx \vee \overline{Fx})$ must always be true because the open part is always true, then the denial of this formula, namely $- (\exists x)(Fx \vee \overline{Fx})$, must always be false. Thus we can now state the rule for all forms of group B:

Given any Canonical Form of group B, drop the quantifier (but not the negation sign preceding it) and test truth functionally for consistency.

Thus in $-(\exists x)(Gx \cdot \overline{Fx} \cdot \overline{Rx})$ we drop the quantifier and then test $- (Gx \cdot \overline{Fx} \cdot \overline{Rx})$ for consistency by a truth-functional—that is, truth-table—test. Since this can be given a true interpretation simply by taking Gx to be false regardless of what value is given to Fx and Rx, $- (Gx \cdot \overline{Fx} \cdot \overline{Rx})$ can be made to turn out true, and $- (\exists x)(Gx \cdot \overline{Fx} \cdot \overline{Rx})$ is consistent.

Now let us look at sentences with the Canonical Form of group C. Note that $(\exists x)Gx \cdot (\exists x)Fx$ says "Something has the property G and something has the property F." Can this be made true? Of course. Think of G standing for "blue" and F for "green." Then the example yields the true sentence "Something has the property of being blue and something has the property of being green." But again there is always the possibility that one of the open parts could be a contradiction, and then the whole formula would be inconsistent. Thus if the example was $(\exists x)Gx \cdot (\exists x)(Fx \cdot \overline{Fx})$, then since the second open part, $Fx \cdot \overline{Fx}$, is a contradiction, $(\exists x)(Fx \cdot \overline{Fx})$ is always false. But since a conjunction is false when any component part of it is false, $(\exists x)Gx \cdot (\exists x)(Fx \cdot \overline{Fx})$ is always false, i.e., inconsistent. Thus even though Canonical Forms of (C) are usually consistent, we test them by means of the following rule:

Given any Canonical Form of group C, test each quantified form of the con-

*junction in accordance with the test for group A. If each one is consistent,
the whole conjunction is consistent.*

Thus we test $(\exists x)\big[Gx \vee (\overline{Rx} \cdot Hx)\big] \cdot (\exists x)\big[(Gx \cdot Rx) \vee Hx\big]$ by testing
each component part of this conjunction by means of the test for (A). It turns
out that both components are consistent, and therefore the whole conjunction is consistent. (Note that we cannot simplify matters by just dropping the
quantifiers simultaneously and then testing the conjunction of open parts for
consistency. If this were done, then $(\exists x)Fx \cdot (\exists x)\overline{Fx}$, which is consistent,
would turn out to be inconsistent.)

But now examine the forms of group D where all the quantifiers are preceded by negative signs. In words, $- (\exists x)Gx \cdot - (\exists x)Hx$ says, "Nothing
is G and nothing is H." Can some predicate replace G and H which could make
this sentence true? Of course. One can say "Nothing is a dinosaur and nothing
is a unicorn," and since both sentences in this conjunction are true, the entire
conjunction is true. Thus $- (\exists x)Gx \cdot - (\exists x)Hx$ is consistent. But some formulas of group D are inconsistent. Let us examine $- (\exists x)Gx \cdot - (\exists x)\overline{Gx}$.
If G is taken to stand for *green*, this formula says, "Nothing is green and
nothing is not green." But given any thing, it is either green or not green.
Thus this example of a form of group D is inconsistent. No interpretation can
make it come out true. If the reader does not see the inconsistency too clearly,
he might try changing the existential quantifiers to universal ones. Then
$- (\exists x)Gx \cdot - (\exists x)\overline{Gx}$ would become $(x)\overline{Gx} \cdot (x)Gx$. But according to the
rules of distributing the universal quantifier, this latter formula is equivalent
to $(x)(\overline{Gx} \cdot Gx)$, which says, "Everything is both green and not green." The
resulting contradiction is now seen quite clearly.

However, even though we cannot simply make a blanket statement about
all the formulas of group D, we can determine whether or not any given one is
consistent. The rule is:

*Given any Canonical Form of group D, drop the quantifiers (but not the
negation signs preceding them) and then make a truth-table analysis.*

Thus to check the consistency of $- (\exists x)Fx \cdot - (\exists x)Gx$, simply drop the
quantifiers and make a truth-table analysis of $\overline{Fx} \cdot \overline{Gx}$. We leave it to the
reader to make the appropriate truth-table analysis.

Now turn to the formulas of group E which deal with the conjunctions of
groups A and B. We shall take as our first example $(\exists x)Fx \cdot - (\exists x)Gx$. How do
we go about deciding the consistency or inconsistency of such a formula? In
words this reads, "Something is an F and nothing is a G," or "Something is
green and nothing is purple." Here, of course, the consistency is fairly obvious.

We could have a situation in which nothing was purple but something was green. Thus some of the formulas of group E can be consistent. But not all the formulas of group E can be said to be consistent. For example, in words the formula $(\exists x)Fx \cdot - (\exists x)Fx$ says, "Something is green and nothing is green." But obviously this cannot be the case. Both of these sentences "Something is green" and "Nothing is green" cannot be true. Thus their conjunction must always be false. In fact, $(\exists x)Fx \cdot - (\exists x)Fx$ is simply a substitution instance of $p \cdot \overline{p}$.

What is needed is a general rule whereby any formula of group E can be tested for consistency.

Given any Canonical Form of group E, do the following:

a) *If there is only one positive existential quantifier in the form, drop all quantifiers (but not any preceding negative signs) and test for consistency.*

b) *If there is more than one positive existential quantifier, repeat the above test separately for each positive quantifier. If each test comes out consistent, the whole form is consistent.*

A few examples will make this rule clear. Observe the Canonical Form

1. $(\exists x)Fx \cdot - (\exists x)Gx$

Since (1) has only one positive existential quantifier, the rule is easily applicable. Simply drop the quantifiers (but not any preceding negation sign) and test for consistency to obtain

2. $Fx \cdot - Gx$

Obviously, (2) is truth functionally consistent. Thus (1) is consistent. But now let us examine a more complex Canonical Form:

3. $- (\exists x)\big[(Fx \cdot Gx) \vee (Hx \cdot Rx)\big] \cdot (\exists x)(Fx \vee Gx) \cdot (\exists x)\big[(Fx \cdot Gx) \vee Hx\big]$

Since in this example there are two positive existential quantifiers, part (b) of our test comes into operation. First test by using part (a) whether the following is consistent:

4. $- (\exists x)\big[(Fx \cdot Gx) \vee (Hx \cdot Rx)\big] \cdot (\exists x)(Fx \vee Gx)$

Drop the existential quantifiers and test whether the following is consistent:

5. $- \big[(Fx \cdot Gx) \vee (Hx \cdot Rx)\big] \cdot (Fx \vee Gx)$

We could, of course, do an entire truth table. But remember—for consistency we need only know that there is at least one interpretation of (5), that is, at least one assignment of T and F to Fx, Gx, Hx, and Rx that would make (5) turn out to be true. It might take a few moments of manipulating trues and falses, but it should not be long before we become aware that at least one interpretation will make (5) true, namely, when Fx and Hx are taken as true and Gx and Rx are taken as false. Thus (5) is consistent. But now we must proceed to check the consistency involving the second positive existential quantifier. Specifically, we must go on to check the consistency of

6. $- (\exists x)\big[(Fx \cdot Gx) \vee (Hx \cdot Rx)\big] \cdot (\exists x)\big[(Fx \cdot Gx) \vee Hx\big]$

Dropping all existential quantifiers, we test for consistency:

7. $- \big[(Fx \cdot Gx) \vee (Hx \cdot Rx)\big] \cdot \big[(Fx \cdot Gx) \vee Hx\big]$

Here also it should not take us more than a few moments to become aware of some set of truth values for Fx, Gx, Hx, and Rx that would make (7) turn out to be true. One interpretation that would make (7) true would be the one where Fx, Gx, and Rx are false and Hx is true. Thus since (7) is consistent, so is (6). And since both (6) and (4) are consistent, the whole form—namely, (3)—is consistent.

Once we have the rules for testing the consistency of any of the C forms from groups A through E, the test for (F) is almost trivial. Since (F) consists of some combination of (A) through (E) in alternation, the alternants are checked until a consistent one is obtained. And since an alternation is false when all of the alternants are false, if we find one consistent part—i.e., the alternant which can have at least one true case—then the whole alternation is consistent. For example, assume we are asked to test the consistency of

$\big[- (\exists x)Fx \cdot - (\exists x)(Fx \cdot Gx \cdot Hx)\big] \vee \big[- (\exists x)(Gx \cdot Hx) \cdot (\exists x)Hx\big] \vee (\exists x)Fx$

What we would do first is look for the alternant whose consistency is quite easily seen. But if all the alternants are complicated, then each one would be checked to see whether there is a consistent one. In the given example, the last alternant, $(\exists x)Fx$, is the most obvious one to test, since it is an example of group A. Thus we need go no further. The formula we are testing is consistent because one of its alternants has been found to be consistent.

Exercises

1. What is a consistent C form?

2. Show how to prove consistency for each group of C forms.

3. Test for consistency:

a) $- (\exists x)\overline{Fx} \supset (x)\big[Fx \supset (Gx \lor Rx)\big]$

b) $- \big[(\exists x)(Fx \cdot Gx) \supset - (\exists x)Gx\big]$

c) $- \big[(x)(Fx \supset Gx) \supset - (\exists x)(Fx \cdot \overline{Gx})\big]$

d) $- (\exists x)(Fx \cdot Gx) \cdot - (\exists x)(Gx \cdot Rx) \cdot (\exists x)\overline{Gx} \cdot (\exists x)\overline{Rx}$

e) $- (\exists x)(Fx \cdot \overline{Fx}) \supset - (x)\big[(Fx \cdot Gx) \supset \overline{Rx}\big]$

f) $- (\exists x)(Fx \lor Gx) \lor (x)(Fx \equiv Gx)$

VALIDITY

Once the consistency of any argument containing quantified sentences is demonstrable, then the validity of the argument can easily be checked. An old familiar equivalence is employed, namely $(p \supset q) \equiv - (p \cdot \overline{q})$. What this equivalence tells us is that if a given premise, p, or a set of premises, implies a given conclusion, q, then it cannot be the case that these premises, p, in conjunction with the denial of the conclusion, q, could be consistent. Thus to know whether some set of premises does imply a given conclusion, these premises must be placed in conjunction with the denial of the conclusion to determine whether this conjunction can be consistent. If it can be, if the conjunction can have at least one true case, the premises cannot imply the conclusion; if it cannot be, if the conjunction cannot have at least one true case, then the premises do imply the conclusion. With this familiar equivalence in mind and also with the knowledge of how to check the consistency of the various C forms, we can now test the validity of any argument. Let us begin by testing the validity of the following:

All F is G.

Some H is G.

Therefore Some F is H.

First, this argument is symbolized in the appropriate way:

1. $(x)(Fx \supset Gx)$

   $(\exists x)(Hx \cdot Gx)$

   Therefore $(\exists x)(Fx \cdot Hx)$

In accordance with the above equivalence, which states that premises imply a given conclusion, to show that the conjunction of the premises with the denial of the conclusion is inconsistent, simply negate the conclusion and place it into conjunction with the premises:

2. *(x) (Fx ⊃ Gx) · (∃x) (Hx · Gx) · − (∃x) (Fx · Hx)*

We shall now proceed to test this formula 2 for consistency. If it is consistent, then (1), the original argument, is invalid. If it is inconsistent, then (1) is valid.

To test for consistency, change (2) into one of the C forms. Begin by changing all the universal quantifiers of (2) into existential ones. Thus (2) becomes

3. *− (∃x) − (Fx ⊃ Gx) · (∃x) (Hx · Gx) · − (∃x) (Fx · Hx)*

Then proceed to change all free parts into normal form. This affects only the first free part, − *(Fx ⊃ Gx)*, since all the others are in normal form. The knowledge that − *(p ⊃ q)* is equivalent to *p · q̄* permits us to change − *(Fx ⊃ Gx)* to *Fx · Ḡx* which, when substituted in (3), puts all the free parts in the required form. Thus (3) becomes

4. *− (∃x) (Fx · Ḡx) · (∃x) (Hx · Gx) · − (∃x) (Fx · Hx)*

This is a C form of group E, and the test described in the previous section can be used in order to determine whether (4) is consistent. Since there is only one positive existential quantifier in (4), simply drop all quantifiers (but not any preceding negative signs) and test for consistency:

5. *− (Fx · Ḡx) · (Hx · Gx) · − (Fx · Hx)*

It turns out that on truth-table analysis (5) is consistent. Thus (2) is consistent. But since (2) is consistent, that is, since the premises of the original argument and the denial of its conclusion can be consistently conjoined, the original argument (1) is invalid for *p · q̄* means − *(p ⊃ q)*—that is, the consistency of the conjunction of *p* and *q̄* means it is false that *p* implies *q*.

However, the above argument is no more than a syllogism, and we could have used Venn diagrams to determine its validity. But let us see if now we can test the validity of the argument given at the beginning of this chapter, the argument which supposedly could *not* be tested in terms of Venn diagrams.

6. All teachers are critical thinkers.

   If no critical thinker is a conscientious objector, then no extremist is a critical thinker.

   Therefore if some extremists are teachers, then some critical thinkers are conscientious objectors.

Begin by symbolizing the argument. Since the argument is fairly complex, the letters which stand for descriptive terms will be listed: *F* stands for *teachers,*

G stands for *critical thinker*, H stands for *conscientious objector*, K stands for *extremist*. Symbolized the argument reads:

7. $(x)(Fx \supset Gx)$

$(x)(Gx \supset \overline{Hx}) \supset (x)(Kx \supset \overline{Gx})$

Therefore $(\exists x)(Kx \cdot Fx) \supset (\exists x)(Gx \cdot Hx)$

The next step is to negate the conclusion and place it in conjunction with the premises:

8. $(x)(Fx \supset Gx) \cdot \left[(x)(Gx \supset \overline{Hx}) \supset (x)(Kx \supset \overline{Gx}) \right] \cdot$
$- \left[(\exists x)(Kx \cdot Fx) \supset (\exists x)(Gx \cdot Hx) \right]$

If it should turn out that (8) is consistent, then (7) and (6) are invalid; but if (8) is inconsistent, then (7) is valid. The next step must be to change (8) into the appropriate C form. We initiate this move by eliminating all universal quantifiers from (8) in favor of existential ones:

9. $- (\exists x) - (Fx \supset Gx) \cdot \left[- (\exists x) - (Gx \supset \overline{Hx}) \supset - (\exists x) - \right.$
$\left. (Kx \supset \overline{Gx}) \right] \cdot - \left[(\exists x)(Kx \cdot Fx) \supset (\exists x)(Gx \cdot Hx) \right]$

Now proceed to use the equivalence $- (p \supset q) \equiv (p \cdot \overline{q})$ with the first three free parts, namely $- (Fx \supset Gx)$, $- (Gx \supset \overline{Hx})$, and $- (Kx \supset \overline{Gx})$, to obtain

10. $- (\exists x)(Fx \cdot \overline{Gx}) \cdot \left[- (\exists x)(Gx \cdot Hx) \supset - (\exists x)(Kx \cdot Gx) \right] \cdot$
$- \left[(\exists x)(Kx \cdot Fx) \supset (\exists x)(Gx \cdot Hx) \right]$

All free parts are now in Normal Form. However, conditionals still remain in the formula. So now proceed to change the formula as a whole to Normal Form. The outward form of (10) is

11. $\overline{p} \cdot (\overline{r} \supset \overline{q}) \cdot - (s \supset r)$

where p stands for $(\exists x)(Fx \cdot \overline{Gx})$, q for $(\exists x)(Kx \cdot Gx)$, r for $(\exists x)(Gx \cdot Hx)$, and s for $(\exists x)(Kx \cdot Fx)$

Applying the rule of Transposition $\overline{r} \supset \overline{q}$, with r substituted for q and q for p, we find that $\overline{r} \supset \overline{q}$ is equivalent to $q \supset r$. Then applying Material Implication to $q \supset r$, we can change this to $\overline{q} \lor r$, and (11) becomes

12. $\overline{p} \cdot (\overline{q} \lor r) \cdot -(s \supset r)$

Now we apply Material Implication using *and* and *not* to $- (s \supset r)$, and this formula is changed to $- - (s \cdot \overline{r})$ which, by the rule of double negation, becomes $s \cdot \overline{r}$. Thus (12) becomes

13. $\overline{p} \cdot (\overline{q} \vee r) \cdot s \cdot \overline{r}$

We can deal with (13) in various ways. For example, distribute $\overline{p}$ through $\overline{q} \vee r$ and then distribute $s \cdot \overline{r}$ using the rule of Distribution of Conjunction throughout. But probably the easiest method is to use the rule of Commutation of Conjunction, which tells us that in any conjunction we can always rearrange the specific conjuncts. We thus bring $s \cdot \overline{r}$ to the front of the formula, and (13) becomes

14. $s \cdot \overline{r} \cdot \overline{p} \cdot (\overline{q} \vee r)$

Now proceed to use the rule of Distribution of Conjunction to distribute $s \cdot \overline{r} \cdot \overline{p}$ through $q \vee r$. The formula becomes

15. $(s \cdot \overline{r} \cdot \overline{p} \cdot \overline{q}) \vee (s \cdot \overline{r} \cdot \overline{p} \cdot r)$

Since $s \cdot \overline{r} \cdot p \cdot r$ is a contradiction because of $\overline{r} \cdot r$, this part drops away (in accordance with Form 26) and we are left with

16. $s \cdot \overline{r} \cdot \overline{p} \cdot \overline{q}$

We now replace these letters by the quantified forms they stand for:

17. $(\exists x)(Kx \cdot Fx) \cdot - (\exists x)(Gx \cdot Hx) \cdot - (\exists x)(Fx \cdot \overline{Gx}) \cdot - (\exists x)(Kx \cdot Gx)$

This is the Canonical Form of (8).

Since (17) is a Canonical Form of group E we proceed to test it for consistency with the rule that governs all forms of group E. Since there is only one positive quantified form, drop all existential quantifiers. This leaves us with

18. $(Kx \cdot Fx) \cdot - (Gx \cdot Hx) \cdot - (Fx \cdot \overline{Gx}) \cdot - (Kx \cdot Gx)$

Now proceed to test (18) for consistency. We can, of course, construct a truth table for (18) and check its consistency. But again a possible short cut presents itself. Since (18) is a series of conjuncts, and since conjunction is true only when all its component parts are true, check to see whether all the component parts can be made true. The first part, $Kx \cdot Fx$, can be true only if both Kx and Fx are true. So, no matter what else occurs, Kx and Fx must be true in (18) if (18) is consistent. But now consider the last two conjuncts of (18), namely, $- (Fx \cdot \overline{Gx}) \cdot - (Kx \cdot Gx)$. If we substitute T for Fx and T for Kx, then $- (Fx \cdot Gx)$ can be made true only if Gx is T. But then Gx must also be T in $- (Kx \cdot Gx)$ and, since Kx must also be T, the last conjunct, $- (Kx \cdot Gx)$, must turn out false. There is no way of making (18) true, and thus (18) is inconsistent. But if (18) is inconsistent, so is (8) in which we negated the con-

clusion of the original argument and placed it in conjunction with the premises. But if (8) is inconsistent, as we have already shown, then the original
argument (6)—and its symbolization (7)—is valid. So (6) is valid.

Exercises

1. Check for Validity

a) $\left[(x)(Fx \supset Gx) \cdot (\exists x)(Gx \cdot Rx)\right] \supset (\exists x)(Fx \cdot Rx)$

b) $- (\exists x)\overline{Fx} \supset \left[(x)(Fx \vee Gx) \cdot (x)(Fx \vee \overline{Gx})\right]$

c) $(\exists x)Fx \supset \left[(\exists x)(Fx \cdot Gx) \vee (\exists x)(Fx \cdot \overline{Gx})\right]$

d) $(x)Fx \equiv \left[(x)(Fx \vee Gx) \cdot (x)(Fx \vee \overline{Gx})\right]$

 Hint: Use the formula $(p \equiv q) \equiv \left[(p \supset q) \cdot (\overline{q} \supset \overline{p})\right]$

e) $- (\exists x) \quad (Fx \supset Gx)$
 $- (x)(Gx \supset \overline{Hx}) \supset - (x)(\overline{Gx} \vee \overline{Hx})$
 Therefore $- (\exists x)(Gx \cdot Hx) \supset (x)(Kx \supset Fx)$

f) $-(\exists x)(Fx \cdot \overline{Gx}) \supset - (x)\left[- (Fx \cdot Hx) \vee Hx\right]$
 $- (x)(Fx \supset Gx) \supset - (\exists x) - (Fx \supset Hx)$
 Therefore $- (\exists x) - \left[(Fx \cdot Hx) \supset Gx\right] \supset - (x)\left[(Fx \cdot \overline{Hx}) \supset \overline{Gx}\right]$

SUPPLEMENTARY READINGS

Boole, George, "A Logical Calculus," in I. M. Copi and J. A. Gould (eds.),
Readings on Logic. New York: MacMillan, 1964.

Dewey, John, *How We Think*. New York: Henry Regnery Co., 1933.
Chapter 5, "The Process and Product of Reflective Activity."

Reichenbach, Hans, *The Rise of Scientific Philosophy*. Berkeley, Calif.:
University of California Press, 1951. Chapter 13, "Modern Logic."

14

Symbolization of Polyadic Predicates, Proper Names, and Descriptions

SYMBOLIZATION OF POLYADIC PREDICATES

In this chapter, we will introduce some elements of logic that properly belong in more advanced work. The following discussion aims to give the reader at least some small hint of the kind of issues and subject matter involved in the study of advanced logic. Thus we shall discuss some of the problems that arise in the analysis of polyadic predicates, proper names, and certain special kinds of descriptive phrases.

The logic of quantification in the preceding chapter dealt primarily with monadic predicates, with sentences such as "If every man is rational, then some men are rational," which can be symbolized as

1. $(x)(Mx \supset Rx) \supset (\exists x)(Mx \cdot Rx)$

Note that all of the propositional functions in this example are monadic: Mx and Rx. The predicates "man" and "rational" require only one individual to function. On the other hand, consider the sentence "Every man loves every woman." We might think that we can symbolize this simply by using monadic predicates, as in the following:

2. $(x)(Mx \supset Lx)$

where M is "man" and L is "loves every woman." But if we symbolized "Every man loves every woman" as (2), then we could never show why a very obviously valid argument is valid, namely, "If every man loves every woman, then every man loves some woman." If we only employed monadic predicates, then this sentence would be symbolized as

3. $(x)(Mx \supset Lx) \supset (x)(Mx \supset Sx)$

where S stands for "loves some woman." But if we used the technique of Canonical Forms, (3) would turn out to be invalid.

The test showing its invalidity is easy to demonstrate. First, negate the consequent and place it in conjunction with the antecedent which yields

4. $(x)(Mx \supset Lx) \cdot - (x)(Mx \supset Sx)$

Now change (4) to Canonical Form. Change universal quantifiers into existential ones, which results in

5. $- (\exists x) - (Mx \supset Lx) \cdot (\exists x) - (Mx \supset Sx)$

Proceed then to change all open parts to Normal Form. By material implication, $- (Mx \supset Lx)$ and $- (Mx \supset Sx)$ become equivalent to $Mx \cdot \overline{Lx}$ and $Mx \cdot \overline{Sx}$, and this yields

6. $- (\exists x)(Mx \cdot \overline{Lx}) \cdot (\exists x)(Mx \cdot \overline{Sx})$

This is the Canonical Form of (4). This Canonical Form is of type E, and we proceed to perform the prescribed test for consistency. Since there is only one positive existential quantifier in (6) we simply drop all quantifiers. This results in:

7. $- (Mx \cdot \overline{Gx}) \cdot (Mx \cdot \overline{Sx})$

If Mx is interpreted as true as well as Gx, and Sx is considered false, (7) is true and therefore (7) is consistent. But since (7) is consistent, so is (4), and therefore (3) is invalid.

Thus by using the techniques of the Canonical Form, we learn that (3) is invalid even though we know that what it is supposed to symbolize, namely "If every man loves every woman, then every man loves some woman," is valid. Thus to account for the validity of this sentence, we require not only a way of symbolizing polyadic predicates, but also additional rules for showing validity of sentences with polyadic predicates.

It would lead us into a more advanced order of logic to deal with the logic of polyadic predicates. But what we shall do in this chapter is show some of the techniques used to symbolize such predicates in order to prepare them for employment with logical rules.

Let us then return to the sentence "Every man loves every woman." How are we to symbolize this sentence? Consider how we went about symbolizing "Every man is rational." We took this universal sentence to read, "If any x is a man, then x is rational." We then symbolized it as $(x)(Mx \supset Rx)$. Let us try to take a similar approach with "Every man loves every woman." Since this is also a universal sentence in that it also speaks of every man, let us initiate the analysis by treating it as a universal sentence with a more complicated consequent. We shall have it read, "If any x is a man, then x loves every woman." This is an ordinary universal sentence except for the complicated consequent. How can we treat the consequent "x loves every woman"? Well, how would we treat it if it were given as a sentence in its own right, rather than as the consequent of a conditional? What we would probably do is treat it as a universal sentence "If any y is a woman, then x loves y," or in symbols, $(y)(Wy \supset Lxy)$. We are forced here to introduce another letter, y, since otherwise the symbolization would be $(x)(Wx \supset Lxx)$, which says, "If any x is a woman, then she loves herself"—which might be true, but is not what we intended to say. Now our symbolization of "Every man loves every woman" becomes

8. $(x)\big[Mx \supset (y)(Wy \supset Lxy)\big]$

which can be read, "For all x, if x is a man, then for all y, if y is a woman, then x loves y."

What we have done in (8) is substitute the symbolization of "x loves every woman" for the usual consequent. All the previous rules are applicable to (8). The connectors can be changed in accordance with valid forms; the universal quantifiers can be eliminated in favor of existential ones. Note also how we have formed the polyadic predicate Lxy. In the case of monadic predicates the individual variable is placed to the right of the predicate term, as in Rx. In the same way, the individual variable in polyadic predicates is placed to the right of the predicate term; the only difference is that more than one individual variable is placed to the right of the predicate term. Thus in Lxy we have two individual variables to the right of L. Many polyadic predicates take more than two individual variables, as in $Gxyz$, which could be taken as a symbolization of "x gives y to z." Note further that in the case of polyadic predicates it is important to know which variable occurs first. Lxy is not the same as Lyx; "x loves y" does not mean the same as "y loves x."

We might ask why "Every man loves every woman" isn't symbolized in the following way:

9. $(x)Mx \supset (y)(Wy \supset Lxy)$

This seems to say the same thing as (8). But it does not. In (9) since there are no brackets, the x of Lxy is not under the scope or under the control of (x). Thus for all practical purposes the x of Lxy might or might not be the x that is a man. Thus (9) could be taken to read, "If anything is a man, then for all y, if y is a woman, then something or other loves her." Nothing need be implied about all men loving all woman. On the other hand, if we look at (8) we find the scope of (x) to include the x of Fxy. By having the brackets extend over the entire formula that follows (x), we are told that every x in that formula which is not under the scope of any other quantifier is under the scope of the original (x). What this tells us is that whatever man happens to be referred to by the first x will also be the man referred to by the second x.

Having symbolized "Every man loves every woman," let us try a few more examples. In "No man loves every woman," a universal negative appears which is very similar to the E form. The difference is that the E form is symbolized as "No X is Y" where Y always represents ordinary monadic predicates such as *is rational* or *is a conductor*, whereas in the example we are now considering the Y consists of a more complicated form containing a polyadic predicate. But just as in the case of "Every man loves every woman" we were able to begin symbolization by first thinking of the sentence as an ordinary

A form, so also let us consider the example as an ordinary *E* form, "If any *x* is a man, then it is false that *x* loves every woman," which we can symbolize as $(x)[Mx \supset - (x\ loves\ every\ woman)]$. Now simply treat "*x* loves every woman" in the same way it was treated in the previous example, and insert the resulting symbolization into the preceding formula to obtain

10. $(x)[Mx \supset - (y)(Wy \supset Lxy)$

which is the symbolization for "No man loves every woman."

Now consider the sentence "John loves Mary." How is this sentence to be symbolized? There are several techniques, but let us recall how we treated proper names when we were utilizing Venn diagrams. There we said that the sentence "John is a student" is to be treated as if it said, "Any person who is John is a student" and then symbolized it as $(x)(Jx \supset Sx)$. Let us apply this same technique to "John Loves Mary." To begin, we can treat this sentence as "Any person who is John loves Mary," which can be partially symbolized as $(x)(Jx \supset x\ loves\ Mary)$. Now we must deal with the clause *x loves Mary* which, in accordance with the rule that changes sentences with proper names into quantified sentences, becomes $(y)(My \supset Lxy)$, which states that if any person is Mary, then he loves her. Inserting this into the consequent of $(x)(Jx \supset x\ loves\ Mary)$ we obtain

11. $(x)[Jx \supset (y)(My \supset Lxy)]$

which is the symbolization of "John loves Mary."

Finally, let us consider the sentence "Some students admire all professors." This sentence is similar to the *I* form of sentence, namely, "Some *X* is *Y*," or "There is an *X* which is also *Y*." The only difference is that *Y* now consists of a polyadic predicate combined with a universal quantifier. What we do is precisely what we did in the case of "Every man loves every woman"; we isolate the polyadic predicate and its conjoined quantifier and symbolize it. Thus the sentence would read, "There is an *x* such that *x* is a student and *x* admires all professors," which is partially symbolizable as $(\exists x)(Sx \cdot x\ admires\ all\ professors)$. We now symbolize "*x* admires all professors" just as we previously symbolized "*x* loves every woman." It becomes $(y)(Py \supset Axy)$, that is, "For all *y* if *y* is a professor, then *x* admires *y*." We insert this into the sentence $(\exists x)(Sx \cdot x\ admires\ all\ professors)$ and we obtain:

12. $(\exists x)[Sx \cdot (y)(Py \supset Axy)]$

which symbolizes "Some students admire all professors."

Of course, adequate symbolization is crucial for determining the consistency and validity of arguments containing polyadic predicates. However, neither consistency nor validity can be determined unless we are aware of certain special characteristics which accrue to polyadic relationships. For example:

> John is bigger than Bill.
> Bill is bigger than Robert.
> Therefore John is bigger than Robert.

is valid. But neither symbolization nor a knowledge of the logical rules governing polyadic predicates would be sufficient for testing the validity of this argument if we did not include the premise "If a thing A is bigger than another thing B, and B is bigger than some other thing C, then A is bigger than C." In other words, the polyadic predicate must have certain kinds of characteristics. To make this point clearer and simpler, we shall see in the next section what these characteristics are.

Exercise

1. Symbolize the following:
   a) Neither John nor Frank loves Mary.
      If John loves Mary, then Mary loves John.
      John loves Mary if and only if Mary loves John.
   b) If no English scholar loves Shakespeare, then no English scholar loves Milton.
   c) Either no one loves Shakespeare or if he does love Shakespeare, then he does love Milton.
   d) All children who love Shakespeare also love Milton.
   e) Either all who are attentive love Beethoven or they do not love him.
   f) Every person admires some actor.
   g) All parents love all children.
   h) Mary hates Bill.

SYMMETRY, TRANSITIVITY, REFLEXIVITY

In order to deal effectively with the characteristics of polyadic predicates, there is a modification that must be made in the forms of quantification. Up to this point the quantification forms have been strictly of the singular sort. There has never been more than one quantifier in front of any free sentimential function. Thus we used examples such as $(x)(Fx \supset Gx)$, or $(\exists x)(Fx \cdot Gx)$, or $(x)(Lxa \supset (\exists x) Lxy)$, where the sole quantifier was (x), or $(\exists x)$, or their negations. But in the following example,

$$(x)(y)(Sxy \supset Syx)$$

we have *two* quantifiers before the free form $Sxy \supset Syx$. What is the difference between the single and the multiple quantifier forms? The answer is that the single quantifier form simply speaks of some object or another having a given property or a given relation. Thus $(x)(Fx \supset Gx)$, where F stands for *metal* and G for *conductor*, tells us that if any given thing, whatever it may be, has the property of being a metal, then it also has the property of being a conductor. Similarly, $(x)\left[Jx \supset (y)(My \supset Lxy)\right]$, where L stands for *lighter than*, J is *John*, and M is *Mary*, tells us that if any given thing is identical to John, then it is lighter than Mary. In this formula only one *it* is indicated. But now look again at $(x)(y)(Sxy \supset Syx)$, where S stands for *is as short as*. Here we are saying that given any *two* things, whatever they may be, if one is as short as the other, then the latter is as short as the former. Whereas in the single quantifier form only one *it* is admitted, in the multiple quantifier form a second *it* is admitted. A similar analysis can be made with forms that have three or more quantifiers. Thus

$$(x)(y)(z)\left[(Txy \cdot Tyz) \supset Txz\right]$$

where T stands for *is taller than*, says that given any three things, whatever they may be, if the first is taller than the second and the second is taller than the third, then the first is taller than the third; x, y, and z are used to indicate the first, second, and third things respectively.

Multiple quantification, i.e., quantification consisting of two or more quantifiers in front of a given form, does not necessarily consist of all universal quantifiers as in the examples above. The following also is an example of multiple quantification:

$$(x)(\exists y)Axy$$

If A stands for *likes*, this reads, "Everybody likes somebody or other." Whereas the arrangement is unimportant in multiple quantification consisting solely of universal or solely of existential quantifiers, the arrangement is important where there are mixed quantifiers. Thus $(x)(y)(Fx \supset Gxy)$ is the same as $(y)(x)(Fx \supset Gxy)$. But $(x)(\exists y)Axy$ is *not* the same as $(\exists y)(x)$ Axy. The latter says, "There is somebody whom everybody likes." It tells us that some one person is liked by everybody. On the other hand, $(x)(\exists y) Axy$

tells us "Everybody likes somebody or other." This means everybody likes somebody, but not necessarily the same person. Mixed quantification involves many interesting problems. However, our concern will be only with multiple quantification consisting solely of universal quantifiers.

With this understanding of multiple quantification, we can turn again to the analysis of dyadic predicates. Let us speak of any relation designated by a dyadic predicate as consisting of a left-hand term, a relation, and a right-hand term. Thus if I say, "John loves Mary," then *John* is the left-hand term, *loves* is the relation, and *Mary* is the right-hand term. It is important not to confuse left-hand terms with right-hand ones and conversely, since such terms cannot be interchanged at will. "John loves Mary" does not say what "Mary loves John" says. However, sometimes left- and right-hand terms can be interchanged with certain kinds of relations. Thus "John is accompanying Philip" means the same as "Philip is accompanying John." In the case of such a relation as *is accompanying*, both left-hand and right-hand terms are interchangeable. Let us then call a relation *symmetrical* when its left-hand term and its right-hand term are interchangeable. *Is accompanying* is such a relation, as well as *is married to* and *is next to*. In each of these instances it is just as correct to say "*x* is married to *y*" as "*y* is married to *x*" and "*x* is next to *y*" as "*y* is next to *x*". Any symmetrical dyadic predicate can be symbolized simply by using more than one quantifier. Thus if a dyadic predicate, *F*, is symmetrical, then the following holds:

$$(x)(y)\ (Fxy \supset Fyx)$$

This states that given any two things *x* and *y*, if one has the relation *F* to the other, then the latter also has the relation to the former.

On the other hand, a relation will be called *asymmetrical* when the interchanging of right-hand with left-hand terms is not permitted. *Is the parent of* is such a relation, since if *A* is the parent of *B*, then it cannot be that *B* is the parent of *A*. Similarly, *is sitting on* is an asymmetrical relation, since if *A* is sitting on *B*, then of course *B* cannot be sitting on *A*. Again using multiple quantification, asymmetry can be symbolized as

$$(x)(y)(Fxy \supset \overline{Fyx})$$

which indicates that given any two things, *x* and *y*, if *x* has the relation *F* to *y*, then *y* does not have the relation to *x*.

Finally, in *nonsymmetrical* relations *A* is sometimes interchangeable with *B* and sometimes it is not. *Loves* is such a relation, since if *A* loves *B*, *B* might or might not love *A*. Another nonsymmetrical relation is *is a friend of,* since if A is a friend of B, it might or might not be the case that B is a friend of A.

Frequently, determining the symmetry or lack of symmetry of a relation is no easy matter. Consider, for example, *is to the right of*. On first analysis this would obviously be an asymmetrical relation. If A is to the right of B, then B is not to the right of A. But one might argue that if I look at A and B from the front, then A may well be to the right of B and B is not to the right of A. But if I look at A and B from the rear, then A would not be to the right of B, and B would be to the right of A. Thus in some cases the symmetry or lack of symmetry of a relation depends upon a specific context.

Another feature of dyadic predicates is that they can be *transitive, intransitive, or nontransitive*. Transitivity here does not mean what the grammarian means by the term. He uses it in relation to verbs to signify whether they take or do not take a direct object. Perhaps the best way to explain the logician's use of transitivity is to give a few examples. Assume that A has a given relation to B, and B has this relation to C. If it automatically follows that A must also have this relation to C, then the relation is called *transitive*. For example, assume that A weighs as much as B, and B weighs as much as C. Then it must also follow that A weighs as much as C. *Weighs as much as* is thus a transitive relation. Similarly, if A is heavier than B, and B is heavier than C, then it follows that A is heavier than C. Thus *is heavier than* is a transitive relation. This characteristic of relations can also be defined by means of multiple quantifiers:

$$(x)(y)(z)\big[(Fxy \cdot Fyz) \supset Fxz\big]$$

which states that given any three objects, x, y, and z, if x has the relation to y, and y has it to z, then x also has it to z.

On the other hand, assume that A is the mother of B and that B is the mother of C. Then, of course, A could not be the mother of C. Thus *is the mother of* is intransitive. Similarly, if A is the father of B, and B is the father of C, then A cannot be the father of C. Rather, A is the grandfather of C. Thus *is the father of* is intransitive. Intransitivity is defined as follows:

$$(x)(y)(z)\big[(Fxy \cdot Fyz) \supset \overline{Fxz}\big]$$

There is also the *nontransitive* relation where A can have the relation to B, and B can have the relation to C, but A may or may not have the relation to C. Thus *loves*, which is nonsymmetrical, is also nontransitive. If A loves B, and B loves C, it does not at all follow that A must love C. A may or may not love C. Similarly, if A is the enemy of B, and B is the enemy of C, it may or may not be the case that A is the enemy of C.

Another important characteristic of dyadic relations is that they can be either *reflexive, irreflexive,* or *nonreflexive.* A relation is *reflexive* if the right-hand member can be replaced by the left-hand member, that is, if the relation is not only applicable to A and B but to A and B individually. Thus *is the same age as* is reflexive, since not only can we say, "A is the same age as B," but also we can say, "A is the same age as A," and "B is the same age as B." A similar analysis can be made for *the same nationality as,* which is always applicable to both the left-hand side and the right-hand side of the relation. Symbolized, this becomes

$$(x)(y)\big[Fxy \supset (Fxx \cdot Fyy)\big]$$

that is, "Given any two things, x and y, if x has the relation F to y, then x has the relation to itself and y has the relation to itself." There is also what might be called *total reflexivity,* which is quite rare and trivial. It states that everything has the relation solely to itself, as in *is identical to,* and is symbolized as $(x)Fxx$.

An irreflexive relation is one in which the right-hand member cannot be replaced by the left-hand member. Thus it is possible that "A is married to B," but it is not possible that "A is married to A" or "B is married to B." Similarly, we can say, "A is to the right of B," but we cannot say, "A is to the right of A." An irreflexive relation is symbolized as $(x)(y)(Fxy \supset \overline{Fxx})$.

Finally, a predicate can be nonreflexive in that it *might* contain a left-hand member which could be substituted for a right-hand member. For example, *loves* is nonreflexive. A person could love someone else and either love himself or not. Similarly, A might hate B, but he also might or might not hate himself, A.

All three characteristics—symmetry, transitivity, and reflexivity—are applicable to dyadic predicates. Thus *heavier than* is asymmetrical, since if A is heavier than B, then B cannot be heavier than A. It is also transitive, since if A is heavier than B, and B is heavier than C, then it follows that A is heavier than C. It is also irreflexive, since neither in the case of A, B, nor C can it be said that they are heavier than themselves.

In concluding this section on relations we should emphasize an important point. The discussion of symmetry, transitivity, and reflexivity has only served to complicate the philosophical problems concerning relations. For what is it that actually determines a relation to be symmetrical or nonsymmetrical, transitive or intransitive, reflexive or irreflexive? What kind of truth is it to state that from "*A* is heavier than *B*" it can be inferred that "*B* is not heavier than *A*." Is it a stipulated kind of truth determined by the way *heavier than* is used in our language? Or is it an absolute truth because in the actual universe if one thing is heavier than another, then the latter cannot be heavier than the former? Those who have some acquaintance with philosophy will see in this discussion the initial stages of inquiry into whether there are *synthetic a priori* truths, truths about the universe which seemingly cannot be falsified and which are contrary to the scientific view that all statements about the universe are at least in principle capable of being false. Some have argued that concern with *synthetic a priori* truths arises only in connection with profound theological beliefs. But such a concern is also manifested on even the most pedestrian level. Is "If *A* is heavier than *B*, then *B* is not heavier than *A*" an absolute truth?

Exercises

1. Give the transitivity, symmetry, and reflexivity of the following:

   a) is larger than

   b) to the left of

   c) is friendly with

   d) is similar to

   e) is a cousin of

   f) is a brother of

2. Give examples of predicates, each one of which has one of the following set of characteristics:

   a) symmetrical, intransitive, irreflexive

   b) asymmetrical, transitive, reflexive

   c) symmetrical, transitive, reflexive

   d) asymmetrical, intransitive, irreflexive

3. Discuss

   All truths are relative. It might be that in some places in the universe if one object is heavier than another object, then the latter is heavier than the former.

PROPER NAMES AND DESCRIPTIONS

To know the extension and intension of a descriptive sign is to know its meaning. This is fairly clear in relation to most predicates. If I know the extension of *brown*, namely, the class of objects to which it applies, and I know its intension, namely, the property or color these objects have in common, then I know the meaning of *brown*. But certain predicates, e.g., *human being over 12 feet tall*, do not have an extension. Since there are no human beings over 12 feet tall, how can we speak of the class of objects referred to by *human being over 12 feet tall*? The answer is that some predicates have no extension even though they do have an intension, and for this reason they still retain a meaning. Thus *human being over 12 feet tall* has a meaning even though there are no human beings over 12 feet tall. Also, some predicates are not so easily explicable in terms of intensions and extensions. Consider "This bar of metal is magnetic." *Magnetic* is a predicate in this sentence, but it is not a predicate in the same sense as *red* or *large*. The magnetism of an object is not seen or experienced in the way we might see or experience its color or its size. When conditions are adequate I will actually see a property of an object— a property I will call *red*. But under no conditions will I ever see a property I will call *magnetic*. The property of being magnetic, like the property of being atomic, is not directly observable. Thus if we say an object is magnetic, we are referring to its *power* or *disposition* to act in certain ways under certain conditions. We can never see the power or the disposition in the same way we can see an explicit property such as color. But even though dispositional properties are less apparent than other properties, they can still be analyzed in terms of extensions and intensions. When an object is magnetic, then it is disposed to function in certain ways under certain conditions. The ways in which it functions can be regarded as its intension, and the class of objects that function in this same way under similar conditions is the extension. Thus even in the case of predicates which refer to dispositions, the extension-intension dichotomy remains the primary means for explaining the meaning of predicates.

Perhaps the most difficult problem concerning extensions and intensions involves three main categories:

1. Expressions that seem to have extensions but no intensions, e.g., proper names such as *Richard Nixon* and *Charlie Chaplin*.

2. Expressions that seem to have neither extensions nor intensions, e.g., proper names such as *Pegasus* and *Hamlet*.

3. Certain kinds of descriptive phrases that seem to have intensions but

no extensions, e.g., phrases such as *the present king of France*, and *the winged horse of Bellerophon.*

Let us analyze each category. As was noted in Chapter 9, proper names apparently have no intension, since they do not designate any set of properties. *Green* describes something green, but *Albert Einstein* does not describe the property *Albert Einstein.* This name is merely a label that tells us nothing about the man as a person, how he looks and how he acts. Furthermore, intensions are always applicable to a group or class of one or more objects. For example, *is human* applies to the class of humans, no matter how many human beings there are. Analogously, a proper name with an intension should be able to apply to several objects. But by definition proper names refer to one and only one object. (However, sometimes a normally proper name can be used as a descriptive phrase, as in "He is a Napoleon." But then, of course, the expression is no longer functioning as a proper name.) We do not speak of *an Albert Einstein* as we might speak of *a pale man.* Thus the notion of an intension does not seem to be applicable to proper names.

It might be possible to account for the oddity of proper names by simply admitting that some expressions have only extensions. This would then account for the expressions of category 1. However, some proper names obviously have no extension, and thus we would be led to the admission of certain terms with neither extensions nor intensions. These are the expressions of category 2. Neither *Hamlet* nor *Pegasus* have extensions, since neither one ever existed; and since they are proper names, they have no intensions. Yet it is surely undeniable that these names mean something in such sentences as "Hamlet killed his stepfather" and "Pegasus never existed." But how can they mean something and yet have neither intension nor extension? The answer to this question rests on what shall be said about the expressions of category 3. So let us now turn to this last category of expressions.

The expressions of category 3 consist of those phrases that begin with *a, an* or *the*—e.g., *a man, an elephant, the boy next door.* They are intended either to refer to some object or other, as in "A man is walking on the sidewalk," where we mean "Some man or other is walking on the sidewalk," or to refer to one and only one object, as when we say, "The boy next door is rude," meaning "There is one and only one boy next door and he is rude."

Unfortunately, descriptive phrases sometimes refer to nothing at all and yet they are taken to be meaningful, for example, *the winged horse of Bellerophon* and *the present king of France.* It has sometimes been argued that while these phrases do not refer to an existent object, they must refer to something existent in the same way as ideas, concepts, or other psychological phenomena. We have the idea of a winged horse, even though we do not have the winged horse itself. But reference to such entities serves to confuse rather than to clarify. Most of us have probably sat on many chairs, but it is rather doubtful that anyone has actually sat on the idea of a chair. Furthermore, to say that "the winged horse of Bellerophon weighed 400 pounds," does not mean that the idea of the horse weighs this much. Very few ideas are this weighty. We shall want to deal with these descriptive phrases in such a way as to avoid attributing existence to nonexistent entities.

Most descriptive phrases do operate like proper names in that they usually refer to one and only one object, as in *the present president of the United States*. However, in natural language a descriptive phrase such as *the boy next door* is occasionally ambiguous because it might be taken to refer to one or more boys. But in most contexts when *the* is used, it signifies a specific individual or object. Otherwise *a* would be employed to signify that one or more objects are being discussed. For this reason a distinction is made between *definite* and *indefinite descriptive phrases*, the former introduced by the definite article *the* and the latter introduced by the indefinite article *a* or *an*. However, it should be noted that in ordinary usage *a* and *the* sometimes take on the meaning of *all*, as in "The lion is a noble animal" and "A man is a creature of divinity." These examples are properly translated into "All lions are noble animals" and "All men are creatures of divinity." *The lion* and *a man* are therefore not descriptive phrases at all. They are part of quantified sentences which have already been analyzed. Similarly, *the dogs owned by Jones* in the sentence "The dogs owned by Jones were expensive" is not a descriptive phrase, since the sentence really states, "All the dogs owned by Jones were expensive" or "All dogs owned by Jones were expensive," and these are also quantified sentences. Finally, even though definite descriptions are usually introduced by *the*, some exceptions occur. Thus instead of "The person who bore Robert was ill," with a readily identifiable description, we could have (and normally would have) said, "Robert's mother was ill." Similarly, the sentence "What John lost was irreplaceable" might be used instead of "The object that John lost was irreplaceable" with the presence of the familiar *the*.

The distinction between *a* and *the* might seem to be rather trivial. Traditionally, grammarians have not concerned themselves with analyzing the function of these words. When they are no longer called articles and instead are labeled *determiners*, as in the new analysis of grammar, we really have nothing more than new labels on old bottles. But the distinction between *a* and *the* is actually quite significant for inference purposes, because indefinite descriptive phrases can be easily translated into expressions which can be explained in terms of intensions and extensions. That is to say, indefinite descriptions can be explained in terms of the categories that produce meaning. Thus the sentence.

A man is walking

can be changed without any loss of meaning into

Someone is walking and is a man.

The latter sentence consists of (a) a quantifier expression which, as we know, is not a descriptive term and (b) two ordinary predicates, *is walking* and *is a man*. Both predicates can easily be defined in terms of intensions and extensions. What this means is that all indefinite descriptive phrases can be changed into those which contain only quantifiers and ordinary predicates. Thus there is no problem in dealing with indefinite descriptive phrases. These can always be explained in terms of intensions and extensions. But what shall be done with definite descriptive phrases? Of course, if all definite descriptive phrases could be transformed into indefinite ones, then a major problem would be solved. Sentences containing such expressions as *the present king of France* and *the winged horse of Bellerophon* could then be transformed into sentences containing only quantifiers and predicates having intensions and extensions. This would then eliminate the curious dilemma of seeming to use expressions that refer to nonexistent things. But can definite descriptive phrases be changed into indefinite ones? Our answer will be affirmative, but before we show how this change can be accomplished we might note the significance of our analysis so far for the expressions of category 2.

Proper names such as *Pegasus* are baffling, for they seem to have neither an extension nor an intension. How do we deal with them? *Pegasus* looks like a proper name, but it cannot be placed in the same group with such other proper names as *Albert Einstein* and *Mae West*. The answer would seem to be that *Pegasus* is not a proper name at all, but merely a more abbreviated form of description. It is only because *Pegasus* can be identified as meaning the same as, for example, "the winged horse of Bellerophon" that *Pegasus* attains the status of respectability as a proper name in the language. Take away this possibility of adding a description and we would simply be left with a meaningless sound in the language. Thus whenever a proper name is encountered without an extension, it ought to be thought of as a substitute for some description. In fact, it is sometimes argued that all proper names, regardless of whether they have an extension, are no more than substitutes for definite descriptions. But for our purposes all that is required is the admission that proper names without extensions are no more than disguised definite descriptions.

Sometimes the proper name is known, but not the description. I might have heard about Pegasus and yet not know that Pegasus was the winged horse of Bellerophon. However, even though I might not know that Pegasus was the winged horse of Bellerophon, I would have to know some description if *Pegasus* is to be gainfully employed in the language. Perhaps I might only know that Pegasus is the thing described in certain mythology books as having wings and looking like a horse. Or the description might be even more minimal than this. But I would still be required to supply some description if *Pegasus* is to be an allowable word. Otherwise, if I had no description to give, it would be as if I had introduced the expression *Gurbi* and then refused to state what it meant or what it was a symbol of. Under such conditions, the expression would not be accepted as a meaningful member of the language.

Thus we find on closer examination that the words of category 2 can be transformed into those of category 3. But now everything rests on whether category 3 can be adequately explained. Does it make sense to speak of a description of something when no object exists which fits such a description? One of the easiest ways of answering this question is to say that every description refers to something or other, but not all descriptions refer to existent entities. *The present president of the United States* refers to someone who does exist. *The present king of France* also refers to someone, but he *subsists* rather than exists. Or to put it differently, the present king of France exists on a different level from that of ordinary objects. This was the answer given by the philosopher Alexius Meinong[1] (1853–1921) and it did seem to be a convenient answer, since it gave a general explanation for all descriptions. All of them had a reference, but each reference had its own existential level.

As Bertrand Russell[2] pointed out, the major problem in Meinong's thesis was that it caused a sudden population explosion. The population of the universe tripled, quadrupled, and finally became infinite in number, since every conceivable description now described some entities which either existed or subsisted. But they were all apparently present in the universe. Added to the population explosion was the fact that subsistent entities were decidedly

---

1. A. Meinong, "The Theory of Objects," in R. M. Chisholm (ed.), *Realism and the Background of Phenomenology*. New York: The Free Press, 1960.
2. Bertrand Russell, *Introduction to Mathematical Philosophy*, Second Edition. London: George Allen and Unwin, 1920, p. 169.

elusive. No test could be devised to find them. No matter where one searched, he could not find a trace of the subsistent being described as *the present king of France.*

Bertrand Russell rejected this reliance on subsistent entities and introduced a new theory which would explain the descriptions of category 3 and yet would not require any commitment to a realm of subsistent beings. To put it more specifically, Russell showed how the descriptions of category 3 could be translated in such a way that the sentences containing them did have meaning yet they did not require any reference to some abstract subsistent entity. The population explosion could be avoided.

Consider the following sentence:

1. The winged horse of Bellerophon is beautiful.

Without using any description, let us determine what is the minimum amount of information given in this sentence? To begin with, the sentence tells us

2. Something is winged.

It also tells us

3. Something (the same thing referred to in sentence 2) is a horse of Bellerophon.

And it also states

4. Something (the same thing referred to in sentence 2) is beautiful.

Putting (2), (3), and (4) together we obtain

5. Something is winged and is a horse of Bellerophon and is beautiful.

This gives almost the same meaning as (1), but not quite. What is lacking is the condition of uniqueness that the description of (1) conveys but which (5) does not. The description tells us that one unique entity is being indicated. Can this uniqueness be formulated without using a description? Russell claimed that this could be done by adding the following sentence to (5), namely,

6. Nothing else is winged and is a horse of Bellerophon and is beautiful.

Combine (6) with (5) to obtain

7. Something is winged and is a horse of Bellerophon and is beautiful and nothing else is winged and is a horse of Bellerophon and is beautiful.

Using the symbolism W for *winged*, H for *horse of Bellerophon*, I for *is identical to*, and B for *beautiful* we obtain

8. $(\exists x)\{Wx \cdot Hx \cdot Bx \cdot (y)[(Wy \cdot Hy \cdot By) \supset Iyx]\}$

which literally reads, "There is something, x, which is winged and is a horse of Bellerophon and is beautiful, and if any other thing, y, is winged and is a horse of Bellerophon and is beautiful, then y is identical to x."

Both (7) and (8) turn out to be the kinds of sentences with all the information contained in (1). Thus we have been able to show how descriptive phrases can be symbolized and therefore utilized in a logical system. Also, definite descriptive phrases have been converted so that they no longer refer to any subsistent entities. Sentence (8) shows us clearly that in symbolizing a definite descriptive phrase only the quantifiers, $(\exists x)$ and (x), and the predicates, W, H, B, and I, are required. All the descriptive predicates can be explicated in terms of intensions and extensions. Thus, following Russell, we have been able to account for all descriptive phrases and all proper names without being committed to some strange unscientific domain of beings. In the case of (8) simply check its truth or falsity by discovering whether anything is winged and a horse of Bellerophon. If something is winged and is a horse of Bellerophon, (8) is true; if not, then it is false. As it turns out (8) is false, since the conjunct, $Wx \cdot Hx \cdot Bx$, is false—nothing is winged, beautiful, and a horse of Bellerophon—and this makes the entire sentence false. However, if (7) is to be regarded contextually, that is, if it is a statement whose truth or falsity depends solely on what is asserted in books on mythology or various fictitious works, then in accordance with the use of contextual existential quantifiers (see p. 170) $(\exists x)$ in (8) would have to be changed to $(\exists x_c)$. With this change (8) could then turn out to be true, since mythology books might indeed maintain that the winged horse of Bellerophon was beautiful.

Exercises

1. Distinguish the definite from the indefinite description in the following sentences.

    a) The dog is a noble animal.

    b) His father is my brother.

    c) A man ran down the street.

    d) He is the strongest man.

    e) People are foolish.

2. Symbolize:

    a) The king of the United States is wise.

    b) The moody Prince of Denmark killed his stepfather.
    (Hint: Take *the moody Prince of Denmark* to be equivalent to *Hamlet.*)

    c) Washington was a famous American.

    d) Santa Claus is coming.

    e) Cyclops was cruel.

3. Discuss:

    a) Given any proper name, one can always find a legitimate definite description that can replace it.

    b) Perhaps there is a definite description for every proper name, but this does not mean a proper name means the same as the definite description that can replace it. *The author of Waverly*, for example, is the definite description that can replace *Sir Walter Scott*, but surely these expressions do not have the same meaning. Thus a language requires both proper names and descriptions.

    c) Proper names may some day be nonexistent in our language. Doesn't Orwell speak of a society in which each person is given a number rather than a name?

SUPPLEMENTARY READINGS

Lemmon, E. J., "Sentences, Statements, and Propositions," in J. F. Rosenberg and C. Travis (eds.), *Readings in the Philosophy of Language.* Englewood Cliffs, N.J.: Prentice-Hall, 1971.

Meinong, A., "Kinds of Being," in G. Iseminger (ed.), *Logic and Philosophy.* New York: Appleton-Century-Crofts, 1968.

Russell, B., *The Problems of Philosophy.* London: Clarendon Press, 1912. Chapter 5, "Knowledge by Acquaintance and Knowledge by Description."

15

Induction

Throughout this text we have been dealing with what is traditionally known as *deductive* reasoning. Given some set of premises, by using the various rules and techniques indicated, we can determine once and for all whether a given conclusion follows from these premises. Furthermore, once we determine that a given conclusion follows, we know it *must* follow. There is no element of probability. Given "All men are rational" and "Socrates is a man," the conclusion "Socrates is rational" does not *probably* follow; it *necessarily* follows. And if the premises are true, then the conclusion *must* be true and not probably true.

Now much of our reasoning is of this deductive kind. Very often we want to know whether the evidence presented to us regarding some view is such that there can be no alternative to the acceptance of the conclusion. We want to know whether the argument is, so to speak, "open and shut"; given the evidence, the conclusion is inescapable. But frequently our arguments are not this conclusive. We have premises and a conclusion but no rules such as those of deduction which can tell us that if an argument has such-and-such a formal structure, therefore the conclusion must follow. We can only say that given the truth of the premises, then the conclusion is *confirmed* or *disconfirmed*; that is, the truth of the conclusion is made either more probable or less probable. Thus in arguments of this sort the connection between premises and conclusion is *probabilistic* rather than necessary. We can only say the evidence "points to" a certain conclusion, or that the evidence makes a certain conclusion "plausible" or "implausible." In this kind of reasoning, which is called *inductive* reasoning or simply *induction*, no guarantee can be given that the conclusion must follow or that it is true. The following examples employ inductive reasoning.

1. This apple in the barrel is ripe.
   That apple in the barrel is ripe.
   This other apple in the barrel is ripe.
   Therefore all the apples in this barrel are ripe.

2. Last March John Smith was observed running away from the scene of a crime with a gun in his hand and he turned out to be the murderer.

   Last May Robert Doe was observed running away from the scene of a crime with a gun in his hand and he turned out to be the murderer.

   Last July Donald Futsenheimet was observed running away from the scene of a crime with a gun in his hand and he turned out to be the murderer.

Therefore whenever someone is observed running away from the scene of a crime with a gun in his hand, then he is the murderer.

3. Jim Jones had wine, cheese, pie, and coffee at the party and got ptomaine poisoning.

Bill Smith had wine, cheese, pie, and coffee at the party and got ptomaine poisoning.

Frank Doe had wine, pie, and coffee at the party but no cheese and he did *not* get ptomaine poisoning.

Therefore the cheese was the cause of the ptomaine poisoning.

In these arguments the premises are such that none of the deductive techniques could be used to show that the various conclusions follow. We could symbolize each premise and each conclusion and we would find that if we used the previous deductive rules of inference, each argument (1) through (3) would turn out to be invalid. But yet it would seem to be clear that there is some sense in which the respective conclusions follow from their premises. Surely if we have examined a certain percentage of apples in the barrel, and they are ripe, then we should be able to say something about the rest of the apples in the barrel. Similarly, if someone is seen at the scene of a crime and is running with a gun in his hand, then it is certainly plausible to infer that he is the murderer. If everyone or most of the people at the party had drunk wine and coffee, and eaten cheese and pie, and become ill with ptomaine poisoning, but Frank Doe was the only one who had not eaten the cheese and he had not become ill, it is not unreasonable to infer that the cheese was poisoned and had caused the illness. But in all these cases the conclusion does not *necessarily* follow. We may have examined a certain percentage of apples in the barrel, but this does not necessarily mean that all the other apples are ripe as well. The bottom layer of apples may be spoiled. Someone—say, John Smith— may have been seen at the scene of the crime; he may have been running from the victim's room with a gun in his hand. But this does not necessitate the fact that he is the murderer. He could have been running after the actual murderer or he could have panicked and mistakenly picked up the gun. Similarly, everyone except Frank Doe might have eaten the cheese and then become ill, but this does not necessarily mean that the cheese caused the illness. The wine, which everyone including Frank Doe had drunk, could have been the cause, but Frank Doe, being accustomed to drinking a great deal of wine, could have become inured to drinking any kind of wine including the bad kind. Thus in all these cases the evidence does not logically imply the conclusion, yet there is a sense in which we can say there is some relationship between the premises and the conclusion. Given the truth of the premises, there is some degree of probability that the conclusion is also true.

Inductive reasoning is concerned with the probability that certain statements relating to evidence imply a given conclusion. The element of logical necessity disappears. In induction we take a chance; a leap is made from incomplete evidence to an unguaranteed conclusion. In this chapter, we will deal with some of the complications of this kind of reasoning. But we should be forewarned that the inductive procedure lacks the comfortable certainty of deduction. Premises of an induction may be true; but they lead to what *may be* not what *must be* true.

PROBABILITY

One of the most popular and most frequent uses of inductive reasoning occurs when a generalization is made on the basis of similar experiences. Thus, for example, boys sometimes find themselves reasoning in the following way: "Last week Hank went out with Geraldine and he kissed her on the first date. The week before, Frank went out with Geraldine and he also kissed her the very first time out. The week before that Moe went out with Geraldine and he also was lucky enough to kiss her on the first date. I'm making a date with Geraldine."

In this example a generalization has been made on the basis of similar happenings. Geraldine has kissed boys in the past on the first date; therefore she will continue to be cooperative in the future. This sort of inference, one which moves from past instances to a generalization of all instances of the same kind, uses as its basis the *frequency theory of probabilistic inference*, which says that the relative frequency of a given result among unobserved events of a given kind will be the same as the relative frequency among observed events of this kind. In other words, if under certain conditions a certain kind of event has constantly or very frequently occurred in the past, then under similar conditions the same kind of event will constantly or very frequently occur in the future.

The frequency theory permeates our day-to-day living. Not only do we use it to estimate our chances with Geraldine, but also we use it to decide our most fundamental actions: "Brand X had delicious peaches in every can I bought in the past. Therefore it will continue to be an excellent brand of peaches in the future. So I will buy it now and in the future." "Mary has been very sweet and sensitive during our entire courtship, and therefore she will

continue to be very sweet and sensitive after I marry her. So I will marry her."
"Professor X has given a grade of B or better to all his students in the past.
This means he will continue to do this in the future. So I'll take his course
next summer."

The frequency theory of probabilistic inference is used not only in ordinary everyday contexts, but also in more sophisticated inquiries as well.
Since Halley's comet has been appearing at intervals of every $75\frac{1}{2}$ years after
its first recorded appearance, astronomers might argue that it would appear
in 1758 (and it did), that it would appear in 1835 (and it did), that it would
appear in 1910 (and it did), and therefore that it would appear again in 1985.
Oswald Spengler (1880–1936) argued that every culture in the past—Indian,
Chinese, Arabian, and so on— has gone through four phases: spring, summer,
autumn, and winter (or birth, maturity, decay, and death). Similarly, Western
culture, which includes Europe and the United States, has been going through
these phases. Indeed, said Spengler, we are already in the winter phase of our
culture and nothing can be done to escape our inevitable demise. Thus the
belief that the recurrence of past events will continue on into the future is an
important one for human beings. We ought to examine how justified it really is.

The first difficulty in the frequency theory is that if one is not careful,
it can lead him into the fallacies of hasty generalization and *post hoc ergo
propter hoc*. (See Chapter 3, "Fallacies.") It might be the case that both John
Smith and Robert Doe had heart attacks after they had eaten certain food.
Then on the basis of this data we might conclude that the probability is high
that anyone who eats such food may have a heart attack immediately afterwards. But two instances in which men had heart attacks after eating certain
food certainly does not seem to be sufficient data from which to draw a general
conclusion that probably everyone will have a heart attack after eating such
food. The two cases might have been coincidences. It just happened that John
Smith and Robert Doe had heart attacks after eating the food. They may very
well have had heart attacks even if they had not eaten what they did. Surely
we would want much more evidence; we would want to be shown many more
cases before we accept the view that there is indeed a correlation between the
occurrence of heart attacks and the eating of the food. Thus when we move
from evidence to generalization, we should be very cautious. We should always
be asking ourselves: Are we being too hasty here? Is our sample large enough?
Are we mistaking a mere coincidence with a genuine relationship between
evidence and conclusion? Have we taken into consideration the fact that
similarity of events does not necessarily mean that some causative factor is
present. When we examine Mill's Methods in the fifth section of this chapter,

we shall see that the mere fact that A occurs just before B occurs does not mean that therefore A is the cause of B.

It is interesting that drawing hasty conclusions very often occurs when there is some bias or prejudice involved. A person can be very fair-minded and careful about drawing conclusions involving metals or other data that do not concern his own personal life. But if he has one or two bad experiences with people of some race, color, or creed, he will often quickly conclude that *all* people of that race, color, or creed are nasty. In brief, in both our everyday and our scientific views we should constantly be critical of ourselves. Too often we are ready to accept conclusions which are based on skimpy evidence if they fit into our own preconceived biases, just as we are also ready to reject conclusions based on good evidence if they do *not* fit into our preconceived biases. Let us not forget Galileo!

Although hasty conclusions are not genuine inductions, this does not mean that there can be no cases in which one or two instances are sufficient to draw a general conclusion. Scientists and trained observers sometimes perform what they call *crucial experiments*, in which conditions are very carefully controlled or very carefully specified. Thus Columbus was said to have argued that the earth was round since an observer who watched a ship go out to sea would see the upper parts of the ship long after the lower parts were no longer visible. This would not be the case if the earth were flat. Obviously, in this case it would not be necessary to bring in hundreds of observers; nor would the probability that the earth is round have increased as more and more observers witnessed the same phenomenon of the distant ship. One, two, perhaps three observers would be all that would be required to make Columbus' theory highly probable. Similarly, it is not necessary to keep repeating the experiment in which sodium combined with chlorine under the proper catalytic conditions can be shown to result in ordinary table salt. After two or three times we take it to be always very highly probable that under the same conditions salt will be produced. But in these examples the conditions are very carefully specified or very carefully controlled. The observer must have good eyesight and be at the beach on a good clear day. The sodium and the chlorine must be combined with special instruments and with an appropriate catalyst, such as manganese dioxide. Yet even here, it should be pointed out, we are still always dealing with probabilities. On the basis of what observers see when they watch a ship at sea, it is highly probable that the earth is round. But there might be other explanations. Perhaps the eye does not really see properly when there is a large distance involved, or perhaps the water gives us reflections that distort the way the bottom part of the ship would look to some observer. Similarly, it is highly probable that sodium combined with chlorine under laboratory conditions will produce salt. But as any student who is first introduced to chemistry knows, the laboratory experiment does not always turn out correctly. A subtle, perhaps undetected change in the laboratory atmosphere or even in the general atmosphere could change the conditions under which sodium and chlorine can normally be combined to produce salt. Thus even crucial experiments are not free from the reliance on simple probability.

The second difficulty in using the frequency theory for drawing inferences is that we sometimes unwittingly change what is solely an inductive inference into a deductive one. The probability element tends to be ignored. If a certain kind of event has been constantly recurring, it is psychologically easy to take the next step and assert that it will occur today, tomorrow, and perhaps forever. This is the way things have been in the past, and this is the way they will be in the future. *Will be* replaced *probably will be.* But as David Hume implied, there is no glue in the universe that guarantees that the future will be like the past. While the evidence seems to be clear that the sun has risen every morning since the very beginning of the creation of the earth, this does not mean that such information gives us the right to assert that the sun *must* therefore arise tomorrow morning and every morning in the future. We know that suns also die and are destroyed for various reasons. But even without such knowledge, no guarantee can be forthcoming about tomorrow's world. Nothing can give us absolute certainty about the rising of the sun tomorrow. An inductive inference can state that something probably will occur or that there is a high degree of probability that something of a certain kind will occur, but we must not take this to be a license for asserting that some given event *must* occur or that it is determined "by the very nature of things" that some given event must occur. The natural world around us does indeed show many regularities. Acorns give rise to oaks; human beings mature, become old, and die. But acorns sometimes do *not* give rise to oaks. And—who knows—some day scientists may discover the secret of prolonging life indefinitely.

Oswald Spengler's analysis is a good example of how easily induction can mistakenly be taken as deduction. Spengler tries to show in great detail that one can speak of various cultures of the past and that these have evolved to a certain high peak and then declined. He then goes on to argue that this data shows that every society *must* go through these stages. But, of course, Spengler only has a right to say that every society *probably* will go through these stages. Similarly, someone might argue that because the last five models of Buicks have been heavy gasoline consumers, therefore every model of Buick throughout the future must also be a heavy gasoline consumer. But this, of course, is false. Buicks might improve their motors; gasoline motors might give way to electric ones. Thus an inductive argument should not be taken for a deductive one.

The Spengler example also reveals certain other difficulties that frequently beset inductive reasoning. It would seem to be much easier to mistake induction for deduction when the argument consists of vague terminology than when the terms are precisely understood. If we inspect ten peas in a barrel and find them to be spoiled, we might argue that the rest are probably spoiled as well, but we would not insist that the rest *must* be spoiled. Similarly, when we are dealing with specific things which are clearly and precisely known to us, such as metals, we might argue that since the ones we encountered are electromagnetic, therefore probably all of them are. But it is unlikely that we would insist that all of them *must* be. (But here also it is interesting to note that when a basic bias or prejudice is involved, the move from induction to deduction becomes easier. If, to begin with, we don't like a particular group of people, it is easy to accept the argument that since some of them have turned out to be criminals, therefore *naturally* there *must* be a criminal tendency in all of them.) On the other hand, when the descriptive terms used are vague, they lead to glib dogmatic statements. Thus people are prone to assert: "Mankind will survive." "Freedom will always triumph over tyranny." "Justice will eventually win out." But as we have seen when we examined similar statements in Chapter 3, when we think of men specifically, we recognize that they do die and that therefore men could be killed. Assuming we understand what freedom is, we might want to qualify the dogmatic statement and claim that free people can be destroyed if they are not careful and are not ready to fight for their freedom. Similarly, while we talk about justice in the abstract, we do know that just men are sometimes sent to prison and even hanged. Thus vague terminology makes it easier to mistake an ordinary induction for a necessary deduction; this indeed is the second problem in Spengler's analysis. He assumes that he has stated his premises unambiguously. India's culture has risen and declined; China's culture has risen and declined, and so on. But what is meant by a culture's *rise* and *decline*? Are cultures like organic things which are born, mature, and then die? Some philosophers and sociologists have tried to picture societies as if they were comparable to enlarged human beings of whom it could be said that they are dying or they are maturing. Are societies comparable to human beings? Perhaps human beings must go through the stages of birth, maturity, and death, but societies may simply change in accordance with how they deal with their problems. Furthermore, whereas one can easily define what is meant by *old age* when it relates to a human being, it is not at all easy to define old age when it relates to society. What may seem to be a decline to one person may appear to another to be an advance. Some people feel American society is progressing and they point with pride to its great scientific feats, its complex technology, and its humanitarian attempts to abolish ignorance and poverty. But others who claim that America is deteriorating point to its increasing violence, its political corruption, and its laxity in moral and sexual matters. Indeed, the same evidence can often be used to buttress either the theory of decline or of progress. Thus the Supreme Court decision 'on abortion is regarded as progressive by pro-abortion groups while it is stigmatized as immoral and degenerate by the leadership of the Catholic Church.

The truth may well be that there are no reasons for assuming that American society is developing in one way or another. The United States consists of a complicated society of men who may or may not settle the problems they face. If the right officials are elected to run the government, they may solve the problems in such a way as to make life more comfortable for the mass of people; if solutions are not forthcoming, then society experiences disruptions caused by those who are not satisfied with the quality of their lives. In other words, *society* is not an entity—some specific thing—with its own life force, but rather it is a group of human beings whose choices build or destroy the group. Thus by using certain vague and undefined expressions, Spengler makes it appear as if his argument has the necessity of a deduction. But if it is any kind of argument, it is an inductive one.

To overcome the difficulties of probabilistic inference, we simply decide to be more scrupulous about our predictions and to avoid the use of ambiguous expressions. The evidence of the past may sometimes seem conclusive, but it never makes some specific future inevitable. A more serious difficulty arises in relation to the determination of the *degree* of probability. How do we determine an increase or decrease in the probability of the occurrence of some event? Even more problematic is the question of whether probability can be determined mathematically. Is there some way in which we can affirm that given such-and-such evidence, then the probability is 80 percent or 65 percent or 32.5 percent that a given event will take place? We can begin to deal with these issues by asking whether it is possible to speak of higher and lower degrees of probability without specifying any number.

If one green pea is taken from a huge barrel of peas, and then another green pea is removed, what is the probability that all the peas in the barrel are green or that the next pea selected will be green? If four peas had been picked instead of two, if the sample had been increased from two to four, and if in all four cases the peas were found to be green, would this have increased the probability that the next selected pea would also be green? Perhaps we can claim that as the number of green peas picked from the barrel increases, the higher the probability that the next selected pea will be green. In other words, the more times the event occurs, the higher the probability that the event will recur the next time. This notion of degree of probability is used in everyday contexts: "The meat from Chaikin the butcher has been very good every time I have bought it from him. Therefore the probability is high that it will be very good tomorrow when I buy some meat for my mother-in-law." However, the mere recurrence of events might have little to do with the probability that the event will continue to recur, or to recur with an increased probability. If the horse *Never-lose* has never lost a race, are his chances of winning a race tomorrow increased? It is a serious mistake to assume that the probability of *Never-lose*'s winning is increased because he has constantly won. In many cases the more times a given event occurs, the less chance there is that it will continue to occur in the future. The horse is growing older; after a certain time its muscles begin to grow weaker rather than stronger; age brings on diseases which are not present when the horse is younger. Thus the probability of the horse's winning would actually be decreasing as the horse continued to win. Former heavyweight champions Joe Frazier and Muhammad Ali won a great many fights, but eventually each victory made the next one a little less likely.

But how about the case of the green peas? Would the probability increase that all the peas in the barrel were green if we kept continually enlarging the sample and coming up with green peas? In this situation it might be possible to posit increased probability since time is not much of a variable. If within a given period of time we keep picking peas at random, and they continually turn out to be green, then we can assert that the more times we come up with green peas, the higher the probability that the next pea will be green. However, under certain circumstances time could become a factor. If we pick a pea a day, then we might say that the factor of time will become a variable in this instance just as it was in our example of the prizefighters. Peas do deteriorate and turn brown after a certain length of time. Thus if too much time elapses in obtaining the sampling of peas, the probability that the next selected pea will be green begins to decrease.

Therefore it is not possible to make a blanket statement about the frequency of certain kinds of events, namely, that the more times they recur, the higher the probability of their recurrence when the conditions are similar. In all such cases we mean "all things being equal," in other words, if time is not a factor or other factors are not involved. The peas might all be green up to a certain point in the selection procedure, but some chemical in the growing process could make them deteriorate rapidly and thus the sampling of green peas could not be used to give us information about what the next pea will be. We might not know whether the sample of the green peas is really a good sample. Have we really picked peas at random from various parts of the barrel, or have we simply selected a few peas from the top? Are we sure we know what it is to make a fair and impartial selection? The truth is that the frequency theory of probabilistic inference can barely be used in a simple, enumerative way. We cannot say, "This has happened over and over again. Therefore the probability is high that it will happen again." We must always ask, "Is the time element a factor?" If the time element is not relevant, we must constantly ask whether the conditions have changed, or whether new information has become available. Thus, for example, if the peas were selected in the past when the temperature was low, and they are now selected when the temperature is higher, temperature might possibly be a relevant factor which makes the peas green or brown. In drawing the probability inference, we must be sensitive to the possibility that only certain factors might be relevant to the inference. Temperature might well be responsible for making the peas in the barrel green or brown, while the fact that the barrel is made of wood might be irrelevant. Thus we must have some understanding of what is meant by relevant or irrelevant factors.

Exercises

1. Discuss the adequacy of the following arguments:
   a) The belief in God is to be found in every past and present society. Therefore God exists.
   b) According to Marxist ideology, capitalist society is doomed. It is inevitable that the workers of the world will unite and take over the means of production.
   c) Dr. Jones is a great doctor. He cured his last eight patients.
   d) The country is going to the dogs. You pick up any New York paper and you find rape, murder, robbery, and prostitution.
   e) Two things are inevitable—death and taxes.

2. Comment on the following:

   But history does tell us that societies rise and fall in certain determined ways. According to some historians, the Second World War was inevitable because of the various economic and political forces that were at work during that time.

RELEVANCY

How can we determine whether some factor is or is not significant for drawing an inductive inference? How do we know that the barrel is an irrelevant factor? Perhaps the wood emits a chemical substance which increases or decreases the probability that the peas will continue to remain green. Thus in this instance something that seemed at first glance to be irrelevant turns out to be relevant. Anyone who has read detective stories knows how often an insignificant scrap of paper near the murdered man's body becomes very important when it is revealed to be the special paper of a cigarette that only the murderer smoked. In a sense everything has the possibility of being relevant. Three hundred miles away from the murder scene a mailman delivers a letter written by the murdered man before his death. The letter becomes significant only if it contains information about the murderer. Otherwise it might be unimportant and irrelevant. How then do we discover what is relevant in any given situation?

There is no positive foolproof way of discovering whether some incident, object, or person is relevant to a particular inference. Very often the discovery of what is germane data comes through a hunch, a lucky accident, or a sudden insight. The discovery that molds could be useful in combating disease came about by accident. Dr. Alexander Fleming noticed that a small mold had developed on one of his glass plates containing colonies of bacteria. For some unaccountable reason he decided to observe what happened on the glass plate, instead of following his usual practice of discarding the plates with molds on them. He observed that the bacteria were destroyed by the molds. Thus when an irrelevant factor suddenly became a relevant one, penicillin was discovered. But even though there are no foolproof techniques for determining relevancy, some rules of thumb are available.

First, knowledge of the area in question helps us to determine the significant elements involved in making legitimate probable inferences. The trained doctor or physicist is more apt to see that something may or may not be relevant to a given inquiry. Perhaps something is being overlooked in contemporary cancer research, but the chances are that whatever this something is, its relevance will be made apparent by a person who is trained in cancer research. Even though in television programs and the movies anyone can be a detective and solve the most complicated crimes, in actual life it is usually the practicing detective who has been involved in numerous similar cases who obtains the insight as to what is or is not relevant in order to solve the mystery.

Second, by having special knowledge in the area under investigation we acquire the ability to see analogies among things, and this is important for determining relevancy. Because the professional detective can draw analogies between cases he has handled, he can more readily discern what is relevant than can the layman. In Case A the lipstick on a cigarette butt led to the discovery that Mrs. Jones had been present at the scene of the crime. In Case B, which is analogous to Case A, the lipstick on a cigarette butt had a similar relevance. A scientist might think, "An atom seems to be similar to the solar system. Thus perhaps we might find particles circling the electrons of the atom just as we find satellites circling many of our planets." Or we might say, in the manner of early inventors, "Birds fly because they have wings that move up and down. Then why not build airplanes with flapping wings?" In all of these examples, analogy plays a role in stressing the importance of what has been ignored. But, of course, analogy never takes the place of an inductive argument.

In this connection we must be aware of the following important distinction. In an inductive argument the claim is made that because things of the same kind have in the past had a given characteristic, therefore things of the same kind will in the future have the same characteristic. We are talking about objects or events which we would be inclined to group together, such as men, metals, and animals. But in analogical reasoning we are talking about objects which we normally would *not* group together. Thus atoms are not grouped with solar systems; birds are not grouped with airplanes. The detective working with Case A might have a murder on his hands, while Case B might involve a robbery—two different kinds of crime. In using analogy we take a calculated chance that if two different kinds of things have two or three similar characteristics, then the third characteristic of one might also be found in the other. But these inferences are no more than suggestions. Birds can fly by flapping their wings. But so far as we know, airplanes do not do very well with flapping wings. They usually crash. Atoms may in some ways be comparable to solar systems. But atoms are obviously different from solar systems in significant ways. For example, electrons move from orbit to orbit and seem to disappear during this movement. But planets do not behave in this fashion. An analogy can *lead* to an induction. If on the basis of analogy we conclude that electrons also might have smaller particles circling them just as planets have satellites, then we could check whether electrons do indeed have such satellite particles and then draw the inductive inference that electrons probably do (or do not) have such satellites.

It is interesting to note that analogies have often been used to bolster certain views which would not be acceptable if strictly inductive procedures were employed. Thus it would be difficult to argue that because there have been many monarchies in the past, therefore monarchy is the best form of government. Yet some have argued analogically that in our solar system there is a sun around which planets revolve, and similarly this same kind of structure is to be found in atoms. Therefore the natural kind of government is one which employs one-man rule with the mass of people obeying the rules of this one man. This, of course, is not even a good analogy. But it has been used to try to bolster support for a certain view of government. Sometimes such abbreviated forms of analogy as metaphors or similes (see Chapter 3) are used, and they function like enthymemes. To say of John, "He is an ostrich" (metaphor) or "He is like an ox" (simile) is to omit reference to the specific nature of the comparison, and to permit the reader or listener to draw his own conclusions—conclusions which might be detrimental to poor John.

Third, something is very often relevant to the occurrence of a particular event when, on investigation, it is found to accompany the same kind of event. Thus the penicillin mold became significant when it was found that bacteria constantly disappeared when the mold was present. But in such a situation there is still no absolute certainty that the accompaniment of one factor with another means that a relevant element has been uncovered. Suppose every time a child is born in Chicago there is a burst of sunspots. This would hardly serve to make sunspots relevant to childbirth in Chicago. However, if something is found to accompany a given event, and on further inquiry is found to be causally related to the event, then that something can be said to be relevant. If additional information reveals the sunspots to be atomic phenomena which are usually followed by certain cloud formations in the vicinity of Chicago, and these cloud formations lead to rain which in turn stimulates certain female and male sex hormones, then there might indeed be a connection between sunspots and childbirth in Chicago. Thus analogy used with discretion can be useful in furthering the process of legitimate deduction.

Exercises

1. It is sometimes said that Cleopatra's nose was a highly relevant factor in

the decline of the Roman Empire. If her nose had been quite a bit longer, Marc Antony would not have loved her and he would have remained loyal to Rome. Discuss.

2. Imagine you are a detective. What factors would you investigate in the case of a middle-aged businessman whose wife reports that he is missing. What are your reasons for considering these factors to be relevant? Are you sure they are good reasons?

3. Imagine you are a mother (or a father). How would you judge whether your son is a *good* or a *bad* child? What are your reasons for considering certain factors to be relevant in making this judgment? Are you sure that they are good reasons?

4. In the following, can any analogies be drawn? What, if any, legitimate inductive inferences might be drawn?

a) Stars and human eyes

b) Soviet Union and Bears

c) United States and the unshaven G.I.

d) United States and a greedy miser

e) Playing ball and politics

f) The human body and machines

SAMPLING

Perhaps the most interesting and in a sense most socially significant use of probability theory occurs when we deal with samples of large groups of objects. Such sampling is of special significance when the groups are human beings and polls are taken to determine how the group as a whole can be expected to react to some past, present, or future event. In every case in which a poll is taken, remissness in identifying certain important factors can lead to an incorrect inference.

To begin we must ask, "Are we sure we have a fair sample?" If we want to know for whom the majority of American people will vote in an election, then the sample should reflect all major segments of American voters. But can we identify the major segments? What else beside the union vote, the Black vote, the Jewish vote should be considered? The Gallup Poll first divides the country into different classes in terms of age, sex, economic status, political party, and so on, and then takes random samples from each group. But even under such conditions where great care is taken to obtain a fair sample, the polls can go wrong. Thus the polls predicted a strong Dewey victory in 1948, but it was Harry Truman who won.

What went wrong? Either the samples were not large enough and therefore they did not truly represent their group, or the sampling in one or more of the various segments was not random, or some unknown or unpredictable event which occurred after the poll was taken affected the outcome. Perhaps the sample of the union was too small and did not really represent how unionists would vote. Perhaps the sample from the Blacks came from only a certain economic group and this did not represent the Black community as a whole. Sometimes something happens which upsets all predictions after a poll is taken. Did Dewey speak too arrogantly after the poll predicted he would win and in this way cause many people to change their minds about him? Polls can sometimes serve to defeat themselves, since a predicted sure loser is cast as the underdog and this makes more people vote for him. Everyone is for the underdog! During the McGovern-Nixon campaign, McGovern thought that the polls predicting a major defeat for him would make people vote for him, since they would see him as the underdog trying to catch up to a powerful Nixon. But in this case the polls were right. McGovern was soundly defeated.

Polls can also go awry because the questions have been incorrectly phrased so that the possibilities for misinterpretation are highly increased. The question "Are you against war?" could not be used to prove one way or the other whether Americans would oppose entering any future war. It is possible to be against war in general but to approve of a certain specific war. Very few people would ever say they are *for* war. But the United States fought in the First and Second World Wars rather enthusiastically. Similarly, a question such as "Should the government vitiate its actions against those who divulge arcane government paraphernalia?" could hardly be used to determine how the American feels towards those who reveal secret government documents. What do such words really mean? Assuming we did make sense of them, the question would still be inadequate since we might want the government not to be too harsh towards offenders, while we would still expect offenders to be punished in some way. Similarly, if a pollster were not aware of the various taboos which relate to such a question as "Is your sex life satisfactory?" he would hardly receive meaningful results from any answers.

Polls dealing with the probability that people believe such-and-such and therefore will probably vote in a certain way are inherently always capable of being wrong. Beliefs very often change rapidly so that even a staunch Republican might vote for Democrats if he objected to some particular policy of his party. The Watergate scandal might change the voting habits of many Republicans. Many Democrats voted for Nixon rather than McGovern because they felt that McGovern's economic policies might produce economic difficulties for them. However, fairly objective and unchanging data can be obtained about human beings, and this can form the basis of more reliable predictions. Thus, for example, if one wished to know the average height of a 15-year-old boy in a given school he could use simple mechanical techniques to find out. He could obtain the height of every 15-year-old boy in the school, add up all the heights, and then divide by the number of 15-year-old boys. Thus let us say there are 40 boys aged 15 in the school, and when we add up their individual heights we come up with the number 230 feet. If we now divide this number by 40, the number of students, we obtain 5 feet $7\frac{1}{2}$ inches, which would be the average height of the 15 year-old boys in the selected school. We call this the *average mean height* of the students. It does not mean that all the students are this height, but rather that if the school ordered sweatshirts which would fit a 5-foot-$7\frac{1}{2}$-inch student give or take an inch one way or the other, the probability is that the sweatshirts would be sold without too much difficulty. Of course, if we were dealing with all the 15-year-old schoolboys in a large city, we might have to do a great deal of adding and dividing. In this case we might simply take several schools as samples, add up the available data, divide by the number of students recorded, and then take the resultant figure as an average for the whole city. This would not have the certainty that is present when we can take every student into account, but it would still give us an average that can be reliably used in many cases. The superintendent of schools would feel fairly confident about the number of sweatshirts he ordered for all the schools in the city.

Sometimes the average mean does not really give us the kind of information we want. Suppose we wished to know the average salary of factory workers in a given city or perhaps in the nation. We could then proceed to select several factories located throughout the nation, add up the salaries of the workers at these factories, divide by the number of workers in the sample, and in this way come up with an average wage for the average factory worker in the United States. But the use of this method might obtain a very deceptive average. For if in one or two of the factories there were a few specialized workers receiving very high pay, this could throw the entire average off. Suppose we wished to know the average salary of workers at one of these factories. Now imagine that there were ten workers here, and their salaries were the following: $8000, $6500, $25,000, $7000, $25,500, $7300, $7200, $6900, $7100, and $7500. Now if we add these figures up, we will obtain $108,000, which, if we divide by 10, will give us $10,800 as the average wage in this factory. But of course this is deceptive, since eight out of ten of these workers are making far below $10,800. What has gone wrong here is that the two workers making $25,000 and $25,500, respectively, have made the average seem much higher than it is.

Thus the average mean is significant when there is prior knowledge that the sample does not include any great extremes. Had we known about the two very high salaries in the above sample we might have left them out and then obtained a truer picture of the salary of the average worker. But once we know about such extremes we can place everything in proper perspective by using what is known as the *mode*. The mode is that object in a group which appears most often. Thus if *A* is making $7000, *B* is making $5800, *C* is making $7000, *D* is making $9500, *E* is making $7000, and *F* is making $7000, we can obtain some idea of the average salary by simply taking that figure which appears most often on the list of salaries. Thus we can ignore the very low salary of $5800 and also the very high salary of $9500, and simply say that $7000 is the average salary—that is, it is the salary that most of the workers at the factory are making. The mode, then, very often gives the more informative data.

But sometimes even the mode will not be adequate. Consider a case such as the following: *A* makes $9000 a year; *B* makes $9200; *C* makes $9300; *D* makes $9400; *E* makes $15,000; and *F* makes $15,000. Here the mode would be $15,000 since it is the figure that is repeated in the list and thus appears most often. But, of course, this would give an incorrect view of the average salary of the factory worker. Thus where the mode does not take in a good number of those included in the sample, we ought to use the *median*. The median is the middle term when a series of items are arranged in an order going from lower to higher, such as the median of the following set of numbers: 6, 3, 9, 8, 7, 2, 4. In order to find the median we first rearrange the numbers in terms of an increasing magnitude: 2, 3, 4, 6, 7, 8, 9. The median is then the middle number of this group, namely, 6. When the group consists of an even number of numbers arranged in increasing magnitude, the median is that number which lies half-way between the two middle numbers. Thus the median of 2, 3, 4, 7, 8, 9 is that number which lies half way between the two middle numbers namely, 4 and 7, that is, $5\frac{1}{2}$. In the previous example in which the mode gave us an incorrect view, namely, where the salaries are the following: *A* makes $9000, *B* makes $9200, *C* makes $9300, *D* makes $9400, *E* makes $15,000, and *F* makes $15,000, the median turns out to be the number between $9300 and $9400, namely, $9350, which is clearly a less deceptive figure than the mode.

Exercises

1. Which of the following are adequate questions for a poll?

   a) In the next election will you vote for the best man?

   b) Are you still a member of the Communist Party?

   c) Do you believe that those who refused to serve in the army during the last war should be given amnesty?

   d) Should Einstein's theory of relativity be accepted by physicists?

   e) In the next election will you vote Democrat?

2. Assume you are working for the Gallup Poll Company and you wish to know what the chances are that Mr. X will be elected governor of California. From what groups would you select your sample?

3. Give the mean, the mode, and the median of the following groups:

   a) 8, 9, 12, 3, 6, 2, 2

   b) 5000, 6000, 7000, 3000, 3000, 2000

   c) 3 students get 50
      2 students get 70
      1 student gets 20
      2 students get 90
      1 student gets 80

MATHEMATICAL PROBABILITY

Thus far probability has been discussed primarily from a relative viewpoint. The probability changes as the evidence changes or as new evidence becomes available. Even in those instances involving the mean, the mode, and the median, the numbers could clearly change if more salaries or other numbers were added. There is no such thing as *the* probability of the occurrence of a given event. But sometimes it is said that all the evidence is in. We know all the possible alternatives and on this basis we can derive a strict notion of probability. What is the probability that a toss of a coin will turn up head? In this example the probability can apparently be completely and absolutely determined. The coin can come down either head or tail. A mathematical formula can determine what the probability of a head will be. The formula states that the favorable cases are divided by the combination of favorable and unfavorable cases, i.e. $f/(f + u)$. In the case of the coin there is only one favorable case, when the coin turns up head; and there is only one unfavorable case, when the coin turns up tail. Thus using the mathematical formula we obtain

1/(1 + 1). The mathematical probability that the coin will turn up head in the next throw is 1/2. What is the probability that a die will land with an even face up on the next throw? Since the die has six faces and the numbers 2, 4, and 6 are the only favorable cases, while 1, 3, and 5 are the unfavorable ones, the mathematical formula is used to obtain 3/(3 + 3). Since 3/(3 + 3) equals 1/2 the probability that the die will land with an even face is 1/2. In other words there is a *fifty-fifty* chance that the coin will turn up head or that the die will turn up with an even face.

Mathematical probability can also be used with more complicated examples. What is the probability of getting two heads if two coins are tossed? Again we can compute that there is only one favorable case, namely, where both coins turn up heads. But there are three unfavorable cases: where the first coin is a head and the second a tail, or where the second coin is a head and the first coin is a tail, or where both are tails. This gives us a formula of 1/(1 + 3). Thus the probability of getting two heads with a toss of two coins is 1/4. Similarly, we can compute the probability of obtaining a ten in a single throw of two dice. There are three favorable cases; the first die shows a 5 and the second die shows a 5, the first die shows a 4 and the second die shows a 6, the first die shows a 6 and the second die shows a 4. Now how many unfavorable cases are there? What we can do is simply list all the possible cases which may occur when two dice are rolled. It turns out that there are 36 cases; the first die shows a 1 and the second a 1, the first die shows a 1 and the second a 2, the first die shows a 1 and the second a 3, and so on, until the first die shows a 6 and the second a 6. Thus if 3 of these 36 cases are favorable, then the 33 that are left are unfavorable. Using our formula we obtain 3/(3 + 33). Thus the probability of obtaining a ten in a single throw of two dice is 1/12.

When we deal with two or more separate and independent events, i.e., when the outcome of one does not affect the outcome of the other, it is sometimes easier to use a formula that combines the probability of each event. Thus, for example, we could have dealt with the probability of getting two heads with a toss of two coins by simply multiplying the probabilities of each event separately. The probability of getting a head with a toss of one of the coins is, as we have seen, 1/2. Similarly, the probability of getting a head with the other coin is 1/2. Multiplying 1/2 by 1/2 we obtain 1/4, which is the probability of getting two heads with the toss of two coins. In cases of this kind where we try to determine the probability of the occurrence of two or more events which are unrelated to one another, we simply multiply probabilities.

$$\frac{f}{u + f} \times \frac{f}{u + f}$$

We might want to know what the probability is of drawing three hearts out of a deck of cards, where after each draw the card is placed back in the deck. Each draw is an independent event, since the card is replaced each time and thus any of the 52 cards in the deck has an equal chance of being drawn each time. This means we have 13 favorable possibilities—since there are 13 hearts —and thus 39 unfavorable ones. Using the formula f/(u + f) multiplied 3 times, we obtain

$$\tfrac{13}{52} \times \tfrac{13}{52} \times \tfrac{13}{52} = \tfrac{1}{4} \times \tfrac{1}{4} \times \tfrac{1}{4} = \tfrac{1}{64}$$

Thus the probability of drawing three hearts is 1/64.

The same technique can be used to determine the probability of obtaining three hearts when each card is *not* replaced in the deck. Thus we first ask what is the probability of drawing a heart from a deck of 52 cards. Here we have 13 favorable possibilities and 39 unfavorable ones. Using the formula f/(u + f) the probability is 13/52. But in the second draw we want to know what is the probability of drawing a second heart if the first draw yielded a heart that was not returned to the deck. In this second draw we are dealing with a deck of 51 cards and 12 hearts. In this case we have 12 favorable possibilities and 39 unfavorable ones. Thus the probability of drawing a heart in this second drawing is 12/(12 + 39), i.e., 12/51. For the third drawing we follow a similar procedure, only now the deck contains 50 cards and 11 hearts. The probability of drawing a third heart in this third draw is 11/50. Now if we multiply all these individual probabilities together, namely,

$$\tfrac{13}{52} \times \tfrac{12}{51} \times \tfrac{11}{50}$$

we will obtain 11/850 as the probability that three hearts can be drawn from a deck of cards without each heart being replaced.

Sometimes we want to know the probability of getting one or the other of several alternative events. That is, we might want to know what is the probability of obtaining either 4 or 6 on a die. In this case we are dealing not with independent events but with *mutually exclusive* ones. If one occurs, the other cannot. In such cases we simply add the separate probabilities, since the events are not independent. If a die turns up 4, then it cannot be 6. The probability of obtaining a 4 on a die is 1/6; of obtaining a 6, also 1/6. Adding both probabilities we obtain

$$\tfrac{1}{6} + \tfrac{1}{6} = \tfrac{1}{3}$$

Thus the probability of obtaining a 4 or a 6 on a die is 1/3. Using this technique of dealing with dependent events we can simplify the above example of trying to obtain the probability of getting a ten in a single throw of two dice. There are three favorable but mutually exclusive cases. The first die shows a 5 and the second a 5; the first die shows a 4 and the second a 6; the first shows a 6 and the second a 4. The probability of getting a 5 on one die and a 5 on the other is found by multiplying $1/6 \times 1/6$ which equals $1/36$. This applies also to getting 4 and 6, and 6 and 4. Each event has a probability of $1/36$. But since all three events are such that when one occurs the other cannot occur, we add

$$\tfrac{1}{36} + \tfrac{1}{36} + \tfrac{1}{36} = \tfrac{3}{36} = \tfrac{1}{12}$$

Thus we show again how we obtain the probability of getting a ten in a single throw of two dice.

There are times when the events considered are neither independent nor mutually exclusive. What is the probability of obtaining at least one tail with two throws of a coin? The two events are not independent, since if the first throw is a tail, then, regardless of what the second throw is, these two throws will be a favorable case. On the other hand, if the first throw is heads, then the second throw will determine whether the case is favorable or not. For similar reasons the two events are not mutually exclusive since one favorable case depends upon both throws turning up tails. In such cases what we do is first determine all the possible cases that could occur with two throws. Only four possibilities exist: head-head, head-tail, tail-head, tail-tail. Each one of these cases is mutually exclusive. The occurrence of head-head, for example, cannot be the same as any of the others. Thus we now proceed to use the addition formula we used previously. The favorable cases in which at least one tail appears are: head-tail, tail-head, tail-tail. Now in relation to each one of these cases we can ask what is the probability that the specific combination will occur. In other words, we first ask what is the probability of obtaining a head-tail combination in two throws of the coin. Since there is only one favorable possibility here—when the first throw is a head and the second a tail—and three unfavorable ones, the probability of a head-tail combination is $1/4$. Similarly, the probability of obtaining a tail-head combination is determined by the fact that there is only one favorable case, namely the tail-head combination, and three unfavorable ones. So here also the probability is $1/4$. The same analysis is made for the tail-tail combination. Adding the probabilities of all these three cases together we obtain

$$\tfrac{1}{4} + \tfrac{1}{4} + \tfrac{1}{4}$$

Thus the probability of getting at least one tail in two throws of a coin turns out to be $3/4$.

Of course, there are more complicated cases of mathematical probability, but they all claim to have in common the view that a specific unchanging probability figure can be attained. Once we know all the possible alternatives, as we apparently do when dealing with coins and dice, we can determine without fear of error what the probability of the occurrence of a given event will be. But this view is mistaken. For even the examples dealing with coins and dice require that "all conditions be equal." For we are assuming that if our coin is a penny, there is not more copper on the side showing Lincoln than on the other side. Otherwise the head side would be more heavily weighted and the tail would show up more than the head. We are also assuming that the coin could not stand on its edge and that there are no erratic weather conditions that could affect the free fall of the coin. Similarly, in the case of the dice we have to assume that the dice are not *loaded*; in other words, nothing has happened to them that makes one face more apt to turn up than another. All possibilities must be regarded as equally likely. Thus even in these so-called *pure* cases of probability, intangibles could affect the inference of a given probability.

Dice and cards usually reveal the clearest examples in which mathematical probability seems to have a genuine application. But this should not be taken to mean that mathematical probability has not been applied in other areas. We know that insurance companies employ mathematical inferences in order to determine the longevity that can be attributed to different groups of individuals. The use of mathematical probability is also seen in such diverse fields as economics, sociology, and the construction of missiles. The prediction of weather is another area in which mathematical probability is said to be increasingly used. We might, for example, have the following data: for 110 days in the last two years clouds of a certain kind appear in the sky and the humidity is at a certain level; during 70 of those 110 days it rains, while during the 40 other days it does not rain. On the basis of this data we can obtain a probability figure relating favorable to unfavorable cases: 70/110, i.e., 7/11. That is, on the basis of the data we have for the last two years we can say that the probability is almost 64 percent that when the same conditions prevail tomorrow or some other time in the future, then it will rain. Presumably, as we gather information about what happens to the weather under different conditions for three, four, or more years, our probability figure will improve. But it is unlikely that the prediction of the weather will ever have that degree of mathematical certainty that is found when we analyze probability relating to cards and dice or balls in an urn. For this reason even with the most careful weather prediction, one that takes in as many conditions as are known, it is advisable to take an umbrella.

Exercises

1. Give the mathematical probability of obtaining the following:

   a) A 6 in the roll of a single die.

   b) A 6 in the roll of two dice.

   c) Two aces in two draws from a deck of cards. (Each card is returned after each draw.)

   d) Four diamonds in four draws from a deck of cards. (Each card is not replaced after each draw.)

   e) An 18 in the roll of three dice.

   f) Not getting a 4 in the roll of a single die.

   g) Not getting an 8 in the roll of two dice.

   h) At least one head in three throws of a coin.

2. Show how you might determine the probability that the United States will have an energy crisis within a few years.

MILL'S METHODS

It is sometimes maintained that under special conditions an inductive inference can have the kind of necessity attributed to deductive inference. Suppose a specific kind of virus is found to be the *cause* of cancer. Now if we label something as a *cause*, it means that when that something is present, a certain event necessarily occurs. Therefore the establishment of a causal relation between two or more events would mean that an inference concerning one event can be made concerning some other event. But this inference is not deductive, since none of the preceding deductive rules are applicable to it, yet the inference is necessary. We would be reasoning in the following way: Given that p is the cause of q, then we can deduce necessarily that if p occurs, then q. The problem, however, revolves around the notion of causation. Is it true to say that there are causal relations in the world such that if one event occurs, then another one will necessarily occur?

Causation has been the subject of much controversy both among philosophers and scientists. This book could add another two hundred pages on the subject of causation and barely touch upon the interesting and puzzling facets of this problem. What we shall do is mention only briefly one or two of the issues relating to causation. Then we shall turn to the attempt of John Stuart Mill (1806–1873) to explain what causation is and how one can discover a causal relationship.

David Hume, the great English philosopher, rejected the notion of causal relations. To say, "*A* is the cause of *B*," means no more than that *A* has frequently been found to occur just before *B* occurred, and as a result we gradually came to believe that *A* not only occurred just before *B*, but also that in some way it was instrumental in making *B* happen. But this belief is purely psychological and has no basis in fact. There is no hook or magnetic force in *A* by means of which it necessitates *B*. Even scientific laws are no more than generalizations about the past. When we say, "All metals are conductors," we mean no more than that metals in the past usually have been conductors and we expect that future metals will also be conductors. We expect this, but there is no guarantee.

Some scientists try to distinguish between a law and a statistical generalization. They think we ought to distinguish between statements that assert mere enumerative generalizations and statements that attempt to explain such generalizations. Thus "All metals are conductors" may mean "All metals tested have been conductors." But then we might go on to ask why metals are conductors, and this would lead us to speak of atomic structures and the like. In other words, we would be led to say, "Metals are conductors *because* certain atoms react in a certain way to produce the phenomenon we call *conductivity*." Thus from enumerative or statistical generalizations we are led to causal relations. But the argument does not end here, for the causal relation itself must now be examined, and it might turn out to be an enumerative generalization. Certain atoms react in a certain way to produce conductivity. Why? Again we seem to be able to answer only by saying, "This is what all similar atoms produce when they react to one another." In other words, the so-called causal relation seems to evaporate into an enumerative generalization.

The problem of causation—whether there are fundamental causal principles in the universe—is still, however, very controversial. In the last century, John Stuart Mill proposed several methods which he believed could explain and also uncover causal relations. Mill proposed five methods, but we shall examine only the following three, which are fundamental: the *Method of Agreement*, the *Method of Difference*, and the *Method of Concomitant Variation*.

The Method of Agreement. This method can be explicated by means of an example: five students are stricken with ptomaine poisoning, and we want to know what caused the poisoning. We find the following:

Student *A* ate soup, chicken, rolls and butter, coffee, and apple pie.

Student *B* ate soup, chicken, coffee, and apple pie.

Student C ate soup, rolls and butter, coffee, and apple pie.

Student D ate soup, coffee, and apple pie.

Student E ate soup, chicken, rolls and butter.

This list reveals that only one item had been eaten by all of them, namely soup. Soup therefore seems to be the cause of the ptomaine poisoning. Generalizing from this example we can define the Method of Agreement as follows: *If two or more instances of the phenomenon under investigation have only one circumstance in common, the circumstance in which alone all instances agree is the cause of the given phenomena.*

The Method of Agreement is useful and is often used to give us some understanding of what it means to call something a cause of something else. But it must still be used with care, since it can never guarantee that a given circumstance is truly *the* cause of some event. In the preceding example we must assume we have listed *all* the factors which might have caused the ptomaine poisoning: either the soup, the chicken, the rolls and butter, the coffee, or the apple pie, and nothing else. But this assumption might be false. All the students might have used dirty plates, and this, rather than the soup, could have been the cause of the poisoning. Furthermore, *common circumstance* can be ambiguous or misleading terminology, since there are always an indefinite number of circumstances common to a group. Thus the students in our example may have had the same color hair or they all may have been wearing the same style clothes. Of course, we do not consider these latter factors to be relevant. But before we can decide the cause of the ptomaine poisoning, we must have some sense of what the relevant factors are, and as we have already seen, relevance is not an easy concept to define. Finally, there is a famous example showing how the Method of Agreement might lead to what would be recognized as an incorrect induction.

Jones drank rye and water on Monday and got drunk. Then he drank scotch and water on Tuesday and got drunk. Then on Wednesday he drank bourbon and water and got drunk. Finally, on Thursday he drank rum and water and got drunk. Using the Method of Agreement (during his sober moments), he decided that the water, which was common to all the instances of inebriation, was the cause of his drunkenness. Therefore he vowed never again to use water with his drinks.

The Method of Difference. Now let us consider the following example: Student A eats soup, chicken, rolls and butter, coffee, and apple pie, and then he becomes ill with ptomaine poisoning. Student B eats soup, chicken, rolls and butter, and coffee, but he does not develop ptomaine poisoning. On Mill's view, we can then conclude that the apple pie must have caused the ptomaine poisoning in Student A, since the only difference between what he ate and what student B ate was that A ate apple pie. Generalizing from this instance we can formulate Mill's Method of Difference in the following way: *If an instance in which the phenomenon under investigation occurs and an instance in which it does not occur have every circumstance in common save one, that one occurring only in the former, the circumstance in which alone the two instances differ is the cause of the phenomenon.*

The Method of Difference is often used. If you moan about an upset stomach after eating a meal at a restaurant, someone will say, "You should not have had that rich dessert. Everyone at the table ate moderately and avoided any rich dessert and all of them are fine. But you had to make a hog of yourself and you had to order that cheesecake with whipped-cream filling which is the cause of your upset." Here the Method of Difference used indicates the one factor which seems to differentiate your eating habits from those of the rest of the group in the restaurant. But again the method of difference must be used cautiously. The cheesecake with the whipped-cream filling might not have been the cause at all. Possibly you alone of the group were allergic to the main dish of Chinese food and sour pickles. Here again, as in the Method of Agreement, the notion of relevance becomes very important. How are we to understand "have every circumstance in common save one"? What if all the circumstances were the same except for the fact that you wore a tie, while none of the others did, that you had a wart on your nose, while none of the others did? While each one of these factors might very well have been the one which differentiated your circumstances from those of everyone else, such factors cannot be judged to be relevant. But again the issue arises as to how we are to distinguish relevant from irrelevant elements. Before applying Mill's methods, we would have to be able to say that having a different tie is not relevant to your getting an upset stomach, while eating the peculiar cheese dish might be relevant.

The Method of Concomitant Variation. In still another hypothetical example, let us assume we are medical research scientists at Bellevue Medical Center, where we are searching for a cure for cancer. After years and years of experimenting, we observe that the following occurs to a live cancer cell when unknown drug X is injected into it. When 1 cc. of the drug is injected into the cell, the cell becomes smaller. When 2 cc. is injected, the cell becomes still smaller. When 3 cc. of the drug is injected, the cell breaks up into parts and disappears. We do this many times and every time the same results occur. After this miraculous experience, we announce to the world that we have found a cure for cancer.

What has happened is that we have been led to identify the drug as the cause of the cure since, whenever the amount of the drug varies, the size of the cancer cell varies as well. Generalizing from this example we can now formulate Mill's Method of Concomitant Variation: *Whatever phenomenon varies in any manner whatever when another phenomenon varies in some particular manner, is the cause of that phenomenon or is connected with it through some fact of causation.*

But this method must also be used with reservation. Even in the case of the cancer, for example, we cannot simply assert that drug X is a cure for cancer. Perhaps drug X combines with some unknown element in the particular human beings tested, and it is this combination which causes the cancer to be destroyed. Perhaps each of these human beings has a particular blood condition which makes the drug work with them but not necessarily with other people. Perhaps some other factor besides the drug varies whenever the cancer cell varies in size.

Those who might wish to deny that smoking is a cause of lung cancer will argue that there might be some other component besides smoking whose variations might be correlated with variations in the growth of lung cancer—for example, pollution in the air, or the increased or decreased consumption of certain foods, or even some psychological factor such as being introverted, which causes both the desire to smoke and cancer. This does not mean we must discount the probability that smoking is a primary cause of cancer. If evidence continues to mount that in the vast majority of cases lung cancer varies as smoking varies, then we ought to regard smoking as a highly probable cause. But we cannot be absolutely certain.

Mill's methods, then, are useful in that they suggest to us ways of approaching the search for possible causal relationships. Look for the factor which events might have in common and which when it is absent also reveals the event to be absent. And finally, if these techniques do not work, look for factors that seem to change in relation to one another. All these methods might give us a clue as to why certain things occur and hence how they might be avoided —or at least how they can be used beneficially. But Mill's methods do not guarantee success.

Exercises

1. Analyze the following in terms of Mill's Methods:

    a) Ten men had dinner together and they all developed a rash. They ate different foods, but an hour before the dinner they each drank two martinis. Therefore two martinis were the cause of the rash.

b) At this same dinner an eleventh man did not eat the same food as the other ten men, nor did he drink any martinis, nor did he develop a rash. Therefore this strengthens the belief that the two martinis were the cause of the rash.

c) All of the ten men at the dinner had olives with their martinis. Therefore perhaps the olives and not the martinis were the cause of the rash.

d) Even though all ten men each had two martinis, the four men who each had only one olive had a less severe rash than the other six men who had eaten two olives apiece. Therefore the olives caused the rash.

e) The four men who had a less severe rash not only had just one olive, but also were much younger and more physically fit than the other six. Thus the martinis, rather than the olives, might still have caused the rash.

f) The four who had a less severe rash were black men. Therefore black people are more immune to rashes than white people.

2. a) In maternity ward A at City Hospital during a given week, 20 out of 30 infants were born malformed. All 20 were delivered by Dr. Jones. Therefore Dr. Jones was inadequate as a deliverer of babies.

b) Dr. Jones also delivered the other 10 babies who were not malformed. Therefore Jones was blameless.

c) The mothers of the 20 malformed children were undernourished, while the other 10 mothers were well nourished. Therefore the malformation was caused by a lack of proper nourishment.

d) In maternity ward B undernourished mothers did not give birth to malformed children. Therefore undernourishment is not the cause of malformation.

e) In maternity ward A a Chinese nurse cared for the mothers of the 20 malformed children, but not for the other 10 mothers. Therefore the Chinese nurse was the cause of the malformation.

f) In maternity ward A and B only those who took drug X during their pregnancy had malformed children. Therefore drug X was the cause.

g) Those who took less of drug X had less malformed children than those who took more of drug X. Therefore drug X was clearly the cause of malformation.

h) Those who used more of drug X also used more aspirins, and those who used less of drug X used fewer aspirins. Therefore aspirins, rather than drug X, were the cause of the malformation.

i) But those who took many aspirins but did not use drug X had healthy babies. Therefore drug X was the cause.

3. a) Ten out of fourteen P-47 airplanes crashed within the same week while on a routine flight. These ten airplanes used brand X fuel while the four other airplanes used brand Y fuel. Therefore brand X was the cause of the crashes.

b) Many other P-47 airplanes used brand X fuel and they did not crash. Therefore it is unlikely that brand X was the cause.

c) Actually, only the ten downed airplanes used a new brand X containing additives. Therefore a new brand X was the cause.

d) A certain part of the engines of the ten downed planes had cracks, but none of the other planes had such cracks. Therefore the cracks caused the crashes.

e) Tests revealed that even though parts of the engine referred to above were cracked, the planes still functioned smoothly. Therefore the cracks were not the cause.

f) All ten planes soared to a much higher altitude than any of the other planes and at such an altitude the fuel solidified, making it unusable. Thus the higher altitude and the characteristics of the fuel at such an altitude caused the crashes.

SUPPLEMENTARY READINGS

Copi, I., "Mill's Methods," *Introduction to Logic*, Third Edition. New York: Macmillan, 1968, Chapter 12.

Mill, J. S., "Of the Four Methods of Experimental Inquiry," *A System of Logic: Ratiocinative and Inductive*, Vol. I, Ninth Edition. London: Longmans, Green, Reader, and Dyer, 1875, Chapter 8.

Russell, B., "On Induction," *The Problems of Philosophy*. London: Clarendon Press, 1912, Chapter 6.

Answers

CHAPTER 1

Pages 9–10

1. People need language in order to communicate with one another. They use language to express the most basic and the most complex feelings and ideas, ranging from the desire for aid in time of danger, to the revelation of a discovery of a cure for a dread disease, to the aesthetic response to a beautiful work of art.

2. Obviously the sound functions in this example like a religious symbol, having the same psychological effect as any words used in a religious service. The guru performs the same function as priests, ministers, and rabbis when they lead their groups in meditation and prayer to bring them closer to divinity and freedom from the stress of life. Such is the power of the word and the sound as religious symbols.

    The most infamous example of how language can be used to relieve tensions is that of Hitler's power to arouse in the German people an ability to express their emotions through the act of killing. F.D.R. used language to relieve tensions when, during the depression, he said, "The only thing we have to fear is fear itself."

3. Yes. It can, for example, use hand signs like the blind do.

4. It would probably survive, but losing the power to speak or write might so handicap the present civilization that it would either deteriorate or be transformed into a radically different kind of world.

5. *Bow-wow*: man's conscious imitation of the sounds of nature.
    Pooh-pooh: instinctual vocal sounds caused by feelings of pleasure and pain, and so on.
    Sing-song: mechanical chanting to show respect for the gods.
    Yo-he-ho: physical exertion led to grunts which became words.
    Ta-ta: sounds automatically arise when the body moves.

    Perhaps the *bow-wow* and *pooh-pooh* theories are more warranted, and the *sing-song* is the least. However, they are all merely theories.

6. A universal language might help to facilitate communication and minimize misunderstanding among people. But unfortunately, Esperanto cannot eliminate human deficiencies and that is what usually causes the most difficulty.

7. Some have maintained that thinking is just talking internally.

8. But if thinking is just talking internally, and if you cannot talk, would you be able to think? Helen Keller could not read or talk or hear, but apparently she could think. Perhaps there is some way of thinking that does not use words.

9. What would Gulliver's linguists use to describe freedom or other abstract concepts? Furthermore, they would obviously have some difficulty in attempting to carry around a cyclotron.

10. Very often illogical reasoning is simply the reasoning of the person with whom you disagree. This text will attempt to reveal what it really means to be illogical.

CHAPTER 2

Pages 23–26

1. a) Narrative

   b) Argumentative

   c) Argumentative

   d) Descriptive

2. a) Explicit Argument. Sex is pleasurable because of friction in the body. Sex is also pleasant because it is a necessary function of the body and also because by being pleasant it fosters the continuous production of living creatures.

   b) Implicit Argument. All civilized nations have gun control which cuts down crime. Therefore the United States, which is a civilized nation, ought to have gun control.

   c) Explicit Argument. College students are spoiled and live luxuriously. Therefore they look for easy ways of getting out of schoolwork.

   d) Explicit Argument. Society breeds respect for the law, which has no conscience. But men ought to live by their own consciences. Therefore men ought to be men first, social beings second.

   e) Explicit Argument. We should have stayed out of the Vietnam War. It was a civil war, not a struggle against Communism.

   f) Explicit Argument. Chaucer was a great writer, but at least one of his stories is anti-Semitic. Therefore Chaucer, like most men of his time, was anti-Semitic.

   g) Explicit Argument. We say this is more or less than that. *More or less* implies the most. Therefore if there is more or less good, then there must be that which is most good, i.e. the best, and this is God.

   h) Not really an argument. This statement consists of arbitrary judgments about masculine and feminine traits. No specific evidence is offered.

CHAPTER 3

Pages 37–38

1. Misused analogy

2. Hypostatization—*brotherhood of man*

3. Amphiboly—dangling modifier

4. Equivocation. However, Dick Gregory deliberately uses the word *serve* to comment sarcastically on the color bias of Southerners. Thus this is not a fallacious use of equivocation.

5. Lexical ambiguity—the word *some*

6. Structural ambiguity—the word *revolting*. Is it part of the verb or is it to be regarded as an adjective?

7. Equivocation—obviously not fallacious if used for a humorous effect!

8. Hypostatization—*un-American*

9. Hypostatization—*freedom*

10. Accent

Pages 47–49

1. Bifurcation, appeal to force

2. Accident

3. Poisoning the wells, ad hominem

4. Hasty generalization

5. Argument of the beard

6. Extension, diversion—humor

7. Begging the question

8. Appeal to ignorance

9. Post hoc

10. Appeal to ignorance

11. Genetic fallacy, ad hominem

12. Accident, misuse of emotive words

13. Division

14. Composition

15. Appeal to force

16. Special pleading

17. Oversimplification, post hoc, hypostatization—*conformity*

18. Appeal to authority

19. Diversion—humor

20. Lifting out of context

21. Red herring

22. Pettifogging

23. Appeal to the people, accident

24. Appeal to force

25. Tu quoque

CHAPTER 4

Pages 60–61

1. a) From a grammatical point of view *it* is the subject and *is raining* is the predicate. However, *it* does not have an identifiable antecedent in this idiomatic expression. Thus while the sentence has correct grammatical form, from a logical point of view this is a puzzling construction since whatever *it* is, it clearly is not doing the raining. What this idiom says is that rain is falling.

   b) *No ghosts* is the subject and *are really there* is the predicate.

   c) The verb is not expressed in this exclamation. It is understood, however, to be present in the sense of "What a ring this is"! Then the subject can be identified as *this* and the predicate is *what a ring is*.

   d) The subject *you* is understood; *don't do that* is the predicate.

   e) *I* is the subject; *ten books to read* is the predicate.

   f) *It* is the subject and *is a pleasure to meet you* is the predicate. The explanation is the same as for (a). *It* does not have an identifiable antecedent in this idiomatic expression. "It is a pleasure to meet you" really means "I feel pleasure when I meet you."

2. a) What Faulkner does in this expression is to omit the signs of punctuation and capitalization that are required if a sentence is to be regarded as correct from a grammatical point of view. When these signs are added, then the reader can readily discern that Faulkner is employing the conventional word order of an English sentence: "What have I done to have been given children like these? Benjamin was punishment enough and now for her to have no more regard for me, her own mother! I've suffered for her, dreamed, planned, and sacrificed. I went down into the valley."

   b) Part of this expression can be described as following the normal pattern of subject-verb-object order: "I could hear my watch whenever the car stopped, but not often. They were already eating." However, the rest of the passage defies such classification and is utilized by the author to reflect the random, stream-of-consciousness pattern of thinking.

   c) In *Finnegan's Wake* James Joyce deliberately uses multiple meanings and many kinds of linguistic effect to convey his complex allegory of the fall and resurrection of mankind. J. Campbell and H. Robinson in *A Skeleton Key to Finnegan's Wake* (New York, Viking, 1944, p. 163) read the lines as follows: "Here we are, whence have we come, and where, after all, are we? For whether we be mere tomtit-tots or the sum total of existence, here it is we are! And here too is the motherly cup of tea." Thus while all the quoted passages in this exercise are not strictly speaking sentences, they can be interpreted to read like sentences.

d) This is a complex sentence consisting of two subordinate clauses (*during which* to *heterogeneity* and *during which* to *transformation*). *Evolution* is the subject and *is* to *transformation* makes up the predicate.

e) *Wake* seems to be the subject, *falls* the verb, and *fruit* the object, that is if we assume that the expression follows the normal subject-verb-object word order we expect to find in most sentences. But *true* or *false* is not applicable to this group of words, and it is not a sentence.

f) *Metals* is the subject; *are vegetables* is the predicate. *False* is applicable to this group of words and it is a sentence.

g) Gertrude Stein's famous remark repeats the predicate *is a rose*. It seems to be no more than a circumlocution, but it obviously has profound significance for Gertrude Stein. She would therefore regard it as a sentence. Who else would?

3. He had to find ways of translating Bimoba into our language forms. We probably could not understand a language that we could not translate into our language forms.

4. To a logician a sentence is a linguistic unit which can be taken as true or false whereas to a grammarian a sentence must contain a special kind of structure (usually involving a subject and a predicate) which does not necessarily have to be taken as true or false.

5. When we speak of negative matter we mean an entity that always behaves in a fashion that is diametrically opposite to the way in which positive matter behaves. Both types of matter refer to a material entity. But a negative state of affairs is supposed to deny that such a state of affairs actually exists. It is not merely the positing of a state of affairs which is different from a positive one.

6. What are ideas? Has anyone ever seen an idea?

Page 64

1. a) Future events might reveal that this judgment is not a correct one.

b) Can we really think of a language which does not employ subjects and predicates? Can a language function without words for space or time? Some characteristics of a grammar seem to make the concept of the relativity of grammar questionable.

c) Perhaps the rule that any sentence that is self-contradictory, such as "John is false and John is not false," must be false. Again try to think of a sentence without a subject.

d) It is difficult to believe that mathematics, for example, is relative to one's culture. Also does any culture believe that a self-contradictory statement is true?

e) Who knows what *decadent* means in this context? In fact, this statement is probably false.

2. One example might be: "I exist." But some have argued that even this sentence could be false. If by *exist* we mean physical existence and if it makes sense to speak of ghosts, then if a ghost says "I exist," he would be mistaken.

3. a) *True* means sincere, or has integrity, or is loyal.

   b) *True* means faithful.

   c) *Truly* when used as part of the conventional closing of a letter really means very little if anything to the person who employs it. It is a way of ending a letter in a formal, businesslike fashion.

   d) *Truth* means knowledge

   e) *False* means not true. But this sentence is paradoxical. It is both true and false. If it is true, it is false; if it is false, it is true. This kind of sentence led Bertrand Russell to posit his theory of different levels of language in which no sentence could refer to itself. Thus "this sentence is false" would not be allowable since the sentence refers to itself.

   f) *False* means deceitful.

CHAPTER 5

Pages 68–69

1. a) If he comes through the door, then I will shoot him.

   b) If a man hesitates, then he is lost.

   c) He tried and he failed and he won the battle.

   d) Either I shall not fire or he runs.

   e) If you go, then I will go.

   f) If you want to leave, then you leave.

   g) He cried and I did not care.

   h) I will fight and my heart is not in it.

   i) The lady next door is not too bright, and she happens to be my mistress.

Page 70

1. a) If p then q

   b) If p then q

   c) p and q and r

d) *p* or *q**

e) If *p* then *q*

f) If *p* then *q*

g) *p* and *q**

h) *p* and *q**

i) *p* and *q**

2. a) *Y* and *H*, or *I*

b) If *p* or *q* then, *r* and *s*

c) *J* and *M*

d) *p* if and only if *q* and *r*

Page 78

1. a) Equivalent since both final columns are the same.

p	*q*	*r*	*q* ∨ *r*	*p* ∨ (*q* ∨ *r*)
T	T	T	T	T
T	T	F	T	T
T	F	T	T	T
T	F	F	F	T
F	T	T	T	T
F	T	F	T	T
F	F	T	T	T
F	F	F	F	F

p	*q*	*r*	*q* ∨ *r*	(*q* ∨ *r*) ∨ *p*
T	T	T	T	T
T	T	F	T	T
T	F	T	T	T
T	F	F	F	T
F	T	T	T	T
F	T	F	T	T
F	F	T	T	T
F	F	F	F	F

*In the forthcoming section of negation, negative sentences will be symbolized differently.

b) Equivalent since both final columns are the same. The last two columns are the final columns.

p	q	r	s	$s \vee r$	$p \vee (s \vee r)$	$p \vee q$	$s \vee (p \vee q)$	$p \vee (s \vee r) \vee q$	$s \vee (p \vee q) \vee r$
T	T	T	T	T	T	T	T	T	T
T	T	T	F	T	T	T	T	T	T
T	T	F	T	T	T	T	T	T	T
T	T	F	F	F	T	T	T	T	T
T	F	T	T	T	T	T	T	T	T
T	F	T	F	T	T	T	T	T	T
T	F	F	T	T	T	T	T	T	T
T	F	F	F	F	T	T	T	T	T
F	T	T	T	T	T	T	T	T	T
F	T	T	F	T	T	T	T	T	T
F	T	F	T	T	T	T	T	T	T
F	T	F	F	F	F	T	T	T	T
F	F	T	T	T	T	F	T	T	T
F	F	T	F	T	T	F	F	T	T
F	F	F	T	T	T	F	T	T	T
F	F	F	F	F	F	F	F	F	F

c) Equivalent since the last two columns are the same.

p	p	p	$p \vee (p \vee p) \vee p$
T	T	T	T
F	F	F	F

d) Equivalent since the last two columns are the same.

p	q	s	$q \vee s$	$(q \vee s) \vee p$	$q \vee s \vee p$
T	T	T	T	T	T
T	T	F	T	T	T
T	F	T	T	T	T
T	F	F	F	T	T
F	T	T	T	T	T
F	T	F	T	T	T
F	F	T	T	T	T
F	F	F	F	F	F

e) Equivalent since the last two columns are the same.

p	q	r	s	$q \vee s$	$p \vee q \vee r \vee s$	$r \vee p \vee (q \vee s)$
T	T	T	T	T	T	T
T	T	T	F	T	T	T
T	T	F	T	T	T	T
T	T	F	F	T	T	T
T	F	T	T	T	T	T
T	F	T	F	F	T	T
T	F	F	T	T	T	T
T	F	F	F	F	T	T
F	T	T	T	T	T	T
F	T	T	F	T	T	T
F	T	F	T	T	T	T
F	T	F	F	T	T	T
F	F	T	T	T	T	T
F	F	T	F	F	T	T
F	F	F	T	T	T	T
F	F	F	F	F	F	F

f) Not equivalent since the last two columns are not the same.

p	q	r	s	$p \vee q$	$r \vee s$	$(p \vee q) \vee (r \vee s)$	$p \vee q \vee r$
T	T	T	T	T	T	T	T
T	T	T	F	T	T	T	T
T	T	F	T	T	T	T	T
T	T	F	F	T	F	T	T
T	F	T	T	T	T	T	T
T	F	T	F	T	T	T	T
T	F	F	T	T	T	T	T
T	F	F	F	T	F	T	T
F	T	T	T	T	T	T	T
F	T	T	F	T	T	T	T
F	T	F	T	T	T	T	T
F	T	F	F	T	F	T	T
F	F	T	T	F	T	T	T
F	F	T	F	F	T	T	T
F	F	F	T	F	T	T	F
F	F	F	F	F	F	F	F

g) Equivalent since the last two columns are the same.

p	q	r	s	p ∨ q	r ∨ s	p ∨ s ∨ q	(p ∨ q) ∨ (r ∨ s)	(p ∨ s ∨ q) ∨ r
T	T	T	T	T	T	T	T	T
T	T	T	F	T	T	T	T	T
T	T	F	T	T	T	T	T	T
T	T	F	F	T	F	T	T	T
T	F	T	T	T	T	T	T	T
T	F	T	F	T	T	T	T	T
T	F	F	T	T	T	T	T	T
T	F	F	F	T	F	T	T	T
F	T	T	T	T	T	T	T	T
F	T	T	F	T	T	T	T	T
F	T	F	T	T	T	T	T	T
F	T	F	F	T	F	T	T	T
F	F	T	T	F	T	T	T	T
F	F	T	F	F	T	F	T	T
F	F	F	T	F	T	T	T	T
F	F	F	F	F	F	F	F	F

Page 82

1. a) p = he stays; $\bar{q}$ = I do not go.

p	q	$\bar{q}$	p ∨ $\bar{q}$
T	T	F	T
T	F	T	T
F	T	F	F
F	F	T	T

b) $\bar{p}$ = I do not stay; $\bar{q}$ = he does not go.

p	q	$\bar{p}$	$\bar{q}$	$\bar{p}$ ∨ $\bar{q}$	− ($\bar{p}$ ∨ $\bar{q}$)
T	T	F	F	F	T
T	F	F	T	T	F
F	T	T	F	T	F
F	F	T	T	T	F

c) $\bar{p}$ = I do not stay; $\bar{q}$ = he does not go.

p	q	$\bar{p}$	$\bar{q}$	$\bar{p} \vee \bar{q}$	$-(\bar{p} \vee \bar{q})$	$--(\bar{p} \vee \bar{q})$
T	T	F	F	F	T	F
T	F	F	T	T	F	T
F	T	T	F	T	F	T
F	F	T	T	T	F	T

d) $\bar{p}$ = presidential candidates do not keep their promises after they are elected; q = they find sneaky ways of pretending that they have kept their promises.

p	q	$\bar{p}$	$\bar{p} \vee q$
T	T	F	T
T	F	F	F
F	T	T	T
F	F	T	T

2. a)

p	q	r	$\bar{p}$	$\bar{r}$	$\bar{p} \vee q$	$\bar{p} \vee q \vee \bar{r}$	$-(\bar{p} \vee q \vee \bar{r})$
T	T	T	F	F	T	T	F
T	T	F	F	T	T	T	F
T	F	T	F	F	F	F	T
T	F	F	F	T	F	T	F
F	T	T	T	F	T	T	F
F	T	F	T	T	T	T	F
F	F	T	T	F	T	T	F
F	F	F	T	T	T	T	F

b)

p	q	r	$\bar{p}$	$\bar{r}$	$\bar{p} \vee \bar{r}$	$-(\bar{p} \vee \bar{r})$	$\bar{p} \vee q \vee -(\bar{p} \vee \bar{r})$
T	T	T	F	F	F	T	T
T	T	F	F	T	T	F	T
T	F	T	F	F	F	T	T
T	F	F	F	T	T	F	F
F	T	T	T	F	T	F	T
F	T	F	T	T	T	F	T
F	F	T	T	F	T	F	T
F	F	F	T	T	T	F	T

c)

p	q	r	$p \vee q$	$-(p \vee q)$	$\bar{p}$	$\bar{r}$	$\bar{p} \vee \bar{r}$	$-(p \vee q) \vee (\bar{p} \vee \bar{r})$
T	T	T	T	F	F	F	F	F
T	T	F	T	F	F	T	T	T
T	F	T	T	F	F	F	F	F
T	F	F	T	F	F	T	T	T
F	T	T	T	F	T	F	T	T
F	T	F	T	F	T	T	T	T
F	F	T	F	T	T	F	T	T
F	F	F	F	T	T	T	T	T

d)

p	q	r	$p \vee q \vee q \vee q \vee r$	$-(p \vee q \vee q \vee q \vee r)$
T	T	T	T	F
T	T	F	T	F
T	F	T	T	F
T	F	F	T	F
F	T	T	T	F
F	T	F	T	F
F	F	T	T	F
F	F	F	F	T

3. a) Equivalent since the last two columns are the same.

p	q	r	$\bar{p}$	$\bar{p} \vee q \vee r$	$r \vee q \vee \bar{p}$
T	T	T	F	T	T
T	T	F	F	T	T
T	F	T	F	T	T
T	F	F	F	F	F
F	T	T	T	T	T
F	T	F	T	T	T
F	F	T	T	T	T
F	F	F	T	T	T

b) Equivalent since the last two columns are the same.

p	q	r	$\bar{p}$	$\bar{q}$	$\bar{q} \vee r$	$r \vee \bar{q}$	$\bar{p} \vee (\bar{q} \vee r)$	$(r \vee \bar{q}) \vee \bar{p}$
T	T	T	F	F	T	T	T	T
T	T	F	F	F	F	F	F	F
T	F	T	F	T	T	T	T	T
T	F	F	F	T	T	T	T	T
F	T	T	T	F	T	T	T	T
F	T	F	T	F	F	F	T	T
F	F	T	T	T	T	T	T	T
F	F	F	T	T	T	T	T	T

c) Equivalent since the last two columns are the same.

p	q	r	$\bar{p}$	$\bar{q}$	$\bar{r}$	$\bar{p} \vee \bar{q} \vee \bar{r}$	$\bar{q} \vee \bar{r}$	$(\bar{p} \vee \bar{q} \vee \bar{r}) \vee \bar{r}$.	$\bar{p} \vee (\bar{q} \vee \bar{r})$
T	T	T	F	F	F	F	F	F	F
T	T	F	F	F	T	T	T	T	T
T	F	T	F	T	F	T	T	T	T
T	F	F	F	T	T	T	T	T	T
F	T	T	T	F	F	T	F	T	T
F	T	F	T	F	T	T	T	T	T
F	F	T	T	T	F	T	T	T	T
F	F	F	T	T	T	T	T	T	T

d) Not equivalent

e) Not equivalent

f) Equivalent

4. a) In the examples mentioned, negation refers to objects and behavior which are different from other objects and behavior. Thus *negative electrons* means electrons with a different charge. Unhappy people are people who behave in certain ways, and their behavior is different from the behavior of happy people. But this might be different from saying that a certain negative sentence refers to what is not the case. How can a sentence refer to nothing?

b) It could be cloudy or it could even be sunny, but this need not mean the same as "It is not raining."

c) By "There is nothing," we might mean "The universe is empty." But what would *empty* mean? There are no chairs, no planets, and so on. We are still involved with the negative.

5. You would have to include the final statement. Otherwise you could not be sure that all the objects had been named.

Page 86

1. a) p = he went to the store; q = he saw Mary; r = he saw Jean.

p	q	r	$q \vee r$	$p \cdot (q \vee r)$
T	T	T	T	T
T	T	F	T	T
T	F	T	T	T
T	F	F	F	F
F	T	T	T	F
F	T	F	T	F
F	F	T	T	F
F	F	F	F	F

b) p = he stays; q = I go; r — I get the police.

p	q	r	$q \cdot r$	$p \vee (q \cdot r)$
T	T	T	T	T
T	T	F	F	T
T	F	T	F	T
T	F	F	F	T
F	T	T	T	T
F	T	F	F	F
F	F	T	F	F
F	F	F	F	F

c) $\bar{p}$ = I did not see the movie; q = he did see the movie; r = he liked the movie.

p	q	r	$\bar{p}$	$\bar{r}$	$\bar{p} \cdot q \cdot \bar{r}$
T	T	T	F	F	F
T	T	F	F	T	F
T	F	T	F	F	F
T	F	F	F	T	F
F	T	T	T	F	F
F	T	F	T	T	T
F	F	T	T	F	F
F	F	F	T	T	F

d)

p	q	r	$\bar{q}$	$\bar{r}$	$p \vee \bar{q}$	$(p \vee \bar{q}) \cdot \bar{r}$
T	T	T	F	F	T	F
T	T	F	F	T	T	T
T	F	T	T	F	T	F
T	F	F	T	T	T	T
F	T	T	F	F	F	F
F	T	F	F	T	F	F
F	F	T	T	F	T	F
F	F	F	T	T	T	T

e)

p	q	r	$\bar{r}$	$q \vee \bar{r}$	$p \cdot (q \vee \bar{r}) \cdot q$
T	T	T	F	T	T
T	T	F	T	T	T
T	F	T	F	F	F
T	F	F	T	T	F
F	T	T	F	T	F
F	T	F	T	T	F
F	F	T	F	F	F
F	F	F	T	T	F

f) p = you can study; q = you can join the radicals.

p	q	$p \vee q$	$p \cdot q$	$-(p \cdot q)$	$(p \vee q) \cdot -(p \cdot q)$
T	T	T	T	F	F
T	F	T	F	T	T
F	T	T	F	T	T
F	F	F	F	T	F

2. a) Equivalent
   b) Equivalent
   c) Equivalent
   d) Not equivalent
   e) Not equivalent
   f) Equivalent
   g) Equivalent.

CHAPTER 6

Page 93

1. a) p = I go to the movies; q = I see my friends; $\bar{r}$ = I will not be home early. The sentence is then symbolized as $(p \cdot q) \supset \bar{r}$.

p	q	r	$\bar{r}$	$p \cdot q$	$(p \cdot q) \supset \bar{r}$
T	T	T	F	T	F
T	T	F	T	T	T
T	F	T	F	F	T
T	F	F	T	F	T
F	T	T	F	F	T
F	T	F	T	F	T
F	F	T	F	F	T
F	F	F	T	F	T

b) p = he stays indoors; q = he goes outside; r = he will be caught. The sentence is then symbolized as $(p \lor q \lor r) \cdot \bar{q}$.

p	q	r	$\bar{q}$	$p \lor q$	$p \lor q \lor r$	$(p \lor q \lor r) \cdot \bar{q}$
T	T	T	F	T	T	F
T	T	F	F	T	T	F
T	F	T	T	T	T	T
T	F	F	T	T	T	T
F	T	T	F	T	T	F
F	T	F	F	T	T	F
F	F	T	T	F	T	T
F	F	F	T	F	F	F

c) p = he goes to the theater; $\bar{q}$ = he does not see Bridget Bardahl; $\bar{r}$ = he will not be happy. The sentence can then be symbolized as $(p \cdot \bar{q}) \supset \bar{r}$.

p	q	r	$\bar{q}$	$\bar{r}$	$p \cdot \bar{q}$	$(p \cdot \bar{q}) \supset \bar{r}$
T	T	T	F	F	F	T
T	T	F	F	T	F	T
T	F	T	T	F	T	F
T	F	F	T	T	T	T
F	T	T	F	F	F	T
F	T	F	F	T	F	T
F	F	T	T	F	F	T
F	F	F	T	T	F	T

d)

p	q	r	$\bar{p}$	$\bar{q}$	$\bar{r}$	$\bar{p} \supset \bar{q}$	$q \cdot \bar{r}$	$(\bar{p} \supset \bar{q}) \lor (q \cdot \bar{r})$
T	T	T	F	F	F	T	F	T
T	T	F	F	F	T	T	T	T
T	F	T	F	T	F	T	F	T
T	F	F	F	T	T	T	F	T
F	T	T	T	F	F	F	F	F
F	T	F	T	F	T	F	T	T
F	F	T	T	T	F	T	F	T
F	F	F	T	T	T	T	F	T

e) $p =$ he does go too; $q =$ I will go.

p	q	$p \supset q$
T	T	T
T	F	F
F	T	T
F	F	T

f) $p =$ he sees *Hamlet*; $q =$ he gets free tickets.

p	q	$p \supset q$
T	T	T
T	F	F
F	T	T
F	F	T

2. a) $p =$ I go to the store; $q =$ I see Fats Waller.

p	q	$\bar{p}$	$p \supset q$	$\bar{p} \lor q$
T	T	F	T	T
T	F	F	F	F
F	T	T	T	T
F	F	T	T	T

Final columns are equivalent.

b) No, since the final columns would then not be equivalent.

3. a) Equivalent since the last two columns are the same.

p	q	r	$q \cdot r$	$p \supset q$	$p \supset r$	$p \supset (q \cdot r)$	$(p \supset q) \cdot (p \supset r)$
T	T	T	T	T	T	T	T
T	T	F	F	T	F	F	F
T	F	T	F	F	T	F	F
T	F	F	F	F	F	F	F
F	T	T	T	T	T	T	T
F	T	F	F	T	T	T	T
F	F	T	F	T	T	T	T
F	F	F	F	T	T	T	T

b) Equivalent since the last two columns are the same.

p	q	r	$\bar{p}$	$q \supset r$	$\bar{p} \vee q$	$\bar{p} \vee r$	$(\bar{p} \vee q) \supset (\bar{p} \vee r)$	$\bar{p} \vee (q \subset r)$
T	T	T	F	T	T	T	T	T
T	T	F	F	F	T	F	F	F
T	F	T	F	T	F	T	T	T
T	F	F	F	T	F	F	T	T
F	T	T	T	T	T	T	T	T
F	T	F	T	F	T	T	T	T
F	F	T	T	T	T	T	T	T
F	F	F	T	T	T	T	T	T

c) Not equivalent since the last two columns are not the same.

p	q	r	$\bar{p}$	$\bar{q}$	$\bar{r}$	$p \vee q \vee r$	$\bar{p} \vee \bar{q} \vee \bar{r}$	$-(p \vee q \vee r)$	$--(p \vee q \vee r)$	$-(\bar{p} \vee \bar{q} \vee \bar{r})$
T	T	T	F	F	F	T	F	F	T	T
T	T	F	F	F	T	T	T	F	T	F
T	F	T	F	T	F	T	T	F	T	F
T	F	F	F	T	T	T	T	F	T	F
F	T	T	T	F	F	T	T	F	T	F
F	T	F	T	F	T	T	T	F	T	F
F	F	T	T	T	F	T	T	F	T	F
F	F	F	T	T	T	F	T	T	F	F

Pages 98–99

1. a) The subjunctive sentence does *not* say, "I will not go to the movies and I will not see Sophia Toothless." It says, "Perhaps I might go to the movies and then I will see Sophia Toothless." But what is meant by *might*?

b) If I say, "All metals are conductors," I am not simply stating that the last 50, 60, or 1000 metals I looked at were conductors. I am also saying, "If the next object were to be a metal, then it would be a conductor." I am also making a prediction about what would be, and not about what is or has been.

c) Actually *being to the right of* is relative to one's perspective.

2. a) If anyone who is like me with my good traits were president, he would vote everyone a bonus. If this is true then (a) is true; otherwise it is false.

b) True. Generalizing this would result in a scientifically acceptable truth.

c) False. Historians do not accept causal generalizations based on noses.

d) True, if Sophia Toothless is really appearing in the movies, since anyone can see her there.

e) False, since the generalization would be scientifically false. Objects fall 32 feet per second per second.

Pages 100–101

1. $(p \supset q) \cdot r$

2. $\left[p \vee (q \supset r) \right] \cdot \left[s \vee (t \supset q) \right]$

3. $\left[(p \cdot q) \vee r \right] \supset \left[(s \cdot t) \vee u \right]$

4. $p =$ I stay home; $q =$ I watch the late show; $r =$ I will do my homework; $s =$ I will eat sandwiches; $t =$ I will neck with my boyfriend. This is symbolized as $(p \cdot q) \supset \left[r \vee (s \cdot t) \right]$.

5. $p =$ he loves me; $q =$ I will respond; $r =$ he brings me a ring; $s =$ he has a talk with my father; $t =$ my father happens to be a justice of the peace. This is symbolized as: $p \cdot \left\{ q \supset \left[r \vee (s \cdot t) \right] \right\}$.

6. $p =$ the reptiles reelect a President; $q =$ the demons will be out for four more years; $\bar{r} =$ the panthers will not be happy; $\bar{s} =$ the panthers will not be successful. The sentence is symbolized as $p \supset (q \cdot \bar{r} \cdot \bar{s})$.

Page 103

1. a) Equivalent

p	q	$p \supset q$	$-(p \cdot \bar{q})$	$(p \supset q) \equiv -(p \cdot \bar{q})$
T	T	T	T	T
T	F	F	F	T
F	T	T	T	T
F	F	T	T	T

b) Not equivalent

p	q	$\bar{p}$	$\bar{q}$	$\bar{p} \vee \bar{q}$	$-(\bar{p} \cdot \bar{q})$	$(\bar{p} \vee \bar{q}) \equiv -(\bar{p} \cdot \bar{q})$
T	T	F	F	F	T	F
T	F	F	T	T	T	T
F	T	T	F	T	T	T
F	F	T	T	T	F	F

c) Equivalent

p	q	$\bar{p}$	$\bar{p} \equiv q$	$\bar{p} \supset q$	$q \supset \bar{p}$	$(\bar{p} \supset q) \cdot (q \supset \bar{p})$	$(\bar{p} \equiv q) \equiv [(\bar{p} \supset q) \cdot (q \supset \bar{p})]$
T	T	F	F	T	F	F	T
T	F	F	T	T	T	T	T
F	T	T	T	T	T	T	T
F	F	T	F	F	T	F	T

d) Equivalent

e) Equivalent

f) Not equivalent

2. a) p = I will permit you to take a make-up exam; q = you promise to study every night.

p	q	$p \equiv q$
T	T	T
T	F	F
F	T	F
F	F	T

b) p = John passes the course; q = the teacher likes me; $\bar{r}$ = the teacher does not like John. The sentence is then symbolized as $p \vee [p \equiv (q \cdot \bar{r})]$.

p	q	r	$\bar{r}$	$q \cdot \bar{r}$	$p \equiv (q \cdot \bar{r})$	$p \vee [p \equiv (q \cdot \bar{r})]$
T	T	T	F	F	F	T
T	T	F	T	T	T	T
T	F	T	F	F	F	T
T	F	F	T	F	F	T
F	T	T	F	F	T	T
F	T	F	T	T	F	F
F	F	T	F	F	T	T
F	F	F	T	F	T	T

c) p = John wins; q = he will be permitted to compete.

p	q	$p \equiv q$
T	T	T
T	F	F
F	T	F
F	F	T

CHAPTER 7

Page 108

1. a) p = I stay home; q = I watch television; r = I will pass the test. The sentence is symbolized as $(p \cdot q) \supset \left[r \vee (\overline{p} \cdot \overline{q}) \right]$.

p	q	r	$\overline{p}$	$\overline{q}$	$p \cdot q$	$\overline{p} \cdot \overline{q}$	$r \vee (\overline{p} \cdot \overline{q})$	$(p \cdot q) \supset \left[r \vee (\overline{p} \cdot \overline{q}) \right]$
T	T	T	F	F	T	F	T	T
T	T	F	F	F	T	F	F	F
T	F	T	F	T	F	F	T	T
T	F	F	F	T	F	F	F	T
F	T	T	T	F	F	F	T	T
F	T	F	T	F	F	F	F	T
F	F	T	T	T	F	T	T	T
F	F	F	T	T	F	T	T	T

b) p = Jones stays; q = Mary leaves; r = her friend stays. The sentence is symbolized as $\left\{ (p \cdot q) \cdot \left[(q \cdot r) \supset \overline{p} \right] \right\} \supset q$.

p	q	r	$\overline{p}$	$p \cdot q$	$q \cdot r$	$(q \cdot r) \supset \overline{p}$	$(p \cdot q) \cdot \left[(q \cdot r) \supset \overline{p} \right]$	$\left\{ (p \cdot q) \cdot \left[(q \cdot r) \supset \overline{p} \right] \right\} \supset q$
T	T	T	F	T	T	F	F	T
T	T	F	F	T	F	T	T	T
T	F	T	F	F	F	T	F	T
T	F	F	F	F	F	T	F	T
F	T	T	T	F	T	T	F	T
F	T	F	T	F	F	T	F	T
F	F	T	T	F	F	T	F	T
F	F	F	T	F	F	T	F	T

2. First of all, robots break down, too; second, what does one mean by *better*? Furthermore, even if robots reason correctly, they cannot love or hope or feel pleasure, can they? And perhaps those who can love and reason are better off than those who can only reason.

Page 115

1. a) p = I decide to go; $\overline{q}$ = you cannot go. Consistent

p	q	$\overline{q}$	$p \supset \overline{q}$
T	T	F	F
T	F	T	T
F	T	F	T
F	F	T	T

b) p = John loves Mary; q = Mary loves John. Valid

p	q	$\overline{p}$	$\overline{q}$	$\overline{q} \supset \overline{p}$	$q \supset (\overline{q} \supset \overline{p})$	$p \supset [q \supset (\overline{q} \supset \overline{p})]$
T	T	F	F	T	T	T
T	F	F	T	F	T	T
F	T	T	F	T	T	T
F	F	T	T	T	T	T

c) p = I may go. Valid

p	$\overline{p}$	$p \vee \overline{p}$
T	F	T
F	T	T

d) This seems to be an instance of $p \cdot \overline{p}$, a contradiction. But it really says, "Part of the table is brown and another part is not brown." Thus it is symbolized as: $p \cdot \overline{q}$. Consistent

e) p = Nixon wins; q = Wallace wins. Symbolized as $[(p \vee q) \cdot \overline{p}] \supset q$. Valid

f) p = Bill wins the race; q = he will make a great deal of money; r = he will retire. Symbolized as $[(p \supset q) \cdot (q \supset r)] \supset (\overline{p} \vee r)$. Valid

p	q	r	$\bar{p}$	$p \supset q$	$q \supset r$	$(p \supset q) \cdot (q \supset r)$	$\bar{p} \vee r$	$[(p \supset q) \cdot (q \supset r)] \supset (\bar{p} \vee r)$
T	T	T	F	T	T	T	T	T
T	T	F	F	T	F	F	F	T
T	F	T	F	F	T	F	T	T
T	F	F	F	F	T	F	F	T
F	T	T	T	T	T	T	T	T
F	T	F	T	T	F	F	T	T
F	F	T	T	T	T	T	T	T
F	F	F	T	T	T	T	T	T

g) $p \cdot \bar{p}$ F Inconsistent—unless *good and bad* means *very bad*; then it is simply p, and thus consistent.

h) $p \cdot \bar{p}$ F Inconsistent—if it means *happy* in one way and *unhappy* in another, then it is consistent $p \cdot \bar{q}$.

i) Valid

p	$\bar{p}$	q	$\bar{q}$	r	$\bar{r}$	$q \vee r$	$p \supset (q \vee r)$	$\bar{q} \cdot \bar{r}$	$(\bar{q} \cdot \bar{r}) \supset \bar{p}$	$[p \supset (q \vee r)] \supset [(\bar{q} \cdot \bar{r}) \supset \bar{p}]$
T	F	T	F	T	F	T	T	F	T	T
T	F	T	F	F	T	T	T	F	T	T
T	F	F	T	T	F	T	T	F	T	T
T	F	F	T	F	T	F	F	T	F	T
F	T	T	F	T	F	T	T	F	T	T
F	T	T	F	F	T	T	T	F	T	T
F	T	F	T	T	F	T	T	F	T	T
F	T	F	T	F	T	F	T	F	T	T

j) Valid

p	$\bar{p}$	r	$\bar{p} \cdot r$	$(\bar{p} \cdot r) \supset \bar{p}$
T	F	T	F	T
T	F	F	F	T
F	T	T	T	T
F	T	F	F	T

k) Inconsistent

p	r	$p \cdot r$	$(p \cdot r) \supset p$	$-[(p \cdot r) \supset p]$
T	T	T	T	F
T	F	F	T	F
F	T	F	T	F
F	F	F	T	F

2. a) p = Mary loves John; q = Mary loves Bill. The sentence is symbolized as $(p \cdot q) \supset (\overline{p} \cdot \overline{q})$. Implication does not hold.

p	$\overline{p}$	q	$\overline{q}$	$p \cdot q$	$\overline{p} \cdot \overline{q}$	$(p \cdot q) \supset (\overline{p} \cdot \overline{q})$
T	F	T	F	T	F	F
T	F	F	1	F	F	T
F	T	T	F	F	F	T
F	T	F	T	F	T	T

b) $p \supset q$ Implication does not hold.

3. a) First, society does not decide whether contradictions are true or false; logicians make this decision. Also, if contradictions were true, then we would be required to change our analyses of conjunction and negation, changes that would make these connectives unusable in any known language.

b) But surely you can think of things that could stop your being crushed; for example, if you jumped out of a window on the top floor of the Empire State Building, you might fall on the mattresses in an open truck.

Page 117

1. p = Republicans win; q = Democrats win. The sentence is symbolized as $\overline{p} \supset - (p \cdot \overline{q})$. The antecedent p can be true in only one way, namely when p is F. We substitute F for p in the consequent and ask whether it can be made F by some substitution for q. No substitution for q can make $- (p \cdot \overline{q})$ false if p is F. Thus the consequent must be true and the sentence is valid. Also if we negate the consequent and place it into conjunction with the antecedent, we obtain $\overline{p} \cdot p \cdot \overline{q}$, a contradiction. Thus $\overline{p} \supset - (p \cdot \overline{q})$ is valid.

2. p = Republicans win; q = Democrats win. The sentence is symbolized as $p \supset - (p \cdot \overline{q})$, and p can be true only if p is T. But $- (p \cdot \overline{q})$ can be made false if q is false and p is t. Invalid. Also if the consequent is negated and placed into conjunction with the antecedent, we obtain $p \cdot p \cdot \overline{q}$. No contradiction. Therefore the formula is invalid.

3. p = Maddox is nominated; q = I shall vote for Nixon. The sentence is symbolized as $[(p \supset \overline{q}) \cdot \overline{q}] \supset \overline{q}$, and $\overline{q}$ is false only if q is true. But if q is true in the antecedent, then the antecedent must be false. Valid.

4. The consequent, $p \supset r$, is false only if p is T and r is F. But the antecedent can be made T when p is T and r is F, namely when q is T. Thus it is invalid.

5. The antecedent $p \cdot q$ is true only when p is T and q is T. When we substitute T for q in the consequent, it must be T regardless of what is substituted for r. Valid.

6. The consequent is false only when p is T and q is F. Substituting these truth values in the antecedent, we find the antecedent must also turn out false. Valid.

7. Only when p is T is p true. Substituting in the consequent, we find it can be made false if T is true. Invalid.

8. The consequent is false if and only if M is T, U is F, and N is T. Substituting these truth values into the antecedent, it turns out that the antecedent also must be false. Valid.

CHAPTER 8

Pages 123 to 125

1. See list of valid forms on pp. 120–121.

2. See list of valid forms on p. 121.

3. a) Using valid form 19, Material Implication, replace $\overline{p} \vee q$ by $p \supset q$. Then by valid form 1, Modus Ponens, the formula is valid.

b) Using valid form 20, Material Implication, replace $-(p \cdot \overline{q})$ by $p \supset q$. Then by valid form 2, Modus Tollens, the formula is valid.

c) Valid by rule 6, Disjunctive Syllogism.

d) Use rule 18, Transposition, to obtain $p \supset q$ from $\overline{q} \supset \overline{p}$. Then by using rule 19, Material Implication, substitute $\overline{p} \vee q$ for $p \supset q$. $(\overline{p} \vee q) \equiv (\overline{p} \vee q)$ is valid, being a substitution instance of $p \equiv p$, which is valid.

e) Use rule 21, Material Equivalence. Then by using rule 22, replace $p \equiv q$ by $[(p \cdot q) \vee (\overline{p} \cdot \overline{q})] \cdot [(p \cdot q) \vee (\overline{p} \cdot \overline{q})] \equiv [(p \cdot q) \vee (\overline{p} \cdot \overline{q})]$ is valid, being a substitution instance of $p \equiv p$, which is valid.

f) Use rule 21, Material Equivalence, but substitute, by rule 19, $p \supset q$ for $\overline{p} \vee q$. Valid.

Page 126

1. a) Use valid form 2, Modus Tollens. But substitute $q \vee r$ for q.

b) Use valid form 7, Constructive Dilemma, but substitute $p \cdot q$ for p, $r \cdot q$ for q, $s \cdot p$ for r, and $r \cdot s$ for s.

c) Use valid form 10, but substitute p for q.

d) Use valid form 25, Exportation, but substitute $p \vee r$ for p, s for q, and $M \cdot q$ for r.

e) Use valid form 16, Distribution of Alternation, but substitute $\bar{s}$ for p. Then use valid form 10, but substitute $\bar{p}$ for p and $\bar{q}$ for q. This changes valid form 10 to $-(\bar{p} \vee \bar{q}) \equiv (\bar{p} \cdot \bar{q})$ which by rule 17, Double Negation, becomes $-(\bar{p} \vee \bar{q}) \equiv (p \cdot q)$. Replace p by q and q by r. This results in $-(\bar{q} \vee \bar{r}) \equiv (q \cdot r)$. Then replace $q \cdot r$ by $-(\bar{q} \vee \bar{r})$.

f) Use valid form 25, Exportation. But first substitute r for s. Then replace $p \cdot q$ by $-(\bar{p} \vee \bar{q})$ in the way it is done in exercise e. This results in $\left[-(\bar{p} \vee \bar{q}) \supset s\right] \equiv \left[p \supset (q \supset s)\right]$. Then using valid form 19 twice, change $\left[p \supset (q \supset s)\right]$ to $\left[\bar{p} \vee (\bar{q} \vee s)\right]$.

Pages 132 to 134

1. a)	3.	1,2, Conjunction
	4.	3, Modus Ponens
b)	3.	1, Exportation
	4.	2,3, Conjunction
	5.	4, Modus Ponens
c)	4.	1, Distribution of Alternation
	5.	4, Simplification
	6.	5, Material Implication
	7.	2, Material Implication
	8.	6,7, Conjunction
	9.	8, Hypothetical Syllogism
	10.	9,3, Conjunction
	11.	10, Modus Ponens
d)	4.	3, DeMorgan's Theorem
	5.	4, Transposition
	6.	5,2, Conjunction
	7.	1, Distribution of Conjunction
	8.	6,7, Conjunction
	9.	8, Constructive Dilemma
	10.	9, Material Equivalence
e)	3.	1, Material Implication
	4.	3, Double Negation
	5.	4, Association of Alternation
	6.	5, Association of Alternation
	7.	6, Idempotency

8.	7, Material Implication
9.	2, Material Implication
10.	9, Double Negation
11.	10, Association of Alternation
12.	11, Association of Alternation
13.	12, Idempotency
14.	13, Material Implication
15.	14,8, Conjunction
16.	15, Material Equivalence
17.	16, Material Equivalence
18.	17, Material Implication

2. Using obvious symbolism, i.e. J stands for "John wins":

a)
1.	$J \supset M$	
2.	$F \supset S$	
3.	$(B \supset S) \cdot (P \supset M)$	
4.	$\overline{S} \vee \overline{M}$	
5.	$\overline{F} \vee \overline{B} / \therefore (\overline{B} \vee \overline{P}) \cdot (\overline{F} \vee \overline{J})$	
6.	$S \supset \overline{M}$	4, Material Implication
7.	$F \supset \overline{B}$	5, Material Implication
8.	$\overline{M} \supset \overline{J}$	1, Contraposition
9.	$(F \supset S) \cdot (S \supset \overline{M})$	2,6, Conjunction
10.	$F \supset \overline{M}$	9, Hypothetical Syllogism
11.	$(F \supset \overline{M}) \cdot (\overline{M} \supset \overline{J})$	8,10, Conjunction
12.	$F \supset \overline{J}$	11, Hypothetical Syllogism
13.	$\overline{F} \vee \overline{J}$	12, Material Implication
14.	$B \supset S$	3, Simplification
15.	$S \supset \overline{M}$	4, Material Implication
16.	$P \supset M$	3, Simplification
17.	$\overline{M} \supset \overline{P}$	16, Contraposition
18.	$(B \supset S) \cdot (S \supset \overline{M})$	14,15, Conjunction
19.	$B \supset \overline{M}$	18, Hypothetical Syllogism
20.	$(B \supset \overline{M}) \cdot (\overline{M} \supset \overline{P})$	17,19, Conjunction
21.	$B \supset \overline{P}$	20, Hypothetical Syllogism
22.	$\overline{B} \vee \overline{P}$	21, Material Implication
23.	$(\overline{B} \vee \overline{P}) \cdot (\overline{F} \vee \overline{J})$	22,13, Conjunction

b)
1.	$\overline{C} \vee V$	
2.	$V \supset O / \therefore -(C \cdot \overline{O})$	
3.	$C \supset V$	1, Material Implication
4.	$(C \supset V) \cdot (V \supset O)$	3,2, Conjunction
5.	$C \supset O$	4, Hypothetical Syllogism
6.	$-(C \cdot \overline{O})$	5, Material Implication

c) 1. $B \supset (R \supset E)$
    2. $E \supset (K \vee L)$
    3. $B \cdot R \cdot \overline{K} /\therefore L$
    4. $(B \cdot R) \supset E$ 1, Exportation
    5. $B \cdot R$ 3, Simplification
    6. $\left[(B \cdot R) \supset E\right] \cdot (B \cdot R)$ 4,5, Conjunction
    7. E 6, Modus Ponens
    8. $\left[E \supset (K \vee L)\right] \cdot E$ 2,8, Conjunction
    9. $K \vee L$ 8, Modus Ponens
    10. $\overline{K}$ 3, Simplification
    11. $(K \vee L) \cdot \overline{K}$ 9,10, Conjunction
    12. L 11, Disjunctive Syllogism

d) 1. $-(p \cdot \overline{q})$
    2. $\overline{r} \supset \overline{q}$
    3. $\overline{r} \vee s /\therefore \overline{p} \vee s$
    4. $p \supset q$ 1, Material Implication
    5. $q \supset r$ 2, Transposition
    6. $(p \supset q) \cdot (q \supset r)$ 4,5, Conjunction
    7. $p \supset r$ 6, Hypothetical Syllogism
    8. $r \supset s$ 3, Material Implication
    9. $(p \supset r) \cdot (r \supset s)$ 7,8, Conjunction
    10. $p \supset s$ 9, Hypothetical Syllogism
    11. $\overline{p} \vee s$ 10, Material Implication

e) 1. $\overline{p} \vee \overline{q} \vee r$
    2. $(\overline{p} \vee r) \supset s$
    3. $q \supset t /\therefore q \supset (s \cdot t)$
    4. $\overline{q} \vee (\overline{p} \vee r)$ 1, Association of Alternation
    5. $q \supset (\overline{p} \vee r)$ 4, Material Implication
    6. $\left[q (\overline{p} \vee r)\right] \cdot \left[(\overline{p} \vee r) \supset s\right]$ 2,5, Conjunction
    7. $q \supset s$ 6, Hypothetical Syllogism
    8. $(q \vee s) \cdot (q \supset t)$ 3,7, Conjunction
    9. $-(q \cdot \overline{s}) \cdot -(q \cdot \overline{t})$ 8, Material Implication
    10. $-\left[(q \cdot \overline{s}) \vee (q \cdot \overline{t})\right]$ 9, DeMorgan's Theorem
    11. $-\left[q \cdot (\overline{s} \vee \overline{t})\right]$ 10, Distribution of Conjunction
    12. $\overline{q} \vee -(\overline{s} \vee \overline{t})$ 11, DeMorgan's Theorem
    13. $\overline{q} \vee (\overline{\overline{s}} \cdot \overline{\overline{t}})$ 12, DeMorgan's Theorem
    13. $\overline{q} \vee (s \cdot t)$ 13, Double Negation
    14. $q \supset (s \cdot t)$ 14, Material Implication

f) 1. $(p \vee q) \cdot (r \vee s) /\therefore (p \cdot r) \vee (p \cdot s) \vee (q \cdot r) \vee (q \cdot s)$
    2. $\left[(p \vee q) \cdot r\right] \vee \left[(p \vee q) \cdot s\right]$ 1, Distribution of Conjunction
    3. $(p \cdot r) \vee (q \cdot r) \vee (p \cdot s) \vee (q \cdot s)$ 2, Distribution of Conjunction
    4. $(p \cdot r) \vee (p \cdot s) \vee (q \cdot r) \vee (q \cdot s)$ 3, Commutation of Alternation

CHAPTER 9

Page 142

1. Words are any group of letters to which a meaning is attached. Words are groups of letters which form an ideogram. Words are groups of letters used to describe, to express, or to connect.

2. a) The form is "All *X* is *Y*."

   b) The form is "No *X* is *Y*."

   c) There is no common form.

3. a) All the expressions—*he, hit, the tree, with his car,* etc.—are descriptive except *consequently* which is a connector term.

   b) All descriptive terms except *if* and *then*.

   c) *I, Joe Smith, his art work* are descriptive; *hate* and *love* are expressive; *but* is connective.

   d) *She* is descriptive; *boy* and *is lovely* are expressive.

   e) All are descriptive.

   f) *The soul of man* is descriptive if you are religious, expressive if you are not. *Will endure* is probably descriptive.

4. a) *Cat* is mentioned.

   b) *Melanie* is mentioned.

   c) *Joanna* is mentioned.

   d) *Paradise Lost* is used.

   e) Both *Dianes* are used.

   f) The first two *Marys* are mentioned. The last is used.

   g) *Friendship* is merely mentioned if we are only speaking of the word; otherwise, if we are speaking of the concept or the meaning, then the word is being used.

5. I might know who John is and who Mary is and also what *loves* means, but this would not mean that I know that "John loves Mary" is different in meaning from "Mary loves John."

6. But has anyone ever seen or otherwise experienced someone else's pain? If someone else's pain cannot be experienced, then how can one know it exists?

Page 147

1. a) dog: *conventional intension*—having four legs and a bushy tail, barking occasionally, having a snout and paws (or any other group of properties which are normally taken to identify a dog); *subjective intension*—dirty, odoriferous, ready to bite someone at a moment's notice, and so on (of course, if one likes dogs, the subjective intension would state other properties such as being friendly and play-

ful); *extension*—all those objects having the properties of the conventional intension.

b) Nazi: *conventional intension*—being a member of the German government or of certain specified German political groups from about 1933 to 1946, being a member of any Nazi party anywhere, being committed to the destruction of Jews, Christians, and proponents of democracy; *subjective intension*—dirty bastards, miserable sadistic beasts, and so on; *extension*—the class of those objects having the properties of the conventional intension.

c) Communist: *conventional intension*—being a member of the Communist Party of the Soviet Union or of any other country, believing in the totalitarianism of the proletariate, believing in the destruction of capitalism; *subjective intension*—believing in the subversion of governments, fifth columnists; *extension*—the class of those persons having the properties of the conventional intension.

d) book: *conventional intension*—having printed pages; *subjective intension*—taking up shelf space, filled with lies; *extension*—the class of objects having the properties of the conventional intension.

e) baby: *conventional intension*—newborn child of the human species; *subjective intension*—little cuddly cutie pie; *extension*—the class of objects having the properties of the conventional intension.

2. A term can have an intension without having an extension, e.g., dinosaur. Intensions may be behavioral properties. Couldn't a mood be defined in terms of how a person behaves?

3. animal, human being, Christian, American, John Smith

CHAPTER 10

Pages 156 to 157

1. The grammarian takes everything except the subject as the predicate; the logician takes only that expression or set of expressions that refers to the property as the predicate.

2. a) is happy, monadic

   b) is happier than, polyadic, dyadic

   c) is friendly, monadic

   d) is friendlier, probably an implicit polyadic predicate which would be clear in a context. For example, the sentence probably means "John is friendlier than X," where the name of X would be understood in the context. Then *is friendlier than* would be polyadic, dyadic.

   e) Should be interpreted as "Muskie is a contemporary of Nixon," where *is a contemporary of* is polyadic, dyadic.

f) *gives . . . to*, polyadic, triadic

g) *sold . . . to . . . for*, polyadic, quadratic

3. a) If they look alike, then they have something in common. But what is this *something*? Similarly what is that which is *alike* when things behave alike?

b) This is a difficult problem. Relations do seem to be abstract. They certainly seem to exist, but not in the same way things exist. Some philosophers seem to think relations may be creations of the human mind. But would this mean that if all human beings died, *A* would suddenly not be to the left of *B*? Odd.

c) *Five* has as its extension the class of all classes having one object plus another object plus another object plus another object plus another object, regardless of what objects they are.

d) Maybe his genes hold him together.

e) But when are two terms "used in the same way"? Are *bachelor* and *unmarried man* used in the same way? Well, how about the sentence "He received his Bachelor-of-Arts degree"? Can we say "He received his unmarried-man-of-arts degree"?

4. a) This something would be the soul or self. But has anyone ever seen it?

b) This means there is no soul, or self. But everyone has a self, and is it no more than the human body? Then why is it the human body always changes but the self remains the same? Maybe the self is not material like the human body. But then how can something immaterial die?

c) Well, perhaps everything material, i.e., atomic, is determined. But we are not sure that the human psyche is strictly material.

CHAPTER 11

Page 164

1. But does an infinite number of numbers mean that there must be an infinite number of objects? Numbers are not things.

2. But *all* sentences are true or false. Commands are not true or false. "Open the window" is neither true nor false.

3. Are there any essential properties? Think of something having a property that you consider to be essential. But must it be essential? Can't there be a metal that is not a conductor?

4. If *metal* means *being a conductor*, then why all the experimentation and scientific inquiry to determine whether all metals are conductors?

5. If the universe is a big empty box, what is outside of the box?

Page 168

1. a) $(x)(Mx \supset Rx)$

   b) $(x)(Sx \supset \overline{Rx}) \vee (x)(Px \supset Wx)$

   c) This means "No person is perfect"; thus $(x)(Px \supset \overline{Fx})$.

   d) This means "If all the people here go to the party, then no one of the people will be unhappy"; thus $(x)(Px \supset Gx) \supset (x)(Px \supset \overline{Hx})$.

   e) $(x)(Ax \supset Sx)$

   f) We can take this to mean "Each man does his own thing"; thus $(x)(Mx \supset Dx)$.

   g) $(x)(Mx \supset \overline{Ax})$

   h) $(x)(Lx \supset Nx)$

   i) $(x)(Sx \supset \overline{Cx})$

   j) $(x)(Ax \supset Mx)$

Page 175

1. a) If numbers are no more than certain marks on paper, then by "Some numbers are even" we mean "There exist certain marks which are characterized as even." If more than such marks are meant, then numbers exist in the way relations exist. No one sees *to the left of*, but it exists.

   b) "Possibilities exist" could be taken to mean "Some statements about the future are more probable than others."

   c) "Goals exist" could be taken to mean "Some statements about the future ought to be made true."

2. a) $(\exists x)(Mx \cdot \overline{Cx})$

   b) $(\exists x)(Sx \cdot Ex) \supset (x)(Px \supset Rx)$

   c) $(x)(Sx \supset \overline{Rx}) \vee (x)(Sx \supset Rx)$

   d) We treat this as "Every (descriptive) expression in the language has an extension," i.e., $(x)(Px \supset Ex)$.

   e) We treat this as "No (descriptive) expression has an extension," i.e., $(x)(Px \supset \overline{Ex})$

   f) $(\exists x)(Mx \cdot Fx)$

   g) $(\exists x)(Px \cdot \overline{Ex}) \supset (x)(Px \supset \overline{Dx})$

3. a) Then there must be different levels of existence? How could we prove this?

   b) But there really seems to be only one level of existence that anyone knows anything about. No one has ever visited the level of existence where Hamlet resides.

CHAPTER 12

Pages 184 to 185

1. a)

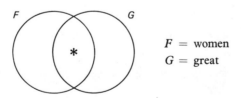

F = men
G = immoral

b)

F = man
G = is an island

c)

F = is a person
G = is unhappy about the war

d) The second *some* obviously means *great* or *terrific*. Thus the sentence means "Some women are great."

F = women
G = great

e)

F = man
G = sacrosanct

f)

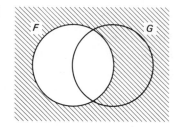

F = atomic
Everything except F is shaded out,
even what is outside the circles.

g)

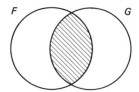

F = unicorns
G = happy

h)

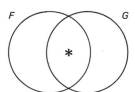

F = man
G = has told the truth

i)

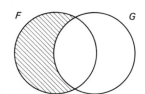

F = elephants
G = big

2. (a), (c), (d), (e) are true; (b) and (f) are false.

3. None

4. Yes, (a) would be true.

Page 193

1. a)

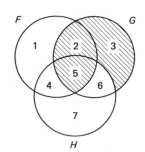

F = democrats
G = liberals   Invalid
H = republicans

b)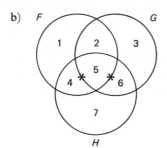

F = McCarthyite
G = republicans   Invalid, since it is
H = disillusioned   not certain that
                      anything exists in
                      part 5.

c)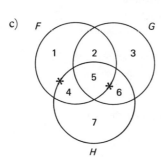

F = men
G = rational   Invalid
H = kind

d)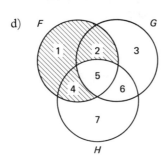

F = person
G = entitled to vote   Invalid
Ч = capable of reading

e)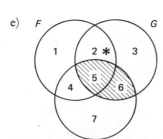

F = men
G = strong   Invalid
H = John

f)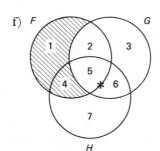

$$F = y$$
$$G = x \qquad \text{Invalid}$$
$$H = z$$

2. a) No, there are only two terms.

b) Yes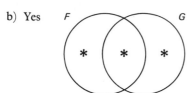

$F = $ metals
$G - $ automobiles   Valid

c) Yes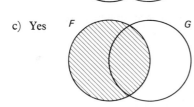

$F = $ metals
$G = $ conductors   Valid

Page 196

1. a)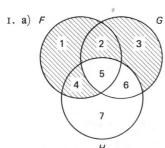

$F = $ metals   All metals are conductors.
$G = $ conductors   All conductors are magnetic.
$H = $ magnetic   Therefore all metals are
                   magnetic

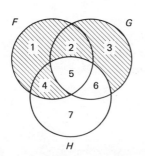

$F = $ metals   All metals are magnetic.
$G = $ magnetic   All magnetic objects are
                   dangerous.
$H = $ dangerous   Therefore, all metals are
                   dangerous.
                   Both are valid. Therefore the
                   whole argument is valid.

b) Enthymeme, should be stated as:
   All hippies are homosexual.
   All homosexuals are security risks. (implicit premise)
   Therefore, all hippies are security risks.

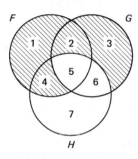

F = hippies
G = homosexuals
H = security risks

Valid, but unsound since the first and implicit premises are false.

c) Enthymeme, should be stated as:
   No hippies are good, clean-cut Americans.
   No good, clean-cut Americans should be arrested. (implicit premise)
   Therefore, all hippies should be arrested.

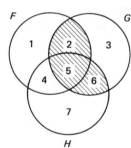

F = hippies
G = good, clean-cut Americans
H = should be arrested

Invalid

d) Enthymeme, should be stated as:
   Some of her friends wore mini skirts.
   All who wear mini skirts are real swingers. (implicit premise)
   Therefore, some of her friends are real swingers.

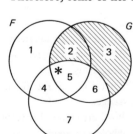

F = her friends
G = wore mini skirts
H = real swingers

Valid

2. Probably none of them.

3. a) Probably this particular college student means:

   Anyone who wants to be mature and enlightened as the people are in this movie ought to be sexually free.
   You want to be mature and enlightened as the people in this movie.
   Therefore, you ought to be sexually free.

We symbolize this as:

   All *F* is *G*.
   All *G* is *H*.
   Therefore, all *F* is *H*.

The argument is valid, although probably unsound since the first premise is questionable.

   b) This probably says:

   Any woman who wants to be kissed by a tall, dark, handsome, muscular, rich-looking man ought to smoke Chesterfields.
   You are a woman who wants to be kissed by a tall, dark, handsome, muscular, rich-looking man.
   Therefore, you ought to smoke Chesterfields.

The argument is valid but unsound, since the first premise is questionable.

4. These might be advertisements for cars (particularly Cadillacs), soaps, deodorants, shampoos, and don't forget the Winchester man for cigars.

Page 199

The following are the problems on pp. 193–194.

1. a) No *d* are *d*.   *d* stands for distributed; *u* for undistributed.
   Every *d* is *u*.   Invalid since *republicans* is *d* in conclusion,
   Therefore, no *d* are *d*.   but *u* in premise.

   b) Some *u* are *u*.   Invalid since the middle term, disillusioned, is
   Some *u* are *u*.   undistributed in both cases.
   Therefore, some *u* are *u*.

   c) Some *u* are not *d*.   Invalid since the middle term, *men*, is undistrib-
   Some *u* are *u*.   uted in both cases.
   Therefore some *u* are not *d*.

   d) All *d* is *u*.   Invalid since *entitled to vote* is *u* in premise,
   All *d* is *u*.   but *d* in conclusion.
   Therefore, all *d* is *u*.

e) Some *u* are *u*.   Invalid since *man* is *u* in premise, but *d* in
   No *d* is *d*.   conclusion.
   Therefore, no *d* is *d*.

f) All *d* is *u*.   Invalid since the middle term *x* is undistributed
   Some *u* is *u*.   in both cases.
   Therefore, some *u* is *u*.

The following are the problems on p. 196.

1. a) All *d* is *u*.
      All *d* is *u*.   Both of these arguments are valid by distribu-
      Therefore, all *d* is *u*.   tion rules. Thus the sorites is valid.
      All *d* is *u*.
      All *d* is *u*.
      Therefore all *d* is *u*.

   b) All *d* is *u*.   Valid.
      All *d* is *u*.
      Therefore, all *d* is *u*.

   c) No *d* is *d*.   Invalid. Premise negative, conclusion must be
      No *d* is *d*.   negative.
      Therefore, all *d* is *u*.

   d) Some *u* is *u*.
      All *d* is *u*.   Valid.
      Therefore, some *u* is *u*.

CHAPTER 13

Page 205

1. Bound formula—all variables are bound by quantifiers; free formulas are not
   bound by quantifiers. Examples: Bound Formula: $(Ex)Fx$; Free Formula: Fx.

2. Yes, $Fx \cdot (x)Fx$. The first x is free; therefore the formula is free.

3. a) This is a substitution instance of the valid formula $(p \cdot q) \supset p$.

   b) This is a substitution instance of the rule of Transposition, $p \supset q$, therefore
   $\bar{q} \supset \bar{p}$. Since they are both equivalent, obviously one implies the other.

   c) In the two free parts of the formula, use the rule of Material Implication with
   or and *not* first; then the rule of Distribution of Alternation is applied to the
   first free part. Result: A substitution instance of the valid formula $p \equiv p$.

4. *Part 1*

    c)   3. 1, Transposition.

    d)   4. 3, Double Negation

    e)   5. 4, Exportation

    f)   6. 5, Idempotence

    g)   7. 6, Material Implication

    h)   8. 7, DeMorgan's Theorem

    i)   9. 2, Material Equivalence

    j)   10. 8, 9, Conjunction and Disjunctive Syllogism

Part 2

    c)   3. 2, Addition

    d)   4. 3, DeMorgan and Double Negation

    e)   5. 4, DeMorgan's Theorem

    f)   6. 5, DeMorgan's Theorem

    g)   7. 6, Commutation

    h)   8. 7, Simplification

Pages 209–210

1. a) Existential quantifier can be distributed over alternation but not over conjunction; not valid.

    b) By Quantifier Conversion change $-(x) - (Fx \cdot Gx)$ to $(\exists x) - (Fx \cdot Gx)$. Then change $-(Fx \cdot Gx)$, by DeMorgan's Theorem, to $\overline{Fx} \vee \overline{Gx}$. Then distribute the existential quantifier; the result is a substitution instance of the valid formula, $p \equiv p$.

    c) The universal quantifier can be distributed through Conjunction; valid.

    d) The positive but not the negative universal quantifier can be distributed through Conjunction. To see this, first distribute the universal quantifier, then the negative sign; $-(x)(Fx \cdot Gx)$ would then be equal to $-(x)Fx \vee -(x)Gx$; thus invalid.

2. a) $-(\exists x) - (Fx \supset Gx)$

    b) $-(\exists x) - (Fx \vee Gx) \supset -(\exists x) - - (Gx \equiv Rx)$

    c) $-(\exists x)\overline{Fx} \vee - -(\exists x) - (Gx \supset Rx)$

    d) $- -(\exists x)\overline{\overline{Fx}} \vee - -(\exists x) - - - (Fx \cdot Gx)$

3. a) $Fx \supset Gx$ can be changed by Material Implication, to $\overline{Fx} \vee Gx$. But universal quantification *cannot* be distributed through alternation; not valid.

b) Change $-(\overline{Fx \cdot Gx})$ to $Fx \vee Gx$ by using DeMorgan's Theorem and Double Negation. Then distribute the existential quantifier; valid.

c) Change universal quantifier to existential quantifier. This results in $-(\exists x)---$ $(\overline{Fx \vee Gx}) \equiv -(\exists x)\overline{Fx} \cdot -(\exists x)Gx$. Using Double Negation and distribution of existential quantification we obtain $-\left[(\exists x)\overline{Fx} \vee (\exists x)Gx\right] \equiv -(\exists x)\overline{Fx} \cdot$ $-(\exists x)Gx$. Distributing negation we obtain $-(\exists x)\overline{Fx} \cdot -(\exists x)Gx \equiv -(\exists x)\overline{Fx} \cdot$ $-(\exists x)Gx$, which is a substitution instance of $p \equiv p$; valid.

Page 213

1. a) Change the formula by going through the following steps:

(1) $\left[(p \supset q) \supset (\overline{q} \supset \overline{p})\right] \cdot \left[(\overline{q} \supset \overline{p}) \supset (p \supset q)\right]$, using Rule of Equivalence

(2) $\left[-(\overline{p} \vee q) \vee (q \vee \overline{p})\right] \cdot \left[-(q \vee \overline{p}) \vee (\overline{p} \vee q)\right]$, using Material Implication and Double Negation

(3) $\left[(p \cdot \overline{q}) \vee (q \vee \overline{p})\right] \cdot \left[(\overline{q} \cdot p) \vee (\overline{p} \vee q)\right]$, using DeMorgan's Theorem and Double Negation and Association of Alternation

(4) $\left[(\overline{q} \cdot p) \vee (\overline{p} \vee q)\right] \cdot \left[(\overline{q} \cdot p) \vee (\overline{p} \vee q)\right]$, using Association and Commutation

(5) $(\overline{q} \cdot p) \vee (\overline{p} \vee q)$, using the rule of Idempotency. This is the normal form.

b) Change the formula by going through the following steps:

(1) $\left[-(p \vee \overline{q}) \cdot -(p \cdot q)\right] \vee \left[(p \vee \overline{q}) \cdot (p \cdot q)\right]$, using Material Equivalence

(2) $\left[(\overline{p} \cdot q) \cdot (\overline{p} \vee \overline{q})\right] \vee \left[(p \vee \overline{q}) \cdot (p \cdot q)\right]$, using DeMorgan's Theorem and Double Negation

(3) $(\overline{p} \cdot q \cdot \overline{p}) \vee (\overline{p} \cdot q \cdot \overline{q}) \vee (p \cdot q \cdot p) \vee (p \cdot q \cdot \overline{q})$, using Distribution of Conjunction

(4) $(\overline{p} \cdot q) \vee (p \cdot q)$, using Idempotency and Contradiction with Alternation. This is the normal form.

c) Change the formula by going through the following steps:

(1) $\left[\overline{p} \vee (q \cdot r)\right] \vee (p \equiv r)$, using Material Implication

(2) $\overline{p} \vee (q \cdot r) \vee (p \cdot r) \vee (\overline{p} \cdot \overline{r})$, using Equivalence. This is the normal form.

d) Change the formula by going through the following steps:

(1) $(p \cdot q) \vee -\left[p (q \cdot r)\right]$, using Material Implication

(2) $(p \cdot q) \vee -\left[\overline{p} \vee (q \cdot r)\right]$, using Material Implication

(3) $(p \cdot q) \vee \left[p \cdot -(q \cdot r)\right]$, using DeMorgan's Theorem

(4) $(p \cdot q) \vee [p \cdot (\bar{q} \vee \bar{r})]$, using DeMorgan's Theorem

(5) $(p \cdot q) \vee (p \cdot \bar{q}) \vee (p \cdot \bar{r})$, using Distribution through Conjunction. This is the normal form.

Pages 214–215

1. Change universal quantifiers to existential ones; change all free parts of formulas to normal form; change the formula as a whole to normal form.

2. c and d.

3. a) Change the formula by going through the following steps:

(1) $-(\exists x) - (Fx \supset Gx)$, changing universal to existential quantification

(2) $-(\exists x) - (\overline{Fx} \vee Gx)$, using Material Implication

(3) $-(\exists x)(Fx \cdot \overline{Gx})$, using DeMorgan's Theorem. This is the C form

b) Change the formula by going through the following steps:

(1) $-(\exists x) - [(Fx \cdot Gx) \supset (Hx \cdot Gx)]$, changing universal to existential quantification

(2) $- (\exists x)[(Fx \cdot Gx) \cdot - (Hx \cdot Gx)]$, using Material Implication and De-Morgan's Theorem

(3) $- (\exists x)[(Fx \cdot Gx) \cdot (\overline{Hx} \vee \overline{Gx})]$, using DeMorgan's Theorem

(4) $- (\exists x)[(Fx \cdot Gx \cdot \overline{Hx}) \vee (Fx \cdot Gx \cdot \overline{Gx})]$, Distribution through Conjunction

(5) $-(\exists x)(Fx \cdot Gx \cdot \overline{Hx})$, Contradiction with Alternation. This is the C form.

c) Change the formula by going through the following steps:

(1) $- (\exists x) - (Gx \cdot Rx) \supset - (\exists x) \overline{Gx}$, changing universal to existential quantification

(2) $(\exists x)(\overline{Gx} \vee \overline{Rx}) \vee - (\exists x)\overline{Gx}$, using Material Implication and DeMorgan's Theorem. This is the C form.

d) Change the formula by going through the following steps:

(1) $- [(x)Fx \vee - (x)Fx] \vee (\exists x)(Fx \cdot \overline{Fx})$, using Material Implication

(2) $- (x)Fx \cdot (x)Fx$, using DeMorgan's Theorem, Double Negation, and Alternation with Contradiction

(3) $(\exists x)\overline{Fx} \cdot - (\exists x)\overline{Fx}$, changing universal to existential quantification. This is a substitution instance of $p \cdot \bar{p}$; thus it is false.

e) Change the formula by going through the following steps:

(1) $(x)(Fx \supset Fx) \vee (\exists x)(Fx \vee \overline{Gx})$, using Material Implication

(2) $- (\exists x) - (Fx \supset Fx) \vee (\exists x)(Fx \vee \overline{Gx})$, changing universal to existential quantification

(3) $- (\exists x) - (\overline{Fx} \vee Fx) \vee (\exists x)(Fx \vee \overline{Gx})$, Material Implication

(4) $- (\exists x)(Fx \cdot \overline{Fx}) \vee (\exists x)(Fx \vee \overline{Gx})$, DeMorgan's Theorem. This reduces to true since $(\exists x)(Fx \cdot \overline{Fx})$ is false and the denial of it is true. An alternation with a true alternant is always true.

f) Change the formula by taking the following step:

T; since one component of the antecedent is a contradiction the whole antecedent is false; thus the conditional must be true.

g) Change the formula by going through the following steps:

(1) $(\exists x)\overline{Fx} \vee \big[(x)(Gx \cdot Fx) \vee (x)(Fx \cdot Gx)\big]$, Material Implication and changing universal to existential quantification.

(2) $(\exists x)\overline{Fx} \vee - (\exists x) - (Gx \cdot Fx) \vee (\exists x) - (Fx \cdot Gx)$, changing universal to existential quantification

(3) $(\exists x)\overline{Fx} \vee - (\exists x)(\overline{Gx} \vee \overline{Fx}) \vee - (\exists x)(\overline{Fx} \vee \overline{Gx})$, DeMorgan's Theorem. This is the C Form.

Pages 220–221

1. See the list of Canonical Forms A through F, p. 215.

2. See pp. 216–220.

3. a) Change to Canonical Form and then use the appropriate test:

(1) $- (\exists x)\overline{Fx} \supset (x)(\overline{Fx} \vee Gx \vee Rx)$, Material Implication

(2) $- (\exists x)\overline{Fx} \supset - (\exists x) - (\overline{Fx} \vee Gx \vee Rx)$, change universal to existential quantification

(3) $- (\exists x)\overline{Fx} \supset - (\exists x)(Fx \cdot \overline{Gx} \cdot \overline{Rx})$, DeMorgan's Theorem

(4) $- (\exists x)\overline{Fx} \vee - (\exists x)(Fx \cdot \overline{Gx} \cdot \overline{Rx})$, Material Implication. This is the C form.

(5) Consistent, since $(\exists x)\overline{Fx}$ is of group A and $\overline{Fx}$ is consistent

b) (1) $(\exists x)(Fx \cdot Gx) \cdot (\exists x)Gx$, Material Implication and Double Negation. This is the C form.

(2) Consistent, since both conjuncts are consistent.

c) (1) $(x)(Fx \supset Gx) \cdot (\exists x)(Fx \cdot \overline{Gx})$, Material Implication and Double Negation

(2) $- (\exists x) - (Fx \supset Gx) \cdot (\exists x)(Fx \cdot \overline{Gx})$, universal to existential quantification

(3) $- (\exists x)(Fx \cdot \overline{Gx}) \cdot (\exists x)(Fx \cdot \overline{Gx})$, Material Implication and Double Negation. This is the C Form.

(4) Inconsistent, since $- (Fx \cdot \overline{Gx}) \cdot (Fx \cdot \overline{Gx})$ is inconsistent.

d) This is already in C Form and is of Group E. Thus we test the following two for consistency:

$- (Fx \cdot Gx) \cdot -(Gx \cdot Rx) \cdot \overline{Gx}$ consistent

$- (Fx \cdot Gx) \cdot - (Gx \cdot Rx) \cdot \overline{Rx}$ consistent

Both are consistent. Therefore the entire formula is consistent.

e) (1) $(\exists x)(Fx \cdot \overline{Fx}) \vee - (x)\left[(Fx \cdot Gx) \supset \overline{Rx}\right]$, Material Implication

(2) $- (x)\left[(Fx \cdot Gx) \supset \overline{Rx}\right]$, Alternation with Contradiction

(3) $(\exists x) - \left[(Fx \cdot Gx) \supset \overline{Rx}\right]$, universal to existential quantification

(4) $(\exists x)(Fx \cdot Gx \cdot \overline{Rx})$, Material Implication and Double Negation. This is the C Form.

(5) Form of Group A; consistent, since $Fx \cdot Gx \cdot \overline{Rx}$ is consistent.

f) (1) $- (\exists x)(Fx \vee Gx) \vee - (\exists x) - (Fx \equiv Gx)$, universal to existential quantification

(2) $- (\exists x)(Fx \vee Gx) \vee - (\exists x) - \left[(Fx \cdot Gx) \vee (\overline{Fx} \cdot \overline{Gx})\right]$, Equivalence

(3) $- (\exists x)(Fx \vee Gx) \vee (\exists x)\left[- (Fx \cdot Gx) \cdot - (\overline{Fx} \cdot \overline{Gx})\right]$, DeMorgan's Theorem

(4) $- (\exists x)(Fx \vee Gx) \vee - (\exists x)\left[(\overline{Fx} \vee \overline{Gx}) \cdot (Fx \vee Gx)\right]$, DeMorgan's Theorem and Double Negation

(5) $- (\exists x)(Fx \vee Gx) \vee - (\exists x)\left[(\overline{Fx} \cdot Gx) \vee (\overline{Gx} \cdot Fx)\right]$, Distribution through Conjunction. This is the C Form.

(6) Form of Group F; $- (\exists x)(Fx \vee Gx)$ is consistent, since $- (Fx \vee Gx)$ is consistent. Thus the entire formula is consistent.

Page 225

1. a) Step 1. Negate the consequent and place it in conjunction with the antecedent:

$(x)(Fx \supset Gx) \cdot (\exists x)(Gx \cdot Rx) \cdot - (\exists x)(Fx \cdot Rx)$

Step 2. Change to Canonical Form. First eliminate universal quantifiers:

$- (\exists x) - (Fx \supset Gx) \cdot (\exists x)(Gx \cdot Rx) \cdot - (\exists x)(Fx \cdot Rx)$

Step 3. Eliminate implication sign by Material Implication:

$- (\exists x)(Fx \cdot \overline{Gx}) \cdot (\exists x)(Gx \cdot Rx) \cdot - (\exists x)(Fx \cdot Rx)$

This is the C Form.

Step 4. Use rules for group E of Canonical Forms. Since there is only one positive existential quantification, we can drop all quantifiers and test for consistency:

$- (Fx \cdot \overline{Gx}) \cdot (Gx \cdot Rx). - (Fx \cdot Rx)$

Consistent. Therefore the original formula is invalid.

b) Step 1. Negate the consequent and place it in conjunction with the antecedent:

$$- (\exists x)\overline{Fx} \cdot - \left[(x)(Fx \lor Gx) \cdot (x)(Fx \lor \overline{Gx}) \right]$$

Step 2. Change to Canonical Form. First eliminate universal quantifiers:

$$- (\exists x)\overline{Fx} \cdot - \left[- (\exists x) - (Fx \lor Gx) \cdot - (\exists x) - (Fx \lor \overline{Gx}) \right]$$

Second, eliminate extended negation signs:

$$- (\exists x)\overline{Fx} \cdot \left[(\exists x) - (Fx \lor Gx) \lor (\exists x) - (Fx \lor \overline{Gx}) \right]$$

We obtain this by using DeMorgan's Second Theorem and Double Negation. Then we use the same theorem on the free parts to obtain:

$$- (\exists x)\overline{Fx} \cdot \left[(\exists x)(\overline{Fx} \cdot \overline{Gx}) \lor (\exists x)(\overline{Fx} \cdot Gx) \right]$$

Third, distribute $-(\exists x)\overline{Fx}$:

$$\left[- (\exists x)\overline{Fx} \cdot (\exists x)(\overline{Fx} \cdot \overline{Gx}) \right] \lor \left[- (\exists x)\overline{Fx} \cdot (\exists x)(\overline{Fx} \cdot Gx) \right]$$

This is the C Form.

Step 3. Test for consistency. We test both alternants by using the test for canonical group E. When the quantifiers are dropped, both are inconsistent. Thus the conjoining of the original antecedent with the negation of the consequent is inconsistent. Therefore the original conditional is valid.

c) Step 1. Negate the consequent and place it in conjunction with the antecedent:

$$(\exists x)Fx \cdot - \left[(\exists x)(Fx \cdot Gx) \lor (\exists x)(Fx \cdot \overline{Gx}) \right]$$

Step 2. Change to Canonical Form. Eliminate extended negation sign

$$(\exists x)Fx \cdot - (\exists x)(Fx \cdot Gx) \cdot - (\exists x)(Fx \cdot \overline{Gx})$$

by using DeMorgan's Theorem. This is the C Form.

Step 3. Test for consistency using rule for Group E of Canonical Forms. Since there is only one positive existential quantification we can drop all quantifiers and test for consistency:

$$Fx \cdot - (Fx \cdot Gx) \cdot - (Fx \cdot \overline{Gx})$$

Inconsistent. Therefore the original formula is valid.

d) We can use the canonical form to test this for validity. The equivalence is eliminated in favor of the conditional and then each conjunct is tested for validity. Thus we would test $(x)Fx \supset \left[(x)(Fx \lor Gx) \cdot (x)(Fx \lor \overline{Gx}) \right]$ and $\left[(x)(Fx \lor Gx) \cdot (x)(Fx \lor \overline{Gx}) \right] \supset (x)Fx$. If our canonical forms show them both to be valid, then the original formula (with the equivalence sign) is valid. But a much simpler way to deal with this example is simply to use the rule by which the universal can be distributed over Conjunction. Thus the formula becomes $(x)Fx \equiv (x)(Fx \lor Gx \cdot Fx \lor \overline{Gx})$. Then by Distribution over Alternation this becomes $(x)Fx \equiv (x)\left[Fx \lor (Gx \cdot \overline{Gx}) \right]$. Then by Alternation with Contradiction this becomes $(x)Fx \equiv (x)Fx$, which is a substitution instance of the valid form $p \equiv p$.

e) Step 1. Negate the consequent and place it in conjunction with the antecedent:

$$- (\exists x) - (Fx \supset Gx) \cdot \big[- (x)(Gx \supset \overline{Hx}) \supset - (x)(\overline{Gx} \vee \overline{Hx}) \big] \cdot$$
$$- \big[- (\exists x)(Gx \cdot Hx) \supset (x)(Kx \supset Fx) \big]$$

Step 2. Change to canonical form. First eliminate universal quantifiers:

$$- (\exists x) - (Fx \supset Gx) \cdot \big[(\exists x) - (Gx \supset \overline{Hx}) \supset (\exists x) - (\overline{Gx} \vee \overline{Hx}) \big] \cdot -$$
$$\big[- (\exists x)(Gx \cdot Hx) \supset - (\exists x) - (Kx \supset Fx) \big]$$

Step 3. Eliminate implication signs by using Material Implication and Double Negation:

$$- (\exists x)(Fx \cdot \overline{Gx}) \cdot \big[-(\exists x)(Gx \cdot Hx) \vee (\exists x) - (\overline{Gx} \vee \overline{Hx}) \big] \cdot \big[- (\exists x)$$
$$(Gx \cdot Hx) \cdot (\exists x)(Kx \cdot \overline{Fx}) \big]$$

Step 4. Eliminate extended negation signs by using DeMorgan's Theorem:

$$- (\exists x)(Fx \cdot \overline{Gx}) \cdot \big[- (\exists x)(Gx \cdot Hx) \vee (\exists x)(Gx \cdot Hx) \big] \cdot$$
$$\big[- (\exists x)(Gx \cdot Hx) \cdot (\exists x)(Kx \cdot \overline{Fx}) \big]$$

Step 5. Using Distribution of Conjunction we obtain:

$$\big\{ \big[- (\exists x)(Fx \cdot Gx) \cdot - (\exists x)(Gx \cdot Hx) \big] \vee \big[- (\exists x)(Fx \cdot Gx) \cdot (\exists x)(Gx \cdot Hx) \big] \big\} \cdot$$
$$\big[- (\exists x)(Gx \cdot Hx) \cdot (\exists x)(Kx \cdot \overline{Fx}) \big]$$

Step 6. Again using Commutation and Distribution of Conjunction in which we distribute $\big[- (\exists x)(Gx \cdot Hx) \cdot (\exists x)(Kx \cdot \overline{Fx}) \big]$ we obtain:

$$\big[- (\exists x)(Gx \cdot Hx) \cdot (\exists x)(Kx \cdot \overline{Fx}) \cdot - (\exists x)(Fx \cdot Gx) \cdot - (\exists x)(Gx \cdot Hx) \big] \vee$$
$$\big[- (\exists x)(Gx \cdot Hx) \cdot (\exists x)(Kx \cdot \overline{Fx}) \cdot - (\exists x)(Fx \cdot Gx) \cdot (\exists x)(Gx \cdot Hx) \big]$$

Step 7. Using Idempotency and Alternation with Contradiction we obtain:

$$- (\exists x)(Gx \cdot Hx) \cdot (\exists x)(Kx \cdot \overline{Fx}) \cdot - (\exists x)(Fx \cdot Gx). \text{ This is the } C \text{ form.}$$

f) Step 8. Test for consistency by using rules of group E. Since there is only one positive existential quantifier, we drop all existential quantifiers and test for consistency:

$$- (Gx \cdot Hx) \cdot Kx \cdot \overline{Fx} \cdot - (Fx \cdot Gx)$$

This is consistent since it is T if Gx and Kx are interpreted as T and Hx and Fx as F. Therefore, the formula of step 1 is consistent. Therefore, the original is invalid.

CHAPTER 14

Page 232

1. a) $(x)\big[Jx \supset - (y)(My \supset Lxy) \big] \cdot (x)\big[Fx \supset - (y)(My \supset Lxy) \big]$
   $(x)\big[Jx \supset (y)(My \supset Lxy) \big] \supset (x)\big[Mx \supset (y)(Jy \supset Lxy) \big]$
   $(x)\big[Jx \supset (y)(My \supset Lxy) \big] \equiv (x)\big[Mx \supset (y)(Jy \supset Lxy) \big]$

   b) $(x)(Cx \supset x$ does not love Shakespeare) where Cx stands for *is an English scholar.* We then proceed to symbolize "x does not love Shakespeare," which becomes:
   $(y)(Sy \supset \overline{Lxy})$

That is, "for all y, if y is identical to Shakespeare, then x does not love y." Substituting this symbolism for "x does not love Shakespeare" in the original, we obtain:

$$(x)\big[\, Cx \supset (y)(Sy \supset \overline{Lxy})\,\big]$$

We make a similar analysis of "No contemporary loves Milton." Then, using the conditional to symbolize *if–then*, (b) becomes:

$$(x)\big[\, Cx \supset (y)(Sy \supset \overline{Lxy})\,\big] \supset (x)\big[\, Cx \supset (y)(My \supset \overline{Lxy})\,\big]$$

(c) $(x)\big[Px \supset (y)(Sy \supset \overline{Lxy}) \big] \vee \big\{ (x)\big[Px \supset (y)(Sy \supset Lxy) \big] \supset (x)\big[Px \supset (y)(My \supset Lxy) \big] \big\}$, where P = person, S = is identical to Shakespeare, M = is identical to Milton, L = loves.

d) $(x)\big\{ \big[Cx \cdot (y)(Sy \supset Lxy) \big] \supset (y)(My \supset Lxy) \big\}$ using obvious symbolism

e) $(x)\big\{ Ax \supset (y)\big[By \supset (Lxy \vee \overline{Lxy}) \big] \big\}$

f) $(x)\big[Px \supset (\exists y)(Ay \cdot Mxy) \big]$ where M = admires; A = actor; P = person.

g) $(x)\big[Px \supset (y)(Cy \supset Lxy) \big]$

h) $(x)\big[Mx \supset (y)(By \supset Hxy) \big]$, where M = is identical to Mary; B = is identical to Bill; H = hates.

Page 237

1. a) transitive, asymmetrical, irreflexive

   b) nontransitive, asymmetrical, irreflexive

   c) nontransitive, symmetrical, nonreflexive

   d) nontransitive, symmetrical, reflexive

   e) transitive, asymmetrical, irreflexive

   f) transitive, nonsymmetrical, irreflexive

2. a) marry

   b) include

   c) as tall as

   d) larger by one, restricted to positive integers

3. It is difficult to believe that there could be a situation in which if A is heavier than B, then B could be heavier than A. Russell thought certain relationships were necessary truths. Others have thought that they are simply truths we have stipulated about the world.

Pages 244–245

1. a) *A noble animal* is indefinite; there are no definite descriptions.

   b) This really means "The father of him is the brother of me," where *the father of him* and *the brother of me* are definite descriptions.

c) There are no definite descriptions unless *the street* means *this street*.

d) *The strongest man* is a definite description; *He* is a definite description, referring to some specific person.

e) No definite descriptions here.

2. a) $(\exists x_c) \{ Kx \cdot Wx \cdot (y)[(Ky \cdot Wy) \supset Iyx] \}$ where K = king; W = of the U.S; I = is identical to.

b) $(\exists x_c) \{ Mx \cdot Vx \cdot (y)[(My \cdot Vy) \supset Iyx] \}$

c) We could symbolize this as: $(y)[Wy \supset Fy)$. Or if we treat *Washington* as a definite description, such as *The father of our country*, we would symbolize it as:

$$(\exists x) \{ Fx \cdot Ax \cdot (y)[(Fy \cdot Ay) \supset Ixy] \}$$

where F = father; A − of our country.

d) Since *Santa Claus* has no denotation, we change it into a description such as *The jolly bringer of gifts at Christmas*. Then we symbolize the sentence as:

$$(\exists x_c) \{ Jx \cdot (y)[Jy \supset Ixy] \}$$

e) We take Cyclops to be *the one-eyed monster of Sicily*. The sentence then becomes:

$$(\exists x) \{ Ox \cdot Mx \cdot Cx \cdot (y)[(Oy \cdot My \cdot Cy) \supset Iyx] \}.$$

where O stands for one-eyed, M for *monster*, I for *is identical to*, and C for *cruel*.

3. a) It could be difficult, as it might have been with *Santa Claus*. But we could always simply change the name itself into a definite description. Thus *Santa Claus* could become *that which Santa Clauses*.

b) But could a name have any meaning at all if there were no definite description that could be substituted for it? Thus it could seem that a language has to have definite descriptions but it can function without proper names.

c) But then the number would be equivalent to a name.

CHAPTER 15

Pages 257–258

1. a) Does a belief in something mean that it exists? Believing is a psychological state just as hoping and thinking are. But surely no amount of hoping or thinking that it is going to rain necessitates that it will rain.

b) Is anything inevitable? Think of something you take to be inevitable. Then ask yourself whether it really is.

c) Are eight patients sufficient evidence to prove Jones is a great doctor? Perhaps the last eight patients only had slight colds. How did he do with really serious cases?

d) New York may be going to the dogs, but this does not mean the country is going to the dogs. Furthermore, newspapers find rape, murder, and the like to be great newspaper material. So they may be exaggerating. And even if they aren't, New York is a big city and the fact that there is some crime does not mean that New York is not a great and important city.

e) Perhaps death may some day be conquered, but taxes . . .???

2. It is highly questionable whether societies rise and fall in certain determined ways. What does it mean for a society to *rise* or *fall*? And is any war inevitable? If Hitler had suddenly died, would this have affected the possibility of war?

Pages 260–261

1. Cleopatra's hairdresser could also be a relevant factor, since she made Cleo's hair look beautiful. So then Cleo's hairdresser might be considered a relevant factor in the decline of Rome. Also, for that matter, the perfume makers who made Cleo's perfumes might be relevant factors.

2. (a) Was there something wrong with his business? (b) Was there another woman? (c) Did he have any illness that might have made him despondent? (d) Was his wife a nag? (e) How did his neighbors regard him and his wife? These are relevant factors since men have been known to disappear for these reasons.

3. He's good if he keeps out of trouble with the law. He's good if he accepts your values and obeys you. He's good if he is courteous, loyal, honest, has consideration for others, and so on. But, of course, what is good to one parent might be bad to another.

4. a) Only in poetry is this analogy effective. We would not argue that human eyes operate in the same way that stars do.

b) This could be an effective analogy, since both the Soviet Union and bears are big, very often brutal. But it probably could not be used for inductive inferences.

c) In World War Two the unshaven soldier symbolized America to many Europeans: crude, vulgar, not caring for the aesthetic things in life. But no inductive inference can be made here. What certain soldiers are under war conditions can be very different from what they are under ordinary circumstances.

d) Again, to many Europeans the United States is like the rich old miser who is ready to sacrifice anything for the dollar. But this analogy really says very little about what America is really like.

e) This may be a good analogy in that it might lead us to think of politics as being played in accordance with certain rules of fair play, just as we play ballgames in accordance with rules of fair play. Then we might be led to find out what these rules of politics are or ought to be.

f) This is a very good analogy. Many scientists make this analogy and then go on to make inductions that since this mechanical heart works in A and B, then it will also work in C, D, and so on.

Page 265

1. a) This is not adequate, as everyone thinks he will be voting for the best man.

b) This could be a very bad question since, if there were some stigma attached to being a member of the party, a yes or no answer could condemn you. During the McCarthy era this was a very frequent type of question. Sometimes we call it a loaded question which people would refuse to answer.

c) This seems to be an adequate question. It is fairly clear and the person who answers could answer without fear of being intimidated.

d) This is not an adequate question. One can't take a poll on a question that only physicists can decide.

e) Here we have an adequate question even though a person might change his mind a hundred times before the next election.

2. Fruit pickers, farmers, and those earning an average wage might be polled, as well as actors and actresses.

3. a) mean, 6; mode, 2; median, 6.

b) mean, 4333; mode, 3000; median, 4000

c) mean, $63\frac{1}{3}$; mode, 50; median, 70

Page 270

a) $\frac{1}{6}$

b) Five favorable cases; 31 unfavorable cases out of 36 possible ones. Thus probability is $\frac{5}{36}$.

c) Each draw has probability of $\frac{13}{52}$. Thus $\frac{13}{52} \times \frac{13}{52} = \frac{1}{16}$.

d) $\frac{13}{52} \times \frac{12}{51} \times \frac{11}{50} \times \frac{10}{49} = \frac{11}{4165}$.

e) One favorable case; 216 possibilities; probability is $\frac{1}{216}$.

f) Five favorable, one unfavorable, probability is $\frac{5}{6}$.

g) Thirty-one favorable, 5 unfavorable; probability is $\frac{31}{36}$.

h) Seven favorable, 1 unfavorable; probability is $\frac{7}{8}$.

2. Our oil and gas deposits have been steadily decreasing during the last decade. In recent years especially they have been decreasing rapidly. Therefore, they will continue to decrease rapidly in the future.

Pages 274–276

1. a) The Method of Agreement is used. But think of everything these men might have shared before dinner, including hearing each other's jokes.

b) The Method of Difference is used. In this case, however, all the people in the restaurant might be used as evidence, since they might have eaten different foods, but they had no martinis and did not develop rashes. In fact, perhaps $\frac{3}{4}$ of the United States could be used as evidence. Also, the fact that the eleventh man did not get a rash and did not drink martinis proves nothing about martinis being the cause of the rash. He might have drunk the martinis and still not have had any rash.

c) To test if the olives or the martinis were the cause, then we have to find a case of someone who had the olives but not the martinis or conversely, and see if any rashes resulted. But if everyone had martinis and olives, then, on Mill's analysis, the cause cannot be determined.

d) The Method of Concomitant Variation is used. This seems possible. But there might have been something else that made the rash milder and stronger, perhaps the physical well-being of the men. See the following question.

e) But again the question arises as to whether there might not have been something else besides the martinis they all had in common.

f) The Method of Agreement is used. All the blacks had less severe rashes. Also the Method of Difference is used. Those who were not black had more severe rashes. But could this be a coincidence? Could there be something the blacks by accident had in common which the whites did not?

2. a) Method of Agreement is used. But Dr. Jones could be blameless. It might have been something given to just these 20 babies at the hospital, or, as in the case of thalidomide, some drug the mothers of these babies took.

b) Since Jones delivered both the healthy and unhealthy babies, he could not be the cause. But he could be at fault. There might have been something special he did in the case of the 20 babies. Methods of Agreement and Difference are being used here. We are looking for something common to all 20 babies and different from the other 10 cases.

c) But again there could be other factors. See (d).

d) Undernourishment could still be the cause. It is just that in Ward B undernourished mothers were given special vitamins and drugs and this produced healthy infants.

e) This would seem to be a pure coincidence equivalent to our whiskey and water example in the context.

f) Methods of Agreement and Difference. All those who had Drug X had malformed children; those who were under the same conditions and did not have the drug did not have malformed children. The drug looks like a good candidate for the cause.

g) Method of Concomitant Variation. This in conjunction with (f) makes the drug look like a good candidate.

h) Aspirins, however, had been used by many pregnant women without bad effect. Therefore, the drug was the cause.

i) Methods of agreement and difference; aspirin had been used by those who had malformed children, but it was also used by those who had healthy children. Thus it could not be the cause.

3. a) Methods of Agreement and Difference are used here. Ten planes used the same brand of gasoline and crashed; four others did not and did not crash. But this could have been a coincidence. Could there have been something else that the 10 planes had in common, but did not share with the other planes?

b) This is probably correct. If something is present in cases where the event occurs and where it does not occur, then probably it is not the cause.

c) The Method of Agreement is used. The new brand X could have been the cause. But again we have to ask whether there might not have been something else all 10 planes had in common. See (d).

d) Yes, the cracks could have been the cause. But now see (e).

e) But the cracks could have been the cause if they became larger as time passed and the engines were used.

f) Here we have what really could be the cause. Not only did each of the 10 planes have a common altitude and the same kind of fuel but scientific knowledge makes it even more probable that the altitude and the fuel caused the crash.

Index

IMPORTANT RULES AND FORMULAS

I. Listed below are the formulas whose validity shall be taken for granted. (Of course, if any question arises about the validity of any formula, the formula can be tested by changing *therefore* to $\supset$ and using the truth table technique.)

Conditional Valid Forms

1. $(p \supset q) \cdot p$ therefore q — Modus Ponens
2. $(p \supset q) \cdot \bar{q}$ therefore $\bar{p}$ — Modus Tollens
3. $p \cdot q$ therefore p — Simplification
   $p \cdot q$ therefore q
4. p therefore $p \vee q$ — Addition
5. $(p \supset q) \cdot (q \supset r)$ therefore $p \supset r$ — Hypothetical Syllogism
6. $(p \vee q) \cdot \bar{p}$ therefore q — Disjunctive Syllogism
   $(p \vee q) \cdot \bar{q}$ therefore p
7. $(p \supset q) \cdot (r \supset s) \cdot (p \vee r)$ therefore $q \vee s$ — Constructive Dilemma
8. p, q therefore $p \cdot q$ — Conjunction

Equivalent Valid Forms

9. $-(p \cdot q) \equiv (\bar{p} \vee \bar{q})$ — DeMorgan's First Theorem
10. $-(p \vee q) \equiv (\bar{p} \cdot \bar{q})$ — DeMorgan's Second Theorem
11. $(p \vee q) \equiv (q \vee p)$ — Commutation of Alternation
12. $(p \cdot q) \equiv (q \cdot p)$ — Commutation of Conjunction
13. $\left[p \vee (q \vee r) \right] \equiv \left[(p \vee q) \vee r \right] \equiv (p \vee q \vee r)$ — Association of Alternation
14. $\left[p \cdot (q \cdot r) \right] \equiv \left[(p \cdot q) \cdot r \right] \equiv (p \cdot q \cdot r)$ — Association of Conjunction
15. $\left[p \cdot (q \vee r) \right] \equiv \left[(p \cdot q) \vee (p \cdot r) \right]$ — Distribution of Conjunction
16. $\left[p \vee (q \cdot r) \right] \equiv \left[(p \vee q) \cdot (p \vee r) \right]$ — Distribution of Alternation
17. $p \equiv \bar{\bar{p}}$ — Double Negation
18. $(p \supset q) \equiv (\bar{q} \supset \bar{p})$ — Transposition (or Contra position)
19. $(p \supset q) \equiv (\bar{p} \vee q)$ — Material Implication (using *or* and *not*)
20. $(p \supset q) \equiv -(p \cdot \bar{q})$ — Material Implication (using *and* and *not*)